Poetry and Translation in Northern Ireland

Poetry and Translation in Northern Ireland

Dislocations in Contemporary Writing

Rui Carvalho Homem

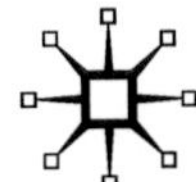

First published 2009 by
PALGRAVE MACMILLAN

Palgrave Macmillan in the UK is an imprint of Macmillan Publishers Limited, registered in England, company number 785998, of Houndmills, Basingstoke, Hampshire RG21 6XS.

Palgrave Macmillan in the US is a division of St Martin's Press LLC, 175 Fifth Avenue, New York, NY 10010.

Palgrave Macmillan is the global academic imprint of the above companies and has companies and representatives throughout the world.

Palgrave® and Macmillan® are registered trademarks in the United States, the United Kingdom, Europe and other countries.

ISBN-13: 978-0-230-22116-1   hardback

This book is printed on paper suitable for recycling and made from fully managed and sustained forest sources. Logging, pulping and manufacturing processes are expected to conform to the environmental regulations of the country of origin.

A catalogue record for this book is available from the British Library.

A catalog record for this book is available from the Library of Congress.

10 9 8 7 6 5 4 3 2 1
18 17 16 15 14 13 12 11 10 09

Printed and bound in Great Britain by
CPI Antony Rowe, Chippenham and Eastbourne

Contents

Acknowledgements

Thanks are due, first of all, to my family for their continued patience and affection. I also wish to thank my colleagues at the Department of Anglo-American Studies (University of Oporto) and CETAPS (the Centre for English, Translation and Anglo-Portuguese Studies) for providing a congenial and supportive research environment. I am grateful to the University of Oporto for a much-valued sabbatical leave, and to FCT (Fundação para a Ciência e a Tecnologia) and the Calouste Gulbenkian Foundation for research grants that have allowed me to spend short but decisive study periods abroad.

I gratefully acknowledge that lines of poetry are here reproduced by permission of the following entities from the following works: Faber and Faber and Farrar, Straus and Giroux from Seamus Heaney's *Death of a Naturalist, Door Into the Dark, Wintering Out, North, Field Work, Sweeney Astray, Station Island, The Haw Lantern, The Cure at Troy, Seeing Things, The Spirit Level, Electric Light, The Burial at Thebes*, and *District and Circle*; The Gallery Press from Derek Mahon's *The Chimeras, High Time, The School for Wives, The Bacchae, Racine's Phaedra, Words in the Air, Collected Poems, Saint-John Perse – Birds, Cyrano de Bergerac, Oedipus, Harbour Lights* and *Life on Earth*; The Random House Group Ltd from Michael Longley's *Collected Poems*, published by Jonathan Cape; Faber and Faber and Farrar, Straus and Giroux from Paul Muldoon's *Shining Brow, Bandanna, Poems 1968–1998, Moy Sand and Gravel* and *Horse Latitudes*; The Gallery Press from Paul Muldoon's *The Prince of the Quotidian, Six Honest Serving Men, The Birds* and *Vera of Las Vegas*; Paul Muldoon from *When the Pie Was Opened*; The Gallery Press from Ciaran Carson's *Collected Poems* and *The Midnight Court*; Granta Books from Ciaran Carson's *The Inferno of Dante Alighieri*; the Trustees of the Estate of the late Katherine B. Kavanagh (through the John Williams Literary Agency) from Patrick Kavanagh's *Collected Poems* (ed. Antoinette Quinn); Carcanet Press from Sinéad Morrissey's *There Was Fire in Vancouver* and *Between Here and There*; The Random House Group Ltd from Leontia Flynn's *These Days*, published by Jonathan Cape; The Gallery Press from Alan Gillis's *Somebody, Somewhere* and *Hawks and Doves*. I am deeply grateful to painter João Vieira for allowing me to reproduce one of his emblematic works on the jacket of this book.

Portions of some of the chapters in this book have been revised from essays originally published in *Colby Quarterly* XXXIX: 3 (September 2003); *New Hibernia Review* 8:4 (Winter 2004); *Beyond Borders: IASIL Essays on Modern Irish Writing*, ed. Neil Sammells (Bath: Sulis Press, 2004); *Irish University Review* 35:2 (Autumn/Winter 2005); *Estudios Irlandeses* no. 0 (2005), http://www.estudio sirlandeses.org; *Back to the Present, Forward to the Past: Irish Writing and History since 1798, vol. II*, ed. Patricia A. Lynch et al. (Amsterdam and New York: Rodopi, 2006); and *Études Britanniques Contemporaines* 31 (Novembre 2006).

1
Introduction: On Rewriting as Dislocation

> Wordsworth? ... no. I'm afraid we're not familiar with your literature, Lieutenant.
> We feel closer to the warm Mediterranean
>
> —Friel 1981: 41

> [T]he translation process has much in common with paradox, metaphor and discovery. Hence, the creative consequences of the state of translation that is modern Ireland
>
> —Cronin 1996: 4

The remarks above are, in distinct ways, privileged starting points for this study of contemporary poetry and translation in Northern Ireland. Michael Cronin's focus on 'process' is complemented and confirmed by his equation, in the same sentence, of 'translation' with 'metaphor': the two terms have often been construed as synonyms, on the basis of their respective etymologies (Latin and Greek), which lend them a common meaning of 'displacement' or 'transport'. But the transit that the second quotation brings to our attention is hardly linear or uneventful, as suggested by the elements of 'paradox' and 'discovery'. Cronin, whose contributions to translation studies show him especially sensitive to matters of identity and cultural difference (see Cronin 1996, 2000, 2003, 2006), is thus seeking productive analogies for translation, not in a nexus of equivalence or necessary correspondence, but rather in confrontations with perplexity and the unexpected meaning. This sense of perturbed transit is hence brought to bear on the Irish predicament, in its linguistic as much as political and territorial dimensions, by Cronin's description of Ireland as (in) a 'state of translation'. The interlingual process, both active component and telling representation of a historically complex scene – with the epicentre of such complexity in the long unresolved condition of Northern Ireland – thus becomes an apt synecdoche of the unstable relations that define the Irish experience.[1]

These troubled relations are also the core theme of Brian Friel's *Translations*, source of the first quotation above and indeed the most famous dramatisation of the fraught connections between language, territory and identity in Irish history. Friel's play is hardly about 'modern' (in the sense of present-day) Ireland, evoking rather the threshold of the transformations that decisively contributed to defining it. His text confronts us with a moment, the early 1830s, that antedates by little more than a decade the social and economic hecatomb of the Famine. The Famine's destruction of traditional bonds between people and land was to be compounded by a drastic reduction in the number of native speakers of Irish, and by the ineluctable course towards the replacement of Irish by English as the language not only of education and official practices, but increasingly also of ordinary daily exchanges. *Translations* dramatises a historical antecedent for that linguistic shift: the particular, imposed anglicisation that took place with the Ordnance Survey (1824–46). Ostensibly aimed at a more accurate mapping of the Irish territory for tax and governance purposes, it had a closer political control as its inevitable corollary. But the aspect that made the Ordnance Survey famous beyond the confines of historiography is also the one that foregrounds the links between language, territory and identity: the initiative of rendering place names into English, the 'translations' from which the play derives its title.[2]

Hugh, the character to whom Friel attributes the remark quoted above is a hedge-schoolmaster who teaches Latin and Greek in an Irish-speaking rural community where English has hardly penetrated, and under conditions that still exhibit the legacy of the Penal Laws (formally superseded in 1829). His quixotic pride in a supposed closer proximity of his culture to the Mediterranean world (through its Greco-Latin heritage) than to England and Anglophone culture could, indeed, boast a lineage and a substance that historians have not failed to acknowledge. Indeed, evidence abounds of a continued interest in the Classics within Irish culture (and in the Irish language) from the Middle Ages onwards, often materialised in translation, as well as in a habit of equating local figures and circumstances with those represented in Classical texts.[3] The schoolmaster's pride is promptly rendered ironical by the fact that his character, who in the dramatic fiction has Gaelic for his mother tongue and Greek or Latin for his professional languages, in fact exists and produces the remark in question in a play in English, the language that has since become the dominant medium of Irish culture and indeed the vehicle for its global circulation and recognition. The irony is first and foremost grounded in the tense relationship (similarity or difference?) between the 'then' of the dramatic action and the 'now' of its reception; but it also involves our present-day awareness that Hugh's boast is endowed by Friel (who situates his play in 1833) with proleptic force, since it anticipates the inclination shown by Irish writers and intellectuals in our time to claim a privileged relationship with other, non-Anglophone,

European cultures, so as to counter the gravitational pull of English culture and literature.

Friel's dramatic fiction of a search for empowerment and self-definition through a relationship with other places thus becomes an enlightening antecedent for recent Irish writing that addresses, referentially and intertextually, the elsewheres that energise Hugh's discourse. This is prominently the case with the translations of texts from 'the warm Mediterranean' – whether ancient, medieval, or modern – in the work of the five Northern Irish poets centrally considered in this book: Seamus Heaney, Derek Mahon, Michael Longley, Paul Muldoon and Ciaran Carson. Studying them requires a careful acknowledgement of the particularities of their place of reading and writing. This certainly means the political topicality of Northern Ireland, and the formative impact (personal as much as literary) of the ethical, social and linguistic complexities of a place that for so long was afflicted by dissension and sectarian violence. But the consequence of the locale for one's reading and (re)writing can be taken in wider terms, geographically and culturally: it can mean balancing the specificity of the Northern Irish formative location against the acknowledgement that it also belongs in a context, as one instance of a broader practice. One such context is provided by northern European appropriations of texts that originated in the space of Romance and Mediterranean cultures; (needless to say, the current cultural resonance of such texts is fundamentally different when they are read from within any southern culture that happens to see itself as a cultural and linguistic heir and legatee of the past greatness that they epitomise).

The tension between perceptions of what is specific and what is shared acquires, however, a complexity of its own in the Northern Irish situation. This reflects the different ways of seeking legitimation in the specific sense of place (involving a heightened combination of language, power, and belief) that historically characterised the territory's two traditions. Indeed, the nationalist-Catholic tradition predicated its endorsement of an Irish autarky (vis-à-vis the rest of the British Isles) not only on the cultural and linguistic particularity of the Gael, but also, fundamentally, on its continued allegiance to a transnational Christendom whose *lingua franca* of many centuries (Latin) also signalled continuity with the Classical past (cf. Stanford 1976: passim). Conversely, the unionist-Protestant tradition emphatically grounded the Planter's right and righteousness in steadfast loyalty to the political and religious consequence of the momentous *rejection* of the transnational empire of Christendom that, with the Reformation, vindicated the autarky of the rising nation state and the dignity of the English vernacular (for the pursuit of spiritual and worldly callings alike).

The relevant contexts, however, for a critical reading of such complexities and their importance in the work of the poets in question are also defined by features of the present intellectual moment, and especially by the discourses that have prevailed in recent years with regard to the literary construction of place, self, and other. The epigraphs chosen for this Introduction, and their brief discussion above, have already highlighted a seductive interchangeability between local and textual references. It is important now to recognise that critical readings in which that seduction is manifest are hardly idiosyncratic, but rather congenial to current intellectual tendencies. These include the growing emphasis on spatial dynamics and relations that has come to mark the discrete but overlapping disciplinary domains of literary and translation studies; as regards the latter, this critical emphasis has accompanied the expanding semantic scope of 'translation', and indeed its emergence as an autonomous field of inquiry.

1.1   An 'epoch of space'?

As has often been noted, the humanities and social sciences have been marked since the 1980s by an increasingly influential interest in space. The extent of this influence can be gauged from the breadth and diversity of the theoretical references that inform what is already commonly described as 'spatiality studies'. Such enabling references range from phenomenology and existentialism through structuralism to theories of post- or late modernity. They include Heidegger's reflections on the grounding or emplacement of being (in his later writings on 'Building Dwelling Thinking' – Heidegger 2001: 141–59); also Foucault's pronouncement, in his essay on heterotopias (today often accorded a quasi-prophetic value), on the advent of an 'epoch of space [. . .] of simultaneity [. . .] [and] juxtaposition', which was to follow and supersede the 'great obsession of the nineteenth century [. . .] [with] history' (Foucault 1986: 22); and (to cite a more recent and equally momentous contribution) Fredric Jameson's endorsement of the prevalence of spatial categories as a characteristic of postmodernity, and his 'cognitive cartography' as an enabling model for a sense of place under the global conditions of 'late capitalism' (Jameson 1991: 16 and passim).

Despite the variousness of their intellectual and ideological leanings, the combined effect of such contributions to the current interest in space has been to emphasise that places obtain their meanings, not from features that one might dub 'essential', but rather from a process that is both discursive and relational. As proposed by the editors of a collection focused on the late twentieth-century's unsettling of self and location, 'If places are no longer the clear supports of our identity, they nonetheless play a potentially important part in the symbolic and psychical dimension of our identifications'. They go on to add: 'How [. . .] does space become place? By being named [. . .] Place is space to which meaning has been ascribed' (Carter et al. 1993: xii). The acknowledgement that the significance of place is verbally constructed brings with it another recognition: that those forms of location and delimitation that invest space with meaning, instituting places and contributing to the emergence of identities, are based on the relationships that mutually position and define them (cf. Harvey 1996: 264, 270).

The argument that this process is eminently relational and dynamic rescues the 'spatial imagination' from accusations of being 'reactionary' (an indictment sometimes levelled at spatially determined analyses because of their conventional associations with a logic of stasis, which would construe them as the opposite to the historical 'awareness' afforded by temporally based approaches).[4] David Harvey endorses the 'dynamic' argument on behalf of the spatial concern when he suggests that the sense of place involves an articulation of permanence and retrospection with an active and prospective import: 'The preservation or construction of a sense of place is [. . .] *an active moment* in the passage from memory to hope, *from past to future*' (Harvey 1996: 306; my emphasis). A non-static understanding of the making of place and identity also converges with views on the concept and realities of nationhood, and its arguable historical transformation into 'postnationality'. A signal example is Richard Kearney's inquiry into the political possibility of 'a postnational model of interdependence', and his characterisation (following Jean-François Lyotard) of 'the postmodern critique of power' as contemplating 'a community where identity is part of a permanent process of narrative retelling', predicated on the 'reminder that every citizen's story is related to every other's' (Kearney 1997: 62–3). Kearney's is partly an analysis of current conditions, partly a vision of an imminent future, but scholars of national images have long pointed out that identity and location have always depended on relations and representations, rather than intrinsic features. In the words of Joep Leerssen, 'national characterizations take place in a polarity between self and Other [. . .] [the relation] between "auto-image" and "hetero-image" tends to show invariant dynamics in various different national and cross-cultural confrontations' (Leerssen 2000: 271).

Besides their plea for a dynamic and relational – as against static and essential – understanding of place and identity, contributions such as those cited above have a common denominator in their focus on discourse: the relations they describe are discursively constituted, and 'narrative' and 'representation' are recurrent keywords in their characterisation. This defines a context in which the study of writing and the study of space cannot but acknowledge and practise their convergence. In other words, the rise of what Edward Soja has called 'a distinctively postmodern and critical human geography' is found to belong within the same moment in intellectual history that has seen the assumption into mainstream literary studies of the poststructuralist emphasis on the inevitably intertextual basis of all processes of signification.[5] Such developments have involved the acknowledgement that geography cannot go unaffected by the crisis of representation, that is, the demise of the notion that 'writing mirrors the world'; that (e.g.) maps are not a transparent, unmediated access to reality, but rather 'constructed images', 'texts', 'socially produced, as discursive tools by which to persuade others': indeed, 'Maps are too important to be left to cartographers alone'.[6] Extending the concept of 'text' to embrace the object as much as the inscribed record of geographic study has allowed for the landscape itself (understood as 'a cultural image, a pictorial way of representing, structuring or symbolising surroundings') to be treated in similar terms to literary representations of place (cf. Cosgrove and Daniels 1988: 1). And these approximations have been fully reciprocated and met by literary studies – as suggested above, and reinforced by John Kerrigan's reminder that, etymologically, geography is 'earth writing' (Kerrigan 1998).

The notion that the study both of space and text cannot productively happen outside of a relational logic is thus compounded by the argument that such relations – 'interlocal' and intertextual – indeed overlap and intersect; moreover, their correlated dynamics have to be understood as processes that happen *in time* (as forcefully underlined by Harvey's remark on the temporal dynamics of the construction of place). These combined perceptions provide the necessary apparatus for a reading of translations that become a decisive part of the poetic output of their authors precisely by appropriating and rewriting texts that pointedly refer to other places and other times. And, again, Friel's play proves inspiring, since *Translations* combines an interlocal with a transtemporal imaginative design. Some of its characters are vocally conscious that the renaming of their places is grounded in history and change, and find imaginative redress in balancing their nominally compromised location against the elsewheres of long ago. But the play also appeals to its audience's historical awareness of everything that followed the momentous verbal and political intervention (the 'translations') in the space and time that the play evokes, and suggests that evoking such a past moment can contribute decisively to a reflection on identity in the audience's present circumstance. Both production and reception, writing and reading, are thus arguably defined by these relational designs of text, space and time; and a critical attitude informed by this awareness could derive its motto from remarks such as the following:

> writing about worlds reveals as much about ourselves as it does about the worlds represented. [. . .]
> when we write we do so from a necessarily local setting [. . .]
> it is not simply our accounts of the world that are intertextual: the world itself is intertextual. Places are intertextual sites because various texts and discursive practices based on previous texts are deeply inscribed in their landscapes and institutions [. . .]
> new worlds are made out of old texts, and old worlds are the basis of new texts.
>
> (Barnes and Duncan 1992: 2–3, 7–8)

1.2   Place and text, home and elsewhere

This study of poems and translations by contemporary Northern Irish poets combines an acknowledgement of such currently influential notions with close attention to their particular relevance for a culture that has long brooded on the emplacement of identity. This cultural particularity should also be assessed in the light of the conditions proper to regions and small nations, vindicated as they have been – their smallness often construed as an ethico-political entitlement – vis-à-vis the homogenising challenges posed by global conditions.[7] In literary terms, this involves reading the authors to be studied as (in Robert Crawford's phrase) 'identifying poets', '[who] construct for themselves an identity which allows them to identify with or to be identified with a particular territory' (1993: 1–2). But Crawford concurs with the nexus of definition by relation and dislocation emphasised above when he adds, 'it is those writers who look abroad who are often [the] most valuable territorial voices [. . .] [with their] transforming open-ness to the other' (1993: 13). As, in another context, Fintan O'Toole has put it, 'Ireland is something that often happens elsewhere' (1994: 27).

In the generation that preceded the first poets studied in this book, this defining tension between home and elsewhere, same and other, particular and universal, found a memorable formulation in the work of Patrick Kavanagh. Long before the discourse of difference and relational identities became current, Kavanagh (whose influence on Heaney has often been acknowledged, notably by Heaney himself) claimed dignity and self-confidence for the local anchoring of identity. In his essay 'The Parish and the Universe', he hailed that trust in 'the social and artistic validity of [one's] parish' which he styled 'parochialism', as against the 'provincialism' of those who permanently appeal to the values of a metropolis for validation of what they are and do (1967: 282). And yet Kavanagh's 'parochial' claim for centrality is not a form of cultural solipsism; his denunciation, throughout his prose writings, was explicitly aimed at the self-abasing fascination of Irish writers with London and its literary establishment, and does not preclude searching the broader panorama of literary history for enabling analogues to his favoured authorial stance. Indeed, Kavanagh himself summons the Classics to empower the triumphant close of 'Epic', a poem on the imaginative clout of the local reference (in all the specificity of its names):

> I inclined
> To lose my faith in Ballyrush and Gortin
> Till Homer's ghost came whispering to my mind
> He said: I made the Iliad from such
> A local row. Gods make their own importance.
>
> (Kavanagh 2005: 184)

Besides a small number of poems (that include 'Epic' but also 'On Looking into E. V. Rieu's Homer', another paean to the imaginative consequence of the Classics and also a tribute to a famous translator of Homer), and a few other incidental allusions, Kavanagh did not become noted for a systematic appropriation of the Classics. And yet the close connection, in those few pieces, between his claims for the dignity of 'the parish' and the culturally energising import of the Ancients, despite or because of their remoteness, has become an important dimension of Kavanagh's value as inspiring precursor. Irrespective of whether the allusion is deliberate or not on Friel's part, audiences familiar with Irish literature are bound to be reminded of Kavanagh's *dicta* when a character in *Translations*, with the ease of one who does not doubt the centrality of his place in the world, casually refers to the 'parish of Athens' (Friel 1981: 13).

Again, Friel's play about English soldiers and administrators, (dis)placed in Ireland, translating the Gaelic place names as they map the territory, and in the process facing a blend of collaboration and resistance from locals whose literacy and imaginative empowerment come from sustained use of Ancient Greek texts, prompts a reflection on the complex relevance of translation, as concept and practice, for considering the physically limited and historically fractured space of Ireland: 'Great hatred, little room', as Yeats famously remarked (1990: 288). Constraint and release, hindrance and enablement, vie with each other for prevalence when one tries to characterise the inter-lingual practices that have marked the Irish experience. Linguistic dispossession and forced anglicisation (epitomised in John Montague's image of the 'grafted tongue'[8]) loom large on the negative side of the equation. But, for Irish poetry, translation has historically proved a liberating device, affording a way out of the dysphoric inwardness induced by a consciousness of trauma and discontinuity – a consciousness that, in Thomas Kinsella's famous diagnosis of the late 1960s, afflicts 'every writer in the modern world', but in Ireland derives particular poignancy from that 'calamity', 'the death of a language' (1967: 15, 10).

Kinsella's commitment to the translation and circulation of Gaelic texts was his chosen strategy for reconnecting 'with the significant past' (15). But a belief in the potential of verbal transits (both as practice and concept) to offer imaginative redress straddles several poetic generations and indeed proves ubiquitous. Just a few years after Kinsella's remarks on the predicament faced by 'The Irish Writer', Seamus Heaney, then already the best-known poet writing out of the complexities of Northern Ireland at the height of the Troubles, was to include in *Wintering Out* a series of poems that memorably troped political, cultural and territorial dispossession as a linguistic affair, imaginary verbal transactions with the value of a vindication, since (as in 'A New Song') it is from a sense of release and positiveness that 'river tongues' issue and 'rise / From licking deep in native haunts / To flood' wider, repossessed territories (Heaney 1972: 33). When poets take the further step of writing under names other than their own, that release may coincide with an extended verbal and imaginary scope, afforded by a diction and a referential range that can be markedly distinct from those that characterise 'their own' writing. Translation (or, in some cases, poems couched in the diction of highly differentiated *personae*) can extricate the lyric voice from its historical and cultural circumstance, allowing it to vaunt in its sufficiency while it paradoxically denies itself by assuming another diction and another set of references. But the release brought by translation does not always equate the particular relief of self-effacement, of yielding to unqualified alterity. Poets may want (and pointedly *have* wanted) to repress the politically motivated voice within themselves; but this voice may be unfettered through the assumption of an enunciation with an *ostensibly* distinct source and another's name. Passing itself off as the mere rendering of another poet's pronouncements, the committed voice may then enjoy a new lease of freedom, *while retaining the recognisable diction* of its 'holder', the poet-translator who authors the target text.

For obvious reasons, this poetics of translation as unconstraint has a particular relevance with regard to the work of Northern Irish poet-translators through (and in the wake of) the Troubles, spawning a practice of vicarious pronouncement on historical adversity, sectarianism, and the various political dysfunctions in the recent history of the territory of their personal and cultural origins.[9] This textual practice becomes in fact an important body of evidence for the particularly 'living and special' sense that (according to Edna Longley) applies to the concept of intertextuality when considered with regard to Northern Irish poetry; for in that body of literature, it emerges 'not as a theoretical dead letter, but as a creative dynamic', precisely because it offers a wealth of evidence that 'no poet or poem ever quite stands alone. Each has a place within various systems of cultural and aesthetic relations.'[10] Further, the notion that textual dynamics of various sorts prevail to an unusual extent in the writerly practices characteristic of contemporary Northern Ireland can be seen as a specific realisation of the tropes of liminality and transit that some commentators (focusing on the cultural upside of the panorama of strife that the North presented to the world throughout the Troubles) have favoured in their political and cultural characterisation of that territory. One such description was offered (again) by Edna Longley in her controversial remark, produced in the late 1980s, on the North as 'culturally a corridor, permeable to influences from Dublin – Glasgow – London'.[11]

The context for such a remark was one of enhanced controversy over the relative unity or plurality of the body of writing that bears the name of 'contemporary Irish poetry', a controversy that to a large extent has coincided with the question of whether the political and social reality of partition finds a correspondence in the realm of poetry.[12] The renewed cultural energy shown by Northern Ireland (Belfast, in particular) from the 1960s, which

proved especially visible in the realm of poetry – with the attention generated by the early work of Heaney, Mahon and Longley – fostered the critical
notion of a 'Northern Poetic Renaissance', which in turn led to sometimes
virulent discussions that were as much about the polity as the poetry. This
double focus reflected the island's rich variety of political positions and
their literary implications; and the controversy was decisively boosted by
the coincidence in time between the rise to prominence of the 1960s poets
and the post-1969 Troubles – although, as both the poets themselves (in
interviews or memoirs) and various commentators have pointed out, the
surge in poetic production in fact predated the civic crisis (cf. Brearton 2003:
94, 101). The notion of a 'Renaissance' certainly abetted the recognition of
the generation of Northern poets with whom it was associated, although
they have hardly ever endorsed it in unqualified terms, and some in fact
have denied it. On being asked, in an interview published in 1991, whether
'the literature from the North should be considered separately from the
literature of the Republic', and whether he believed in a Northern 'renascence', Mahon quipped, 'You can't renasce something that was never nasce.
There is, however, as always, an Irish renascence' (Scammell 1991: 5). The
latter remark highlighted how frequently the model of the early twentieth-
century Revival, with its hopes of a combined upward dynamics of literature
and the nation, has been conjured in Ireland, at the risk of banality: by the
middle years of the century, Patrick Kavanagh had already offered the satirical
proclamation, voiced by the 'devil Mediocrity' in his mock-epic 'The Paddiad',
that 'a great renaissance is under way' (Kavanagh 2005: 151).

As suggested above, however, most objections to the acknowledgement
and celebration of a 'Northern Renaissance' concerned not so much the fatu-
ity of any such construction, but rather the separateness that inhered in the
notion; and it therefore inevitably rekindled discussions centred on matters
of identity and nationality (with all the risks that Claudio Guillén once highlighted, by pointing out how easily debates on 'national literature' have 'led
to determinism, ethnomania, and various reactionary attitudes' – 1971: 500).
As regards the writers, the notion of a distinctive post-1960s Northern Irish
poetry proved especially disturbing to poets from the preceding generation,
who for various reasons will have felt excluded by (or from) it. A poet like
John Montague, who had his roots in the North but had pursued his writing
both in the South and abroad, seeking in fact an international validation to
counter the provinciality of mid-twentieth-century Ireland, reacted to critical
representations of a poetically re-energised Northern Ireland by reminding
readers of his precedence, as a forerunner of themes and modes of writing that
were now celebrated as new: 'I have described myself as the missing link of
Ulster poetry' (O'Driscoll 1989: 60). For a Dublin poet like Thomas Kinsella,
the sense of a generationally and regionally determined exclusion was compounded by the clash between arguments for an Ulster specificity in poetry
and his own active concern with contributing to 'healing' Ireland's 'mutilated'

literary tradition. As seen above, this concern found a fundamental weapon in translation from the Irish, practised in ways that better allow readers to recognise recurrence and continuity. This was a project whose best-known realisation remains *The New Oxford Book of Irish Verse* (1986), edited by Kinsella, who was also the translator of most of its many pieces rendered from the Irish – an anthology that remains to date 'the last attempt [. . .] to cover Irish poetry as a whole', since 'most recent anthologies have given up the attempt to be all inclusive' (O'Donoghue 2005: 183).

Significantly, Kinsella's Introduction included one of the most damning pronouncements on the notion of a distinct 'Northern poetry': 'The idea of such a renaissance [. . .] has acquired an aspect of official acceptance and support. But it is largely a journalistic entity' (1986: xxx). The crucial link between the virulence of these debates, in the 1980s and early '90s, and the lingering issue of partition is reflected in the promptness with which territorial references emerge in pronouncements by major protagonists in the polemics. Kinsella went on to dismiss 'a provincial Ulster poetic Renaissance addressing its work toward the British mainland and finding an identity there' (cited in Johnston 1991: 26); Edna Longley grounded her argument for the specificity of Ulster poetry on a consciousness of the pull of three capital cities as an enabling force, 'the tension of Belfast-Dublin-London' (1987: 4); and Terence Brown, even while ascribing the particularity of that body of poetry to its dominant formal model, could not but represent the 'Northern Renaissance' as dislocation and relocation: 'the well-made empirical lyric found in the northern counties of Ireland a [. . .] new territory in which to be rejuvenated. The Northern Renaissance was a renaissance for a particular kind of poem' (1988: 215).[13]

The two decades that have elapsed since the height of this controversy have largely deflated it: a changed political atmosphere (more recently, the declared end of the Troubles era) has combined with the intense attention of professional and non-professional readers to entitle Northern Irish poetry as a hardly questioned object of discrete critical consideration – a critical construction, no doubt, but as such no different from any of the other constructions on which the work of criticism depends. The terms of the polemics briefly outlined above remain, nonetheless, especially cogent for this book's concerns: as epitomised in Terence Brown's remark, the controversy often combined an attention to a particular arrangement of and in language with a heightened sense of transit that invites recognition of the links between identity and place. Indeed, to varying degrees, each of the five poets whose translations are read in the chapters below reveal a sharp attention to the dynamics of language; as highlighted by their poems as (in some cases) by their critical prose and other forms of commentary, the attractions of an authorially deflected utterance become closely implicated with the spatial reference. The latter dimension is patent in Seamus Heaney's recurrent interest in 'The Sense of Place', 'Place and Displacement' or *The Place of*

Writing (to cite just three titles from the bulk of his essays, also known for the critical self-commentary they frequently offer, embedded in discussions of other writers); but it is also variously present in the obliqueness of Derek Mahon's representations of places in and beyond history, and in his probing of the sources and entrenchments of sectarian conformations; in the variety of inscriptions that compound the poignancy of Michael Longley's sites of memory and mourning, alternating as heritage and nature; in the liminality (playful or otherwise) of Paul Muldoon's writing, the frontiers and indecisive territories over which his poetry, essays, libretti recurrently joke and brood; and in the palimpsestic topographies, the urban spaces erased and reinscribed with which the work of Ciaran Carson has been juxtaposing Belfast and the world.

1.3   The scope of translation

In recent years, the concept of translation has been extended to include processes and practices that go far beyond questions of interlingual transit. This tendency in fact predates the theoretical contributions resulting from the emergence of 'Translation Studies' as a characteristically porous field of academic inquiry. Early pleas for a broader understanding of 'translation' included Octavio Paz's *dictum* 'when we learn to speak, we are learning to translate' (1971),[14] and George Steiner's influential work *After Babel*, which claimed, amongst other things, that 'translation is formally and pragmatically implicit in *every* act of communication, in the emission and reception of each and every mode of meaning' (1992: xii). Recent contributions have at times transcended the verbal communicational model to construe translation as an 'interdiscipline', or rather, as a macro-model for an indefinite range of ways of accessing and circulating information – at its most extreme, encompassing any quest for knowledge and all semiosis. Translation conferences cater for large academic and professional audiences under titles such as 'Translation (Studies): A Crossroads of Disciplines' and 'Translation and Interpreting at the Hub of Disciplines',[15] a comprehensiveness that has also appealed to scholars of Irish literature, as proved by Robert Welch's belief that 'All legitimate intellectual inquiry is translation of one kind or another' (1993: xi).

However, this indefinite extension of the concept of 'translation', which becomes invested with a vocation for totality, inevitably brings with it the risk of a loss of heuristic and operative value. The vagueness of such an all-inclusive concept may prove a liability rather than an asset for critical discussion of a body of writing whose potential for *signifying* depends on recognition of the generic distinctions that structure and enable the web of its intra- and intertextual relations. This is an important *caveat* that needs to be borne in mind when attempting to derive critical insights from theoretical considerations that have shown themselves remarkably prone to random but resounding analogies: the protean object of Translation Studies has, at different times, been described in terms that range from the somatic and physiological (e.g., sex and the circulatory system) to the commercial (e.g., the form of real-estate business known as 'time-sharing').[16]

The rise of Translation Studies to disciplinary prominence has also involved a certain amount of self-justification; indeed, it has retained and reproduced a discourse of legitimation that has persisted far beyond the obstacles that first prompted it. This has characteristically focused upon the subaltern position of translation in the academic world, and its narrative of disciplinary growth and emancipation remains its rhetorical trump card even when the tale is retold from positions that are no longer marginal to the academic establishment. A case in point is *The Manipulation of Literature: Studies in Literary Translation*, a 1985 landmark collection of essays. Introducing the collection, editor Theo Hermans characterised 'the position occupied by Translation Studies in the study of literature [. . .] [as], at best, marginal', marked by 'barely veiled condescension' or 'neglect' (1985: 7) – despite the fact that many of the contributors were already academically and institutionally influential players in a variety of sub-domains within literary studies. Indeed, it was precisely their academic distinction and influence that lent credibility to the programmatic design announced in the title of Hermans's Introduction, 'Translation Studies and a New Paradigm'.

The centre vs periphery model, with its Foucauldian resonance (e.g., Foucault 1995: 195–228), is just one of a number of recurring notions that show Translation Studies' indebtedness to tendencies in contemporary 'theory'. At the same time, some of these notions have been applied to complex political situations like that of Northern Ireland – so often described in terms of tensions that destabilise conventional perceptions of centrality/peripherality and authenticity. The target of Hermans's rather vehement denunciation was a centre of academic power whose very logic is easily assimilated to the entities against which a non-metropolitan culture defines itself. Indeed, the rise of Translation Studies was strongly aided by the querying of 'national literatures' as self-centred and self-contained objects of study that also proved fundamental for the legitimation of comparative literary studies. This congeniality is compounded by the significant overlap between the study of national literatures and a dominantly canonical rationale, as illustrated by the resistance of traditional literary historiography to acknowledging translations as an integral part of a nationally defined literary system and hence a worthy object of study. The minor status traditionally accorded to translated works certainly reflected a sharp hierarchical distinction between 'original' and 'derivative' writing, and the concomitant opposition between the uniqueness of authorship and the secondary role of the translator. Again, such distinctions were decisively eroded by the combined effect of various strands within poststructuralist theory, such as deconstruction's exposure of the fallacy of a sense of origin, with the Derridean insistence rather on the inevitability of 'repetition' and 'deferral' (the play of *différance*), the foundational notion of intertextuality that all writing is always already rewriting, and the much-echoed Barthesian proclamation of 'the death of the author.'[17]

These counter-hierarchical, countercanonical and decentring notions, which have become conceptual landmarks in contemporary literary studies since the late 1960s, were crucial for the academic legitimation of translation. They also prove critically productive for a consideration of writerly practices in a peripheral territory such as Northern Ireland, torn between allegiances that can easily polarise (politically and culturally) around London and Dublin, and which seek either to confirm such attachments or deny them by developing elective textual affinities with a literary elsewhere. Other related critical contributions may be more specific, such as those derived from the so-called 'cultural turn' that brought Translation Studies closer to the study of cultural conformations in their integrity (i.e. in their relations). As argued by influential commentators, 'cross-cultural relations [. . .] all [. . .] appear to be modes of translation'; 'the study of translation *is* the study of cultural interaction'.[18]

The currency of the 'cultural turn', and its close association with the perceived coming-of-age of Translation Studies, owe much to the insights of two scholars in particular, Susan Bassnett and André Lefevere: in different ways, their work underlies the reading strategies that inform this book. Bassnett's contributions have sometimes taken the form of claims for disciplinary comprehensiveness, such as when she argued that the initial relationship of containment between comparative literature and translation studies had been reversed: 'the revised view of the translation-comparative literature position makes Translation Studies the principle discipline, with comparative literature as an important branch of that discipline' (Bassnett 1991: 136). Her triumphant assertion, in 1996, that 'there has never been a better time to study translations' (Bassnett 1996: 22) not only acknowledged the success of the discipline (arguably also a form of critical enablement, to the extent that it further encourages translation criticism), but also implicitly recognised that the time had passed when translation could be plaintively described as the underdog of the academic world. As for Lefevere, his vast influence[19] has centred upon a cluster of concepts that he proposed or fostered and which have enjoyed increasing currency. These include an insistence on translation as one of various forms of 'rewriting'; a development of the notion of 'manipulation', highlighting the affinities between translation and canon formation; and, above all, the notion of 'refraction', an optical metaphor that Lefevere applies to a process of semantic and rhetorical inflection. This involves a combination of 'misunderstandings and misconceptions' that paradoxically extend the consequences of any text when it is rewritten and thus made to cross the spectrum of cultural features and expectations that characterises the target system – that is, the context within which the translated text 'arrives' and is assimilated (Lefevere 1985, 1992, 2004).

Lefevere equates refraction with all the textual dynamics, crucially including processes of transformative assimilation, on which the life of a literary culture depends: 'refractions are what keeps a literary system going' (Lefevere 2004: 252). It is a broad concept, which refers not only to what happens in translation, but also to the reception of 'criticism [. . .], commentary, historiography' and other forms of cross-cultural reading and rewriting (241). This makes refraction a particularly useful concept for considering the inter- and intratextual practices of writers who are also critics and (under their own name, or through translation) practitioners of various genres. Further, an awareness of the complementary relations that take place within the generic range of those writers also contributes to an understanding of the dimension of compromise in the processes of refraction, and of the constraints that define the target system. Of particular relevance to the concerns of this book, in view of the tensions that have beset Northern Irish culture throughout most of its recent history, is Lefevere's alertness to the complex factors that determine and shape the assumption of any translated writer into a given culture: 'The degree to which the foreign writer is accepted into the native system will [. . .] be determined by the need that native system has of him in a certain phase of its evolution' (Lefevere 2004: 243).

This sharp sense of necessity and circumstance, foregrounded by Lefevere's conceptual and terminological emphases (e.g., 'the native system', 'acceptance'), is characteristic of a target-culture-oriented understanding of translation. Indeed, the passages just quoted highlight Lefevere's culturalist contribution to 'descriptive translation studies', the theoretical framework that has come to prevail within the discipline since the 1980s. Deriving its name and some of its founding notions from groundbreaking work by Gideon Toury and Itamar Even-Zohar, the 'descriptive' orientation rather obviously seeks its defining antithesis in the *prescriptive* concerns that characterised earlier approaches to translation, and it is crucially based on a view of translation as indissociable from other forms of textual production and relations within 'the literary polysystem'.[20] A key principle of descriptive translation studies (one which this book endorses and critically pursues) is that translations are 'facts of the target system' (Toury 1985: 19), versions that in this case come to integrate the poetic work of their authors and hence the literary (poly)system within which they write and publish, in the full variety of its literary and cultural relations.

This concentration on the target system has a specific methodological implication: it deflects one's reading from a concern with matching target text against source text, from predicating one's critical work on expectations of strict equivalence – and judging it accordingly. And this is also a case in which my methodological attitude, itself a reflection of broader critical and intellectual mores, converges with strategies that prevailed at the genesis of the texts in question. Indeed only a few of the poet-translators considered here are thoroughly knowledgeable in what are (nominally) the source languages of the texts they render – be they Classical Greek, Latin, medieval Italian, or modern languages. As they usually acknowledge themselves, they often produce their versions aided by other translations, in their own or a third language; in some cases it is explicitly conceded that theirs was a strictly intralingual translation, a literary English rendering of earlier English versions (often of an academic type).

This practice, whose currency on the literary scene, Irish or otherwise, has often been critically noted – with varying degrees of (dis)approval[21] – lends a sharper edge to the *dictum* that translations are 'facts of the target culture'. Realising that a significant part of the work of the Northern Irish poet-translators consists of intra-lingual versions in fact adds to the complexity of the relational reading to be carried out. Since the actual source texts for such intralingual renderings are earlier English versions, these (the translations that have materialised the tradition of bringing the texts in question over into English) join the poems that the poet-translators publish under their own names on a grid of texts to which their translations creatively relate *in the target language*. As for the *primary* source texts (those with which the relation is *inter*lingual), they certainly retain their relational relevance, but paradoxically relegated to a *secondary* order, both because of the indirectness of their appropriation and the prevalent focus on the target system proper to a descriptivist programme. Should one feel outraged by an assessment of translations that focuses on same-language relations, one can always derive some comfort from the realisation that this somehow approximates (albeit from a radically different perspective on authorship and the canon) the conditions of reception in many different periods. That is to say, for generations of readers, the 'classics' (Ancient or Modern) they cherished were scarcely perceived as translations: in their cultural experience, the 'classics' were always already in the readers' mother tongue (cf. Bassnett and Lefevere 1998: 9).

A critical attitude predicated on effacing traditional distinctions between 'original' and 'derivative' texts and on the understanding that poets' translations are to be read on a par with their 'own' poems, may, however, clash to some extent with other notions that have recently enjoyed substantial critical favour. A case in point is the expectation that, out of respect for the cultural difference of the translated text, its condition *as a translation* be duly signalled by the translator; this also involves decrying the 'domestication' of texts rewritten in such a way that they read as if they originated in the target language. Pleas on behalf of 'foreignising' translation, as put forward by Lawrence Venuti from the early 1990s, are largely a retrieval and adaptation to the present-day ethics and politics of alterity of a discussion that has long marked the history of translation theory (a discussion that probably had its most characteristic presentation in Friedrich Schleiermacher's 1813 essay 'On the Different Methods of Translating'): whether the translator should aim to offer the reader an experience of familiarity or strangeness.[22] Venuti's quarrel with translations that are predicated on the translators' self-effacement and 'invisibility' (creating the illusion of a 'transparent' appropriation, cancelling the text's otherness), and his endorsement rather of strategies that highlight the translators' intervention, may at first reading seem congenial to the rewritings carried out by highly *visible* writers (whose names are often more prominent on the books' covers than those of the original authors). But his critically influential argument on behalf of 'foreignizing translation [which] seeks to restrain the ethnocentric violence of translation', countering its drive to 'bring back a cultural other as the same, the recognizable, even the familiar' (Venuti 1995: 18), will appear to be irremediably at odds with versions that call attention to themselves precisely by starkly domesticating the appropriated texts in the translators' recognisable voice. The acts of textual and cultural appropriation carried out by contemporary Northern Irish poet-translators inscribe the texts with a diction and a set of meanings that they could only have by originating in the target culture.

And yet these appropriations are prominently *not* the gratification of mainstream taste, the accommodation to sameness that Venuti associates with domesticating strategies. On the contrary, making Sophocles, Dante or indeed modern canonical authors (writing in modern languages) sound like Northern Irish writers confronting the predicament of their time and place in their characteristic diction is a counter-hegemonic gesture, often a form of 'radical witness' (to borrow Seamus Heaney's phrase – Heaney 1988: xix). This in fact shows that, in order to make critical sense of the textual body considered in this book, Venuti's domesticating vs foreignising model is bound to prove inadequate – mostly because of the cultural standpoint that determined its founding assumptions. Indeed, Venuti's denunciation of a politics of translation that erases difference and normalises texts reflects the insider's experience – and ultimate resentment – of a majority culture, with its gravitational pull, its intractable self-confidence, a culture that (in its mainstream) is little used to minding linguistic diversity and even less to inquiring into the texts and representations of alien cultures and literatures: in short, features that Venuti identifies as determining most translation and publishing policies in contemporary America (Venuti 1995; Venuti 1998). Writing in English, Northern Irish poets partake of the global centrality of an Anglophone literary culture – while on the other hand the place of their formative experience, persistently the dominant referential territory of their writing (even when no longer of their abode), carries a ballast of conflict, entrenchment, divergent politics of language, and uncertainties regarding identity that sets them firmly on the outside of that centripetal and self-confident culture (even when they enjoy global fame).

1.4   Culture of shadows

The territory that predominantly grounds these poets' imagination, haunted by the spectres of recent and remote violence, often resisting attempts to shed light on sensitive areas of history and collective memory, is therefore home to a 'culture of shadows' (to adapt a notion that has been coined for translation history).[23] And it is surely ironical that a culture that was subject to various oppressions, despite having achieved a visibility rarely granted to other oppressed communities, should bear so many conspicuous examples of translations of culturally central texts carried out in such a way that they sharply bring out the shadows of the target culture.[24] This has also involved regular appropriations of texts that represent descents to the realm of the dead and ghostly revisitations: it is hardly by chance that the text which will better allow us to interconnect our reading of the first and last of the poet-translators studied in this book, Heaney and Carson, is Dante's *Inferno*. Memorable tableaux of a world of shadows are thus regularly refigured through the 'afterlife' of texts (to borrow Benjamin's felicitous phrase – Benjamin [1923] 1999: passim).

Contemporary Irish poetry, taken within its boundaries – before one even considers the additional set of relations, the other voices and 'shadows' that are brought into it by translation – arguably comes across as an already haunted setting. The mutual awareness that its current protagonists have shown is enriched by a no lesser awareness of ghostly presences, those of renowned and influential literary predecessors. Such awareness helps account for the totemic value that a term like 'tradition' has long acquired in Irish critical discourse; and, insofar as it can foster a sense of empowerment, inhibition, or both, it has led to suggestions that a Harold Bloomian notion of influence might find its 'natural' laboratory in a literary scene so strongly marked by that play of desired and spurned parental and filial relationships which has tended to organise around Yeats and Joyce as alternative father-figures.[25] Diagnoses of a complex sense of lineage have more often been produced with regard to the mid-twentieth-century writers, whose chronological proximity to those forebears enhanced such complex responses; but the post-1960s poets manifest, in their various ways, a sharp and indeed broader awareness of those they write *after* – in the potentially triple sense of posterity, derivation, and minority. Practitioners of the lyric might reasonably be expected to relate more promptly, be it in appreciative or reactive ways, to Yeats, as the most canonical exponent of the genre in the tradition; but contemporary Irish poetry also contains abundant examples of attempts to exorcise his shadow by deliberately summoning an alternative precursor. This has often been Joyce – a case of the forebear's prevalent genre proving less important than cultural congeniality;[26] if Yeats's notorious championing of the Protestant Ascendancy, and his generally outrageous politics, have allowed him to be construed (in the words of Thomas Kinsella) as standing for 'the Irish tradition as broken', Joyce's subversiveness, and his scepticism regarding nationalist shibboleths (including the matter of the Irish language), have not prevented recognition of his ability to epitomise defining features of the Irish Catholic mindset. This, together with the more libertarian traits of his ethics and politics, has led to Joyce being hailed as standing for the tradition 'as healed – or healing – from its mutilation' (Kinsella 1967: 14), or indeed as 'a great democrat of literature' (Montague 1982: 52). In broader terms, his fundamental concern with the wealth and plurality of language(s), a defining trait (semantic as much as formal) of his legacy for contemporary writing, combines with his personal and literary history of exile and cosmopolitan mobility to ensure his centrality with regard to the present study's concerns.

Kinsella's and Montague's pronouncements, several decades ago, on matters of tradition and continuity can also remind us that, for more recent poets, the search for an enabling forebear has often prompted affinities with literary figures of the intervening generation, either because such mediating figures proved able to exorcise Yeats, or to assimilate and inflect his voice so as to make it an empowering force for the present-day poet. As regards the Northern Irish poets whose careers began in the late 1960s or later, this mediating role began by being ascribed to mid-twentieth-century figures whose values, outlook and referential scope arguably correspond to the dominant cultural traditions in the community. For a poet like Seamus Heaney, the appointed mediator was Patrick Kavanagh, through his vindication of localism and an ordinary, non-idyllic, non-mythologised rurality as a worthy referential domain for poetry; for those like Michael Longley and Derek Mahon, originating in distinct urban and Protestant backgrounds, the sceptical, brooding Louis MacNeice, with his *odi atque amo* stance towards Ireland, and his cosmopolitan ballast of represented experience.

Such (s)elective affinities can also partly be accounted for by the formative consequence of the 'well-made lyric', to which (in Terence Brown's already mentioned thesis) these poets are joint heirs – since this particular allegiance arguably restricts the range of their assimilation of the lessons of Anglo-American Modernism, recognised at their most obvious in a formal transgressiveness that is hardly characteristic of their verse. But these all too neat distinctions and lines of descent, primarily applied to the work of this generation, are hardly continued in the more recent developments that have marked both their work and that of more recent poets. The closeness between the inflection in Heaney's work from the late 1980s and the changed emphasis in his critical celebration of Kavanagh (from rural champion of the local muse, with a strong element of socio-historical awareness, to unconstrained lyric proclaimer of a sense of wonder[27]) is a revealing instance of altered congenialities. Likewise, Mahon's and Longley's acknowledgements of MacNeice's example, firmly established in their contributions of several decades to restoring MacNeice (otherwise read as an 'English' poet) to his Northern Irish birthright,[28] has evolved in its core emphases, accompanying the extension of the imaginative scope and literary affinities of 'MacNeice's spiritual sons' (Dawe 1995: 161). This tendency for a widening of the range of possible models, also increasingly plurilingual and pluricultural, becomes even more marked in the work of Paul Muldoon and Ciaran Carson – both, in their different ways, defined by the appeal of balancing an often playful gallery of international references against the perplexities posed by Ireland's languages and cultures.

This rich framework of allegiances and cross-influences includes but also supersedes the dynamics of descent suggested by such notions as the poet's assumption or rejection of 'the burden of the past', or the power struggle between 'strong precursors' and 'latecomers' (to cite two of the most famous pronouncements on the tense handing down of poetic legacies).[29] On the contemporary poetic scene of Northern Ireland, authorial awareness of contemporaries or potential successors is possibly as important as the concern with predecessors: 'anxieties of succession' (to borrow Edna Longley's phrase – 1996) vie with 'anxieties of influence' for predominance in the power dynamics that shape the tradition. The textual forms that evince this unusual degree of mutual awareness, ranging from tribute to parody, include dedications (of books or single poems), explicit or covert allusion, literal or truncated quotation, and verse letters.[30] This practice of writing *to* and *about* one another, within a relatively small though high-profile literary scene, has its varying degrees of irony and indirection extended when a number of figures on that scene bring in the additional mediations that translation involves – complicating even further the perception of who (and in what tone) writes *after* whom.

Insistence on this 'after' formula, with its various and already mentioned implications, also reminds us of how specious it would be to pretend that all protagonists on this scene enjoy identical status and authority, as if a complex construction of authorship and mutual acknowledgment inevitably fostered a democracy of literary recognition. The effects of canonicity can be mitigated by writerly generosity (of which several of the poets in question have often given unmistakable signs), but they are nonetheless patent in the intensity and manner with which the poets' mutual awareness is manifested. Further, the perplexities of canon construction can contribute strongly to the distinctiveness of poetic voices; literary reputations are often as important, or more so, than the poets' cultural origins (Catholic or Protestant) for determining a difference in poetics – whether we are considering their 'original' writing or their translations. And exacerbating the distinctiveness of one's writing can prove decisive for evading the shadow of a contemporary who has risen to global fame. The place held by Seamus Heaney in the grid of inter-authorial relationships between contemporary Northern Irish poets is in many ways exceptional. Strictly a contemporary of Longley and

Mahon, and only a few years older than Carson and Muldoon, the national and international impact of his work have led to a prominence that easily becomes analogous (in the reactions that it prompts) to precedence.[31] In the face of chronology, Heaney therefore often seems to emerge, in textual responses to his presence in the tradition, as a predecessor *after* and *against* whom one writes: the latter preposition implies in this case contrast rather than antagonism, involving an assertive and self-defining relation towards a canonical reference; and the impulse towards this *counterwriting* can also be gratified in an indirect and mediated way, through translation of other canonical authors whose voices are pitted against that of the major contemporary *qua* predecessor.

An acute consciousness of Heaney's presence on the part of other contemporary Irish poets is matched by recurrent manifestations of Heaney's own awareness of his canonical status, and the privileges and demands that it involves. This awareness includes a backward look and a sense of the contemporary: as regards the former, some of the attention that this book devotes to Heaney's assumption of 'the burden of the past' will highlight the extent to which his work's evolving emphases can be gauged by inflections in his relation to Yeats. It is as if the condition of unofficial laureate, imposed on Heaney as early as the mid-1970s (the moment when Robert Lowell dubbed him 'the best Irish poet since Yeats'[32]), had concentrated on him the responsibility of connecting his generation to the past – a responsibility enhanced by the painful consciousness of discontinuity that has beset the Irish tradition. The tendency for each of Seamus Heaney's utterances to be followed by a spate of critical views has not excluded his options as a translator: his choice of texts, his strategies for rendering them, and what they reveal of the poet's stance on life, history, politics. And, in general, Heaney's consciousness of himself as a writer, of the trajectory of his work, and of the persistent attention that he has obtained, have all regularly become an object of his own poetry. It is precisely this alertness to constant scrutiny that allows for an awareness of predecessors to be balanced against an awareness of contemporaries and successors, a sharp sense that he shares the poetic scene with a variety of others whose writing (and translations) show the marks of his canonical presence.

This authorial consciousness of self and others has strongly determined the content and methods adopted in the chapters that follow. It also largely accounts for the decision to focus on five poet-translators from Northern Ireland whose work is a privileged textual territory for recognising the forms taken by mutual poetic awareness. It is certainly ironical that several of these practitioners of textual dislocations, while retaining an often emphatic interest in the locations of their personal origins, have left Northern Ireland to live elsewhere; however, as John Goodby argues, 'residential' definitions of literary identity can hardly be sustained – and even less so in a tradition that has thrived on the achievements of notable exiles.[33]

Opting out of a comprehensive survey inevitably involves exclusions; but the sharper critical perspectives afforded by a cohesive object should contribute to a clearer understanding of the broader poetic scene. Moreover, this concern with cohesion has to be balanced against the arguments for discreteness and evolution that are abundantly offered by the respective *oeuvres* of Heaney, Mahon, Longley, Muldoon and Carson: those aspects of their writing that emerge as both distinctive and unstable, and thus help define a ground for critical discrimination, will therefore receive as much attention in this study as the recurrent and shared dimensions of their poetics. This will certainly bear on their options as translators.

This Introduction has offered a preliminary argument for the imbrication of original writing and translations as a specificity of contemporary Northern Irish poetry; the chapters below, however, will also inquire into the variety and difference of the individual textual appropriations that help shape that poetic corpus. Different poet-translators are bound to make different choices at different stages in their respective careers, and the weight that translation acquires in the economy of their writing will likewise differ. Beyond such recognition, this study will probe into the extension of the poetic range, in diction as in representation, afforded by the various translational practices to be considered. The daring and ingenuity of an appropriation, by which a poet-translator makes another's utterance his/her own, is certainly one of the attractions of poetry translation; but it is strongly rivalled by the gratifications brought by difference, the awareness of how plural imagination and diction can be. This alertness to translation as a source of variety, a practice that sets up a tension between two distinctive voices to generate new meaning potential (rather than more of the same), has strongly determined the choice of authors and texts explored in the ensuing chapters.

2
Authority and Freedom: Seamus Heaney

The rare popularity that the poetry of Seamus Heaney has enjoyed among a vast and diverse readership, from his first collections in the late 1960s, has recurrently hinged on a compromise between the excitement of the new and the comfort of a recognisable diction. Occasionally this tension between novelty and familiarity has involved Heaney's formal options, but more often than not it has emerged in connection with the poetry's themes, the breadth of its referential range. Heaney's universe of reference predominantly involves: (1) an empirically perceived reality: although his verse can also be abstract in its bearings, much of it involves scenes from a recognisable world, autobiographically mediated or not, which is one of its most consistent attractions; (2) other writings: Heaney's references to other texts and authors are more frequent and varied than the poet or his critics have acknowledged (and this has obvious relevance for the present study, centred as it is on the particular salience of intertextual relations in contemporary Northern Irish poetry); (3) itself: a practice of sly or ostensible self-reference has been present in Heaney's poetry from an early stage, becoming more apparent as time goes on.

Both that recurrent tension between continuity and departure, and the referential interplay of world and text, can be productively read and characterised by focusing on a cluster of interlinked thematic concerns. The sense of a communal 'burden of the past' is often conjured up in Heaney's work by moments in personal and literary history, frequently embodied in haunting father figures featured against the backdrop of his persistent themes of language and writing; and these themes, which have evolved through the empirical and imaginary landscapes of Heaney's verse over more than four decades, materialise in tropes of text and inscription for which the simplest and most frequent referent is the poetic line itself.

Critical identification of this thematic patterning, in its permanence and evolution, is facilitated by an aspect of Seamus Heaney's poetics that distinguishes him from his contemporaries: the limited amount of revision, of reconfiguration of his own work that this poet has ever indulged in.

This might be construed as a consequence of canonicity: a much scrutinised body of poetry that is often remembered and quoted can hardly afford to be changed at will without the risk of alienating sections of its readership. But other reasons for this comparative textual stability may involve its surprising inner consistency, the way in which an appearance of structure, of design, even of some elusive pre-existing 'master plan', seems to be confirmed by each addition to the oeuvre. Jokingly acknowledged by Heaney himself as 'planned retrospectively',[1] such internal coherence, entailing both proleptic and analeptic perceptions, has also meant that poems long recognised as signposting the overall design of his work have retained their relative positions.

Nowhere has this poetic benchmarking been clearer than in the case of 'Digging', the first (and title) poem in Heaney's first collection, *Death of a Naturalist* (1966). In spite of its recognised obviousness (cf. Heaney 1980: 41),[2] 'Digging' has persistently been accorded by the poet the place and status of a starting point, never ejected from such prominence – and indeed usually selected as the opening piece of every public reading. Rather than a mere sentimental gesture, this arguably reflects the poem's rhetorical power, its ability to come across to its readers as the very first statement of a programme, a poetic mindset, and a panoply of favoured tropes – all of which prove relevant to this book's concerns. 'Digging' is firmly based on the assumption of a heritage, proposing a writing whose self-representation coincides with the felt wish to give continuity to the labours that defined the rural existence of the poet's forebears. Despite its tribute to their example and precedence, the poem refuses to idyllise that continuity by allowing the hardness and drudgery of that rural existence to emerge. This underlying anti-pastoral element combines with the poet's half-guilt and sense of privilege at being freed from such a life through education and those writerly skills that the poem instances, in its very existence and in its referentiality. The vow to write *after* the example set by his forebears would seem to construe the act of writing as a tendentially passive enablement, a way of allowing a prior practice to channel itself through the poet. In some of the essays collected in *Preoccupations* Heaney reflects on the difference between passive and active, inspirational or volitional attitudes towards poetic creation (1980: 61–78; 83, 87–8). Just as his critical attitude in those essays balances the attraction to assertive and masterful creation against the seductiveness of the inspirational, vehicular experience, so the passive element in 'Digging', prevalent in the occasion for writing that the poem strives to record vividly, is duly balanced by a strong element of deliberation. This is evident in the programmatic ending to the poem – 'I'll dig with it [the pen]' (1966: 2) – but, above all, in the equation of the writer's implement with 'a gun', an equation which is redolent of the 1960s militant and libertarian ethos, and the ensuing discourses of artistic commitment.

Within the rhetorical and representational economy of *Death of a Naturalist*, 'Digging' has obvious and celebrated continuities in 'Follower' and 'Personal Helicon'. The former poem is known for its ambivalent celebration of the precedence of the poet's ploughman father – followed around by the poet as a child, and then trailing the mildly resentful adult poet in his imagination; but also for its offer of the primary instance of Heaney's use of the 'furrow' as a trope for the line of verse, a trope whose longevity and literality he did not fail to note in his remark on the etymological meaning of *versus* as the ploughman's 'turn [. . .] at the head of the field' (1980: 65). If 'Follower' prompts this eminently visual association of furrow and verse line, 'Personal Helicon' foregrounds the auditory element, which nonetheless is also associated with puzzlement over source and primacy: the echoed shout, the mirrored face; and, like the book's first poem, 'Personal Helicon' (which is the volume's last) combines the inspirational approach to writing suggested by its title with the note of deliberation in its famous closing formula, 'I rhyme / To see myself, to set the darkness echoing' (1966: 44).

In these and other combinations, such tropes of self, territory and writing; such narratives of a craft's ancestry and transmission, inscribed in Heaney's work from his first collection to his latest, have become indissociable from most readers' perception of this poet's place in the canon of contemporary poetry. Delineating the development of these interrelated emphases is arguably the same as tracing the broader continuities and inflections that have shaped his verse. This provides a critical basis from which, later in this chapter, I will approach Heaney's work as a translator, to be read alongside those poems that have ostensibly grown out of the production of his versions.

2.1   From furrow to jet stream: The lineaments of imagination

The relation between self and ground in the early Heaney poems mentioned above, and the sense of emplacement that it fosters, led directly to the emergence of some of the defining strategies of Heaney's writing in the late 1960s and 1970s. They included the extension of the metaphor of excavation in the direction of an archaeology of identity, personal as much as communal; and the mythologising of history, through dislocations in space and time, that had its best-known achievement in his fourth collection, *North* (1975).

This mythopoeic moment in Heaney's poetry, with its conflation of Nordic/Northern geographies (ancient Jutland and present-day Northern Ireland) and its suspension of historical time, proved momentous in the making of his reputation and the extension of his readership. Its central conceit, which seizes upon the ritual practices of a remote place and time to re-signify them in such a way that they illuminate a present-day predicament on the poet's homeground, has obvious relevance for a chapter that progresses towards the study of the textual transits performed by the same poet, through translation, across various temporal and spatial gaps.

Nonetheless, the most characteristic textual realisations of this mythmaking device in Heaney's poetry, which obtained massive critical attention from its inception, will be largely bypassed in this chapter – except for a related linguistic emphasis: in a variety of pieces from the early 1970s, with important continuities in later stages of Heaney's writing, language, in the variety of its implications (from physiological to historical), becomes the ostensible object of an interrogation that is provocatively set against space and time.

A focus on language was to some extent anticipated in the foregrounding of verbal resources that characterises some of Heaney's early poems. Many of these employ onomatopoeia and a rough consonantal diction in order to equate the 'word hoard' with the bounty of an auditory alert, sensuously rich but harsh world. The clearest instances are found in some of the poems in *Wintering Out* (1972), which, while representing the workings of language (the materiality of utterance, as much as the primary signifying power involved in the process of *naming*), are also, revealingly, poems of place. Indeed, several, such as 'Anahorish' and 'Toome', have place names for their titles. In both of these, the vocal experience of pronouncing the place name – 'soft-gradient / of consonant, vowel-meadow', 'My mouth holds round / the soft blastings' (1972: 16, 26) – is both a form of representation and a means of evoking the place itself, not only its topography but also the full sedimented evidence of memory, from pre-history to recorded (i.e., inscribed) history. Since the act of articulating the name is invested with a ritualistic power to conjure up the place in the fullness of its existence in time, such utterance also becomes a means of defining an identity, a sense of community, on the basis of an exclusive vocality: 'like that last / *gh* the strangers found / difficult to manage' ('Broagh', 27).

More than two decades later, in the lecture that marked his acceptance of the Nobel Prize (1995), Heaney recalled the childhood experience of learning foreign place names from the family radio (in a small farm in County Derry), and, prompted by their alien sounds, imaginatively embarking on 'a journey into the wideness of the world. This in turn became a journey into the wideness of language' (1995a: 11). In the toponymic poems in *Wintering Out*, this double exploration of sound and space focuses rather on the home-ground, claimed by those who are able to pronounce its names. From here, it is a small step to representing the historical conflicts acted out on that ground as ineluctably bound up with 'its' language – that is, the 'guttural muse' of Gaelic brutally overwhelmed by the English 'alliterative tradition' ('Traditions', 1972: 31); and another small step from there to the euphoric contemplation of a linguistic redress of political dispossession, a reclamation of lost ancestral ground: 'To flood, with vowelling embrace, / Demesnes staked out in consonants' ('A New Song', 1972: 33).

The dynamics of this imaginary repossession, and the represented verbal utterance that enables it, qualify what might otherwise seem to be a staid link between language and a located memory, often represented in Heaney's poetry from this period through images of tombs, archaeological remains, 'hoards' of one kind or another. 'Lie down / in the word-hoard', 'Compose in darkness' – these are injunctions that, in the title poem of *North*, the poet receives from the 'swimming tongue' of a Viking 'longship' (Heaney 1975: 19–20). But while the early collections often represent the self in close tactile relation to the ground, this relation is not always troped as a penetration, inhumation or passive at-homeness. Indeed, in many pieces there is a progression towards a sense of self, location, direction and (poetic) calling, afforded by mobility or spatial expanse, and assisted by representations of two types of lived experience: agricultural labour or travel of some kind.

Rurality continues to be represented in Heaney's poetry as a fundamental layer of human experience, although its most memorable manifestations are probably found in his early work. 'Digging', as argued above, remains the primordial gesture of a poetics of the 'gravelly ground', the announcement of a poetic calling. Concomitantly, the poet's evocation in 'Follower' of his father as ploughman, 'mapping the furrow exactly' (1966: 12), is emblematic of a relationship with the ground that is presented not only as muscular effort, but also as mobility within definite boundaries, a repeated reconnoitring of a familiar topography, which is recalled in a fundamental equation between rural and poetic incision. In a more clearly socio-historical gesture, imaginative sympathy with hard labour on the surface of the earth also leads the poet to seek a correlative in the hardships of the 'navvy', hailed as 'my brother and keeper // [. . .] / picking along / the welted, stretchmarked / curve of the world' (1972: 51). However, the representational range of the poetry has repeatedly included other, less constrained forms of relating self to landscape and environment, among which travel looms large.

Indeed, the 'driving poem' has become enough of a Heaney subgenre to merit studies specifically dedicated to it (cf. McGuckian 1999). Its inception dates from his second collection, *Door into the Dark* (1969), which includes two poems about driving around or across a territory, with writerly consequences. In 'The Peninsula', it is the untiring repetition of a banal drive, rather than an extraordinary gesture or experience, which offers a verbal way out of the initial, aporetic condition:

> When you have nothing more to say, just drive
> For a day all round the peninsula.
> [. . .]
> And drive back home, still with nothing to say
> Except that now you will uncode all landscapes
> By this: things founded clean on their own shapes,
> Water and ground in their extremity.

> (1969: 21)

Though in a very different register, fulfilment awaits the male subject of 'Night Drive', the record of a strenuous southward journey across France to join the poet's wife 'where Italy / Laid its loin to France on the darkened sphere' (1969: 34). This equation of geography and sexual encounter reminds us of how often in Heaney close contact with a territory becomes erotically troped (the celebration in *North* of a sacral relation to a feminised ground yields an imagery of tactile erotic knowledge: 'my hands, on the sunken / fosse of her spine', 'I estimate / for pleasure / her knuckles' paving' – 1975: 29, 30).[3] But 'Night Drive' also makes the steady progress (rather than circular repetition, as in 'The Peninsula') towards reunion coincide with a verbal, specifically onomastic sequence. The place names literally flash at the driver under the headlights, and reading them, while propelled by desire, becomes indeed the only possible (ac)knowledge(ment) of a nocturnally traversed territory: 'Signposts whitened relentlessly. / Montreuil, Abbéville, Beauvais' (1969: 34).

These two early poems, in their affinities as much as their differences, epitomise a nexus between transit, text and knowledge that runs through Heaney's work and accompanies its landmark inflections. The telluric involvement in Heaney's poetry of the 1970s is matched by images of the poet surveying his homeground from a vantage that already shows the distancing effect of education and other hazards of life, acknowledging that 'I composed habits for those acres' (1972: 21), 'bedding the locale / in the utterance' (1972: 25). In Part II of *North* (whose 'journalistic' drive contributed as much as the mythopoeic Part I to lay the volume open to accusations of sectarianism – cf. Carson 1975, E. Longley 1985), he half-jokingly represents the course of his own education as a roughshod incursion of a rural Ulster accent, with its 'hobnailed boots', over the 'fine / Lawns of elocution' proper to literary English (1975: 64).

Heaney's poetic discourse of ground and progress was to gain in complexity, both of perspective and representation, when his personal move from Northern Ireland to a rural retreat in the South, effected in 1972, had its first acknowledged poetic consequence in *Field Work* (1979). The eminently sedentary nature of the experience it records may seem to make it a characteristically *sited, located* volume. However, in assuming the pastoral mode, the book enacts a transit between the mutually dependent spaces of culture and action (origin) and of nature and contemplation (temporary retreat), with disturbing but enlightening consequences for the subject.[4] *Field Work*'s central sequence, 'Glanmore Sonnets', alludes to a qualification of the rural retreat by signalling the arrival, albeit benignly represented, of all that haunts this poet: 'My ghosts come striding into their spring stations' (1979: 33). These transhumant presences can be literary, as in the playful suggestion of 'Dorothy and William' Wordsworth as analogues for the poet and his wife in Glanmore, or the similar (but possibly less tongue-in-cheek) invocation of precedents in Diarmuid and Grainne, or in Shakespeare's

Lorenzo and Jessica (1979: 35, 42). But they can also be the revenant ghosts of victims of the Troubles, penitently stopping by on their final transit to query the poet who had always balked at enlisting his writing in the cause of the community of his origins.

By poetically staging these hauntings, and the melancholy soul-searching that they provoke in the poet, several poems in *Field Work* – most pointedly, the poet's meeting with a murdered cousin in 'The Strand at Lough Beg' – anticipate the penitential circuits of the 12 'stations' that make up the title sequence of *Station Island* (1984). The *via crucis* that Heaney imagines himself pursuing on St Patrick's Purgatory, Lough Derg, yields (as Heaney phrases it in a note) a structural poetic correlative, a twelvefold 'sequence of dream encounters with familiar ghosts' (Heaney 1984: 122). And again these ghosts stem as much from the poet's divided *polis*, as from a varied literary lineage, since they include both accusing friends and relatives who died in the Troubles, and predecessors variously situated in the Irish literary tradition.[5] Significantly, just as the snatches of translated verse that punctuate 'Station Island' (Horace, Dante, a whole poem by St John of the Cross) bring welcome relief from the dreariness and gloom of the accusing voices, the ghosts of precursors offer him a way out of the moral deadlock and the sterile self-indictment that he spatially projects onto the repeated circuit of an ancestral pilgrimage site. William Carleton, the politically equivocal nineteenth-century author of *The Lough Derg Pilgrim* (1828), impatiently exclaims in section II: 'O holy Jesus Christ, does nothing change?' (1984: 64). And, in the closing section of 'Station Island', Joyce, Heaney's chosen guide at that point, author of emblematic representations of the Irish Catholic psyche that resound through the angst of the sequence, offers advice for freedom. Its power to prompt an *anagnorisis* in the circuit-bound pilgrim poet is enhanced by the combined spatial and metascriptural[6] imagery of Joyce's injunctions to break free of the circuit, to cancel the ordeal of inscribing one's traces around the same definite space and of having the marks of that space (its stones, its rough ground) inscribed on one's body as a penitential consequence:

> Keep at a tangent.
> When they make the circle wide, it's time to swim
>
> out on your own and fill the element
> with signatures on your own frequency.

(1984: 93–4)

These lines reiterate a concern that Heaney regularly manifested in the course of more than a decade – from his lament, in the poem that closes *North*, for an excessive pondering of his civic responsibilities that caused him to miss 'the once-in-a-lifetime portent', the sight of a comet (1975: 73); to the refusal (in an interview) of 'any more doors into the dark', since he longed rather for the exit and furtherance of a 'door into the light' (O'Driscoll 1979: 13); and on to the mentally clear-cut civic and writerly allegories in *The Haw Lantern* (1987), under titles like 'From the Republic of Conscience', 'From the Land of the Unspoken', 'From the Canton of Expectation.'

These allegories, anticipating the major change in Heaney's poetics (from the early 1990s) that he was himself to dub 'the swerve' (Homem 2001: 28), institute imaginary travel destinations, heterotopias that afford the experience of newness even while they propose the features of familiar *loci*, thus redesigning the relation between self and place: 'when we recognize our own, we fall in step / but do not altogether come up level' (1987: 18). The sense of wonder offered by such poems is thus mostly (though not exclusively) ironical. The particular poignancy of the best-known of these pieces, 'From the Frontier of Writing', derives from the analogy between a driver's anxiety when stopped at a checkpoint and the liminality of the moment of writing, a moment of unflinching (self-) scrutiny that has to be endured but then transcended, and whose wonder is not diminished by being experienced over and over: 'And suddenly you're through, arraigned yet freed, / as if you'd passed from behind a waterfall' (1987: 6).

In a repeated contrast with the effort, malaise or melancholy that often characterised the spatially mobile (and writerly) self in earlier poems, it is again wonder that marks the intimation of mortality that is serenely received in 'Hailstones', another poem about driving and inscription:

> that dilation

> when the light opened in silence
> and a car with wipers going still
> laid perfect tracks in the slush.

> (1987: 15)

In fact, at least from *Field Work* onwards a range of positive emotional responses tends to be evoked in Heaney's poetry in connection with marks on the landscape that, by their very form or arrangement, can be experienced and represented as analogues to the line of poetry. Perceiving them as such (when encountered, or in retrospect) is often made possible by travel – though in some cases the poet is static, but sensorially impacted by the evidence of mobility; they are characteristically a road, a line of trees or poles drawn across a landscape glimpsed from inside a car, or yet the much-favoured railway. The metapoetic potential of the latter was highlighted in one of the 'Glanmore Sonnets', from its opening line: 'I used to lie with an ear to the line'; a childhood thrill is recollected in the tranquility of the adult poet's retreat to be endowed with the value of an enlightening precedent – 'an iron tune [. . .] along the ground', sending 'small ripples [. . .] across my heart' (1979: 36). The hold that the mobility and sound associated with the railway had on the poet's imagination was to be confirmed nearly 20 years later, in *The Spirit Level* (1996), with 'A Sofa in the Forties', in which the golden patina of the pastoral of childhood adheres to the memory of playing trains; here, however, the retrospection afforded by history and an adult consciousness signals with bitter irony, through the use of the word 'transported', the contemporariness of that imaginary train and the actual ones that carried thousands to the concentration camps (cf. Corcoran 1998: 192). The gestures and noises of imaginary travels on a sofa nonetheless provide a subtly humourous connection with the language of Heaney's early verse: 'First we shunted, then we whistled', 'Our only job to sit [. . .] and make engine noise' (1996: 7, 9).

This was a particularly late instance of Heaney bowing to 'the auditory imagination' (a phrase that Heaney, the critic, borrowed from Eliot – Heaney 1981: 81), at a stage in his work where an emphasis on the visual conspicuously prevailed. But an earlier poem, in *Station Island*, had seized on a memory of the railway – and the mediation of a 'classic' of children's literature – to trope its imaginative and poetic potential through eminently *visual* imagery. In 'The Railway Children', which derives its title and idyllic resonance from Edith Nesbit's novel, the experience of finding oneself 'eye-level with [. . .] the telegraph poles and the sizzling wires' prompts the scriptural and *geographic* metaphor, the perception that 'like lovely freehand they curved for miles'. But language, landscape and travel become even more strongly welded in this poem through a childhood explanatory myth for that *writing from afar, telegraphy*: 'We thought words travelled the wires / In the shiny pouches of raindrops' (1984: 45).

This interest in word-in/and-transit, the urge to derive metaphors of writing and self-discovery from forms of travel and their evidence on the landscape, straddles the already mentioned divide in Heaney's poetry, the 'swerve' brought about by *Seeing Things* (1991). Over two decades separate *Station Island* (1984) and *District and Circle* (2006), but the former collection opened with a poem, 'The Underground', that has been ostensibly echoed in the more recent book. Contrasting with the childhood memories that marked the railway poems mentioned above, these are poems of adult experience (even when recollected from a certain distance) in an obvious urban setting – and with strong literary mediations. In 'The Underground', the memory of 'honeymooning' as a young adult in London becomes refracted through Ovid's *Metamorphoses* ('me then like a fleet god gaining / Upon you'), the Grimm brothers's *Hansel and Gretel*, and, decisively for the metapoetic implication at the close of the poem, the Orphic myth. The latter reference emerges with the poet's candid posing, in the final lines, as the prototypically perfect poet-as-young-lover, trying to emerge from down under with his beloved – a narrative that he returned to in 1993 when he translated two sections from Ovid's *Metamorphoses*, 'Orpheus and Eurydice' and 'The Death of Orpheus' (1993: 15–19, 39–42).

District and Circle, by contrast, marks its belatedness in various ways. Politically and culturally, this is post-9/11 and – pointedly – post-7/7 verse. By entitling the collection after a London Underground line (which bears a name that itself evokes location and mobility), Heaney reminds readers of the specific setting of a terrorist outrage and of the global conditions that are both relevant to the massacre of July 2005 and to the circulation, within that grid of lines, of people and utterances from all over the world.[7] The perspective afforded by this can in fact be brought to bear on other instances of transit and human outrage. For example, in 'Polish Sleepers' the decorative presence in the poet's own garden of old railway sleepers brought from Poland conflates the childhood memory of the 'ear to the line' exercise (recorded in 'Glanmore Sonnets, IV') and an allusion to the trains carrying prisoners to 1940s death camps (2006: 6). Poetically, the belatedness of this writing is seen in the extent to which it reflects a plurality of other writings that include the poet's own, over 40 years of an output that, in itself, has been consistently intertextual.

In the title poem, the poet's trajectories in the Tube confront him with a hint of the bombings, 'blasted weeping rock-walls', and an intimation of death in finding himself the living bearer of his father's physiognomy and bodily posture (2006: 19). But a sight of the anonymous moving urban crowds – 'A crowd half straggle-ravelled and half strung / Like a human chain, [. . .] / then succumbing to herd-quiet' (2006: 18) – is also reminiscent of Eliot in the *Waste Land* ('A crowd flowed over London Bridge, so many, / I had not thought death had undone so many' – Eliot 1963: 65) and, behind him, of Dante (an intertextual chain to which I will return). The poem's opening section centres on an encounter with a busker that will remind Heaney's readers of the 'encounters with familiar ghosts' in 'Station Island'; in this case, however, the 'watcher on the tiles' is endowed with a moral neutrality – he offers 'an unaccusing look I'd not avoid' – that seems itself a deliberate foil to the indictments that punctuated the earlier sequence. The familiarity of the two acquainted strangers, on what comes across as a regular mute exchange, is acknowledged with an *interrogatio* that might be a motto for much of what the present study is about: 'For was our traffic not in recognition?' (2006: 17).

The poetic acknowledgement of the woes of the *polis* in *District and Circle* is certainly distinct from that which characterised Heaney's poetry 20 and 30 years earlier. However, its very emergence qualifies the critical assumption, defined after the publication of *Seeing Things*, that Heaney's celebrated move into a lyrical practice unfettered by concerns from the world of action would be absolute, unmitigated, and irreversible. The 'swerve' was, nonetheless, momentous. Although it in fact predated *Seeing Things* (as suggested above, and cogently shown by John Wilson Foster – 1991: 188ff.), reviewers and critics hailed that 1991 volume as a landmark in Heaney's epistemological, representational and moral universe, celebrating an apparent supersession of his brooding mode of the 1970s and '80s, which threatened to perpetuate itself as Heaneyspeak.[8] The treatment of space is a fundamental index of the change. At their most characteristic, the poems of *Seeing Things* suspend ordinary spatial constraints and reconfigure the relations between body and world, subject and object:

> Was it you
>
> or the ball that kept going
> beyond you, amazingly
> higher and higher
> and ruefully free?
>
> (1991: 10)

The rhetorical device of *interrogatio*, celebrating release from ordinary physical constraints, or rather from the poet's earlier self-definition as 'Inclined to / The appetites of gravity' (1975: 43), has the effect of suggesting metaphysical perceptions that now gain a dominant position in the poet's work – who half-delightedly, half-ruefully remarks: 'Me waiting until I was nearly fifty / To credit marvels (1991: 50). Representation of unconstrained mobility is thus served by a verbal practice that can be defined as the opening up of a space – that of the surmised, but absent reply, the *locus* of an inferred meaning. As such, Heaney's penchant for *interrogatio* in his poetry of the 1990s becomes a verbal correlative for his celebration of the bright, empty, silent, unlocated space as the source of potential and meaning (rather than the pregnant, dark, vocal places of Heaney's earlier poetics): 'I thought of walking round and round a space / Utterly empty, utterly a source' (1987: 32). These lines from the sonnet sequence 'Clearances', elegising the poet's mother, had been employed by Heaney before, in the third station of 'Station Island', where they were associated with the rhythmic circularity of a place where the body was mortified (1984: 68). In this later poem, though, the same lines (slightly reorganised) assist a celebration of the released spirit, a dislocation which is also a disembodiment, the physical emptying of a space that becomes spiritually replenished, and whose potential seeks confirmation and equivalence in absolute silence.

The transfigurations of the ordinary through release and mobility in *Seeing Things* occasionally involve an element of self-mockery. At one point, a farmyard implement, emblematic of a foundational rurality that Heaney never reneged on, is imaginatively released from its earthbound heaviness and propelled into zero gravity and the absolute silence of outer space, dislocated from the domain of the simplest to that of the most elaborate technology:

> And then when he thought of probes that reached the farthest,
> He would see the shaft of a pitchfork sailing past
> Evenly, imperturbably through space,
> Its prongs starlit and absolutely soundless
>
> (1991: 23)

In an interview given in 1990, Heaney connected the decisive inflection in his work, (and particularly these representations of unconstrained transit) with both 'a slight sense of eeriness and airiness' derived from 'flying on aeroplanes back and forth across the Atlantic' and the experience of 'getting a bit older' (Wilmer 1994: 82). Indeed, ageing has been a frequent concern since the late 1980s, often in association with an acknowledgement of his parents' deaths (commemorated in *The Haw Lantern* and in *Seeing Things*).[9] It can hardly be dissociated from the more transcendental bent in lines like, 'I saw the soul like a white cloth snatched away // Across dark galaxies' (1991: 77; the epiphany, though, is prompted by the very physical action of 'once and only once' firing a gun). The 'frequent traveller' explanation, however, establishes yet another link between images of mobility and a writerly identity, in this case informed by the consciousness of privilege that haunts the lionised but self-aware poet.

In *The Spirit Level* (1996), this consciousness certainly contributes to the irony that pervades some representations of the poet's roamings. Indefiniteness, as regards a sense of space and place, is reclaimed from any negative implication – as much as the phrase 'You are neither here nor there', which defines a liminally positioned poetic self in 'Postscript' (1996: 70); metascriptural from its title, this 'after-writing' thus centres on a formula for the creative ambivalence of location in late Heaney. And ambivalence, indeed, marks the title of the collection itself, which points in the direction of the spiritual, confirming the element of wonder that *Seeing Things* introduced in the perception and representation of space, while at the same time designating a workman's implement.[10] Thus, a short poem evoking a miracle involving displacement and the Virgin Mary puns on the etymology of 'translation' and sees the poet, candid and 'in a light-headed credo, / Discovering what survives translation true' (1996: 45); while candour and irony alternate in 'The Flight Path.'

Two of this poem's central sections relate literally to the title. In one case, the poet 'stand[s] in Wicklow under the flight path', looking up, conscious that the experience conjoins him with 'the stay-at-homes', cherishing the domestic, while also retrieving the memory of being on the other side of that perspective, looking down from a jet plane. The other section takes the converse starting point, the 'jet-sitting' [*sic*] nonchalance of the poet and academic – 'Westering, eastering, the jumbo a school bus' – that is counterpointed by the interspersed call of the place name that has more persistently meant the pastoral in Heaney's work: 'So to Glanmore. Glanmore. Glanmore. Glanmore' (23–4).[11] The very recurrence of glimpses of this academic cosmopolitanism in Heaney's post-1991 poetry underlines its irony and self-directed satire, as when an avowedly 'privileged and belated' poet evokes *Matthew* 4:5–6 to admit to suffering 'temptation on the heights', after climbing 'the Capitol by moonlight'; and he proceeds to proclaim a poetic creed from the rooftops –

> 'Down with form triumphant, long live,' (said I)
> 'Form mendicant and convalescent. We attend
> The come-back of pure water and the prayer-wheel'

– only to be called to his senses, his hubris exposed and deflated by a condescending and very pragmatic voice:

> 'Of course we do.
> But the others are in the Forum Café waiting,
> Wondering where we are. What'll you have?'
>
> (1991: 98)

However, as suggested above in connection with the title of *The Spirit Level*, a degree of ambivalence characterised Heaney's poetry at the turn of the millennium: the recurrent irony often feels like a way of precluding a naive reading of the tone of wonder, of that exhilaration with take-off, air and light that ultimately prevails – as it does in 'The Flight Path'. If the central sections of the poem query the poet's worldly flights between cottage and campus, the opening and closing sections define a framework in which taking to the sky is a feat of the spirit, rather than of an air-travelling body. The former recalls the chagrin felt when a 'paper boat' went 'soggy once you launched it', a paper boat, though, taken from his father's hands with exhilaration and best remembered as an 'ark in air' (1996: 22); the latter departs from 'the sheer exaltation / Of remembering climbing zig-zag up warm steps / To the hermit's eyrie above Rocamadour', and closes with a paean to an imaginative space of light, air and weightlessness:

> Eleven in the morning. I made a note:
> 'Rock-lover, loner, sky-sentry, all hail!'
> And somewhere the dove rose. And kept on rising.
>
> (1996: 26)

2.2   Of banishment, joy, and damnation: Afterwritings

> The song isn't mine,
> It just passes through me sometimes[12]

The aerial and tutelary entity saluted at the end of 'The Flight Path', 'Rock-lover, loner, sky-sentry', is reminiscent of two recurrent figures in Heaney's work. One of these is the watchman, recognisably one of the poet's masks, voicing a solitary preoccupation over a space of struggle or dissension, which is also sometimes a concerned self-scrutiny – the 'lookout posted and forgotten', 'balanced between destiny and dread' (1984: 100; 1996: 29–30). The other lone figure, rather more reverentially approached, has the lineaments of a looming precursor – living 'like a rook in an unroofed tower', in possession of 'a book of withholding' (1984: 110). Crucially, these figures emerge in poems that are directly related, in their genesis and concerns, to Heaney's work as a translator; this enhances their relevance as authorial models, contributing to a critical understanding of a scene of afterwritings that Heaney has alternatively characterised either as defined by tributes and benign transmissions, or (in a more sardonic tone, and through the voice of appropriate *personae*) as a source of 'sulphurous news', and indeed the space of a 'jealous art.'

The latter phrase appeared as the closing words of 'The Scribes', a poem in Part III of *Station Island*, the sequence of 'glosses' entitled 'Sweeney Redivivus' that emerged as the lyrical consequence of Heaney's experience of translating the medieval Irish verse narrative *Buile Suibhne*, published in 1983 as *Sweeney Astray*. Ostensibly about medieval monks in their scriptorium, 'The Scribes' becomes a poem about writing in general, about the text and its margins, and also, as Heaney acknowledged, a poem 'very much about literary life' (Brandes 1996: 59). It follows the more often quoted 'The Master', a piece about poetic descent, masters and disciples, precursors and followers. The two poems, placed side by side at the centre of the poetic sequence, arguably epitomise the designs served by 'Sweeney Redivivus'; and this sequence is in turn central to the designs of a writing that has consistently become more metapoetic, intertextual and self-referential.

As the Introduction has already suggested, considerable critical attention has been given to the intense mutual awareness shown by contemporary Northern Irish poets, possibly only surpassed by their awareness of predecessors. It has likewise suggested that such consciousness of forebears and coevals has its source in each poet's desire to stabilise a literary identity as a participant in a network of poetic relationships, entailing a highly strung self-awareness, manifested in the poetry's tendency to become one of its own more constant referents. This anxious scene might seem alien to a poet as canonical as Seamus Heaney, but a vicarious element in his strategies for self-definition has regularly emerged in the various genres of his writing.

Heaney has also contributed to canon-making ventures, by editing and introducing the section on Yeats in *The Field Day Anthology of Irish Writing* (Deane 1991), or – in less conventional fashion – co-editing, with Ted Hughes, two anthologies: the idiosyncratic *The Rattle Bag* (1982), and the more scholarly and authoritative *The School Bag* (1997). Further, 'the criticism of [this] practitioner' (to retrieve a phrase from Eliot that Heaney has occasionally quoted) has consistently afforded insights into the course of his poetic development and his affinities – and (willingly or not) it has presented the reader with successive instances of self-reading refracted through readings of others.[13] In Heaney's own words, 'I suppose my criticism is some form of autobiography'.[14]

A key piece of Heaney's critical prose, with a particular bearing on the matter of poetic descent, is his 1985 essay 'Envies and Identifications: Dante and the Modern Poet'. The essay begins by quoting Yeats in 'Ego Dominus Tuus' declaring Dante 'the chief imagination of Christendom', and, after a brief critical commentary, it offers the remark:

> I quote these lines at the outset as a reminder that when poets turn to the great masters of the past, they turn to an image of their own creation, one which is likely to be a reflection of their own imaginative needs, their own artistic inclinations and procedures.
>
> (1985: 5)

This is phrased like a truism, a notion requiring no demonstration (it is no more than 'a reminder'), and it follows a two-tier authorial dialogue: Heaney-reading-Yeats-reading-Dante. The notion itself, combined with Heaney's turns of phrase (e.g., 'great masters of the past'), may remind some readers of Harold Bloom's elaboration on the self-directed concerns of the 'latecomer' poet, or 'ephebe', vs the great precursor: indeed, the duality in the title ('Envies and Identifications') and the frequent use of the word 'influence' throughout the essay make this reference inevitable, even if Heaney does not explicitly invoke it (Bloom 1973: 5–16 and passim). Although the essay opens with Yeats, it is Eliot who is given the foreground, confirming an interest that first became apparent in Heaney in the late 1970s, when a longing for authorship as 'authority' became explicit in some of his pronouncements (e.g., Kinahan 1982: 410). 'Envies and Identifications' is pointedly about models for authority: 'Virgil comes to Dante [. . .] as Dante comes to Eliot, a master, a guide and authority' (1985: 11). The balanced equation, the rhetorical clout of the enumerative dynamics, everything suggests an ambition to participate in a great literary lineage. Indeed, Heaney was to describe his essay 'Learning from Eliot' as 'a prolonged gloss' on Eliot's own writings on Dante (1989b: 17); and his more recent '"Apt Admonishment": Wordsworth as an Example' again includes interlocked references to Dante and Eliot, both forebears exalted as 'highly self-conscious artificers' and 'unapologetically literary' in the range of their representations – a set of remarks that might well apply to Heaney himself (2008: 22).

In the earlier essay, though, Heaney seemed to waver between the 'peaceful' and grateful model of literary descent exemplified in the above passage – a kind of descent Eliot himself envisaged and described in 'What is a Classic?' (cf. Eliot 1957: 57–8) – and the hint of a Bloomian *agon*: 'Eliot begins to envy the coherence and certitude [. . .] available to his great predecessor' (1985: 11). This wavering tries to resolve itself by postulating an individual yearning for triumph in recreating the predecessor – while promptly making clear that the ultimate aim is no more than the security of what can be shared and held in common:

> Eliot was recreating Dante in his own image. He had always taken what he needed from the work and [. . .] he needed [. . .] a way of confirming himself as a poet ready to submit his intelligence and sensibility to a framework of beliefs which were inherited and communal.
>
> (1985: 12)

A similar balancing act was offered in one of Heaney's Richard Ellmann Lectures collected as *The Place of Writing*. Here, Heaney quotes and expands on Auden's notion of reception as digestion and recreation, while also representing the attitude of followers towards the canonical precursor as one of wilful distance, instituting a potentially two-way transit of inscription and erasure:

> a dialectic is set in motion in which the new writing does not so much displace the old as strive to displace itself to an enabling distance away from it [. . .] any writing is to some extent an unwriting not only of previous writings but even of itself.
>
> (1989: 55–6)

The closing sentence in this passage chimes with the textual practices to be studied below. But the passage also reminds us that continuity vs confrontation – indeed emulation, in the dual sense of imitation and rivalry – has constantly characterised Heaney's representation of his relationship to precursors, even when (as seen in connection with early poems such as 'Digging' and 'Follower') the precursor is the biological father. The writerly implication of the father–son relationship was extended in some of the elegiac writing of the 1990s, most notably in a short poem in *The Spirit Level*:

> The dotted line my father's ashplant made
> On Sandymount Strand
> Is something else the tide won't wash away.
>
> (1996: 62)

The mixed comfort and unease that surround the father's ghostly return, the persistence of his insignia and inscriptions, confirm Heaney's interest in construing the moment of writing as a manifestation of otherness in the self.[15] 'Widgeon', in Part I of *Station Island*, gave that manifestation an empirical and natural grounding by evoking the moment when someone blew on a dead bird's voice box, thus making its cry sound again (1984: 48) – the posthumous retrieval of a voice which is itself reminiscent of Ezra Pound's dictum on translation as a way of bringing a dead man to life (cf. Bassnett 1991: 83).

That poem on a human borrowing a bird's voice was included in the collection that followed Heaney's publication of *Sweeney Astray*, the Early Medieval tale (by unknown, possibly various authors) of a mad or otherwise displaced king from Ulster who turns bird and takes to the air and trees. Heaney's version of the title retains the uncertainty about Sweeney's displacement or distraction: earlier versions of *Buile Suibhne* styled it *The Madness of Sweeney*, or *The Frenzy of Sweeney* – as in J. G. O'Keeffe's 1913 bilingual edition that Heaney acknowledges as his source, an acknowledgement that is itself relevant for its indication that the translation work was both inter- and intralingual. In his Introduction, as well as in a retrospective essay published in 1989, Heaney provided a significant amount of information on the genesis of *Sweeney Astray*. In Heaney's account, a first version was swiftly produced between 1972 and 1973 in terms that (16 years later) Heaney himself was to consider 'arrogant', brashly appropriative, and unashamedly intralingual – taking O'Keeffe's English version, rather than the Irish text, for his source.[16] However, this was subject to substantial rewriting after 1979, resulting in a version that (again, according to Heaney's later essay) gave considerable attention to the text on the left-hand page (1989a: 16–19). This mitigated the appropriation, the domestication of the text in his own poetic diction – although it remained a target-oriented venture (like most of the translations studied in this book).

The 1983 Introduction to *Sweeney Astray* gave Heaney's readers considerably less detail about the book's genesis, though it opened with a few remarks on sources and literary history. In general terms, it claimed an historically integrative role for writing, in tune with an earlier essay in which Heaney had defined 'poetry [. . .] as a restoration of the culture to itself', and argued that '[the effort] to define and interpret the present by bringing it into significant relationship with the past [. . .] has to be urgently renewed' (1980: 60). The envisaged contribution of his *Sweeney Astray* to that integrative effort was referred (again in the measured tone of his Introduction) to the sectarian landscape of Ulster, by remarking on 'Sweeney's easy sense of cultural affinity with both western Scotland and southern Ireland as exemplary for all men and women in contemporary Ulster' (1983: n.p.). However, in the economy of arguments enlisted by Heaney's Introduction, this pious concern with what a refracted *Sweeney Astray* might do for Northern Ireland is in fact subordinate to his interest in what it might do for himself, the translator-poet. Sweeney is thus construed as 'also a figure of the artist, displaced, guilty, assuaging himself by his utterance', a model for the poet torn between civic and artistic allegiances. Location, through close knowledge of the map evoked by the place names in the text (often poignantly recited to emphasise Sweeney's doleful displacement), is explicitly invoked as a strong reason for identification: 'My fundamental relation with Sweeney [. . .] is topographical'. Autobiography (especially Heaney's move from Belfast to Co. Wicklow shortly before embarking on the Sweeney venture) gains particular cogency, contributing towards a thorough identification, as made clear by the Introduction's closing sentence: 'he seemed to have been with me from the start' (1983: n.p.).[17]

This congeniality also contributed to balancing duty and pleasure in the inclinations and strategic choices of this particular translator. Confronted with the fullness of the text's 87 sections (whose succession offers a textual correlative to the character's itinerancy), Heaney reveals how tempted he felt to render only 'the best lyric moments'. However, he ultimately yielded to the awe commanded by 'a major work in the canon of medieval literature' and translated 'the whole thing', paying due attention to the text's epic dimension, even if indulging the lyrical vocation by 'invest[ing] the poems with a more subjective tone than they possess in Irish' (1983: n.p.). His *Sweeney Astray* derives due rhetorical capital from the stark alternation between the narrative of King Sweeney's distraction and metamorphosis (in the course of a battle, and due to the curse of an offended cleric) and a lyrical celebration, in terms that combine exultation and dolefulness, of the natural settings where Sweeney roams in his dislocated, translated condition. The contrast between the two modes is enhanced by Heaney's poetic investment in the lyrical sections, whose predominantly free verse has nonetheless a measure of regularity (line length conforming mostly to trimeters and tetrameters, but subject to no definite pattern) that makes his quatrains distinct from O'Keeffe's philologically determined version.

Heaney's options occasionally foreground the element of refracted, indirect commentary on the Northern Irish situation, as with the 'stubborn band of Ulstermen' tellingly associated with 'Scotland' – Heaney clarifies the reference by substituting the English (and Scots) version of the Gaelic name – in a stanza from section 45 (O'Keeffe's version provides an apt term of comparison):

<table>
<tr><td>

I'll be overtaken
by a stubborn band
of Ulstermen
faring through Scotland
      (Heaney 1983: 53)

</td><td>

There will overtake me
a warrior-band stubbornly,
far from Ulster,
faring in Alba.
      (O'Keeffe 1913: 95)

</td></tr>
</table>

Versions of place names (whose literary resonance in an Irish context is amplified by awareness of the medieval lyrical subgenre of *dinnseanchas*) also serve a purpose of literary domestication, allowing readers to recognise locations from better-known sources – as is the case with Heaney's preference for the form 'Benn Bulben' over 'Benn Gulbain' (favoured by O'Keeffe). And domestication is arguably also the operative concept when Heaney translates in such a way that his version becomes remarkably similar to well-known lines of his own. This becomes evident when he employs the phrase 'wintering out' (the title of his 1972 collection) in section 27, or when in section 40 he resorts to a diction – 'the wolves behind me / howling and rending – / their vapoury tongues / [. . .] / shaken off like nightmare' – that echoes his poem 'Midnight' (1972: 46).[18]

Sweeney Astray is in many ways a text that bears the signs, in characteristic diction as in defining concerns, of Heaney's poetic output over and beyond the decade of its intermittent translation. The avowed ambition that a new version of a medieval tale of events in Ulster might contribute to a better intercultural and intersectarian understanding brings it into line with the strategy of juxtaposing present and past adversities that defined *North*. Sweeney's brooding, his inner suffering in his roamings anticipates the moral discomfort that was to acquire a spatial projection and a dramatic delineation in the circuit of expiation and the ghostly encounters of 'Station Island.' Conversely, the delighted celebration of natural surroundings in the poem's more luminous sections belongs within the same moment in Heaney's writing as the tendentially pastoral pieces in *Field Work*, which have the Glanmore retreat as a dominant referential space (relationally empowered by a few elsewheres of the mind). *Sweeney Astray* therefore becomes one of the textual locations that highlight the poet's perplexities in the 1970s and 1980s, by virtue of both the textual transit that defines it (as a translation) and the transit that defines the condition of its rambling, transformed central character. Indeed, a text that presents itself (in terms of its primary authorship) as *not by* Heaney, and as coming to us from a remote era, confirms, through various verbal echoes, the characteristic diction and concerns of its poet-translator. The radical otherness of Sweeney's madness and remoteness, dislocated from his original identity and the warring place that grounds it, enters a mutually defining textual play with the long-verbalised malaise of the poet whose name rhymes with this character's, the poet whose displacement to the Glanmore retreat yielded the tale of Sweeney's transformation.

Heaney's 1989 retrospection on his mindset after rendering and publishing *Sweeney Astray* includes the diagnosis that 'I had got fed up with my own mournful bondings to the "matter of Ulster" and valued more the defined otherness of *Buile Suibhne* as art' (1989: 20). The suggestion of a complete break may require some qualification, but this judgement would largely seem to be substantiated by the poems that Heaney published in

1984 as 'Sweeney Redivivus'. This poetic sequence, a direct offshoot of his translation work on the medieval tale, constitutes one of the most substantial poetic treatments of a poet-translator's own afterthoughts in contemporary literature. Besides this immediate relation to *Sweeney Astray*, 'Sweeney Redivivus' was also (again in Heaney's words) 'a very definite reaction against the kind of deliberately unlyrical work I did in the title poem of *Station Island*', a reaction produced 'from the perspective of a liberated, exorcised consciousness' (1996b: 7).

Freedom is then one of the meanings ascribable to the Sweeney persona, a freedom that entails a different and enhanced consciousness of self and world, as suggested in the closing words of 'In the Beech': 'My tree of knowledge. / My thick-tapped, soft-fledged, airy listening post' (1984: 100). However, the mad mythical king turned bird experiences not only release but also estrangement and alienation – and these words, with their etymological implications of enforced or embraced strangeness and distance, are fully relevant here. The same poem makes it clear that the tree as Sweeney's abode is both 'a strangeness and a comfort', and its opening line is: 'I was a lookout posted and forgotten'. Significantly, Heaney would re-employ the image of the lookout as a poetic persona at least twice more: a sense of freedom and possibility predominates in one occurrence, limitation and abandonment in the other. Gloom and estrangement indeed prevail in 'The Watchman's War': 'and me the lookout / [. . .] posted and forgotten', 'My sentry work was fate' (1996: 29–30). In contrast to this experience of constraint, a poem in *Seeing Things* includes the lines: 'You are free as the lookout, / That far-seeing joker posted high over the fog' (1991: 29). These words from 'The Settle Bed' follow an outrageous but liberating injunction to 'Imagine a dower of settle beds tumbled from heaven', a triumph of the imponderable over the ponderous that is made possible by the dictum: 'whatever is given / Can always be reimagined' (1991: 29).

This formula has a considerable latitude of potential meanings; if taken as referring to verbal recreation, it could be a motto for Heaney's notion of 'any writing' as 'an unwriting not only of previous writings but even of itself' (1989: 56). It proclaims a belief in the unlimited possibilities of 'reimagin[ing]' that was arguably enacted to renew Sweeney's voice in the 'Redivivus' poems (following the rewriting of his tale that had already occurred in *Sweeney Astray*). 'The First Gloss' is self-referential, but it also defines the terms in which, from this opening poem, the sequence is to unfold:

> Take hold of the shaft of the pen.
> Subscribe to the first step taken
> from a justified line
> into the margin.

> (1984: 97)

Liberation and transgression combine in this marginal writing, made of 'glosses' – a meta-writing at two removes: these are poems about the experience of translating other poems. With 'Sweeney Redivivus', the *marginalia* take centre stage, a doubly derivative writing that queries priority and originality.

This questioning of precedence and succession, and its extension from experience to representation, from life to writing, becomes even more insistent in the later Heaney, *The Spirit Level* being a case in point. In its first poem the enjoyment afforded by repeated listening to the sound of a toy-like implement ('The Rain Stick') prompts a rejection of any necessary link between the original or once-only event and a potential for pleasure and beauty:

> What happens next
> Is undiminished for having happened once,
> Twice, ten, a thousand times before.
>
> (1996: 1)

The significantly entitled 'The First Words', a translation of a poem by Marin Sorescu, denies the purity of a verbal source: 'The first words got polluted / Like river water in the morning' (1996: 38). And one of Heaney's several poems of bemused or delighted identification with traditional craftsmen explicitly claims descent from 'the journeyman tailor who was my antecedent', a man whose craft is no more than remaking, 'ripping out / A garment he must recut or resew', rather than producing unique and original work ('At Banagher', 1996: 67).

Nearly a decade before this, however, Heaney's attitude towards a notion of his art as always already pre-inscribed was apparently much less content (or much more ironical) than those poems of the mid-1990s were to suggest. *The Haw Lantern* is considerably more ambivalent in this regard: true, it opens with 'Alphabets', the quintessentially autobiographical poem about the mutual implication of self and inscription. This ranges from the young child learning to recognise figuration in 'A shadow his father makes' to 'new calligraphy that felt like home' (a lapidary phrase under this theme), and it includes the acknowledgement that, underlying and empowering the adult poet's scriptural sophistication, the memory of his 'pre-reflective stare' survives, marvelling at 'the plasterer' writing the family's name 'on our gable' (1987: 1–3). However, *The Haw Lantern* also offers the patent and emphatic dissatisfaction of 'The Stone Grinder', where Penelope's work is envied for its 'guarantee of a plot' and contrasted with the frustrated agency, the self-inscription ever under erasure that the persona vocally resents. The craftsman's palimpsestic art in fact induces a dual resentment – of the inevitability of rewriting, but also of impermanence, a denial of posterity that the poem's closing line emphasises by proposing *coitus interruptus* as an apt metaphor for this craft. The poem's middle tercets are explicit about the bitterness and anxiety on this scene of never fresh and never permanent inscription:

> I prepared my surface to survive what came over it –
> cartographers, printmakers, all that lining and inking.
> [. . .]
> For them it was a new start and a clean slate
> every time. For me, it was coming full circle

> (1987: 8)

Some critical readings of Heaney's poetry have suggested that it lends itself particularly well to 'theory'.[19] However, its congeniality to a poetics of indeterminacy, of the demise of origin and authorship, of the contingency of all inscriptions can hardly be taken for granted, as suggested by 'The Stone Grinder.' This poem's discourse of scriptural resentment in fact provides a critical vantage point from which to return to pieces avowedly on translation, those *afterwritings* in 'Sweeney Redivivus.' In particular, 'The Master' and 'The Scribes', which self-containedly face each other on opposite pages, arguably represent an 'anxiety of influence' and 'anxiety of succession' respectively.[20] The self-centred loneliness of 'The Master', combined with his abode 'in an unroofed tower', make it tempting to assume that the figure of literary authority referred to in this poem is Yeats, the foremost and most awkward predecessor for contemporary Irish poets.[21] The represented attitude of the persona towards the Master, together with specific choices in diction and lexicon, also seem deliberately to echo some of Heaney's critical writings on Yeats, which have in fact evolved significantly over the years. In some of Heaney's early essays, collected in *Preoccupations*, admiration is clearly qualified by wariness, bordering on dislike. Yeats' mode of composition is characterised as forceful and assertive – 'masculine', 'theatrical in its triumph', set in a 'rhetorical cast', 'the music of energy reined down, of the mastered beast stirring', 'a mastery, a handling, a struggle towards maximum articulation'; and we are reminded that 'a very great poet can be a very bad influence on other poets' (1980: 73, 75, 109). But this coexisted with the admission that 'one is awed by the achieved and masterful tones of that deliberately pitched voice', and with the recognition that '[Yeats] is, indeed, the ideal example for a poet approaching middle age' (1980: 109–10); (a reminder: Heaney started representing himself *nel mezzo del cammin* at around the age of 40 – which was also when he started to declare his already-mentioned longing for 'authority').[22]

In Heaney's later criticism, the attraction to Yeats became less qualified, as is shown by the fact that he characteristically started highlighting those aspects of Yeats's poetry that were more congenial to his own poetry from the early 1990s onwards. Words and phrases like 'transcendence', 'the marvellous', 'our best-dreamt possibilities', 'a universal symbolic force' recur both in his Introduction to the section on Yeats in *The Field Day Anthology of Irish Writing* (Deane 1991, II: 783–90) and in a lecture included in *The Redress of Poetry* (1995: 146–63). This evolution of Heaney's critical perspective on Yeats is not devoid of irony, an attitude that is sometimes reflected in the poems. One of the pieces in the 'Squarings' sequence of *Seeing Things* poses a series of questions, both mystical and metapoetic, that are ultimately described, in the bracketed closing line, as '(Set questions for the ghost of W. B.)' (1991: 78). The familiar use of the initials, together with the classroom associations of the chosen phrase, could make this poem a half-mocking instance of the final 'revisionary ratio' in Harold Bloom's theory of influence – '*Apophrades*, or the return of the dead' – by which the relative positions of master and disciple are reversed (Bloom 1973: 15).

Other 'revisionary ratios' might be identified in 'The Master', described by Neil Corcoran as 'almost an allegory of [. . .] the "anxiety of influence"' (Corcoran 1998: 128). The connection between 'The Master' and the 'Squarings' poem 'for the ghost of W. B.' also includes the question, in the later text: 'Where does it [spirit] roost at last? On dungy sticks / In a jackdaw's nest up in the old stone tower [?]' (1991: 78). This is compounded by the fact that, in the earlier poem, the rook-like figure of the Master is being approached by the half-bird persona of Sweeney – which also helps conceal the hubris of this approach, allegorised as a difficult 'climb up deserted ramparts', under the Master's dreaded gaze and hearing 'the purpose and venture / in a wingflap above me' (1984: 110). But although contact with the mastery of the great figure leads to a clear acknowledgement of the exactness of his text ('Each maxim given its space'), it ultimately deflates the sense of wonder, since all initiates already know (better or worse) the codes that frame the Master's writing:

> Deliberately he would unclasp
> his book of withholding
> a page at a time and it was nothing
> arcane, just the old rules
> we all had inscribed on our slates.
>
> (110)

Irony may be common to 'The Master' and 'The Scribes', but the sense of awe that dominates the former poem is replaced in the latter, from its opening words, by sheer dislike for the scribes, qualified though this may be by the persona's reluctant sense of having '[his] place' among them. Their asceticism born of spite rather than emotional purification, the scribes become like the implements of their fastidious and ostensibly dutiful craft: 'a black pearl kept gathering in them / like the old dry glut inside their quills' (1984: 111).

Their 'resentment' is again, very clearly, that of derivative writers, copyists who can only vent their frustration for their subaltern status by writing marginal glosses, thus somehow unwriting the subservience of 'texts of praise', on whose margins 'they scratched and clawed'. But this choice of verbs, together with the writing of glosses, effectively brings together the copyists, the bird-man Sweeney (with his 'claws' or talons) and the authorial figure hiding behind the persona – the poet-translator who now writes these glosses 'on the margin' of his translations, themselves a textual tribute to previous writers. To make it more complex, however, the persona also seems to speak in the voice of an 'original' author 'against' whom (in the sense of both confrontation and calque) the scribes ply their craft: '[I] felt them / perfect themselves against me page by page' (1984: 111).

Resentment is mutual: but if the scribes experience that of the derivative writer, the privilege of the first person gives the upper hand to the 'anxiety of succession' of the authorial persona, angry at those who 'perfect themselves against [him]'. It is as if the speaking voice were now that of a translated author, weary of all of his rewriters in their ambition to approximate (or, the translator's hubris, surpass?) the 'original.' But it might also convincingly be, coming from the poem on the opposite page, the voice of 'The Master', weary of disciples who, having learned from him how 'Each character [should be] blocked on the parchment secure', dismiss the mystery of his craft as 'just the old rules' and enviously strive to match him. And why not hear in it the harassed poet, wearied by the over-attention of his critics, often intent on producing a meta-literature by preying on his 'pages'? Or even the much imitated and adulated author, weary of the epigonal trail generated by his work, who hears in his mind the echo of the great predecessor's epigrammatic complaint: 'But was there ever dog that praised his fleas?' (Yeats 1990: 241). However, that concise prodigy of irony and litotes in the closing lines of 'The Scribes' – 'Let them remember this not inconsiderable / contribution to their jealous art' (1984: 111) – demonstrates Heaney's ability to preserve a detached self-assessment, by making clear that 'this [. . .] contribution' (indeterminately, this poem? or this sequence?) is not left out of what he has just represented as a 'jealous art.'

***

Jealousy was the main theme of an earlier Heaney poem about literary life which, hardly by coincidence, was also a poem reflecting Heaney's interests, as a translator, at the time of its presumed composition. In 'An Afterwards', Dante's *Inferno* provides a fictional posthumous vantage point from which to imagine a ghostly encounter between the poet's soul and his widow. She acknowledges his (laudable) aspiration 'to a kind, / Indifferent, faults-on-both-sides tact', but resents his dedication to a literary calling that limited his involvement in family life and remains his dominant concern: 'who wears the bays', which poet proves the 'most dedicated and exemplary?' (1979: 44). This fictional interest in 'the sulphurous news of poets and poetry', this avowal of a concern with fame and posterity is sardonic and self-chastising, because of its transparent hubris: in a satirical re-enactment of a Dantean circuit of hell, the poet's wife appears 'aided and abetted by Virgil's wife' – the implication of this spousal correspondence being, inevitably, that *this* poet is posing as Dante.

In 'An Afterwards' Heaney thus proposes but deflates, (self-)satirically, an ambition that his essay 'Envies and Identifications: Dante and the Modern Poet' was somehow to admit as inevitable, as noted above in connection with his remark that 'Virgil comes to Dante [. . .] as Dante comes to Eliot, a master, a guide and authority' (1985: 11). In fact, this formula paraphrases Dante's apostrophe to Virgil, 'tu duca, tu segnore, e tu maestro' (*Inferno* II.140), which Heaney was a few years later to render as 'you are my guide, my master and my teacher' (1993a: 11). This reverential formula, and the peaceful and grateful mode of inter-authorial relations that it suggests, could not, however, be farther from the scene depicted in 'An Afterwards.' The poem's starting point is the attribution to the poet's wife of a wish to damn all poets, as participants in a universal scene of selfishness and murderous jealousy, which has analogies in the lower levels of hell:

> She would plunge all poets in the ninth circle
> And fix them, tooth in skull, tonguing for brain;
> [. . .]
> Unyielding, spurred, ambitious, unblunted,
> Lockjawed, mantrapped, each a fastened badger
> Jockeying for position, hasped and mounted
> Like Ugolino on Archbishop Roger.
>
> (1979: 44)

Inter-authorial relations are here construed as a very literal case of picking someone's brains, devouring them, somatically appropriating the consciousness (hence, the discourse) of others. The sense of a universality of prey increases with a mise-en-abyme effect: the poet's wife's retributive drive seeks its apt intertext and Dantean metaphor in the gratification of a hunger that is already retribution. Indeed, the allusion implicit in the poem's second line becomes explicit at the end of the second stanza: the ghostly encounter (in Cantos XXXII and XXXIII) with Count Ugolino della Gherardesca, who perpetually gnaws at the head of Archbishop Ruggeri degli Ubaldini in retribution for the death by hunger that he inflicted on him and all his progeny by walling them into a tower and starving them.

This is the most memorable of the infernal encounters with traitors imprisoned in the ice, and it has enjoyed a rich history of appropriations in

English ever since its first rewriting in Chaucer's 'The Monk's Tale.' Heaney translated it as the closing poem in *Field Work* – thus reinforcing the recurrent brooding note that qualifies the book's pastoral dimension, pointing forward to the penitential circuit in 'Station Island.' But the poet's acceptance (albeit ironical) of his inclusion in the predatory scene evoked in 'An Afterwards' means that, when Heaney's readers come upon his version of the Ugolino episode a few pages later, their recognition of the poet's voice and location is rendered considerably more complex. Indeed, when a poet appropriates another poet's voice through translation his/her readers' supposition of authorial identification through a first-person speaker is particularly strong – even if sophisticated readers may be aware of the indirection proper to the use of *personae* or masks. In the case of versions of the *Inferno*, the fact that Dante is both author and key character (the visitor, led by his master and lord, Virgil, on a tour of hell) further enhances the expectation of a substitutive relation between the poet-translator and his great precursor. Readers of Heaney's 'Ugolino' will therefore tend to 'hear' his voice in the 'I' that addresses them and narrates this encounter; but they are also conditioned (after reading 'An Afterwards') to 'see' the poet in the position of the patriarch gnawing at his killer's brains – recognising him, therefore, both as an onlooker and a gazed-at damned soul.

This lends additional poignancy to the stark domestication of Heaney's translation, which bears on the thematic and representational conditions of his own work, as well as on the Irish historical predicament, prominently marked as it is by the theme of hunger through both the traumatic memory of the nineteenth-century Great Famine and the republican tradition of prisoners going on hunger strike. Passages from Heaney's 'Ugolino' that are bound to strike a familiar note include the description of Ugolino and Ruggeri as 'two soldered in a frozen hole / On top of other' (1979: 61), reminiscent of a passage in *North* 'Where two berserks club each other to death / For honour's sake, greaved in a bog, and sinking' (1975: 70). This earlier piece was a reaction to one of the Goya paintings that refracted the poet's qualms (at the height of the Troubles) regarding the relation between art and politics. Echoing it in 'Ugolino' also evokes its association with Northern Irish political violence and the poet's related malaise. Even more pointedly, the simile that has Ugolino gnaw at Roger's brain 'Like a famine victim at a loaf of bread' – for Dante's 'come 'l pan per fame si manduca' (XXXII: 127) – has obvious historical resonance in an Irish context (a reference that is not to be found in other English versions of the *Inferno*[23]). And the other major intersection of hunger and disaster in the Irish historical memory – the tradition of hunger strike, incidentally to be renewed in Northern Ireland the year after 'Ugolino' was published – is also alluded to when Dante's 'muda' is rendered as 'jail' (Heaney's is the only of ten contemporary English-language translations of the *Inferno* to choose that option[24]): 'Others will pine as I pined in that jail / Which is called Hunger after me' (1979: 62).

Almost two decades later, in a section of 'The Flight Path', Heaney was to acknowledge the connection between 'Ugolino' and the then current political situation, recollecting an encounter on a train with a rabid nationalist who badgered him (to no avail) for a sectarian commitment of his writing (1996: 24–5); the context for that encounter, as narrated in the poem, explicitly equates the 'dirty protest' at the Long Kesh prison with 'Dante's scurfy hell', and a few quoted lines from 'Ugolino' give that version (in retrospect) proleptic value with regard to the hunger strikes of the years immediately following.[25]

Heaney's lengthier translation of Dante, the three Cantos that he contributed in 1993 to a collection of translations of the *Inferno* by contemporary poets, was considerably less provocative than his 'Ugolino', and rhetorically much closer to a conventional scholarly translation. Nonetheless, Heaney's appropriation is signalled through a few conspicuous lexical choices, particularly the use of 'astray' in the second line: 'I found myself astray in a dark wood'. This description of Dante's anxiety at losing his way retroactively emphasises the wanderings of Sweeney (rather than the madness element), while it also reminds readers of Heaney's concern with continuity and coherence in his writing. And this concern converges with his careful phrasing of Dante's tribute to Virgil, from their first meeting in the first Canto to the already quoted formula (that Heaney had translated already in 1985, as shown by its use in his essay on Dante): 'you are my guide, my master and my teacher' (II.140).

Confronting the 'second center of the canon' (as Harold Bloom has called Dante – 1995: 76) can be a daunting task – in particular if we bear in mind the jocular suggestion of a voraciously intimidating Dante in Joyce's malaprop version of his name as 'the divine comic Denti Alligator' (Joyce 1975: 440). But several commentators have proposed that a more serious agon occurs among Dante's would-be followers than between any of them and the awe-inspiring precursor; as John Freccero puts it, 'To trace one's poetic lineage to Dante is tantamount to claiming the poet's laurels against all other contenders'. Freccero points out that 'Dante's text [. . .] is too remote in history to create the kind of obstacle described by Harold Bloom in his *Anxiety of Influence*', which deflects the energies of contention to 'the aspiration to poetic or even cultural supremacy, a contemporary struggle masked by the figure of Dante' (Freccero 1986: 3–4).

This combined concern with poetic salience and with cultural empowerment is certainly borne out by Heaney's critical remarks on Dante, both in his 1985 essay – with its opening endorsement of the epithet coined by Yeats, 'chief imagination of Christendom' – and in an interview given in 1989. In it, Heaney, who has otherwise described his relationship to Catholicism as secularised, acknowledges Dante as an exogenous source of cultural self-confidence for the Irish reader and writer (de Petris 1989: 72). He grounds his attraction to the *Divine Comedy* in its combination of epic scope with the 'secret beauty of the lyric' – as indeed he does with regard to *Sweeney*

Astray. With the Irish medieval tale, however, Heaney has performed an act of cultural devolution, retrieving a text from the autochtonous tradition – a text, moreover, that bears the marks of the transition from paganism to Celtic Christianity. Conversely, with his assumption of Dante he vindicates a cultural and spiritual conformation that has remained peripheral within the British Isles, despite being central elsewhere. For in Dante, the Catholic ethical and devotional world, with its aspiration to universality, acquires a validation equivalent to endowing the faith manifested before a 'little roadside altar' with a 'cosmic amplification' (de Petris 1989: 72 and passim).

Heaney's remarks on the devotional pattern centred on 'the little roadside altar' are a telling reflection of his appropriation of Dante in the early 1980s with the sequence of posthumous encounters that defined the poetic *via crucis* of 'Station Island'. In this case, his debts to Dante do not involve direct textual appropriation, but rather a borrowing of a representational pattern and the *Commedia*'s defining verse form (with which Heaney experiments, with considerable freedom). The dominant register in 'Station Island' is one of expiation rather than damnation, anticipated in the elegiac pieces in *Field Work* that mourn victims of the Troubles, such as 'The Strand at Lough Beg', with its three-line epigraph from the *Purgatorio*.[26] The 12 stations on the island known as 'Saint Patrick's Purgatory' include various echoes of Dante, but 'Station Island' consolidates its connections with devotional writings also by honouring other sources in Christian literature – notably the full translation, in section XI, of a poem by St John of the Cross (1984: 89–91). The simplified and fluent approximation of *terza rima* that Heaney uses in several sections of the sequence has had notable continuities in his poetry, when we consider the number of pieces in three-line groups (rhymed, unrhymed, assonantal) in all of his subsequent collections – with a notable concentration in the 48 poems that compose 'Squarings', Part II of *Seeing Things*, which prompted Peter Levi's remark on the 'wonderful new invention for poets' that Heaney's triplets might be.[27]

Two final observations on Dante's continued presence in Heaney should be made, both of them closely related to translation. One of these concerns yet again *Seeing Things*, a collection that is framed by translations: it opens with 'The Golden Bough' (a version of a passage from the *Aeneid*), and it closes with 'The Crossing', the confrontation with Charon in Canto III of the *Inferno*, a passage (with minor variants) of the translation of the first three Cantos that Heaney was to publish two years later, in 1993. *Seeing Things*, a collection celebrated for its luminosity, closes with another gloomy moment from the *Inferno*, but the reasons for this are made clear by its framing device. Just as the opening translation from the *Aeneid* has its hero address the Sibyl to 'pray for one look, one face-to-face meeting with my dear father' (1991: 1), and the core sections of the book include several elegiac pieces for the poet's father, so the closing Charon passage, with its reminder that 'No good spirits ever pass this way' and its injunction for the soul in transit to draw a positive conclusion from Charon's rejection, becomes a valedictory poem, a bid for the mourned soul of an immediate forebear to enjoy a good crossing onto brighter shores than those that one reaches with Charon. But there is yet another poem that combines Dante, deceased forebears and the trope of a journey, and which proves relevant to the structural design of *Seeing Things* – and that is the first poem of the collection (if we do not count the opening and closing translations). Under the title 'The Journey Back', its first line relates another apparition, that of an unlikely forebear offering a no less likely quotation: 'Larkin's shade surprised me. He quoted Dante' (1991: 7).

The sonnet inflects the traditional view of Philip Larkin as champion of 'the heartland of the ordinary' to endow him – through Dante, and despite Heaney's critical characterisation of Larkin's ethics as 'post-Christian' (1995: 156) – with a visionary/aesthetic dimension that may substantiate the epithet, in the closing line, 'A nine-to-five man who had seen poetry.' This association of Larkin with 'vision', in the dual sense of the word that *Seeing Things* consistently promotes, also makes him an enabling precursor to be invoked at the particular moment in Heaney's work that this collection epitomises. This precursor is quoted quoting Dante (another passage from Canto II) – or rather, quoting Dante in Seamus Heaney's translation (which makes this play of precedence and textually defined authority even richer). And the use of Dante allows the poem to reflect yet another aspect both of Larkin's changing reputation, and of Heaney's complex relation to recent literary history: the urban setting against which the Movement poet is glimpsed introduces an Eliotian note – 'rush-hour buses / Bore the drained and laden through the city' – that reminds us, yet again, of the place held by Eliot in Heaney's remarks on poetic descent in 'Envies and Identifications: Dante and the Modern Poet' (1985).[28]

The second of these final notes on Dante also involves a trip, but it is neither an urban 'journey back / Into the heartland of the ordinary', nor a crossing in Charon's boat. It is a boat trip, nonetheless, that the poet remembers in 'The Gaeltacht', a sonnet in *Electric Light* whose title, designating the areas in Ireland where Irish is the spoken vernacular, becomes ironical from its first line – 'I wish, *mon vieux*, that you and Barlo and I' (2001: 44). This opening line quaintly mixes English with a French tag to suggest the familiarity of a past convivial moment shared by a group of friends in a Gaelic-speaking environment, and such polyglot irony accrues with the realisation, explicitly offered towards the end, that the poem is in fact a version of a well-known sonnet by Dante (the one beginning 'Guido, i' vorrei che tu e Lapo ed io'). Heaney takes a 'dolce stil' nuovo' sonnet and brings it home – into English as the target language, certainly and inevitably; but also into the territory of a third language, a territory whose very designation rests on a *resistance* to English, as required by the politico-cultural dream, shared by the young people whose boat trip the poem records, that

Irish might become their community's *first* language. The cultural endowment that this domestication might suggest, however, is severely qualified by any comparison of source and target texts, which is bound to highlight the fact that Heaney's version is close to a burlesque. The source text's love discourse and its praise of the beloved are subjected to erasure and replaced with a nostalgic discourse that allows names of friends and old flames to take up a lot of the tight space of the sonnet, together with self-denouncing empty formulas – 'it would be great [. . .] if the people we are now / Could hear what we were saying.' This is compounded by an ending whose possibly playful intent, enhanced by self-reference, does not reduce the culturally deflationary impact (on the dream evoked by the poem's title, 'The Gaeltacht') of the final images of mismatch and meaningless noise: 'this sonnet [. . .] / Could be the wildtrack of our gabble above the sea' (2001: 44). A translation of a thirteenth-century text by Dante is brought to bear, again, on the cultural realities of a radically other time and location; and the distinct conclusions that it affords, when compared with similar verbal transits carried out by the same poet, prove again the ability of translation to shed light on the most complex lineaments of the cultures that make it one of their central practices.

***

If Heaney has been [. . .] the most subtle, apt and exacting interpreter of events in the North of Ireland, it is not least because he can bring, to the characterizing of those turbulent events, a set of powerful traditional resources – classical, Christian, Celtic and secular.

(Vendler 2002: 196)

This remark by Helen Vendler occurs in an essay on Heaney and 'the usefulness of tradition', written apropos of one of his confrontations with the Classics – specifically, his Aeschylean sequence 'Mycenae Lookout' (1996), the offshoot of an intent to translate the *Oresteia* that ultimately fell through. Both Heaney's actual translations of Classical texts[29] and the poetry that has grown out of those renderings have become one of the constant textual layers of his writing, and a factor in its overall coherence.

As regards the first of his two translations of Sophoclean drama, continuities are evident: after having taken on the displaced and radically othered *persona* of Sweeney, and closely intertwined his various appropriations of Dante with his inner expiatory itineraries, Heaney addresses yet another solitary, marginalised figure by translating Sophocles's *Philoctetes* under the title *The Cure at Troy* (1990). The version was written for a production by The Field Day Theatre Company, and the nature and extent of the refraction and domestication that define it matched the programme and expectations proper to that cultural and theatrical project.[30] It did so by reflecting a particular moment in the recent history of Northern Ireland, as pointed out by Heaney himself in notes written for one of the productions of the play (2002a). Besides the presence throughout *The Cure at Troy* of a 'level of generalized parable meaning' (McDonald 1995: 192), which brings the Sophocles play to bear on a public crisis, there is another and more specific way in which *Philoctetes* is dislocated: Sophocles's tragedy is brought into the poet-translator's frame of reference and rendered in his unmistakable diction at a particular juncture in his work. This drama of a man deserted by companions who can no longer bear the pestilence and wailing caused by his incurable wound, a man nonetheless in possession of a much coveted weapon that makes him the target of deceit and treachery, was translated by Heaney after a period that witnessed the protracted account of his conscience pains, torn between the sense of civic duty stimulated by calls for commitment and a yearning to embrace the detachment and independence of his lyrical calling. The process of outgrowing this dilemma, from the *via crucis* of *Station Island* to the civic allegories of *The Haw Lantern*, had also been critically buttressed by the essays in *The Government of the Tongue* (1988). Strongly informed by the concerns about empowerment and the relation to established powers that the pun in the volume's title suggests, these essays reveal Heaney's attraction to the poetics of evasion of pre-1989 Eastern European poets.[31] The book's central plea for the value of autonomous artistic assertion in the face of oppression was epitomised in Heaney's remark on the Russian poet Osip Mandelstam: 'For him, [. . .] lyric action constituted radical witness' (1988: xix).

Readers and audiences of *The Cure at Troy* who knew their Heaney were duly reminded of the play's antecedents in his poetry, often considered critically or ironically. The opening chorus (one of Heaney's additions to Sophocles's text) refers to

> People so deep into
> Their own self-pity self-pity buoys them up
> [. . .]
> Licking their wounds
> And flashing them around like decorations

> (1990: 1–2)

– a denunciation of egotism and emotional exhibitionism, which, in the light of Heaney's own self-assessment as disclosed in his essays and interviews in the late 1980s and early 1990s, might be a critical self-description of his brooding mode in earlier books. One of Philoctetes's laments brings him blatantly close to the voice of Troubles victims mourned in 'Station Island': 'He's condemning me to a death by hunger. / I'm going to be a ghost before my time' (52). Conversely, Philoctetes is the object of a choric injunction that specifies the ambivalent title of Heaney's quasi-contemporary collection of criticism: 'You should govern your tongue and present a true case' (61). Even more significantly, when Neoptolemus urges Philoctetes to abandon his self-commiseration he is made to anticipate and announce the title of a then imminent collection of poems that was to prove a watershed in Heaney's writing: 'Stop just licking your wounds. Start seeing things' (74).

This is an explicit textual connection between two books that are very different in several respects, although they are separated by just one year in the chronology of Heaney's work. The first (*The Cure at Troy*) is a dramatic version of a Greek tragedy refracted through the Northern Irish predicament; in this text, the images and voices of the Troubles emerge at their most explicit – as in the following lines, added by Heaney to Sophocles's text:

> The innocent in gaols
> Beat on their bars together.
> A hunger-striker's father
> Stands in the graveyard dumb.

> (1990: 77)

The second (*Seeing Things*) is a poetry collection in which Heaney pledged, as we have already seen, to abandon his preoccupied mode in order to surrender to unencumbered 'vision', the beauties of perception and lyrical celebration – 'To credit marvels' (1991: 50). When read in the context of Heaney's writing at the time, the line in question ('Stop just licking your wounds. Start seeing things') signals a concomitance, but also a bifurcation in his literary practice: what was threatening to perpetuate itself as deadlock within one single genre – the poet's inner *agon* over a public quandary not quite fitting the lyric mould – diverges respectively into a generic framework defined by inter-individuality and conflict (drama), and another (the lyric) that lends itself rather more easily to stasis and an exploration of self (cf. Peacock 1992). This sees Heaney venture into drama in a way that reflects an understanding of the genre as pre-eminently an art of the *polis*, as so often critically proposed.[32]

Arguably, the 'swerve' and the 'redress'[33] that the ensuing years have brought to Heaney's sense of public duty have also meant that his second and more recent version of a tragedy by Sophocles, the translation of *Antigone* published as *The Burial at Thebes* (2004), appears to be much less strongly informed by the stridency of the local quarrel. At a moment when Northern Ireland was gradually moving towards a much hoped-for peace and renewed civic life, its yet recent Troubles were hardly absent from the representational scope of this version. However, the local plight was approached rather from the perspective afforded by the broader vistas of world history and world politics. This latitude of political reference seems particularly well-served by a play (*Antigone*) that has so often refracted conflicts between the embattled individual and a repressive state (cf. Arkins 2003: 169). The phrase 'Whoever isn't for us / Is against us in this case' (2004: 3), which Heaney attributes to Creon, is a staple of many autocratic regimes, but it gained a new resonance after 9/11, when it became associated with the moral bludgeon with which America's allies could be coerced into 'the war against terror'. Further, by strewing his *Antigone* with phrases – 'cover-ups', 'the powers that see all' (2004: 6, 7) – that have marked a range of current discourses of and on power, about its uses and abuses, Heaney ensures that the global drift of this *aggiornamento* is not missed by audiences: 'global domestication', though an oxymoron, may be an apt description of Heaney's translation policy in *The Burial at Thebes*.

In the rich context provided by Irish appropriations of the Classics, such a policy also attracts attention from the extent to which it contrasts with another translation of *Antigone* by an Irish poet, Tom Paulin's *The Riot Act*, which premièred two decades earlier (in 1984) as a Field Day production. Although not the most blatantly Hibernicised of Paulin's versions,[34] its Northern Irish implications are made clear by the combination of recognisable formulae from Unionist public speaking – 'loyal citizens', 'public confidence and order', 'your steadfastness and your most exceptional loyalty' – with current slang and the odd Irishism – 'eejit', 'dayligone' (Paulin 1985: 15–17, 18, 44). Paulin's version thus provides a foil to Heaney's own anachronistic strategy in his second Sophoclean venture, much less context-specific in its rationale. The subtle ways in which *The Burial at Thebes* prompts its audience/readership to 'think in public in front of itself' also become apparent when references to the political and current coexist with an emphasis on verbal pleasures, such as those afforded by prosody, in passages that could otherwise be more blatantly employed for external reference: 'Are we sister, sister, brother? / Or traitor, coward, coward?' (2004: 4).[35] Indeed, the comparative regularity and smoothness that seems to characterise Heaney's rhythms through *The Burial at Thebes* foregrounds itself,[36] and may in particular catch the attention of readers of contemporary Irish poetry when we reach the passage, 'Among the many wonders of the world / Where is the equal of this creature, man?' (2004: 16), probably remembered by such readers as, 'Wonders are many and none is more wonderful than man' – the version chosen for the opening line of Derek Mahon's poem of self and place, 'Glengormley' (Mahon 1999: 14).

Some of the forms taken by the mutual awareness of these *coeval* poet-translators will be considered in the next chapter. However, Heaney's awareness of *earlier* translators of the Classics as precursors, a theme that has also occupied him occasionally as a critic (1999a), becomes explicit in ways that highlight the overarching theme of self and (dis)location. *The Cure at Troy* bears the dedication, 'In memory of Robert Fitzgerald, poet and translator, 1910–1985', and this was in fact one of Heaney's various textual tributes to the great classicist, which included an Introduction to Fitzgerald's version of the *Odyssey* (1992) and the elegiac sonnet 'In Memoriam: Robert Fitzgerald' (1987: 22). The Introduction combines literary-historical information with praise for Fitzgerald's 'loose iambic pentameter', and with reminders of the long 'afterlife' of Homer's text, which ensures that many readers who have not read Homer before are nonetheless familiar with Homeric episodes from their consequence in the work of writers from many different periods and traditions; in close though implicit relation to this, this Introduction highlights passages of the *Odyssey* that Heaney's readers are bound to recognise from their echoes in some of his own poems (1992: ix–xi, xix and passim). The sonnet, in turn, is a gloss on the episode (in Book XXI of the *Odyssey*) in which the returned but as yet incognito Odysseus strings his bow and shoots an arrow through 12 axeheads; but this famous feat is represented by Heaney as a shot through a succession of 'doorway[s] to a megalithic tomb'. The extended analogy honours the deceased Fitzgerald, of Irish-American descent, by imaginatively monumentalising his passing, represented as a 'migration' of Odysseus's arrow to and through the pre-historic passage graves that are one of the emblematic elements of Irish heritage (as proved by the attention obtained by the Newgrange site).[37]

Ancient literary and material heritage from two distinct places and cultures is thus made to overlap by means of a refracted representation. A trope from the North is inserted in a poetic account of another text, from a Mediterranean culture, transporting it to a Northern and Atlantic location – a juxtaposition that proves recurrently seductive in later Heaney. And if the archtraveller's homecoming was the theme of that elegiac sonnet dedicated to a translator (a master of textual transits), the bliss of return becomes the theme of a celebratory sonnet glossing a related episode of the *Odyssey* – the moment when 'At last Odysseus and Penelope / Waken together' (1991: 36). The sonnet belongs in a sequence, 'Glanmore Revisited', which is defined already by a sense of return and recurrence within Heaney's oeuvre (it relates to the earlier 'Glanmore Sonnets'); and it relocates the Homeric couple in a cottage in Wicklow, 'translated' into the middle-aged persons of the poet and his wife, as present-day connubial complicity derives a sense of renewal from an Ancient text. Neither the title, 'Bedside Reading', nor the sonnet's lines allow readers to forget the literary mediation: 'I swim in Homer' (1991: 36).

This particular metaphor for the assumption of the oldest of literary heritages, and the transit from epic to lyric brought about by 'Bedside Reading', are both relevant to this study for their combination of free flow and enjoyment, since these have become signal features of Heaney's relationship to Classical texts in some of his more recent work. After the brief resumption of a dark, brooding note under the tragic aegis of Aeschylus in the 'Mycenae Lookout' sequence in *The Spirit Level*, which Heaney himself has explained as an outpouring of pent-up anger with the Troubles, paradoxically released after the 1994 ceasefire (Cole 1997: 136–7), his textual dealings with the Classics in the collections published in the new millennium have tended to favour tropes of light and mobility. In *Electric Light*, the dominant mode for such appropriations – some in the form of translations, others as glosses or afterwritings of some sort – is pastoral, both formally and content-wise. The volume includes a translation of Virgil's Eclogue IX; a Virgilian 'Bann Valley Eclogue' – featuring a dialogue in which the 'Poet' addresses 'Virgil' as 'my hedge schoolmaster' (a stark domestication of the relation previously established, through Dante, with the Latin poet); and a 'Glanmore Eclogue' in which the dialogue, strictly local, features the 'Poet' and 'Myles'. But if the volume brings the Classics to Irish soil, it also takes the (Irish) poet to Greece, a modern Greece that is nonetheless empirically encountered in forms that fit the pastoral expectation, and thus lends itself to representations that allow for regression in time and literary references. Such is the case with 'Into Arcadia', the opening poem in 'Sonnets from Hellas', centred on images of bounty, but imaginatively energised by the perplexities of seeing global forces enter but not fundamentally change a space where farmers can still use methods 'Known in Hellas, probably, since Hesiod'. The sonnet's ending is celebratory but complex, as the lyric form (the eclogue) that has epitomised the pastoral mode across many centuries, and the verbal transit that has given it a new lease of life in many cultures, are declared (despite the commonplaces of literary hubris) less real and durable than the human embodiments of the way of life that gave pastoral its name:

> And then it was the goatherd
> With his goats in the forecourt of the filling station,
> Subsisting beyond eclogue and translation.

(2001: 38)

This closing line, with its self-referential import, may have a sobering effect. Indeed, the hubris of artistic and material success, with a strong autobiographical implication, appears intertwined with the classicising use of pastoral (or rather, 'bucolic'[38]) in *Electric Light*, and nowhere more so than in 'Glanmore Eclogue'. The poet lays himself open to satire as man of property, master of his own time, owner of a 'bay tree' (source and emblem of the laurels that crown his fame), empowered by 'book-learning' in a gentrified rural setting where 'small farmers [. . .] are priced out of the market', and not shirking the humorous epithet for himself as bucolic poet: 'Meliboeus would have called me "Mr Honey"' (2001: 36). But fame and its satiric representation have here a literary–historical association that is no less telling, prompted by a pastoral account of the well-known episode of how a Canadian scholar first allowed the Heaneys use of the cottage they were eventually to buy:

> A woman changed my life. Call her Augusta
> Because we arrived in August, and from now on
> This month's baled hay and blackberries and combines
> Will spell Augusta's bounty.

(2001: 35)

In a collection punctuated by pieces written (in various ways) *after* Virgil, the 'Augustan' implication, with a gender shift, is humorously obvious. But, in an Irish context, a poet that declares himself 'Augusta's tenant', having generously been allowed the use of a country retreat for comfort and writing, inevitably also alludes to Yeats, recurrent guest of the generous Augusta Gregory. The fact that those lines, originally part of a poem in *Electric Light*, were used as an epigraph to the following volume, *District and Circle*, dedicated to Ann Saddlemyer (alias 'Augusta'), leaves no doubt that late Heaney prefers to acknowledge and confront, rather than evade his canonical status, while using the ironies afforded by intertextuality and translation to query the makings of worldly fame.[39]

His translations, while allowing him to pay tribute to authors and texts that proved influential in his intellectual and literary *Bildung*, have also, by their very range, contributed fundamentally to the delineation of Heaney's position with regard to literary history and the traditions that empower his writing. He has translated texts that have previously provided a foundation for the culture(s) of their source language without having travelled much beyond their confines, but also texts that have long enjoyed a reputation for universality, through their influence as fundamental reading for the educated in many cultures, where they were received both in their original languages and in the myriad versions yielded by a long tradition of translation. Rather than just balancing the local against the global, Heaney's practice plainly aims to disrupt the neatness of such distinctions: the classics of the Ancient world and 'the chief imagination of Christendom' are grounded and localised in the translator's culture, and a long poem from the Irish Middle Ages is given a global circulation by being translated by a high-profile poet and issued by a major London publisher.

A defining addition to this corpus arrived in 1999 with Heaney's translation of *Beowulf*, a version whose success retrieved the Old English foundational poem from its condition of classroom chore, or object of arcane academic research, to make it an actual *read* for a global audience. The undertaking had multiple implications – for cultural and language politics, translation strategies, and relations to the translator's own work – discussed in the substantial piece of criticism that Heaney wrote as an Introduction.

Sections of this are an account of an itinerary, from a position on language that emerged from the 'cultural and ideological frame' of his origins, entailing a conception of 'English and Irish as adversarial tongues', to the realisation – significantly afforded by education and research – of linguistic interpenetrations that reflected the history of the British Isles and yielded a perception of shared heritage that would otherwise have gone unnoticed. Passages of this account are reminiscent of the primordial textual *locus* for the politico-cultural consciousness of the Anglophone Irish writer, Stephen's clash with the Dean of Studies in Joyce's *Portrait of the Artist as a Young Man* (already evoked in 'Station Island, XII'). Heaney's terminology for describing his enabling perception, at the level of language(s), of the inadequacy of 'the Irish/English duality, the Celtic/Saxon antithesis', is predominantly spatial and territorial:

> a gleam of recognition flashed through the synapses and I glimpsed an elsewhere of potential that seemed at the same time to be a somewhere being remembered. [. . .] The place on the language map [. . .] [where etymologically connected words] coincided was [. . .] an escape route [. . .] away into some unpartitioned linguistic country, a region where one's language would not be simply a badge of ethnicity or a matter of cultural preference or an official imposition, but an entry into further language.
>
> (1999: xxiv–xxv)

This is then the process by which the Irish poet, schooled in the history of languages, supersedes the quasi-guilt of having made an emblematic contribution to the canon of English – his medium, but also (for many in the community of his origins) an 'adversarial tongue'. Indeed, in a later essay Heaney recognises that some would diagnose his decision to study *Beowulf* and then translate it as 'exhibiting all the symptoms of the colonial subject' (2002: 381). He opposes the notion both in his *Beowulf* Introduction and in this later text, whose title – 'Through-Other Places, Through-Other Times' – borrows the phrase 'through-otherness' significantly from a poet from the Ulster Protestant tradition, W. R. Rodgers, to make it a verbal token of his own commitment to a relational view of language, culture and identity.[40] In both texts, Heaney finds in the overlapping etymologies of the linguistic media of Ireland, England and (indeed) Scotland the arguments to construe his translation of the primordial epic of the English language as a cultural and political enablement, a gesture that uncovers the grounds for a more ecumenical understanding of the traditions on those islands. This reclamation is signalled and furthered in the actual translation by Heaney's occasional employment of words that in present-day usage are peculiar to Ulster, but which were once current in English or in some other way highlight the linguistic interconnections that validate his integrative vision.

Some of these lexical choices, as indeed this overall argument on language and history, will be recognised by most readers not because they are familiar with Heaney's scholarly references or retain some auditory memory of them, but rather because they were used by Heaney before, in particular in the (politically suggestive) philological poems in *Wintering Out*. And it is indeed at this level, rather than in terms of representations, that Heaney's version of *Beowulf* is recognisably the work of this Irish poet: with regard to aspects characteristic of the Germanic/Nordic world (such as the ethics of revenge, the 'formal boast' and the celebration of heroic mayhem), domestication and refraction can hardly be expected to produce the correspondence between the predicament of their characters and the circumstances of the translator's time and place that defined earlier translations.[41] Indeed, Heaney also acknowledges in his Introduction that *Beowulf*, in spite of being 'the first native epic', is bound to come across to most English speakers as much more remote than the Classics, whose onomastics and narrative strands have become familiar through education (1999: xxi–xxii).

Well-known aspects of the translator's characteristic diction, and not just the odd lexical choice, may contribute to mitigating the remoteness of *Beowulf*, for reasons that again involve particularities of the English spoken in Ulster. The consonantal percussion of that variety of English, combined with literary influences such as G. M. Hopkins's 'sprung rhythm', may have accounted for some of the verbal effects in Heaney's earlier poetry, and contribute to his sense of congeniality when rendering the alliterative vividness of Old English (1999: xxiii). This perception on the translator's part in fact results in Heaney's most daring and yet simplest of canonising gestures in connection with *Beowulf*: the suggestion that his 'linguistic and literary' environment determined a fundamental affinity between his beginnings as a poet and the formal features of English at its very beginning as a literary language. For this myth of origins, the ground for prosodic demonstration is provided (with a sense of inevitability) by 'Digging':

> without any conscious intent on my part certain lines in the first poem in my first book conformed to the requirements of Anglo-Saxon metrics. [. . .] Part of me, in other words, had been writing Anglo-Saxon from the start.
>
> (1999: xxiii)

In Heaney's account, this perception 'that I was born into its [*Beowulf*'s] language and that its language was born into me' arrives considerably late, as if a conviction of a 'natural' bond had to follow the consolidation of a process of nurture, first launched with his undergraduate study of Anglo-Saxon poetry. Heaney's deep knowledge of the source language, the fact that in the case of this translation he confronts himself a lot more directly with the Anglo-Saxon text than (admittedly) he did for his versions of Sophocles or Dante, may also contribute to a much more reduced element of icono-clasm (such as the provocative anachronism), although the narrative and discursive fluency of his text distinguishes it from an 'ordinary' scholarly version. But Heaney's insertion of Anglo-Saxon poetry, and *Beowulf* in par-ticular, in the narrative of his intellectual and literary construction predates the publication of this translation by a quarter of a century. The Germanic world of feuds, treasures or 'hoards', of evening pleasures in the well-lit hall is one of the referential layers in *North*, certainly, through phrases such as 'the word hoard', or the imagined regressive movement, 'past / philology and kennings', to recover 'the scop's / twang, the iron / flash of consonants' (1975: 20, 28–9). In the same year as *North*, the bond between a bountiful lord and a brave thane about to venture forth was appropriated in a retro-spective account of an autobiographical episode in which the young Heaney is greeted and praised by his schoolmaster for a scholarship he had won (in the prose poem 'The Wanderer' in *Stations*). This account is followed by the reflection, couched in the diction he was to use abundantly in *Beowulf*: 'I have wandered far from that ring-giver [. . .]. I have seen halls in flames, hearts in cinders, the benches filled and emptied, the circles of companions called and broken' (1975a: 19).

'The Wanderer' is one of several poems that reveal the strong presence of the educational scene in Heaney's autobiographical range. It also instances the close involvement between representations of the poet's formative tra-jectory and his acknowledgment of a gallery of influential authors and texts, some of which he translates. This poetry of autobiography and tribute to (mostly) canonical writers, through whose voices the poet found his own, has in a much more recent and longer piece focused on 'translation' in that other sense of the word that makes it a synonym of staging.[42]

The sequence 'The Real Names' (2001: 45–50) constitutes Heaney's most sustained confrontation to date with 'the center of the canon' (as Harold Bloom has styled Shakespeare – Bloom 1995: 45). Its ten sections on a series of moments in the poet's early experience mark the development of a sense of self and circumstance, represented through images and phrases found in school productions of Shakespeare – their castings, rehearsals and perform-ances. Some sections in the poem suggest that Shakespeare's text was so thoroughly absorbed that it informed the child's or young man's percep-tion and representation of the world. The dire circumstances of a violent storm, combined with memories of sectarian bloodshed and a shipwreck in the North Channel, thus become refracted through *Macbeth*, and the ability to see, name and phrase a familiar riverside scene in lyrical terms is derived from the account of Ophelia's drowning in *Hamlet*. The sense that this conscious afterwriting affords an advancement of learning appears paradoxically bound up with a difficulty in remembering the poet's school-fellows (and fellow actors) as themselves, or as the characters they played, a cognitive and referential ambivalence that accounts for the title: which are

'The Real Names'? The fact that such figures in the poet's life story tend to become indistinct from the canonical literary constructions through which he remembers and knows them signals his concern not just with remembering, but memorialising. This is accomplished by paying homage to people and actions whose significance is initially private, but becomes shared and public when they are refracted through well-known works of literature. It is also made possible by verbally inscribing them in such conditions that they become *memorable* – which has self-canonising implications for a body of writing that might claim for itself (if Heaney were to use Shakespeare yet again to apostrophise any of the holders of 'The Real Names'): 'So long lives this, and this gives life to thee.'

The elegiac note became more prominent in Heaney's poetry with the poetic consequence of his parents' deaths (in *The Haw Lantern* and *Seeing Things*), and has tended to become connected with translation. As seen above, a relation between verbal transit and the soul's 'crossing' was integral to the dynamics between the framework provided by translations and the core parts of the collection *Seeing Things*. In 1995 Heaney also collaborated with the Polish poet and academic Stanisław Barańczak in the translation of Jan Kochanowski's *Laments*, sixteenth-century poems of grief for the death of a young child.[43] And his chosen title for an interview given in 2001 that reviewed his poetics at the turn of the millennium was, significantly, 'On elegies, eclogues, translations, transfusions' (Homem 2001). The enumeration in this title matches the various forms in which *Electric Light* honours a generous gallery of writers from different periods, languages and traditions – almost a secular hagiography, if one considers some of the continuities, provided by translation as practice and as metaphor, from the various poems celebrating saints in *The Spirit Level*.[44] A poem that makes this connection apparent is 'An Invocation', an elegy for the Scottish poet Hugh MacDiarmid whose title, combined with its opening formula – 'Incline to me, MacDiarmid' – equate it with a prayer (1996: 27–8). The poems in *Electric Light* that arguably continue this celebration of forebears and peers include a piece addressing several other Scots, jointly elegised under a Shakespearean title: 'Would They Had Stay'd' (from *Macbeth* 1.3.85).

This poem's often quoted last line, 'Like peat smoke mulling through Byzantium', epitomises Heaney's strategy for juxtaposing locations – actual and fabled, northern and southern – and their associated sensibilities, although the dominant relational dynamics in the poem are 'Britannic' (to use a recently much-favoured adjective[45]). In 'Would They Had Stay'd', Norman MacCaig is summoned to 'come forth from the deer of Magdalen' College and urged to be 'gallowglass' in Shakespeare's Globe; and a reference to 'Englished Iain MacGabhainn' reminds readers (implicitly) that he is probably better-known as Iain Crichton Smith (2001: 68–9). This integrative attention to poets from north of the English border emerges in a period, which includes the moment when Heaney wrote the Introduction

to *Beowulf*, when he was particularly vocal in his interest in contributing to
an acknowledgement of the meeting points and the areas of overlap in the
'Britannic' cultures and languages. His modern English versions of some of
the work of the fifteenth-century Scottish poet Robert Henryson, of which
the first text to emerge (in a limited edition published in 2004) was *The
Testament of Cresseid* (Henryson's sequel to Chaucer's *Troilus and Criseyde*),
have actively materialised this interest and extended the range of Heaney's
translations in several respects. From a philological perspective, a degree
of uncertainty as to whether such versions should be described as interlingual or intralingual translation further enhances the affinities and overlaps
among the different forms of rewriting practised by Heaney. Culturally and
politically, the ongoing project complements his earlier work on texts in
Middle Irish (*Sweeney Astray*) and Old English (*Beowulf*) with versions from
Middle Scots, pursuing the 'Britannic' agenda, as he frankly acknowledged
in 2001: 'Sweeney Astray was my "hidden Ireland," *Beowulf* was my "hidden England," and now I have a "hidden Scotland" coming up' (Homem
2001: 27). Indeed, the Scottish venture has prompted his probably most
explicit political and programmatic statement on translation:

> my writing about Scotland – I've written a couple of essays on Scottish
> poetry, and now there are the versions of Henryson – is meant to question
> the imperatives of identity politics, disestablish the notion that someone
> called Seamus, who did Irish at his Catholic school, will translate Irish,
> and that someone called William will translate Scottish.
>
> (Homem 2001: 27)

Seamus Heaney's latest versions, and the poetry and criticism that parallel them, thus confirm that his translation ventures provide the focus
for his civically most ambitious designs; a case in point is this proposal
that a broader recognition of phonetic proximities between the linguistic
media of the 'Britannic' space (straddling cultural, political and religious
traditions) be construed as the possible 'beginnings of a commonweal or
a common welfare, a *res publica*, or rather a *res phonetica* leading to the *res
publica*' (Homem 2001: 27). This dimension of utopia that comes to the fore
in later Heaney may prove one of the distinctive features of his embrace-
ment of translation, vis-à-vis the warier, less fervent discourses that other
poet-translators considered in this book have produced with regard to
the envisaged consequence of (their) writing.[46] Further, it converges with the
favour that Heaney's recent poetic and critical writing seems to give to the
benign understanding of poetic emulation and descent, which has vied for
prevalence, at important points in Heaney's work, with the contrary model
of inter-authorial *agon* and envy. This ultimate inclination towards a nexus
of generous transmissions, arguably epitomised in the celebration of poetic
forebears and peers that has ever more regularly marked his collections,

'compounds an ethical and an aesthetic judgement'. Ostensibly about others, such celebration of precursors bears decisively on the descendant poet himself, offering him 'a bolstering imaginative system of self-instruction, self-declaration, self-evaluation and self-rebuke' (as argued by Neil Corcoran in his study of Heaney's advocacy of the 'exemplary' status of admired authors – 1999: 95–120). Heaney acknowledges as much when, in his essay '"Apt Admonishment": Wordsworth as an Example' (2008), he removes the question mark that 30 years earlier he had added to the formula borrowed from Auden for the title of an essay on 'Yeats as an Example?' (1978), and proposes from the outset:

> When a practitioner describes an encounter with a living or dead master, or an equivalent moment of epiphany, something fundamental is usually at stake, often having to do with poetic vocation itself. At the level of autobiography, such scenes record crucial events in the growth or reorientation of the poet's mind; at the mythic level, on the other hand, they can be read as evidence of a close encounter between the poet and the muse.
>
> (2008: 19)

The passage is neo-inspirational *as well as* imitative – since 'the muse' is more often than not an earlier writer (Eliot is again at the back of Heaney's mind, arguing that 'the most individual parts of [a poet's] work may be those in which the dead poets, his ancestors, assert their immortality most vigorously' – Eliot 1969: 14). The rationale presented by Heaney, and its appertaining 'sense of election' (2008: 21), have their proper poetic ground in his repeated celebration of writers as secular saints: the integrative utopianism noted above converges with a belief in self-fashioning through authorial mediation. But, crucially for our purposes, this invocation of exemplary figures *after* whom the poet writes, and from whom he derives empowerment, is ever more regularly served by the particular *afterness* of translation. It is certainly by no accident that the resources deemed necessary by Heaney to elegise/eulogise Ted Hughes in the poem 'On His Work in the English Tongue' prominently include invocation and citation of *Beowulf* (in Heaney's version), as well as the lines:

> And the poet draws from his word-hoard a weird tale
> Of a life and love balked, which I reword here
>
> (2001: 62)

These are followed by a slightly revised (reworded) version of ll.2444–66 of Heaney's *Beowulf,* a digressive tale of grief for a son murdered in a way that admits of no redress. The poem includes no hint that Heaney fears any undue hubris or that any irony incompatible with an elegy might be perceived in his paying tribute to Hughes's 'work on the English tongue' by citing such lines of parental grief from *his* (Heaney's) *own* work, as a translator and renovator of the founding text of English literature. And this offers further confirmation of his belief in the mutual enablement derived from inter-authorial bonds (construed, in his words, as 'a web of relationships', 'an overall system of gravitation and association' – 2008: 26), a belief that largely overlaps with an endorsement of the inevitability of rewriting.

3
Of Containment and Unmeasure: Derek Mahon

The particular order in which authors and texts are approached in the course of this book is, by virtue of its relational logic, hardly a matter of critical necessity. And yet there is a strategic advantage in reading Derek Mahon after having focused on Seamus Heaney, if we consider a recurrent argument in discussions of Mahon's reputation. The argument is that Mahon is 'the most underrated Irish poet of the century', the victim of 'a conspicuous critical deficit' (Kiberd 1991: 1380; Kennedy-Andrews 2002: 1), and it is often combined with a comparison that implicitly attributes blame for such neglect: 'the amount of critical and media attention' lavished upon 'his fellow Northern Irish poet, the Nobel laureate Seamus Heaney' (Kennedy-Andrews 2002: 1). There is, it is claimed, a need for 'redress', in view of Mahon's 'equally strong case' to emerge as a major figure in contemporary poetry (Haughton 2007: 2).

The above quotations are taken, respectively, from the editorial apparatus of possibly the best-known comprehensive anthology of Irish writing, and the opening paragraphs of two heavy tomes of criticism integrally dedicated to Mahon. Such solid evidence of canonicity suggests that the argument of neglect is a critical topos that is now largely unfounded and which has been perpetuated due to the appeal of its underlying antithetical design. Derek Mahon's 40-year-long career, materialised in over 20 volumes (almost equally divided between poetry collections and translations), has secured him an esteem that compares well with that of other major contemporary poets – only failing to match Heaney's phenomenal popularity. An awareness of the latter's exceptional fame cannot but clash with the expectations derived from the apparent neatness of Heaney's and Mahon's parallel emergence as supposed representatives of the 'two psychic landscapes'[1] proper to the major cultural traditions (Catholic and Protestant) in Northern Ireland. If this has created a notion of equivalence in cultural function, it has also highlighted the imbalance in the attention obtained by the two poets, making the diagnosis above an inevitable critical factor – as inevitable, indeed, as the dual conformation with which it is so closely interwoven.

Perceptions of the Heaney/Mahon duality have also been fostered by the very different ways in which their respective works have been constructed. In marked contrast to Heaney's well signposted, recognisable textual territory, where poems remain unaltered and in place, as they were first published, textual instability is a characteristic feature of Derek Mahon's work and arguably a principle of his poetics. Mahon's habit of rewriting, retitling and reordering his poems has proved disturbing for some of his readers, though these revisions have afforded fascinating insights into the writing process.[2] Rather than a mere aspect of textual genetics, revision has become a defining dimension of his writing that is of particular interest for this study. It may be described as 'intralingual translation' in accordance with Roman Jakobson's famous threefold model – and indeed, the other two kinds of translation (namely 'interlingual translation or translation proper' and 'intersemiotic translation', cf. Jakobson [1959] 2004: 139) are also very much present in Mahon's work.

Most of Mahon's readers probably become acquainted with his work in the first instance through his *Selected* (1991, 2000, 2006) or *Collected Poems* (1999); however, these volumes can hardly be said to make the shape and course of his writing apparent to anyone who browses through them. They provide no indication of the poems' dates of composition or publication, or of the collections in which they first appeared; although their sequence seems to be mostly chronological, it accommodates a few reorderings, probably determined by thematic concerns; and a few poems were simply excluded from the *Collected Poems* (and hence from the author's canon). This strategy was already employed in *Poems 1962–1978*, which collected the first decade of Mahon's poetic output, dominated by his three (by then, out of print) collections *Night Crossing* (1968), *Lives* (1972) and *The Snow Party* (1975). Offering the poems unframed by any editorial apparatus may have the advantage of prompting readers to focus on the texts themselves in order to recognise the concerns that hold the work together, but it also deprives them of the referential import (empirical, imaginative, cultural, sometimes meta-artistic) of the various collection titles – those listed above and the later ones: *The Hunt by Night* (1982), *Antarctica* (1985), *The Hudson Letter* (1995), *The Yellow Book* (1997), *Harbour Lights* (2005), *Life on Earth* (2008). The very dates of these collections (again, dates are omitted from the *Selected* and *Collected Poems*) have their own relevance for an understanding of some of the phases of this poet's oeuvre, some of the strengths and uncertainties of its reception; in particular, they highlight a ten-year period (after 1985) in which no new collections of poetry appeared.

Any overview of the critical opinion that has surrounded Mahon's work must engage with the reactions that followed a change in the makeup of his verse from the mid-1980s to the 1990s, since his later writing has seemed to many to discontinue highly valued features of his earlier work. Critical assessments of early Mahon tended to value his formal accomplishments: fellow poet Douglas Dunn praised the 'elegance, [. . .] the assurance of his skill' (1975: 78), while an interviewer was to dub him 'a great man for metre and rhyme, a formalist' (Scammell 1991: 5). The sceptical disaffection that accompanied his 'urban' or 'cosmopolitan' imaginative range was also much noted, contrasting as it did with the ruralist discourse of identity that had otherwise dominated Irish verse (as confirmed with his contemporary and fellow Northerner Heaney). Commenting on this aspect of Mahon's writing, Terence Brown pointed out in the mid-1970s that 'Mahon is no eulogist of suburban possibilities nor of industrial society's blessings [. . .] sensing rather a new barbarism beneath a façade of materialist disregard for ideology, social hierarchy and commitment' (Brown 1975: 194–5). Implicitly reinforcing the antithesis to Heaney's belief in poetry's imaginative 'redress', other commentators have stressed the disenchantment of Mahon's poetry vis-à-vis a panorama of alienation and fragmentation, and his scepticism with regard to poetry's ability to offer a positive force or a 'moral voice'.[3] This characterisation has also included some emphasis on Mahon's assumption (in ways and to a degree that has seldom been matched by other Irish poets) of the modernist legacy – both as regards key formal and thematic choices, and the definition of an authorial persona marked by aloofness and expatriation, for which Beckett appears as the prime model.[4]

However, Mahon's weariness of some topoi of his critical appreciation has proved characteristically vocal. He has emphatically dismissed narratives of shared poetic beginnings that other poets of his generation have not altogether shunned (cf. Scammell 1991: 4). This was reinforced by his endorsement, in the Introduction to *The Penguin Book of Contemporary Irish Poetry* (which he co-edited with Peter Fallon), of Thomas Kinsella's denunciation of the 'Northern Renaissance' as 'largely a journalistic entity' (Fallon and Mahon 1990: xx). In an interview given halfway through the silent decade of his poetry, Mahon also took the 'opportunity to correct a few misconceptions. First of all, I am not sophisticated, I am not cosmopolitan' (Murphy et al. 1991: 28). If this suggested a wish to inflect his poetics and hence his reputation (by coincidence, at the same time as Heaney was at pains to flag his own 'swerve'), the two new collections Mahon was to publish in the second half of the 1990s were indeed acknowledged as distinct from his previous work. The responses to this change of tack were mixed, however: the poet's supposed relaxation of both his tight prosodic control and his intellectual severity prompted both damning criticism and spirited defences, in either case predicated on an awareness (explicit or not) of his earlier writing.[5]

Mahon's staunchest supporters and his harshest critics have acknowledged the relevance of his practice of rewriting, both as a translator and an incessant reviser of his poetry, and the extent to which the pervasiveness and inherent instability of this dual practice has moulded his poetry and reputation will become apparent in the course of this chapter. Attention will also be given to two important paradoxes: firstly, the salience of textual uncertainty in the poetics of someone whose early fame was so strongly grounded on an imputation of formal control; and secondly, the decision (in the light of a reputation characterised in part by a 'cosmopolitanism' that demarcated him from the local pieties proper to identity politics) to open his larger and more influential collections with poems titled after Northern Irish place names. Both *Poems 1962–1978* and the more recent *Selected Poems* (2006) open with 'Glengormley'; the 1991 *Selected Poems* starts with 'In Carrowdore Churchyard', while the *Collected Poems* (1999) sets off from 'Spring in Belfast'. These three are, in different but convergent ways, defining pieces in Mahon's oeuvre, and their prominence provides an apt starting-point for a discussion of his writing guided by an attention to place, precedence and the writer's self-awareness.

3.1   Forms and sites of disaffection

The choice of a place name poem to open a collection suggests that the emphasis on location will be decisive, probably part of a narrative of belonging. When the toponym in question is glossed as the place where the poet grew up, readers are led to expect an account of a firmly located formative experience, particularly in the context of the lyric. Derek Mahon's 'Glengormley'[6] relates ironically to these expectations at various levels. It includes elements – 'the terrier', 'the [trimmed] hedge', 'the watering can', 'washing lines' with 'white linen', a sensation of being 'safe' – that might belong within a modern pastoral of suburban life, the *locus amoenus* recreated on the outskirts of Belfast. But the ironies that pre-empt this representation are apparent to all from the clash between the grand celebratory ring of the poem's initial proposition and the risible modesty of its proposed substance:

> Wonders are many and none is more wonderful than man
> Who has tamed the terrier, trimmed the hedge
> And grasped the principle of the watering can.

(14)

This clash becomes even more striking when one realises that the first line is the opening of the second choral ode in Sophocles's *Antigone* (in Richard Jebb's Victorian translation – 1891: l.332), where it is followed by an exaltation of man's sway over sea and land. Both *Poems 1962–1978* and the more recent *Selected Poems* clearly present that opening line as a quotation, between inverted commas – but these are absent both from the 1990 *Selected* and the 1999 *Collected Poems*.

These minutiae are relevant for pointing out the following: Mahon endows this apparent narrative of personal origins with the unique status of a 'first poem', and opens it with an ecstatic celebration of human prowess that is promptly turned into a mock-heroic statement; and this effect is compounded by the unstable, on-and-off acknowledgement that the opening line is a translation of a Classical source, with its appertaining canonical weight. The fact that the (unnamed) source is the *Antigone*, a fundamental locus for the representation of conflict prompted by tyrannical dicta, further highlights the role played by translation and revision in this 'first poem', providing a vehicle for Mahon's trademark ironies at the expense of traditional pieties and certain forms of political optimism. The 'new era' sardonically celebrated in the poem is denounced as a looming order that not only transcends primeval fears of 'monsters' and 'giants' from the mythical past, but also supersedes the historically ennobling ancestry of the 'saint or hero' (so often enlisted by discourses of political legitimation in Ireland), 'landing at night from the conspiring seas'. In such a polity, no 'sticks and stones' cause physical damage, but 'the unreconciled' have 'their metaphysical pain' terminated (or highlighted?) when they 'dangle from lamp-posts'. The poem's dismal picture of post-historical torpidity, however, includes the recognition, with self-referential implications, that 'only words hurt us now'. This belief in a negative verbal effectiveness is pursued with the closing declaration of disaffection, which confirms the dystopian import of such writing of place and proclaims the self's *unwilling* location: 'By / Necessity, if not choice, I live here too' (14).

The second of the poems that have alternated with 'Glengormley' in the initial position described above is possibly the best-known representation of the Northern Irish writer's characteristic malaise, in this case disaffected from the Protestant community of his origins by education and acquaintance with other places. Originally entitled 'In Belfast', then retitled (in succession) 'The Spring Vacation' and 'Spring in Belfast'; excluded from the *Selected*, but given the opening position in the *Collected Poems*, the piece records a failed attempt to resume a sense of belonging in 'this desperate city' (13). It is the first of several poems on this common Irish theme, whose recurrence in Mahon's work also reflects the experience of living elsewhere; with titles such as 'Homecoming', 'Going Home' and 'Afterlives', they never stage a gratifying comeback to a cherished origin: 'Skies change but not / souls change', 'the world grows old' (33). (This contrasts starkly with the imagery of retrieved shelter in Heaney's 'Homecomings' – Heaney 1979: 49).[7] 'Spring in Belfast' describes a space of inter-individual relations ruled by a mistrust that accommodates 'the knowing nod', but finds its epitome in a trope that internalises it – 'the unwieldy images of the squinting heart' (13) – while signalling a satirical symmetry with the *display* of suffering (the 'sacred hearts') proper to Catholic iconography. Memory, kept or erased, is paramount to this community's sense of historical and territorial entitlement – and it is as crucial and vulnerable as suggested by the much-quoted dictum of another disaffected (and rather more exasperated) Protestant

Northerner, Tom Paulin: 'There is so little history / we must remember who we are' (Paulin 1983: 29). In Mahon's 'Spring in Belfast', memory characteristically becomes the object of an equivocal formula: 'I remember not to forget'. It is also through ambiguity that the final stanza registers a misfit condition construed as impaired knowledge: 'One part of my mind must learn to know its place'; but the discomfort of Mahon's persona lies ultimately in his acknowledgement that, rather than passionate dislike, the life of that city obtains only 'casual interest', 'casual pity' from him (13).[8]

A no less ambivalent response to the Northern Irish location characterises the work of the precursor honoured in the third of the inaugural poems of Mahon's anthological collections: 'In Carrowdore Churchyard (*at the grave of Louis MacNeice*)' was the opening poem in the 1991 edition of Mahon's *Selected Poems*, where 'Glengormley' came second (this order was reversed in the 2006 edition). It is of obvious relevance that Mahon alternates, as starting points, a poem titled after the place of his upbringing and an elegy for a poet whose entitlement to being considered (Northern) Irish (rather than English) Mahon was one of the first to champion, with his essay 'MacNeice in England and Ireland' (Mahon 1974). Rather than directly evoke MacNeice's '*Odi atque amo*' perspective on Northern Ireland, the elegy celebrates him through a dominant imagery of springtime energy and passions, when nature is 'igniting flowers', exalting his talent for 'keeping the colours new' (17). Apropos of his and Mahon's landscape of 'hard' hills in need of the softening brought by spring, the elegy also hails MacNeice's ability to inspire a life alert to 'The ironical, loving crush of roses against snow, / Each fragile, solving ambiguity' (17) – an allusion to the celebration of an 'incorrigibly plural' world, and 'the drunkenness of things being various', in the precursor's 'Snow' (MacNeice 2007: 24). By invoking MacNeice's combination of lyrical skill and ethical sense, Mahon allows himself the possibility of pursuing the lyric in spite of his general scepticism and a context that the precursor characterised, in the controversial section XVI of 'Autumn Journal', as uncongenial to the educated, urbane writer.[9]

Although MacNeice's representation of Northern Irish places (closely bound up with a consciousness of self) includes the celebration of natural beauty, as Mahon's elegy emphasises, some of its best-known instances feature harsh landscapes, particularly seascapes. While this is to some extent an empirical reflection of the actual topography and climate, it also corresponds to an existential bleakness,[10] becoming an important part of McNeice's legacy for the next generation (cf. Garratt 1995: 179, 188–9). Bleak or desolate places have long been a hallmark of Mahon's poems, including the emblematic 'A Disused Shed in Co. Wexford', with its disconsolate opening conjecture that 'even now there are places where a thought might grow'. The nondescript locale is equated with the distant desolation of abandoned 'Peruvian mines' and 'Indian compounds', while the 'thousand mushrooms' found abandoned in the shed prompt the politically disturbing (and outrageous?) analogy with the 'lost people of Treblinka and Pompeii' (89–90). Another, almost as famous instance, with a clearer sociological referent in emigration, involves the echoes of past lives that lend poignancy to the run-down premises of 'A Garage in Co. Cork' (130–1). Despite their nominal locations, and Mahon's insistence on the uniqueness of the plights and joys those places have witnessed, such poems also seem to represent a circumstance beyond the known conditions of geography and history. Tom Paulin has commented on Mahon's fascination with 'a place of pure being', and Peter McDonald notes that Mahon's 'poems have always gravitated towards a cold and unpeopled area which exists generally before, or after, anything ordinarily recognizable as historic process' (Paulin 1984: 58; McDonald 1997: 87). Both critical arguments could cite the wish (or mere avowal) to be 'through with history', which occurs twice in Mahon's poetry: in 'Rathlin', which closes on the uncertainty 'whether the future lies before us or behind' (107), and in 'The Last of the Fire Kings', where the mythical persona lives through the paradox of a power that is submission, while 'Perfecting my cold dream / Of a place out of time' (65).

Insistence on this release from history, however, only emphasises its ineluctability, the unfeasibility of the disconsolate hope. The transit that takes place in 'A Disused Shed in Co. Wexford', through analogy, to remote locations and across various histories is countered by the Irish grounding provided by the poem's dedication 'for J. G. Farrell' (89), author of the novel *Troubles* (a title that referred to the 1920s unrest, but would inevitably evoke the post-1960s conflict to Mahon's readers). Likewise, the fire king's 'cold dream' is something that 'the fire-loving / People, rightly perhaps, / Will not countenance', forcing him to remain with them in 'a world of / Sirens, bin-lids / And bricked-up windows' (65). The sway of 'necessity' rather than 'choice' (in the terms of 'Glengormley') again and again becomes manifest. A concise and pointed example of the close links between the discomfort experienced by the subject in Mahon's poems about desolate places, and the cultural and political conformation of the poet's origins, is provided by the closing lines of 'Nostalgias':

> In a tiny stone church
> On a desolate headland
> A lost tribe is singing 'Abide With Me'.
>
> (75)

The starkness of these lines, and indeed of the landscape, brings out the imperative form of the hymn, converting it from a believer's hopeful plea into the sentence pronounced on the sceptic as convict, disaffected but not released. Its tones of doom resound through poems in which the Mahonian-self roams the wilderness, through settings ('these stormy parts') like those of 'North Wind: Portrush', which compares 'the wind / On this benighted coast' to the shrieks of a lost soul (100); or of the 'The Sea in Winter' (one of several verse letters that, with Auden and MacNeice as precursors, punctuate Mahon's oeuvre, usually reporting autobiographically from a new or reencountered location). The yearning for a renewed displacement, albeit imaginative, becomes manifest ('Sometimes, rounding the cliff top / [. . .] / I pretend not to be here at all' – 115), although Mahon's verse is hardly the environment for wishful thinking, or for wish fulfilment either: the fantasy that the place might be any other and milder ('Paros', 'Naxos') is promptly dispelled by evidence of a northern climate, with more than strictly natural implications.

In this sombre scenario, pain combines with irony – a legacy of MacNeice's ostensibly offhand remarks on 'the obscure but powerful ethics of Going North' (MacNeice 2007: 49). Such mixed tones were arguably present in Mahon's 'Girls in their Seasons' (originally published in *Night Crossing*, though omitted from both the *Selected* and *Collected Poems*), which troped the course of life as a journey 'north / Into the night', differing little from 'a trip I took last winter / From dream into bad dream' (Mahon 1979: 23–4). Precisely because Mahon's north is hardly a cardinal point, it can be directionally reversed, and the 'degree zero of place – an uninhabitable place' (Haughton 1992: 113) emerge rather as the extreme south, the deathly site of the title poem of *Antarctica* (166). In every case, features of a specific landscape 'objectify a general spiritual desolation' (Andrews 1992: 239); but this does not, in turn, prevent the more rarefied representations of existential hurt from coexisting with the acknowledgement of objective social and political ills – sectarianism, intra-communal hatred, repression – that contribute no less to the poet's gloom in 'The Sea in Winter'. Hopes of release tend to be suppressed as soon as they are uttered, and in this regard a contrast with Heaney may again prove enlightening, since both poets have offered vignettes of that prototypical instance of renewal which is the calm after the storm; in Heaney's, the bright morning sea-view is declared 'marvellous and actual', and the word 'haven' the verbal correlative of a 'deepening, clearing [. . .] sky' (1979: 39); in Mahon's, the freshness of the scene prompts a regressive analogy with a blissful 'first day', but the illusion is promptly dispelled:

> A false sense of reprieve,
> For the climate is here to stay.
>
> So best prepare for the worst
> That chaos and old night
> Can do to us

(101)

Originally published just three years after Heaney's 'Glanmore Sonnets', these lines from 'North Wind, Portrush' might be Mahon's sardonic answer to the other poet's quasi-sacramental belief in renewal, 'a haven' – counterpointed by the certainty that any solace will be elusive, the temporary occlusion of an impending existential 'worst'.

Heaney's sonnet eventually balanced the 'actual' scene before the speaker's eyes against a variously named 'elsewhere', and this, combined with their renewed critical comparison, reminds us that in his essay on 'Place and Displacement' Heaney remarked on 'Mahon's sense of bilocation', arguing that 'in order for any place to be credible for Mahon, it has to be reimagined in the light of other places' (Heaney 1985a: 168). By suggesting that Mahon's places are characteristically relational, Heaney gives us one of many critical pronouncements on other poets that could be applied to himself; and this also underlines that an inter-authorial set of relations is often imbricated with the interlocal design. Mahon's representations of other places regularly coincide with representations of other authors, usually enduring some form of exile. Any list of Mahon's titles will bring out the onomastic combinations, indicative of this poet's habit of ventriloquising the malaise caused by the place of his origins through the predicament (either biographically grounded, or imagined) of other writers and artists: 'Van Gogh in the Borinage' (later retitled 'A Portrait of the Artist'), 'Camus in Ulster', 'Brecht in Svendborg', 'Ovid in Tomis'.

As suggested by the presence of Van Gogh on the list above, this practice sometimes sees Mahon extend his elective affinities to non-verbal art forms, adding 'intersemiotic translation' (Jakobson [1959] 2004: 139) to his range of rewritings. The visual arts, and painting in particular, are an important part of Mahon's referential universe. They are sometimes included in his 'habit of parody and pastiche' (Denman 1994: 31 and passim), or even evoked as a field for illicit artistic appropriations – whose ironical attractions become manifest in the poignant self-apologia of 'The Forger', couched in the voice of Van Meegeren, who painted and sold 'fake Vermeers to Goering' (24). The Van Meegeren persona confidently asserts that 'my genius will live on', undiminished by the fact that it operated 'at one remove'. This bold plea finds an ethical and political corollary in a discourse of hopeful purpose, as the derivative artist who treaded the line between deceit and collaboration claims that '[I] sheltered in my heart of hearts / A light to transform the world'. The poem's ambiguities increase with the iteration of a formula – 'And I *too* have wandered', 'And I *too* have suffered' (24; my emphasis) – that leaves one in doubt whether the Van Meegeren mask is still on, suggesting the poet's attraction to the equivocal practitioner of an art that would seem to epitomise scepticism, but is here credited with a redemptive design.

Mahon's active interest in ekphrasis – that is, 'a verbal representation of a visual representation' (Heffernan 1993: 3) – has attracted considerable attention (Brown 1994; York 2002), and its best-known instance is likewise marked by a degree of political ambivalence, combined with spatial and temporal dislocations. 'Courtyards in Delft', a poem on several of Pieter de Hooch's mid-seventeenth-century paintings of women involved in domestic chores, invites recognition of their 'thrifty lives', 'modest but adequate', as enactments of the Protestant work ethic, which, with its attendant political values, had revolutionary consequences in the Europe of De Hooch's time – including the inception of Planter culture, the bedrock of Ulster Protestantism. Through various hints, Mahon prompts his readers to equate his description of De Hooch's courtyard(s) with the backyards of the suburban Belfast evoked elsewhere in his poetry, and to recognise his lines on the 'house-proud [. . .] wives / Of artisans' (105) in Early Modern Delft as an echo of his disaffected and despondent perspective on 'the kitchen houses / And echoing back-streets' of mid-twentieth-century Belfast (13). The irruption of the voice of a misfit, combined with the various suggestions of primness and denial of the emotions in the 'trim composure' of the courtyards, unequivocally distances that seventeenth-century scene from a domestic idyll. By declaring that 'I lived there as a boy', the persona confirms the imaginative dislocation, but it also admits to the difficult belonging of

> A strange child with a taste for verse,
> While my hard-nosed companions dream of fire
> And sword upon parched veldt and fields of rain-swept gorse.

> (106)

This oppositional identity, idiosyncratic but also cultural, is offered as a juvenile instance of Mahon's characteristically 'lonely alienated' persona (cf. Horton 2000: 362); and the re-emergence, in other poems, of the prim middle-class Protestant home confirms the autobiographical element (as when the poet's mother is evoked against 'a Dutch interior', with 'bread-bin and laundry basket awash with light', in 'A Bangor Requiem' – 260). But those lines from 'Courtyards in Delft' also bring with them the historical reminder that De Hooch's pictures of domestic placidity are contemporary with a demonstration of how the 'thrifty', dour and disciplined content of the Protestant ethic could prove violently expansive and acquisitive, belying the 'modest' values of the Delft scene.[11] Mahon's lexical choices of 'veldt' and 'gorse' are synecdoches of location: the former, for South Africa – the word is an import from Dutch via Afrikaans, a reminder of the Dutch foundation of Cape Colony and Boer culture; the latter, for Northern Ireland, since 'gorse' is a 'Protestant word for "whins"' (as Mahon himself explained – Scammell 1991: 6), evoking William of Orange's campaigns in Ireland and their long train of consequences.

This interrelation of historical patterns glimpsed in different places and ages, and explored in various Mahon poems, is grounded in a rationale that is political, rather than mythical – a signal difference vis-à-vis Heaney (in particular when we think of a design such as that of *North*). It is one of the dimensions that persist in Mahon's later writing, despite the significant changes that it undergoes. In *The Hudson Letter* (1995) and ensuing collections, the line lengthens and becomes more fluid, as if to match the extended range of longer poems; an irony that characteristically relied on terseness and discipline may now be conveyed through less indirect and more discursive resources; and the range of references likewise broadens to accommodate, sometimes parodically, the forms and manifestations of global culture. But the continuities from Mahon's earlier work are no less striking, ranging from the relational spatial dynamics highlighted above to the textual consequence of this poet's elective affinities.

'Waterfront', in the title sequence 'The Hudson Letter', is ostensibly written from a shore that is 'far from home', and is in fact the ultimate transatlantic and metropolitan context. This does not prevent the New York harbour scene from conjuring a memory from another bleak dockyard:

> and I recall my ten-year-old delight
> at the launch of a P&O liner in Belfast,
> all howling 'O God, Our Help in Ages Past'

> (192)

The original 'delight' is irretrievable, as proved by the lexical choice 'howling', the adult's consciousness imposing his distaste on devotional gestures that evoke the Belfast shipyards as bastion of the siege mentality of working-class Protestantism (the 'lost tribe' on the 'desolate headland' of his earlier poem 'Nostalgias'). Remembering a Belfast ship launch from the vantage of New York harbour involves a half-concealed irony: the most famous product of the Belfast shipyards was a ship that has become inscribed in global memory precisely because it failed to reach New York – the Titanic. This memory, pervaded by irony, works at various interrelated levels. There is a cultural and political dimension (the disaster of the Titanic, and the sense of hubris and nemesis that came to inform its narrative were from an early stage symbolically associated with the decline of Belfast's industrial might); a personal note (Mahon's father and grandfather were shipyard workers); and a literary reference, since a similar childhood memory was evoked by Louis MacNeice in his elegy, 'Death of an old lady', where a child, by Belfast Lough, glimpses a ship that was 'so big it was named Titanic' (MacNeice 2007: 517). Mahon also wrote on the Titanic in the elegiac 'A Refusal to Mourn' (about an old shipyard worker recognisable as his grandfather), where the ship is perceived as emblematic of the passing of the ages, the drift towards post-historical oblivion:

> the earth he inherited
> Is gone like Neanderthal Man
> And no records remain.

(88)

But these lines very clearly gloss another passage by MacNeice, when he envisages humankind '[going] down like palaeolithic man' (MacNeice 2007: 4) – a passage that returns us to 'Waterfront', for the very fact that Mahon used it as an epigraph to this later poem.

Through the textual mediation of MacNeice, Mahon therefore connects his earlier lines anticipating the collapse of human civilisation (troped as the wreck of naval hardware on a desolate seabed) with the motley scene captured in one of his New York poems. His wish to reinforce this connection (with the Titanic in the background) is clear when in the *Collected Poems* he interpolates the line 'where ice confined the crippled *QE2*' ('Waterfront', 192). The MacNeice epigraph and its train of textual and historical memory qualify the sense of recovery or improvement that would otherwise seem to prevail from the poem's first lines, as the poet's isolated, fragile self acknowledges his membership of a (universal) community of 'Chaste convalescents from an exigent world', and 'toddle[s] into the cold' of a New York pier. At this least likely of retreats, visual and auditory echoes of the heyday of transatlantic voyages coexist with graffiti and haunting references retrieved from literary memory (*The Ancient Mariner*, 'Bohemia's desert coast'), but all of these find an ironic correlative in the 'infection and industrial waste' which seem to belie the notion that 'now we emerge from the industrial night' (192).

The ecological concern has had its most prominent and unqualified expression, with celebratory overtones, in Mahon's collection *Life on Earth* (to which I will return); but in earlier poems it helped set off the desolation of locales, often appearing 'intertwined with historical disaster' (Haughton 2007: 93), and occasionally combining with images of displaced writers. A case in point is 'Ovid in Tomis', where glaring anachronism equates 'coarse god' with 'gearbox', 'nereid' with 'unsinkable / Coca-Cola' (157); in the poem's earlier version, this polluting element was 'hair conditioner' (1982: 37) – the 'Coca-Cola' revision accentuating the connection between a blasted environment and global consumerism. By noting this, we lay an emphasis on continuity, and yet there is a significant difference between the ecological and cultural critique in earlier pieces and that which informs poems in *The Hudson Letter* and *The Yellow Book*, as also (in yet other ways) in *Harbour Lights* and *Life on Earth*.

In Mahon's work from the mid-1990s, the relationship between represen-tation and its formal enactment changes, and the rhetorical consequence of this is a degree of ambivalence that paradoxically grows in direct pro-portion to the explicitation. The 'desperate ironies' (rephrased as 'terminal ironies' in the *Collected Poems*) that defined the figure of the 'poet indulging his wretched rage for order' in a well-known early poem were energised by a sense of urgency and authority for which the formal correlative was the tight-lipped diction employed to characterise writing as 'a dying art, / [. . .] In an unstructurable sea' (47). The satiric outspoken wordiness in the title sequence of *The Hudson Letter*, or in 'America Deserta' (a poem in *The Yellow Book* that was originally subtitled 'postscript to "The Hudson Letter"'), or yet in the Paris-based 'Resistance Days' in *Harbour Lights* (2005: 13–18), is fundamentally different, although it also mimics what it denounces.[12] Its abundance, flow and variety mirror the verbal paraphernalia of the 'post-modern': this critical description is invoked in several poems ostensibly to be derided, although it could also be applied to those poems' own garrulous, enumerative, culturally zapping verve, mindful of 'the images forming which will be screened tonight / on CNN and *The McNeil-Lehrer News Hour*' (190), aware of 'the post-Cold war, global-warming age / of corporate rule, McPeace and Mickey Mao' (255). In this regime, the poet acknowledges that

> subscribing eagerly to the post-modern kitsch
> we shirk our noble birthright as the glitch
> in the internet
>
> (255)

The trotting rhythms and rhymes of such verse knowingly prompt and attract laughter, but its satiric clout may slacken when the distinction is eroded between weapon and target, the denouncer and the denounced. Lists of power-names from intellectual and commercial culture, high and low ('Venturi, Thompson, Rowse', 'Klein and Nike, Banana Republic, Gap' – 190, 254) energise the lines and coexist with inscriptions from the metropolitan scene that take pride in their volatility. The (supposedly) reproduced graf-fito that closes 'Waterfront', which in the 1995 edition read 'QUESTION REALITY. DEATH IS BACK. MIGUEL 141' (1995: 44), was (aptly) rephrased for the *Collected Poems* in terms that reflect back rather differently on the poem, as on Mahon's recent poetics: 'SUBVERT THE DOMINANT PARADIGM. GABRIEL 141' (193).

The self-referential import of the latter inscription is paramount to this study, as a quotation purportedly from the least canonical of sources (a wall somewhere in the modern metropolis) foregrounds itself by being rewritten – and the resulting statement is self-descriptive. The sustained coherence of this reconfigured poetics within the broader economy of Derek Mahon's work will be set off more clearly by considering in some detail the various forms and fronts of his rewritings.

3.2 Translation and the uprooted voice

Terms such as 'ambivalence' and 'instability' have recurred in this discussion of Derek Mahon's poetry; they will again be invoked to consider his translations of authors from a broad range of languages and periods, and the place they hold in the 'poetic economy'[13] of his writing. Mahon's numerous versions fully partake in the unstable, fluid nature of his work: they have been relocated, retitled, sometimes discarded, and their publication history requires careful charting.[14] On the other hand, they can also be seen to play an integrative role, affording a vantage on the course of Mahon's work that allows his readers to perceive it in fuller and more coherent terms. The relevance and scale of this enhancement has tended to increase in recent years, fulfilled both by the translations of individual poems that have punctuated the various poetry volumes (some of these versions were collected in *Adaptations* – 2006) and by the versions that were published as autonomous books, irrespective of genre (poetry or drama). Priority will be given here to the collected or book-length versions, while shorter translations will be selectively considered, in combination with other single poems by Mahon.

A reconnaissance of his textual terrain suggests the critical relevance of certain versions emerging at particular points in his career. In the chronology of his translations, the first collected venture was a slim volume containing Gérard de Nerval's *The Chimeras*. This choice confirmed an interest in French poetry that had already resulted in versions of Villon, Corbière, Guillevic, and Jaccottet (included in earlier collections), reflecting the importance of French letters in Mahon's academic training; this commitment to Francophone literature also emphasised his modernist affinities (significantly more relevant to Mahon than to his Northern Irish contemporaries), and hence his interest in the great faultlines of early twentieth-century writing.[15] *The Chimeras* was published in the same year as *The Hunt by Night* (1982), one of Mahon's most celebrated books, but also the last before the conspicuously less productive period (as regards new poetry collections) of 1982–95, which witnessed the publication only of the slim *Antarctica* (1985). This 'gap' proved prolific with regard to translations, however. It is not just the chronology that is intriguing: the mid-1980s yielded both existentially desolate poetry (in *Antarctica*) and versions of comedies by Molière – *L'École des Maris* (1985) and *L'École des Femmes* (1986). Drama and the lyric alternate in Mahon's active commitment to translation from the French, since in 1987 he published his best-known volume of poetry translation by a single author, a selection from the work of the Swiss-born

Francophone poet Philippe Jaccottet (republished, a decade later, as *Words in the Air* – 1998).[16] The next two volumes of translation were plays, Euripides's *The Bacchae* (1991) and Racine's *Phaedra* (1996), two incursions into the tragic whose particularities show a somewhat close relation to the diction and some of the concerns of his collections *The Hudson Letter* (1995) and *The Yellow Book* (1997).

Mahon himself has acknowledged the 'creative charge' that he derived from such translations, and the tension between constraint and release that energises the relation between his dramatic versions and his poetry.[17] This alternation has continued to the present: two of the slightly longer lyrical versions that Mahon published in recent years came out as separate volumes (in limited editions): Paul Valéry's *The Seaside Cemetery* (2001) (later included as 'Part Four' of *Harbour Lights*) and Saint-John Perse's *Birds* (2002); and the series of dramatic versions was pursued with Edmond Rostand's *Cyrano de Bergerac* (2004), and *Oedipus*, a version of Sophocles's *King Oedipus* and *Oedipus at Colonus* (2005). As pointed out below, several of these versions have met with a controversial reception, which has itself become a part of Mahon's reputation and authorial stance.

The volume and range of his translations of individual lyrics – by French, and also Latin, Provençal, Italian, Greek, German and Russian poets – has also expanded since the 1990s, as shown by the space they have tended to occupy in Mahon's more recent collections; indeed, a reviewer was led to remark on the 'real danger of their swamping the original work' (Wheatley 1996: 127). This awareness of a 'danger' of indistinction between original and derivative texts in Mahon's collections reflects not only the continuities, the shared diction that his appropriative strategies often entail, but also his concomitant habit of varying the way in which he signals the status of certain pieces as translations (from the conventional 'after', followed by the source author's name, to mere indication of the name as part of the title or between brackets, or italicisation of appropriated passages inserted in other lyrics). The coexistence, within the collections, of translations and a large number of poems that evoke or pay tribute to writers (Ancient or Modern) – alluded to, cited in epigraphs, honoured by dedications – further blurs the textual boundaries. Such variety in procedure is also related to the degree of freedom with which Mahon renders each translated piece, and to the no less varying command he may have of the source language.

A seductive hypothesis is precisely that variations in Mahon's strategies as a translator, and in particular his appropriative freedoms, evince a pattern that can be related to factors such as the translator's familiarity with the source language, or the relative, compared canonicity of the translated author and the translator. These aspects have implications at the level both of propriety – the decorum observed by the translator, somewhere between the reverential and the subversive – and property – involving the imaginary reply to the imaginary question: 'whose text is this?' The original author's, or the translator's? A preliminary hint of the expected reply may be given by book covers: in most of the volumes listed above the translator's name features in the position conventionally reserved for the author. This is current practice whenever the translator is a well-known writer, and hence an index of his/her fame; but the feasibility of this authorial substitution, without seriously compromising the cover's informative value, also depends on the source authors' canonical stature and the fame enjoyed by their work. Indeed, the readers' prompt recognition that the volume before them is a translation is made possible by their prior knowledge that (e.g.) *Oedipus* is a title that originally *belongs* in the domain of Greek tragedy – even if the name of the original author does not appear on the covers, or features in smaller print below the title (in the space traditionally reserved for the translators' names). The latter practice is to be found in Mahon's volumes of translations to date, with two exceptions: in the case of *Racine's Phaedra*, for the obvious reason that Mahon chose to include the author's name in the title (a curious proprietorial acknowledgement, possibly signalling that this is not the tale of Phaedra as given in Euripides's *Hippolytus* or Seneca's *Phaedra*); with Saint-John Perse's *Birds*, the decision to have title and author feature in larger typeface in the upper section of the book's cover, with the phrase 'a version by Derek Mahon' in smaller print at the bottom, may reflect uncertainty as to the ability of English-language readers to identify Perse's title – although Perse was a Nobel Prize winner. No such doubts seem to have affected the publication of Jaccottet's versions a few years earlier, where 'standard' practice applied.

Mahon's choice of Gérard de Nerval (1808–55) for his first book of translations carried some irony, since the authorial identification/substitution suggested by a book whose cover read 'Derek Mahon, *The Chimeras*' seemed to echo the half-joking label *'poète maudit'*, which (originally coined for a few nineteenth-century poets, prominently including Nerval) was regularly applied to Mahon from early stages in the definition of his literary personality. The epithet responded to his immersion in French poetry, but above all to his disaffected stance, the gloom of some of his settings, and his tendency to offer representations of artist figures in desperate circumstances.[18] The very choice of this sonnet sequence, which Mahon renders with prosodic deftness, was therefore a self-confirming gesture, combined with an effort towards release from his stereotypical description as 'Northern Protestant urban poet'.[19] Due awareness of this should precede and qualify one's perception of aspects of the translation itself that arguably bring Nerval's text home to Mahon's recognisable diction. The scope for such particularities is limited by the expressive and rhetorical gap between Nerval's ecstatic and exclamatory register, his imagery of 'Orient', mysticism and inebriation, and the prevalent diction of a late twentieth-century body of poetry in English that still displays the legacy of the well-made poem, and of a Larkinesque mode of reserve and understatement.[20]

The Chimeras is therefore not a prime example of domestication, although the sequence reveals a few options by the translator that chime with dominant tones in his other writing. These include coupling the adjectives 'dim, disconsolate' (a description that could be applied to the dominant persona of early Mahon) in a line of 'El Desdichado' in which the source for 'dim' is the considerably more thunderous 'ténébreux' (Nerval 1964: 7; Mahon 1982a: 9); as well as, in 'Horus', rendering as 'the old fraud' the epithet given by the goddess Isis to the dying god Kneph, which in Nerval reads 'ce vieux pervers'.[21] In Mahon's version, a more meditative dynamic replaces Nerval's exclamatory glitter; probably the most striking instance of this occurs in the closing 'Pythagorean Lines', where the salutation to man as (literally) 'free thinker' disappears from the first line:

> Homme! libre penseur – te crois-tu seul pensant
> Dans ce monde, où la vie éclate en toute chose
>
> (Nerval 1964: 16)

> Man, do you think yourself the one reflective
> Thing in this lively world?
>
> (Mahon 1982a: 20)

Otherwise, Mahon closely reproduces Nerval's distinctive diction ('Bring me Posilipo and the Tyrrhenian sea', 'Myrtho, dark sorceress, I think of you' – 9, 10) or achieves a congeniality of diction and representation without being boldly appropriative, as in lines that evoke Mahon's typically inhospitable settings:

> Hasard qui, t'avançant
> Parmi les mondes morts sous la neige éternelle
>
> (Nerval 1964: 14)

> as you meander through
> The dead worlds shrouded in eternal snow
>
> (Mahon 1982a: 17)

In Mahon's more extensive versions of poetry in French, congeniality comes across more promptly in his renderings of Philippe Jaccottet (1925–). The importance of these in Mahon's oeuvre was highlighted by the new edition that came out 12 years after the initial 1986 publication under the title *Words in the Air*.[22] The volume is the only translation that Mahon has published as a bilingual edition, the parallel text inviting the perception of a mirrored writing, an authorial dialogue across the page. It also includes a longer Introduction than the brief informative prefaces that Mahon has otherwise tended to write (in tune with his dismissive attitude towards his own critical prose, most of it short reviews collected in 1996 as *Journalism*, with an equally short 'Author's Preface' centred on an apologia for 'the Grub Street hack'[23]). Mahon's Introduction to his Jaccottet selection confirms a deep authorial affinity – in contrast to the othering pull of Nerval's voice (cf. Shields 2000 145–64) – and makes it yet another instance of a writer's self-reading refracted through critical assessment of another. It includes an initial observation that Jaccottet does not confirm those expectations of radical experimentalism often associated with 'contemporary French verse', since his work is 'recognizably circumstantial, and empirical in its relation to "reality"' (1998: 11) – a reassuring caveat to Anglophone readers brought up on the well-made poem. But, above all, readers of the Introduction learn that Jaccottet 'began as an urban poet [. . .] full of alienation, existential fear and the onus of self-definition'; that 'like other minimalists he knows exiguity and exasperation', the voice of a 'solitary inquiry'; and that he 'is an intensely visual poet' (1998: 11–13). These aspects have long been associated with Mahon's own work and literary persona, as epitomised in the 'dying art' and 'semantic scruple' of the isolated poet (47–8), and in his ekphrastic writing. But this Introduction also seems to point forward by noting the *absence* in Jaccottet of a set of characteristics that are proposed as necessary for readers to experience confirmation and fulfilment: 'What do we miss in this poetry? Several things: vitality sometimes, humour, the demotic, the abrasive surfaces of the modern world' (1998: 14). These are recognisable features that the translator's verse exhibited from *The Hudson Letter* onwards (that garrulous metropolitan scene of 'spy cameras, radio heads, McDonald's, rowdytum' – 245). Tribute to a congenial author thus comes to include the imputation of an experiential and representational deficit vis-à-vis the translator's own work – which implicitly claims a totality that cannot be acknowledged in the translated poet.

Mahon's versions of Jaccottet often evince that real affinity which requires no glaring domestication for the source author to be couched in the poet-translator's known diction. Examples include 'the icy places' (almost a calque rendering of 'les espaces glacés') in 'During a Snowstorm' (1998: 49); a line such as 'the sea is dark again on my last night' ('Portovenere', 23); or the anticipation of a posthumous (and post-human?) moment when 'there will be no one left / to visit the grave, [. . .] / not even shadows in that shadowless place' (65). If Mahon's readers find this over-familiar, a glance at the page on the left will not afford the perception of a de-forming (or re-signifying) appropriation. There are passages, however, where the translator's options exacerbate the proximity between his and Jaccottet's imaginative worlds, as with the opening line (and title) of 'The June night is like a city of the dead', where the second term of the comparison is, in the source text, 'une grande cité endormie' (literally, a big sleeping/dormant city) – Mahon's version forcing the funereal trope (16–17). Moreover, some of his options have self-referential implications, or otherwise bear on the verbal and literary systems, as in one of the passages from which he derives the 1998 volume's title: 'all that I say / is only a flight of words in the air' (31); in the source text, this is phrased as a rhetorical question, its rendering as an affirmative emphasising a sceptical view of verbal efficacy. Even more tellingly, in the sonnet beginning 'I know now I possess nothing of my own' Mahon's emphatic phrasing (for the original 'je ne possède rien') enhances the poignancy of this disowned, dispossessed condition; the statement occurs in a translation – the verbal business of dispossessing and repossessing – and its potential for self-referentiality is confirmed when, towards the end of the sonnet, Mahon renders the *interrogatio* 'qui peut dire // quel est son sens?' as 'who can translate // its meaning?' (20–1). 'To say' (the immediate lexical cognate of 'dire') is here provocatively equated with 'to translate', and the relation between this passage and the sonnet's title (its first line) has an obvious textual and authorial import.

In the 1980s, alongside his translations of Jaccottet's poetry of delicate emotions and private epiphanies, Mahon was already producing versions of dramatic texts, which brought a command of new registers, the 'vitality', 'humour' and 'demotic' language whose absence he explicitly noted in Jaccottet. The two Molière comedies, published in 1985 and 1986, are among his most radical translations. *High Time* is described on the title page as 'A comedy in one act based on Molière's *The School for Husbands*', while the blurb announces it as 'Derek Mahon's boisterous comedy'; Mahon himself, in one of his short prefaces, presents it simply as 'a free translation of *L'École des Maris*' (Mahon 1985a: 7). Brief but informative, the preface lets us know that the play was produced and performed in Derry, in 1984, by the Field Day Theatre Company, as part of a double bill in which it was counterpointed by Tom Paulin's *The Riot Act* (his version of *Antigone*). The double billing may have offset the risible outrageousness of *High Time*; it may also have emphasised that both plays, in the diverse ways proper to tragedy and comedy, deal with ethical options (of a public or private nature) that might be found topical by audiences of either persuasion in the Northern Ireland of the 1980s.

The translator's preface to *High Time* focuses almost exclusively on the temporal dislocation of Molière's plot, since 'doing *High Time* in period' (7) was never an option for a 'we' that implicitly includes the translator and the directors of this production, and possibly also the directors of the Field Day project – in view of their high intellectual and literary profile, and their commitment to the contribution that 'a new theatre and a new audience' might give towards an 'explicit and urgent [. . .] reappraisal of Ireland's political and cultural situation' (Field Day 1985: vii). The sense of civic urgency that informed the project may have led them to 'make it *now*, [. . .]

go for immediacy instead of nostalgia' – the nostalgia referring, in this case, to the last of the creative anachronisms they had considered: 'we toyed with the Nineties, the Twenties, and paused for a long time at May 1968' (Mahon 1985a: 7). Their decision made them construe the 'young people' in *High Time* as 'tough punks', rather than the 'gentle hippies' of the 1968 generation that the translator favoured, in his avowed cultural and political 'nostalgia': gentleness was not on the agenda, or at least it was felt not to serve the theatrical rhetoric required by a troubled time and place. The dislocation became not only temporal, but also spatial, as made clear by an opening stage direction: 'The action takes place in Ireland, May, present time' (10); and, before the action itself begins, another one reads, '*Seventeenth-century court music or similar; changes to rock music*' (11).

Mahon's preface leaves no doubt that he favoured a wholesale rewriting and relocation of Molière's text, but the specific way in which it was ultimately done – on stage, as conspicuously also on the page – was the outcome of collaborative work, in which his stated initial preference did not ultimately prevail. *High Time* is therefore an instance of drama translation that is strongly determined by the conditions of a specific production, in terms that involve a conflation of the work of a translator and that of a dramaturg; and it also seems to have been the only case in Mahon's versions in which the translator's strong awareness of a 'commission'[24] fully took over and determined his rewriting. Mahon's conversion of the original three acts into 'a comedy in one act' also suggests a wish to offer a speeded-up action, a continuous plot that can match the supposed greater vivacity imparted by the play's radical refraction.

High Time, however, retains the structural integrity of Molière's plot, with only occasional abridgements and amplifications. The text's radical dislocation becomes manifest above all in its diction and range of references. A few Irishisms punctuate the dialogue, and demotic tones mark the speeches of the younger characters. Val's (Valére's) mock threat, cried out to Isabel's repressive guardian (Sganarelle, who becomes 'Tom' in this version), epitomises this slant: 'To hell with the old fart! I'll break his fucking neck / if he shows up here trying to get you back' (1985: 51).[25] This couplet also brings out one of the most effective resources of *High Time*'s dramatic rhetoric: Mahon renders it in regular metre and rhymed couplets, echoing the alexandrines of seventeenth-century French drama. This option sets off two tensions: firstly, between the signalled foreignness of Molière's text and Mahon's drastic domestication in time, space, diction and references; secondly, between the language's presentness and its stilted formal quality, as imparted by regular metre and rhyme.

Throughout *High Time*, references to seventeenth-century genteel entertainment are predictably replaced by 'Films and dances, parties and discothèques' (18), while some of the mythological references that would be less familiar to the average audience today are simply dropped. Occasional tropes involving other cultures are reformulated in ways that make the point clearer to present-day audiences;[26] possibly the most suggestive example occurs when a reference to the treatment of women among 'les Turcs' is rendered as: 'You'd think you were in some place like Iraq' (17). The passage highlights the change, from the seventeenth century to the late twentieth century, in the postulation of a token 'other,' but the play encounters other refractions through the two decades that followed its première; recent history (the two Iraq wars) has added implications that show how a translator's intervention can become re-signified (within a fairly short timespan) under changed circumstances in the target culture.

The major problem with the dislocation suffered by Molière's *L'École des Maris* in Derek Mahon's *High Time* is the basic verisimilitude of the plot. A dramatic fiction predicated on the power of male guardians to coerce young parentless women into marriage (to themselves, or third parties) is difficult to pull off in a late twentieth-century Western context where such power is socially and legally untenable. However, certain diffuse patriarchal constraints have nevertheless remained in place in more 'traditional' societies, and this, exacerbated by the extreme circumstances of the Troubles, may have contributed to Field Day's decision to set the play in present-day Ireland, offering a new slant to the comic triumph of the liberal ethical option represented by Ariste/Archie over Sganarelle/Tom's repressive stubbornness. Political history has made Ireland, arguably, 'the last English-speaking' society where, '"if you have something to say, you write a play about it"'[27] – or you translate it, one might add. Unlike (e.g.) Seamus Heaney's *The Cure at Troy* (also translated for a Field Day production), Derek Mahon's *High Time* is hardly an obvious case of politically determined appropriation, and yet its updating of Molière and the specific time and place of its initial performance gave it an otherwise unlikely public pertinence.

Mahon's second version of a Molière comedy, *The School for Wives* (1986), was apparently not subject to the constraints of a particular stage production, but nevertheless has much in common with the earlier version. Anachronism is again one of the comedy's main sources of laughter, as the 'young bucks' about town are described as sporting 'their curly hair / by Scaramouche', spending time 'at Rick's', and 'their nights in the Bad Ass Café'; the town where Mahon sets the action acquires a '*rue Molière*'; and the rich man *ex machina* who proves crucial for the happy ending is construed as '*an expansive Texan*' (1986: 38, 60, 69). But anachronism operates here at two different levels: it is perceived because Mahon inserts such present-day references in a seventeenth-century comedy, but also because he pointedly chose to set the action of his *The School for Wives* not in the present, but rather in the early nineteenth century – and in France (with Molière's characters' names unaltered). In the translator's preface, Mahon explains his rationale for moving the action to 1830, and for specifying a location (Avignon) that in Molière remained unnamed. The crucial point is that this opposes, in a quasi-explicit way, the decision taken in *High Time* to 'make it *now*', which led to problems of plausibility. In the translator's words,

> in a Provençal town, on the way to Italy (home of the *commedia dell'arte* from which Molière derived his initial inspiration), it would still be possible to imagine, even in 1830, a curious guardian-ward relationship such as exists between Arnolphe and Agnès.
>
> (Mahon 1986: 8)

The implication is that the identical guardian-ward relationships in *High Time*, transposed to the present, were implausible. *The School for Wives* thus shows us the translator-poet revising the management of time and place in his appropriations of canonical comedy, so that its ethical issues are not lost on contemporary audiences.

In this second Molière version, Mahon foregrounds the implications of the play's date and location in ways that are entertaining, but also potentially detrimental to its coherence. He invests the text with a variety of references, occasionally playing with the cultural resonance of his chosen place: Horace, the young lover, admits that 'I *have* established a liaison / with a young demoiselle of Avignon' (Mahon 1986: 24); but the highbrow allusion to one of the best-known paintings in Western art cannot but be ironical (since Picasso's *Demoiselles* represents a brothel scene), and is promptly balanced by the most popular of the city's associations, as 'Avignong' [*sic*] is 'A fine spot, with a bridge just like in the song' (23). (Mahon resorts often to forced, joking rhymes, suggested by anomalous spelling). The excitement but also the vulnerabilities of the translator's consciously inconsistent strategy are best seen in the play's central character, Arnolphe. The comic theme of the man who wants a stupid wife that does not have the wit to betray him combines with the pretentiousness of his assumed aristocratic name and over-the-top patriarchal discourse (epitomised in his 'Marriage Maxims' – 40–1) to define his dramatic status as the *senex*, the obstructive old man of comedy, whose absurd authoritarianism, belated amorousness and opposition to young love justify his ultimate social humiliation.[28] Mahon's concern with choosing a plausible time and place for Molière's particular use of this age-old basic plot is challenged by the slangy, often taboo language that he gives Arnolphe, albeit counterpointed by the formality of rhymed couplets. The complicities of laughter endow the prig with the contradictory condition of a comic pointer, who wields such locker-room epithets as 'some poor bugger's wife' (12), 'a girl without too much upstairs' (13), 'randy fellers' (50), and above all the resonant proverbial-sounding couplet: 'Better some dumb cow with an ugly face / than a fine beauty full of wit and grace' (13). True, this misogynous excess is denounced both for its ethics and its pragmatic shortcomings; but Arnolphe's rhetorical deftness hardly finds a match in the naïveté of the young lovers. Mahon's addition to Molière's text of a feminist denunciation (also the translator's apology?) in the voice of Agnès enjoys the authority of a quasi-last word, but lacks rhetorical clout: 'His treatment of me has been quite inhuman: / I see this play as a blow struck for women' (74).

Mahon's continued interest in experimenting with conflicting linguistic registers, and in representing the erotic tensions and power games between the sexes was confirmed in his next ventures into drama translation, *The Bacchae – after Euripides* (1991), *Racine's Phaedra* (1996), and *Oedipus* (2005). The decision to translate tragedies (after two comedies of manners) may suggest a wish to confront issues of a graver and more public nature. Indeed, in Ireland, such issues have often been mediated through Greek tragedy, in particular Sophocles, provenly amenable to appropriative designs that foreground a heroic dimension. However, it may be revealing that, for his first version of a tragedy, Mahon chose Euripides, in whose work the ambivalence of ethical judgement has often been noted.[29] Mahon also showed his awareness of translating in a context in which other poet-translators have rendered Classical tragedies, by joking about a competition with Heaney's nearly contemporary first version of Sophocles: 'I've been doing versions of this and that for the Dublin theatre, most recently *The Bacchae* of Euripides, which will knock *The Cure at Troy* into a cocked hat' (Scammell 1991: 6).

Mahon's first version of a tragedy also foregrounds the interaction between translation and original writing in his work, since the theme of maenadic violence is bound up with the most discussed episode of revision in his poetry, involving 'Courtyards in Delft'. First published as the title poem of a slim volume in 1981, it was also the opening piece of *The Hunt by Night* (1982), then featuring a new final stanza that further dwelt on the expansive nature of the Protestant ethos glimpsed in De Hooch's paintings. The extra stanza expressed a yearning for the arrival of 'Maenads [. . .] with fire and sword' to put an end to the propriety and primness that, in earlier lines, the poet had recognised as marking his own formative background (Mahon 1982: 10). Mahon was later to decide that such explicitness was 'inept' and undue (cf. Scammell 1991: 6), and the new stanza was omitted from subsequent republications. However, this happened only after he ensured an even more conspicuous presence for the Maenads in his work: *The Bacchae* was published in the same year (1991) in which Mahon's *Selected Poems* reverted to the shorter version of 'Courtyards in Delft'.

In the different environments of drama and the lyric (and under his own name, or that of a translated author), Mahon has either expressed or implied his sympathy for a breadth of human experience that will not demote the life of the senses. He has directly invoked the Nietzschean duality of the Apollonian and Dionysian, declaring his alertness to 'the subversive Dionysian spirit, which is lyrical and unamenable to rational explanation and control' (Scammell 1991: 6). Unlike the Molière versions, *The Bacchae* does not have a preface, but it is introduced by a page containing three epigraphs – by Nietzsche (on those 'two prime agencies' in one's consciousness), MacNeice (comparing Yeats to Euripides, with regard to the ability to evolve, in 'old age', from 'a sceptical, rationalist attitude' to 'admit[ting] that there was a case for Dionysus'), and the great Classical scholar E. R. Dodds: 'the Maenad, however mythical certain of her acts, is not in essence a mythological character but an observed and still observable human type' (cited in Mahon 1991a: 9).[30]

When we consider Mahon's palimpsestic lines in 'Courtyards in Delft' in the immediate context afforded by the poem, and then set against the broader context provided by his work, we obtain more than a simple endorsement of Dionysian 'release'. Historical alertness causes Mahon to yearn for the Maenads to bring confusion (in)to a culture of denial and repression that he accuses of forceful acquisitiveness. However, he has shown his awareness that the Dionysian also means the frenzy of mindless violence, death, and dismemberment, and is no mere appeasement and gratification of the senses, 'as of right' (1982: 10). His later poem 'Schopenhauer's Day', from *The Yellow Book*, leaves no doubt that a clear-cut opposition between 'the calm light of Dutch interior art' and 'Weimar, a foul Reich and the days of wrath' (233) proves illusory, and that an historically informed perspective will have to detect the nightmare behind a placid surface. Although one of Mahon's most quoted *dicta* is his repeated wish to be 'through with history', 'The Last of the Fire Kings', one of the pieces where the phrase occurs, considers but rejects the dubious comforts of the sacral and ritual as ways of endowing historical violence with a nexus (64).

Together with other moments in Mahon's work, this leaves no doubt that his choice will not be to seek solace in mythopoesis, by moving from history to myth (or commuting between them, as Seamus Heaney memorably did in *North*) in search of order and redress. And yet, when Mahon borrows Wallace Stevens's phrase 'blessed rage for order' (Stevens 1972: 98) to rewrite it as the 'wretched rage for order' that poets indulge in before the nightmare of history, he knows the outcome can only be 'desperate' or 'terminal ironies' (48). The place and time he envisages in striving for release from history will hardly be that of a 'barbarous cycle' of 'fire and sword' (64), but characteristically a 'site of residual aspiration' (E. Longley 1994: 250) reached by 'Perfecting my cold dream / Of a place out of time' (65). By definition, such a dream will ever await fulfilment, as attested by a continued malaise that the playful verbal surfaces of his dramatic rewritings may camouflage but not efface.

Mahon's textual confrontation with that complex instance of the human and the inhumane, the Dionysian rage in Euripides's *The Bacchae*, yields a version that is anything but the work of an 'invisible translator' (to use again a celebrated phrase for translational self-effacement – Venuti 1995). It is true that, as in his Molière versions, Mahon's strategy is, in an immediate sense, 'domesticating', to the extent that his text abounds in references and idioms specific to present-day uses of the English language. However, Euripides's text is brought over to Mahon's contemporary reader in such a radically current language that it becomes highly 'foreignised', in relation to most readers' expectations of what a Classical text 'should' sound like. The effect is to underline that this is a *translation* of a Classical text: an iconoclasm, and a verbal equivalent, indeed, to 'smashing crockery' (a gesture attributed to the Maenads in the deleted final stanza of 'Courtyards in Delft'). Such features are highlighted from Dionysus's opening speech, punctuated by onomatopoeic interjections – 'Whoosh!', 'pow!' – usually found in cartoons or in teen talk (but hardly to be spotted in more conventional English versions of *Bacchae*[31]). In the course of the same speech, Dionysus refers to his dances and rituals as 'my Dionysian stuff' and alludes to Hera as 'the jealous bitch'. The god is here broadly identified with a post-1960s hedonistic youth culture: rock 'n' roll music is mentioned several times, both in dialogue and in stage directions. His characterisation whips up sympathy for his clash with the 'earnest', rational, official discourse represented by Pentheus, who in Mahon's version is made to denounce the Dionysian rituals in the register of a prig: 'The whole thing's an excuse for drink and sex'.[32] Pentheus's repressive 'rationalism' is, in turn, denounced in the authorised voice of his grandfather, Cadmus: 'You're not thinking straight; the rationalism / you prize so much has led you from the truth'.[33]

Many of the translator's options reinforce a prevalent sympathy for what Dionysus represents; colloquialisms contribute rhetorically to a sense of the 'genuine', as when Dionysus is made to tell Pentheus: 'I'm trying to save your *life*, you pompous twit!'[34] And yet the dialogue in which this occurs is craftily turned by Dionysus into the trap that victimises Pentheus and makes evident the ruthlessness and (properly tragic) disproportion of the punishment meted out by the god to those who fail to acknowledge his sway. However much stress Mahon lays on Euripides's point that it is futile and misguided to deny the Dionysian, he cannot suppress the horror of the death and dismemberment of Pentheus, nor the *pathos* of Agave's awakening from her Maenadic frenzy and delusion to recognise her son's head in her own hands, and of Cadmus's recomposition of his grandson's body for the sake of proper exequies. This is the point at which the jocular tone of Dionysus's speeches turns sour, together with the whole boisterous element that Mahon whips up throughout his translation. Although he steers clear of the more obvious strategies of refraction occasionally employed by Northern Irish poets for confronting the Troubles through their translations of the Classics, the Irish implication is hardly absent. It often emerges in the form of echoes of other Mahon poems that carry the implication more obviously, and occasionally as an Irishism, as when Tiresias refers to the Dionysian festivities as 'the famous *céilí*' (1991a: 15). Such moments do not allow us to forget, at the point when King Pentheus's torn body is brought back to his palace, other dismembered bodies that so often brought horror to a place where 'home' rhymed with 'bomb' (as in Mahon's 'Afterlives' – 58).

Mahon's ambivalent attitude towards the Dionysian element in the human experience pervades his representations of women. Dionysus's opening address is fully on the side of idiosyncrasy and laughter, proposing the Bacchae as superannuated partygoing 'aunties' – as if De Hooch's housewives had left their 'courtyards' behind and gone roaming, all containment and decorum lost:

> Not only Cadmus' daughters, but virtually the whole
> feminine population rock'n'roll
> among the rocks, under the moonlit pines;[35]

At the other end of the emotional and representational spectrum, Mahon's text offers the poignancy and pathos of Agave's self-delusion that the 'belovèd body' of her son, whose head she herself has brought on stage in her frenzy, will be 'in one piece' (1991a: 56, 58).

Mahon's continued attraction to rewriting famous terrible women was confirmed with his 1996 version of *Racine's Phaedra*. The option for neoclassical rather than Classical signals continuities and helps construe literary history as a lineage of rewritings: a few years after translating Euripides, Mahon translated Racine's reworking of Euripides (and Seneca), and made both translations relevant to his practice of self-revision. This second translation of a tragedy has similarities with *The Bacchae*, but is also significantly different in tone: the demotic element is considerably downplayed, as if the translator's familiarity with the source language had made inevitable a greater deference for the formal solemnity of Racine's alexandrines. Indeed, a brief 'Translator's Note' remarks on the 'psychological realism and poetic force' of Racine's text, and acknowledges that 'the present version tries to give some indication of these qualities in the original' (1996a: 9). It is, though, a translation that shirks the ambition to propose 'what Racine would have written in his day had he written *Phèdre* in English'. This is precluded by the present-day phrasings that still punctuate Mahon's text – either through ironical effects, as when Hippolytus sneers, 'I can just see us sail off into the sunset!'[36], and 'Oenone' rhymes with 'the cliffs at Navarone' (14, 60); or idioms and references that characterise the discourse of the modern educated European, such as allusions to drugs and 'anorexia', or accusations of 'misogyny' (23, 24).

It is noteworthy that Mahon pursues this strategy with a dramatist (Racine) that George Steiner has singled out as an example of the neoclassical assumption that 'all translation from the canon, all imitation, restatement, citation [. . .] [will be] synchronic', a synchronicity predicated on a 'postulate of timelessness', 'the constancy of general human traits and, consequently, of expressive forms' (Steiner 1992: 452). Mahon rather obviously queries this assumption, be it with regard to the verbal representation of emotions or of intellectual judgment – even if his interest in plots with a Classical and mythical matrix and a long literary–historical lineage suggests an endorsement of the 'timelessness' of basic features of human experience.

Another aspect that lends a strong ironic content to Mahon's strategies as a translator of Racine is what Steiner calls the 'disembodied' nature of Racine's dramatic art: 'The order of physicality [. . .] is alien to French high theatre [. . .] it is at no stage somatic' (Steiner 1992: 390). Mahon does indeed introduce into Racine's text a bodily, 'somatic' dimension, although without the boisterousness he gave to Euripides. When he conjures the image of an 'anorexic ghost' (1996a: 23), he paradoxically represents a tortured *soul* as an emaciated, pathologically deprived (hence, foregrounded) *body*. Hippolytus's self-recrimination for being 'contemptuous of the emotional life', the attitude which also makes him refer to 'my hubristic soul' (28), proves that Mahon's concern with the repression of the Dionysian persists in this version, with particular reference to Hippolytus and his (in)experience of 'sexual love', as opposed to Racine's 'amour' (1996a: 25; Racine 1990: 68). It is hardly irrelevant that this tragedy also ends in dismemberment for the character thus described, and a father 'griev[ing] for [his] dismembered child' (1996a: 64).

Mahon took care to signal the continuities that mattered to him from *The Bacchae* to *Racine's Phaedra*, in particular in a poem in *The Yellow Book* titled 'At the Gate Theatre' (241–2). Dedicated to the actress Dearbhla Molloy, who played Mahon's Phaedra in the première, the poem originally had two epigraphs (excised for inclusion in the *Collected Poems*), the second of which, by Stevie Smith, read: '*Now the story of* Phèdre *is very well known, but perhaps the story of the* Bacchae *is not so well known*' (1997: 30). 'At the Gate Theatre' otherwise opens with self-quotation (a passage from a lament by Mahon's Phaedra), and goes on to exalt those rare actresses who 'now can decently impersonate / the great ones of the tragic repertoire' (241). The rest of the poem expands on the notion that the time for high tragedy was historically over soon after *Phèdre*, the age being rather for those satyr plays that used to follow Greek tragedies 'in the early days', and that Euripides is credited with having brought to the fore in *The Bacchae*. In its original reading, the poem featured a finale of celebratory farewells to 'the tragic sense of life' and satirical imperatives to indulge in 'a soap serial and a dirty laugh', or (a Shakespearian comic note) to 'fornicate / with donkeys, or with a monster fall in love' (1997: 31–2). The final twelve lines of 'At the Gate Theatre', however, which derived from the poem's evocation of the Dionysian rule in *The Bacchae*, but capped it with a satirically festive ending, were excluded from the text published in 1999:

> Dionysus son of Semele is come
> to release us from our servitude to the sublime,

> no further resistance offered by the medium,
> the whole history of creative tension a waste of time.
>
> (242)

This new, abridged ending remains a satirical welcome to Dionysian release construed as the facility of moral, intellectual and artistic defeat; but its terseness probably means that the underlying bitterness, and the equation between this sense of defeat and the unquestionable *pathos* of the end of *The Bacchae*, are more promptly perceptible – as against the longer ending of the 1997 text, whose verbal fireworks and festive tone might easily be misconstrued as a surrender to 'post-modern kitsch' and the overall climate of 'corporate rule, McPeace and Mickey Mao' (255). Again, the *petite histoire* of a poem's revision clarifies Mahon's inflected poetic mode from the mid-1990s, and the internal relations of his (re)writings.

A dimension of Mahon's work that offers a critical vantage on his poetry and translations in this period is his reinforced focus on the artist in a metropolitan context. Imaginatively sustained by the intensity and diversity of urban life, the artist figure nonetheless requires the aloofness and boost afforded by that great *commonplace* of artistic modernity, the attic or garret above the city (Paris, or an elsewhere modelled on Paris). Several poems in *The Yellow Book*, as also 'Resistance Days', the opening piece of *Harbour Lights*, testify to the continued appeal of this model of literary life. But the poetic persona seems much less *maudit*, much less defined by extreme circumstances than when it featured in Mahon's early verse; the view from his 'high window' does not necessarily place him so 'far from his people', nor does it seem to require 'desperate' or 'terminal' as favoured adjectives (47–8). *The Yellow Book* signally opens with a translation of Baudelaire's 'Landscape', acknowledging that, in order to write, 'I need to lie / [. . .] in an attic next the sky', between the moon, 'dispensing its mysterious influence', and the 'workshops full of noise and talk' (223). The imaginative consequence of this self-representation was stressed by a paratextual revision: where in the 1997 collection the poem was marked *'after Baudelaire'*, in the 1999 *Collected Poems* it read *'Context: Baudelaire'* (1997: 11; 1999: 223). The 'contextual' location provided by 'Landscape' is proved relevant by the book's first 'original' poem, 'Night Thoughts', which opens with an epigraph from Paul Fussell's *Abroad* on the late modern devaluation of places into mere tourist sites. 'Night Thoughts' sees the poet 'night-writ[ing]' in Dublin, but implicitly reconnecting with Paris at another *fin-de-siècle*, by 'read[ing] the symbolists as the season dies', and closing the poem with a version of lines from Jules Laforgue's 'L'Hiver qui Vient' (224–5). This link with the nineteenth century is reiterated throughout the collection, both via Parisian settings – the crepuscular 'Dusk' is another Baudelaire translation (249–50) – and

Anglophone urban counterparts, as in the allusions to 'Dowson, Johnson, Symons', 'Yeats's "tragic" generation' that punctuate 'Remembering the '90s' (retitled 'Hangover Square' in the *Collected Poems*), and account for the collection's title (239–40).[37] Concomitantly, the Dublin location is firmly asserted through the perspective from a 'high window' with a 'studious light' on 'the backlit tree-tops of Fitzwilliam Square', and the poet's self-description as 'an armchair explorer in an era of cheap flight' (226–7).

Emplacement thus vies with displacement in the later Mahon. In the New York of *The Hudson Letter*, the expatriate condition of the autobiographical persona contributed much to the sense of global loss and uprootedness in the title sequence; *The Yellow Book*, however, signals a much less ironical homecoming than earlier poems on the theme: 'Autumn in Dublin; safe home from New York' (253).[38] But Dublin is not the only European location where empirical experience and elective memories of literary life afford Mahon a sense of emplacement, since Paris in 'Resistance Days', couched again in the epistolary mode common to several of his longer pieces, finds him relating both to his own memories of the place and those that he knows from literary history: 'Old existentialists, old beats, old punks / sat here of old'; 'the Deux Magots / where as a student I couldn't afford to go' (2005: 13). This is an account of a contented return that wavers between fond nostalgia and a consciousness of the improved circumstances enjoyed by the ageing poet, who derives from both retrospection and an enjoyment of the present the determination to retrieve 'creative anarchy' in an eminently suitable topography for 'a *flâneur* in the dense galaxies of text' (2005: 15, 17).

Textual *flânerie* can indeed be an apt metaphor for a continued involvement in translation, pre-eminently of French sources: the same years that yielded 'Resistance Days' saw Mahon publish Saint-John Perse's sequence of prose poems *Birds* (2002) and Edmond Rostand's *Cyrano de Bergerac* (2004). In *Birds*, a reiterated, exclamatory attraction to 'the asceticism of flight', 'the exhilaration of flight', 'the lightning flash of the artist' (2002: 11, 17, 26) chimes with the urge for a retrieved creative impetus elsewhere troped 'in an attic next the sky' (223). *Cyrano* finds Mahon returning to drama translation (on a commission from the National Theatre in London) to render a play written in Paris in the late nineteenth century, but whose action (in the source text) is set in Molière's and Racine's seventeenth century. *Cyrano de Bergerac* features the dislocations in space and time that marked his Molière versions, compounded by a remarkable willingness to abridge the dialogues. The Foreword declares that 'we are in indeterminate space-time', nominally in 1640, 'though the war looks remarkably like that of 1914–1918. The Gascons are a sort of Ulstermen, the *précieuses* modern feminists' (2004: 12). Unsurprisingly to readers of his earlier dramatic versions, the taverns in *Cyrano*'s Paris have the names of English pubs (or otherwise of global chains), many of the play's characters make abundant use of present-day taboo language, and the translator's attraction to his main character's notion of 'panache' is mimicked in a management of the couplets that does not balk at getting 'Bordeaux' to rhyme with 'H_2O' (2004: 43). Poetic identification with the figure of Cyrano is openly hinted at in the description of the protagonist 'in his bare attic',[39] and in self-referential amplifications like Cyrano's musing (with translational implications) on 'the kind of exercise that tempts a poet – / *ventriloquism*, romance' (2004: 130, 66 – my emphasis). It also involves a cultural claim, following on Mahon's proposal that the Gascons be construed as Ulstermen; when the battleground in *Cyrano*, where the Gascons shout 'over the top!' (124), is equated with the First World War's trenches, it is doubtful that Mahon is including himself in the identity that he so pointedly summons – that of *unionist* Ulster; but the Gascons include and are epitomised by Cyrano himself, which means that their boisterousness is also the poet's own. The implicit claim of a shared excess possibly bears on Mahon's outrageous freedoms with Rostand's text – which hardly went unnoticed, and were not universally applauded.[40]

The strategy of iconoclasm (through anachronism) that Mahon has adopted has seen significant variations. If the paratextual and extratextual remarks on the Dionysian, in connection with *The Bacchae*, seemed to invoke the notion of a textual 'release' for the poet's iconoclastic writing, then the more straightforward translations offered in his *Oedipus – A Version of Sophocles's King Oedipus and Oedipus at Colonus* (2005) are suggestive of a post-cathartic serenity. Mahon's foreword is notably candid in admitting to having worked from 'various literal translations', since 'I know no Greek' (2005a: 10). (A similar admission recurs in the Foreword to *Adaptations*, which begins by describing the book's contents as '[not] translations, properly speaking, but versions of their originals devised [. . .] from "cribs" of one kind or another', and makes a plea for the 'venerable tradition' of versions by poets without a 'working knowledge' of the source languages; the admission of a linguistic limitation in fact leads to a declared ambition for the *ne plus ultra* of poetic translation – the dual hope that his own versions 'will read *almost* like original poems in English', while yet 'allowing their sources to remain audible' – 2006: 11). The assumption that an intralingual version is bound to be freer, since it seeks legitimation and raison d'être through differentiation, by starkly departing from its sources, could apply to Mahon's *The Bacchae*, but hardly to his *Oedipus*. Comparison with scholarly translations indicates that Mahon handles the dialogue and the overall dramatic rhetoric with some freedom, but *Oedipus* does not boast the boldness of diction that characterised Mahon's earlier dramatic versions, compared to which it may appear relatively conventional. The odd (though discreet) joke still emerges in this text, as when Oedipus describes himself as 'a mother-lover', a phrase that evokes but avoids its demotic synonym; and Mahon remains unfearful of anachronism: Oedipus yearns for 'a shock / of electricity', and decries his 'degenerate' sons, who seem 'preoccupied with interior decoration / while women do the work once done by men' (2005a: 51, 55) – but such effects are now the exception, rather than the rule.

In general, it is as if the mature translator, though admitting to having worked intralingually, no longer felt the need to leave a blatant mark on his version. And yet some of those moments in Mahon's *Oedipus* that stand out for their modernity (their anachronism) involve values that have always been a part of his ethical and intellectual makeup, though his poetry often celebrates them only in negative or ironical terms, through their absence. Where, in other versions of *Oedipus at Colonus*, Athens is credited with being 'devout' or having 'reverence for the gods',[41] Mahon opts for secularising it as 'the source of art and science, philosophy, literature' (2005a: 54); and one of his rare additions has Theseus recommend 'our great city' for its 'new enlightenment', 'with drama and philosophy in the air' (60) – a quasi-parodic version of the liberal humanist's dream. The Foreword to *Oedipus* lays some emphasis on the element of 'redemption', on the fact that (through Oedipus's suffering) 'a new life can begin' (9). In favouring this emphasis, as in the self-assuredness and comparative sedateness of its translation strategies, arguably proper to a later moment in a literary career, Mahon's *Oedipus* may seem to approximate Heaney's *Antigone* (*The Burial at Thebes*), published in the previous year – and, maybe not by coincidence, *Oedipus* bears the dedication "*for Seamus Heaney*", in contrast to the boisterous declaration of rivalry with which Mahon had announced in 1991 the publication of *The Bacchae*, shortly after Heaney's *The Cure at Troy*.

It is tempting to extend to Mahon's more recent poetry this challenge to the polarisation that has tended to organise the critical reading of these two poets (and, to resume, towards the end of this chapter, its opening topos). The distinct rapport with nature that emerges in the later Mahon sets a productive terrain for this: 'A Swim in Co. Wicklow', one of the new pieces included in the closing pages of the *Collected Poems*, celebrates a reencountered seascape that has none of the bleakness of his earlier poetry, but offers rather an organic at-homeness represented in quasi-Heaneyesque terms – the onomatopoeic sensuousness, the imagery of immersion and connection: 'warm uterine rinse', 'soft water-lip, soft hand', 'the sensual writhe and snore / of maidenhair and frond' (280). In the title poem of *Harbour Lights*, the located self musing on local and global matters over 'one more sedative evening in Co. Cork', while 'watch[ing] by starlight / the London plane' (2005: 61–2), might remind readers of Heaney's 'The Flight Path' (Heaney 1996: 22). And 'The Seaside Cemetery', Mahon's version of Paul Valéry that closes *Harbour Lights*, has none of the tone of scepticism and loss that in an earlier (elegiac) poem accompanied the self's confrontation with a 'crowded cemetery / That overlooks the sea' (88), but rather the emplacement proposed in the lines: 'to this high point I climb and feel at home / ordering all things with a seaward stare', and indeed the experience of 'bursting with new power' (2005: 72).

Nowhere has Mahon come so close to a convincing representation of malaise overcome as in *Life on Earth*, which also reinforces the link between a reconfigured perspective on nature and ever more blurred boundaries between original writing and translation. The collection opens with the mythologically remote shore of 'Ariadne on Naxos' (another version of Ovid, this time from the *Heroides*), and closes with the exotic Indian shores of 'Turtle Beach' and 'Homage to Goa' – two Goan pieces that blend a delighted immersion in natural and cultural elsewheres with the pastoral of contented ageing. *Life on Earth* stands out for the ecological commitment flagged by its title and expressed at its most vocal and ecstatic in the sequence 'Homage to Gaia', which apologises to 'great Gaia our first mother' for human depletion of resources (2008: 46); muses on 'how to live // in the post-petroleum age', and urges the sun to 'remember life on Earth!' (44–5); declares a zest for healthy and exotic food enjoyed in cosy environments (50–1); and celebrates a pop singer's capacity to sing against 'global warming' in 'Ode to Björk' (54–5). Some of the pieces in the sequence are quasi-parodic in their neo-Futuristic, exclamatory enthusiasm for 'wind turbines', their injunction to the wind to 'Blow [. . .] and seize / the slick rotors!', their didactic discursiveness on the prospect of 'an average annual / thousand kilowatt hours / per photovoltaic panel' (2008: 44, 47–8).

However, as suggested by a framing device that pointedly includes translation, the collection superimposes a self-reflective (and possibly ironical) element on such programmatic, sometimes awkwardly wide-eyed paeans; and it achieves thematic concentration by positioning the poet not only with regard to the earth itself, but also to an array of earth-writings which play with contrast and continuity vis-à-vis the poet's earlier take on experience and the world. One of Mahon's poems on (or after) the *Odyssey*, 'Circe and the Sirens', is a case in point; the poem offers a loose rendering of the narrative mainstream of Books X through XII of the *Odyssey*, and concludes with an (extra-epic) envisaged idyllic ageing prospect: 'He might retire, sea music in his ears, / this micro-climate his last resting place, / and spend his old age in sublime disgrace' (2008: 28). These lines relate closely to the refashioned 'Calypso' episode in *Harbour Lights*, which has Odysseus stay with Calypso and 'never [make] it back' to Ithaca – Mahon twice flagging his rewriting with the formula 'Homer was wrong' (2005: 57–60). 'Circe and the Sirens' signals its link with the earlier poem by opening with the assertion that 'Homer was right' (2008: 27), but this endorsement refers to the forebear's management of the time and structure (rather than the contents) of his narrative.

Indeed, the notion of 'getting' or 'making' things right, with a bearing on earlier writing (by himself or others), pervades *Life on Earth*, possibly finding its two most intriguing examples in the ekphrastic sequence 'Art Notes' – because they relate to a landscape, or living presences, at several removes, and testify to a yearning to constantly reformulate that relationship. The first of these 'Art Notes', 'A Lighthouse in Maine', is a verbal rendering of Edward Hopper's painting – but also a remake of Mahon's earlier poem of the same title, initially published in *The Hunt by Night*, excluded from *Collected Poems* and now rearranged with only a few of the original lines (2008: 31). The fifth poem in the sequence, 'Birds – Georges Braque (after Saint-John Perse)' (2008: 35), is an even more complex afterwriting – a poetic summation of Mahon's earlier version of Perse's sequence *Birds*, itself originally 'written to accompany a series of bird lithographs by Georges Braque' (2002: 9). These mediations seem to find an epistemological and programmatic reflection in the sequence's second piece, 'The Realm of Light – René Magritte', which includes the caveat: 'view this picture with extreme distrust / since what you see is the *trompe l'oeil* of a dream' (2008: 32).

The irony and wariness that such lines impart to *Life on Earth* also reinforce a perception that the element of uplift and optimism in late Mahon appears severely qualified. This was already noticeable in *Harbour Lights*: the nocturnal situation in the title poem is one in which 'the high spirits begin to drop, / remembering buried errors and wasted time'; the postmodern, neoliberal 'crude culture dazed with money' that Mahon decries also entails natural surroundings that are post- (and anti-) pastoral, a 'dark grove / of baths, old cars and fridges'; and the epigraph (from the pioneer ecologist Rachel Carson's *The Edge of the Sea*) has the poet ventriloquising through 'a newcomer' whose elusive roots make for a precarious, 'anachronistic' belonging (2005: 61–3). As for the 'site' conjured up by 'The Seaside Cemetery', its representation may evade the bitter 'ironies' of an earlier mode (nor is the translation iconoclastic or 'radical'), but the place cannot be more 'terminal': indeed, 'The future [is] here already' – but it 'scarcely moves' (73); and the *ubi sunt* formula pointedly dooms the verbal talents: 'Where now are the colloquial turns of phrase, / the individual gifts and singular souls?' (74). A few lines below, a formula (an amplification, with regard to the source 'Tout fuit!') encapsulates one of the poem's prevalent significations, and possibly conjures a familiar precursor: 'everything flows, ourselves the most' (74) – a phrase that Louis MacNeice, ever alert to Heraclitean flux, might have penned.

Evoking this particular Classicist, translator of Greek drama, and author of reflections on translating the Classics may prove apt in more ways than one. Mahon's continued alertness to this predecessor was confirmed in the year he published *Harbour Lights* through the insertion in *Oedipus* of a phrase from MacNeice – when the Chorus envisages 'a brisk return / to the pre-natal night' (2005a: 67). Moreover, the strategy he uses when rendering the Classics has been described as illustrative of MacNeice's notion of 'translation as calculated disruption rather than "cure"' (McDonald 1995: 198). Although the 'site' conjured by Mahon's recent poetry has become less starkly one of 'residual aspiration' (cf. E. Longley 1994: 250), he has hardly converted to a poetics of spiritual redress and existential emplacement.

'Ariadne on Naxos' prefaces *Life on Earth* with a lament uttered 'Above the cold beach and the pounding waves', as, abandoned 'on this bare rock', she acknowledges her likeness to 'a madwoman / or some lost Maenad' (2008: 11). This translation is indeed 'disruptive': it is a free and ultra-concise version (in 41 lines) of a source text that is nearly four times as long, and confirms a continued interest in complex or terrible women that extends to other poems in the book. 'The Lady from the Sea (after Ibsen)' features dialogue which becomes a lyrical abstract of Ellida's crucial option between the sedate emplacement of a landbound life and the alluring unknown of a displacement to the sea (2008: 29–30). The connection between these shoreline poems and the more contented eco-sensibility that otherwise marks the collection is possibly provided by the self-directed advice in 'Research':

> Best to ignore
> 'the great ocean of truth',
> the undiscovered seas of outer space,
> and research this real unconscious conch on the shore
>
> (2008: 41)

This rejection of broader abstract and conceptual expanses (epitomised in the cited Newtonian phrase[42]), to settle for the immediate, small-scale and concrete, also involves forgoing the grander and gloomier tones that defined the 'best prepare for the worst' attitude of an earlier shoreline piece (101). The interrogative rapport with existence and location persists – but its mitigation, in the name of immediacy and the human, provides an apt cue to address the work of Mahon's other contemporary, Michael Longley.

4
Versions of Compassion: Michael Longley

> The lapwing and I
> Watch over each other and we speak in tongues
>
> —243[1]

The poetry of Michael Longley, when approached from the perspective that informs the present book, illustrates a convergence of a different type between a critical design and a favourite object of representation. With Longley, our study of *textual* relations is brought to bear on a body of writing that focuses on the emotional yield of *human* relations, both in the actuality of lived experience, and in real or imagined lineages – biological as much as literary. This means that his poetry is committed to traditional lyrical themes and modes, and in particular to the genre's defining assumption of the emotions that are proper to love and the awareness of death. But it also means that, in his case, the concentration on self that has conventionally defined the lyric is constantly enabled by the emotional bonds between self and other(s), acknowledged (in amorous or elegiac writing) as cherished presence or mourned absence. Such concern with the presence/absence of loved ones extends, with the necessary inflections, to literary relations: this homology becomes noticeable in the form and diction that Longley employs in verse tributes to choice forebears, and in some measure also in his frequent and frank acknowledgement of his contemporaries, in particular Mahon and Heaney.

Of these three poets, it is possibly Longley who has most often evoked shared aspects of their formative experience, though he also partakes of their wariness with regard to notions of a 'poetic generation', or accounts of the beginning of their respective writing careers that unduly stress the dynamics of the 'school or coterie', at the expense of individuality (Allen-Randolph 2003: 299). Despite these reservations, Longley has been less insistent than Mahon on the separateness of their trajectories, reminiscing in interviews, or in his brief autobiographical account, *Tuppenny Stung* (1994), about some of the common joys and challenges of his and Mahon's student life at Trinity College Dublin, and about the much-discussed role played by Philip Hobsbaum's 'Group' in fostering young poetic talent in 1960s Belfast.[2] Likewise, he has also pointed out that it was only on his return from Dublin to Belfast that he made his first friends ever from the Catholic community (which included Seamus Heaney and his future wife) – a revelation that is itself a gauge of the thoroughness of the Ulster sectarian divide, and of the important breakthroughs that literary companionship made possible in Northern Ireland in the late 1960s and early 1970s.[3]

The bonds, personal and literary, that make up Longley's sense of self and energise his writing are paratextually highlighted in the dedicatory lines to his books, which tend to alternate an acknowledgement of the private and familial with his writerly relations. His inaugural collection, *No Continuing City* (1969), bears the dedication *'for Edna'*, followed by lines that ground his writing in a sense of generational flux (the lived themes of birth, growth, and death), and construe his own perception of that grounding as a vicarious reading experience: 'My children and my dead / Coming of age / In the turn of your head / As you turn a page' (1). Conversely, Longley's second collection, *An Exploded View* (1973), is dedicated to 'Derek [Mahon], Seamus [Heaney] & Jimmy [Simmons]'; his acknowledgement of their common attempt 'to make ourselves heard' is equated in the dedicatory lines (by means of three similes) with the paroxystic – hence, sincere, but also primarily intimate – voices of 'the lover [. . .] / In his passion', 'the condemned man / Who makes a last-minute confession', and 'the child who cries out in the dark' (39). In the case of this second book, the dedication was taken up and confirmed in Longley's sequence of verse 'Letters' addressed to the same 'three Irish poets' on a personal celebratory occasion (fatherhood), but nonetheless dealing with political and poetic matters (53–61). Longley's subsequent collections – *Man Lying on a Wall* (1976), *The Echo Gate* (1979), *Gorse Fires* (1991), *The Ghost Orchid* (1995), *The Weather in Japan* (2000), *Snow Water* (2004) – have maintained this practice of dedication either to family or friends, in the latter case mostly writers, which reinforces the inseparability of his poetry and the autobiographical record.

The sense of a continuity between life and its inscribed consequence also helps explain why Longley (starkly contrasting with Mahon in this regard) opts not to revise his poems, 'not to tinker with past effort', since 'this resembles denting cold metal that was red-hot in another life' (as he puts it in the 'Author's Note' to his *Collected Poems* – n.p.). In Heaney's case (as seen above), textual stability emerges as a necessity of an internally tight oeuvre that itself crafts the arguments for each poem's position in the authorial canon to appear as inevitable. With Longley, whose *Collected Poems* neatly reproduce the author's discrete collections in their original order, the *staidness* of the various pieces is rather a formal correlative for the attachments that define this poetics – which, by virtue of the experience underlying it, becomes also an ethic.

This defining importance of attachments to people and locations is certainly a feature that Longley's poetry has in common with Heaney's. However, Longley's poetically enabling links to certain topographies tend to appear mediated, if not determined, by human bonds, rather than paralleling Heaney's grounding of self and writing on a territory invested with historical and ancestral significance – a distinct rootedness that may reflect their origins in different Northern Irish communities. Longley might not reject the fundamentally lyrical interlock of identity, place, and private emotion in a recent Heaney line such as 'If self is a location, so is love' (Heaney 2006: 12), but the relative position of those three terms in the equation would not necessarily be the same. The way in which Longley's poetry thrives on 'the ties of family, home, class and country' is, on the other hand, a fundamental distinction vis-à-vis the perception of 'failed filiative bonds' that from an early stage became a hallmark of Derek Mahon's work (Dawe 1995: 154). The distinction is all the more obvious in view of Mahon's and Longley's origin on the same side of the Northern Irish divide, and their common formative experience as 'old boys of the Royal Belfast Academical Institution' and Trinity College students.[4] The power that the world of nature holds over their poetic imaginations also makes for a fundamental difference, as noted in Gerald Dawe's remark that 'while Longley takes the natural world to heart and humanises it in the process, Mahon's denatured world is calmly mindful, brooding on itself' (Dawe 1995: 157).

These differences reflect the mutually determining impact of experiential and idiosyncratic factors, but also – despite such common (but discrete) legacies as the MacNeice example, and the 'well-made poem' – of different literary models. Mahon's prevalent disaffected, melancholy persona, often glimpsed against a bleak background, owes much to his interest in Beckett, and (in broader terms) is informed by an outlook that acknowledges the modernist legacy (cf. Mahon 2006a; Burton 2005). Longley's celebration of domestic and local environments, as also of natural landscapes (usually around his second home in Mayo, in the west of Ireland), both of which provide confirmation of the self, is empowered by a personal pantheon of authorial references that prominently includes Thomas Hardy, Wilfred Owen, Edward Thomas, and to some extent Philip Larkin – the tradition that has been influentially described as bypassing the consequence of High Modernism to define a continuing strand in 'British' poetry; a tradition whose assumption (to varying degrees) originally led to poets of Longley's generation being dubbed 'neo-Georgian'[5].

Longley's option to remain in Belfast (unlike most other contemporary Northern Irish poets), and his participation, throughout the Troubles and in their wake, in civic efforts to counter the sectarian mindset and its dismal effects are biographical data of obvious relevance (both as cause and consequence) for his poetics of attachment. His endorsement of the liberal stance of moderate Protestants commits him to a liminality that, buttressed by his vocal concern with cultural diversity, distinguishes his position from those that are more conventionally associated with the hyphenated (Anglo-Irish) alternative within Northern Irish identity politics (as suggested by some of his scant autobiographical prose – Longley 1994: 43–76). The representational needs proper to this position have led Longley, at key moments in his writing, to address the textual space provided by the Classics (the object and theme of his student days) as an aptly remote set of resources. His self-description as a 'lapsed classicist' (cited in McDonald 2000: 35) is both belied by the skills confirmed in his appropriations, and ironically echoed in their very latitude and freedom – a strategy that may equally seem unexpected in a poet otherwise so firmly committed to formal rigour.

The sequence of Michael Longley's publications (already delineated above by the dates of his collections) shows some rather obvious similarities to Derek Mahon's. Both published their first collection at the end of the 1960s; both (though for different personal reasons) went through a whole decade without a new collection – in Longley's case, from 1979 to 1991, a period that sees only the publication of a retrospective volume (*Poems 1963–1983*), gathering earlier collections and a few new poems; and in both cases translation has played a decisive role either in precipitating the resurgence of their careers, and/or as an integral structuring factor in their writing. But this chapter will also point out some notable differences. The first is that Longley's translations, which are not always overtly labelled as such, have invariably been included in his collections alongside his other poems, rather than presented as autonomous publications. A second difference is that Longley has not felt attracted to the generically distinct domain of drama, which has so exercised the recreative imagination of Heaney and Mahon.

A brief comparison might also be productive between Longley's and Heaney's respective publication histories, since it reinforces one's perception of affinities within this poetic generation. Such affinities rarely bear the signs of deliberate (ironical or fraternal) emulation. Rather, they reveal the inevitability of the mutual consciousness and assimilation that is bound to develop within a tightly knit tradition, despite possibly being imperceptible to each of the writers involved. Readers will have noted that 1991 was the year both of Longley's long-awaited new collection *Gorse Fires*, which won the Whitbread Poetry Award, and of Heaney's *Seeing Things*, which marked a new direction in his poetry (incidentally, Heaney had won the same award in 1987 with his previous collection). As amply discussed above, this 1991 Heaney volume offered a measure of release from the constraints that political concerns had imposed on the poet's lyrical calling. Likewise, one of the strategies developed by Michael Longley, in his poetry since 1991, has been to address the public crisis indirectly through mediations derived from the intimate landscapes of private experience, as much as from the unexpected transits revealed by translation and other authorial dialogues, and by the imaginative dislocations that define and interrelate his textual topographies.

4.1 Human(e) locations

On being asked, shortly after publishing his first collection, for a brief description of the makings of his poetic self, Michael Longley declared: 'since poetry is about most of the things that happen to most people, I am happy to be a husband and a father' (Murphy 1970: 670). Readers encountering Longley for the first time might find this a strangely diffident or unconcerned visiting card from a poet whose environment (late 1960s Ulster) was then notorious for 'things' that were regrettably outside the scope of private bliss. However, Longley's poetry (from his earliest publications), as well as other remarks he has made on the relation between poetry and 'things that happen', was by no means indifferent to the long and intense public crisis that marked his empirical and imaginative surroundings. At the height of the Troubles, he repeatedly argued in interviews and elsewhere for an artistic ethos that involved responsiveness and responsibility. As a poet writing in traditional forms, he was wary of 'sound[ing] like fiddling while Rome burns' and aware of the need for verbal accuracy to avoid 'dangerous impertinence' and offer 'antidotes to death-dealing dishonesty'.[6] As for his poetry, the impact of the Troubles tends to take the form of representations of moral hurt and mourning afforded by the private experiential and cognitive position that defines and locates the self – and that position, as suggested by Longley's 1970 self-description (quoted above), largely coincides with the space of love, marriage, home, and family.

This centring of identity on the private sphere, from which Longley addresses public circumstances (as they impinge upon the parental, marital or filial consciousness), generates an emphasis on recurrence and permanence. His interest in the generational continuum can also find him anticipating posthumous moments or engaging in a regression (sometimes based on family history) to prenatal conditions. This theme has tended to organise itself around the poet's father, whose reminiscences about the First World War become a fundamental inherited memory for the poet's particular topographies. The war's perplexing spatiality – the entrapment of the trenches, the awful liminality of No Man's Land – becomes a source of recurrent tropes, with metatextual implications. His father's 'place' as an Englishman in Ulster society was partly defined by his military rank as 'Major Longley'; the place he holds in the poet's consciousness is that of a poignancy fostered by past and revenant sufferings, a poignancy that conflates private grief for a father's death and communal remembrance of the fallen of many decades earlier. Participation in the Great War has long been a key trait of the historical identity and proud self-image of Protestant Ulster – and, as such, proved decisive for its sense of territory: entrenchment elsewhere reinforced a community's sense of entitlement to cry 'No Surrender!' over a disputed 'home' ground. But for Longley, the war is far from being the enabling public memory it traditionally was for unionist Ulster. Instead, it is represented in several of his earlier poems as a disabling power, poignantly illustrated by the description of a private wound that almost denied the poet his very existence:

> shrapnel shards that sliced your testicle.
> That instant I, your most unlikely son,
> In No Man's Land was surely left for dead,
> Blotted out from your far horizon.
> As your voice now is locked inside my head,
> I yet was held secure, waiting my turn.
>
> ('In Memoriam', 30)

Imaginatively locating himself on a terrain of death as a suspended life-to-be, the son was later to witness the wound's delayed deadly effect: 'In my twentieth year your old wounds woke / As cancer' (31).

In the aptly entitled 'Wounds', Longley juxtaposes his father's private predicament and deferred death with the public ills of Troubles-stricken Northern Ireland. The memory of his father's deathbed and funeral comes to encompass the burial of 'Three teenage soldiers, bellies full of / Bullets and Irish beer, their flies undone' (62); while the same poem also includes one of several descriptions of sectarian murders made particularly nasty by the fact that they were committed in the very homes of the victims:

> He collapsed beside his carpet-slippers
> Without a murmur, shot through the head
> By a shivering boy who wandered in
> Before they could turn the television down
> Or tidy away the supper dishes.
> To the children, to a bewildered wife,
> I think 'Sorry Missus' was what he said.
>
> (62)

> He was preparing an Ulster fry for breakfast
> When someone walked into the kitchen and shot him:
> A bullet entered his mouth and pierced his skull,
> The books he had read, the music he could play
>
> ('The Civil Servant', 118)

The second of these 'despoliations of domesticity', regarded by a critic as '[Longley's] most successful poems on the Ulster conflict' (Crotty 1991/92: 115–16), comes from a sequence called 'Wreaths', in which the poems are offered as a floral tribute to the dead, or rather stages in the recomposition of bodies and identities that have been profaned. A commitment to restore the dignity of victims dominates 'The Linen Workers', the last poem of 'Wreaths', written in remembrance of a sectarian attack that, as Longley reimagines it, scattered all the loose, private, identity-endowing belongings on that most public of places, a road: 'Wallets, small change, and a set of dentures' (119). This vision of inhuman disorder prompts the poet to envisage how, from his own poetic and familial experience, he could redress it, recollecting the humane gestures of preparing the corpse of a loved one by adding to it those props and prostheses – 'spectacles', 'money', 'the set of teeth' – that dignify it for the public space.[7] This allows suffering to be 're-individualised' (cf. Parker 2007 – II: 22). The dead loved ones from his personal memory and the victims of atrocities in the community are thus assembled in his consciousness – like the children evoked in the brief and poignant 'Kindertotenlieder',[8] which he declares to be 'My unrestricted tenants, fingerprints / Everywhere, teethmarks on this and that' (61).

The poems quoted above were included in collections from the first decade of Michael Longley's published work, but their prevalent tropes have become a continuous strand in his poetics, persisting in the collections published since the early 1990s (i.e., following the hiatus of the 1980s). In *The Ghost Orchid* (1995), war memories resurge, again with both public and private implications. The continued relation between battlefield and home, as key locales in Longley's imagination, foregrounds the tension between the hurt derived from remembering the maimed and dead of a war scenario, and the potential solace afforded by a poetic evocation that claims for itself the status of a memorial.[9] In *The Weather in Japan* (2000) and *Snow Water* (2004), Longley's interest in cultivating the memory of past violence to preclude its recurrence takes the form of poems that become verbal correlatives of those physical memorials that have served to focus the act of remembrance since the First World War. On the one hand, the poems give a verbal content to the muteness of stone and earth, or to the 'cenotaphs' (literally, 'empty tombs') that reify the unretrieved fallen, or those buried elsewhere – re-energising the often empty formula, 'Lest We Forget' ('The Cenotaph', 259). On the other, they exemplify and extend the lists of names of the dead so often inscribed on stone memorials; indeed, amongst them one finds the war poets (Edward Thomas, Wilfred Owen), who have always enjoyed pride of place in Longley's poetic pantheon, as much for their denunciation of the war's irrationality as for other aspects of their poetics (cf. 'The War Graves' – 256). Occasionally, verbal expression seeks a correlative in a sister art, such as the music that happens when 'A tommy drops his harmonica in No Man's Land' (a poem called 'Harmonica' in *Snow Water*); the sound is imagined as issuing from the poet's father, whose breath the evocative poem therefore replicates and extends. The next piece in the same work, entitled 'The Front', combines this evocation with the uncanny experience of confronting his father as his double, or rather as his own son – a reference both to his father's young age when 'marching up to the Front', and to the poet's own advancing years (309).

The association between death and family memory has a broader scope than the shadow cast by the war(s), and its prevalence as a major theme in Longley's more recent poetry was suggested by the dedication of *Gorse Fires* (1991), 'In memory of my parents', followed by a verse epigraph on their imagined *post-mortem* reunion. Rather than merely confirming this association, *Gorse Fires* (dubbed by Bernard O'Donoghue 'a decidedly marmoreal, elegiac book' – 1991: 13), *The Ghost Orchid, The Weather in Japan*, and *Snow Water* add intensity and a sense of design to the concern for memorialisation, as suggested by titles such as 'Headstone' (232). The strong autobiographical element that accompanies this increased emphasis also signals the ageing poet's awareness of being on the front line of generational flux. Consequently, elegiac pieces for forebears coexist in Longley's poetry with personal intimations of death, frequently offering a placid foretaste of the tomb. His imaginings on the subject of family, generation and death are occasionally projected onto remote locations, such as the radically austere, ascetically Protestant rural environment of the New World evoked in 'The Shaker Barn', a poem in *The Weather in Japan*. Poet and wife are here imagined as their own monuments:

> I would lie down with you here, side by side,
> Our own memorials in what amounts to
> The Shakers' cathedral, this circular hay barn
>
> (269)

This poem is one of the examples of Longley's search for correlatives to his poems of home and memory in places and artefacts that, despite their simplicity, are nonetheless endowed with aesthetic (even monumental) dignity, as well as being part of a familial or communal heritage. Some of these are found far beyond the poet's immediate environment, as is the case with a series of pieces on visually attractive quilts and rugs produced by traditional North-American sects. The title poem of a small, interim collection published in 1998 bore the name of an Amish quilt, *Broken Dishes*; and more than half a dozen poems in *The Weather in Japan* offer representations of these homely artefacts and of their consequence on the self. Their metascriptural implication is at times made explicit: 'then [I] stitched together this spell, / A quilt of quilt names to keep you warm in the dark' (270). The poetic emplacement of these quilts may focus on the placidity of a light, the discoveries of a childhood, a shared and lived bliss. But the placidity may be that of death, as when someone is imagined making 'A quilt that will cover the sea bed and the graves / Of submariners in their submarines' (262). Typically used to cover beds – the sites of birth, conception, and death – the quilts embody a memory carried over by the very process of family transmission, and prove decisive for memorialisation.

The breadth and range of Longley's imaginings of the grave mean that the most located and static of conditions can be a source of apt, though para-doxical, representations for an experience of mobility and transit. 'Couchette', recalling a train journey, voices a longing for inhumation within the cosiness of the nuclear family:

> With my wife, son, daughter in layers up the walls
> This room on wheels has become the family vault.
> They have fallen asleep, dreams stopping and starting
> As my long coffin wobbles on the top couchette.

> (179)

Other occurrences, involving also the routines and comforts of ordinary domestic life, deepen this connection between the close family circle and the motif of the tomb. Some of these instances suggest how fine the line can be between the comfort afforded by such a space and its potential oppressiveness. Further, if home-as-shelter can easily become home-as-tomb, then all areas of experience relating to the domestic, and in particular to married love, can also be represented as refuge and inhumation. A poem from the early 1980s, 'Among Waterbirds', closes with the plea: 'Let me use your body like a hide' (155).[10] A bodily object of desire is reshaped as a cocoon in the closing line of 'A Grain of Rice' – 'Your unimaginable breasts become the silk-worm's shrine' (208) – and in another poem from *The Ghost Orchid*, 'Snow Hole', the couple descend from the bed, its site of conjugal love, into a place that is not unlike a tomb, however cosily it may be represented (222).

Gorse Fires in fact provided a clue to this sense of connubiality as shelter and tomb by combining, in a poem entitled 'Icon', the emotional consequence of the poet's mother's death with an awareness of the wife as surrogate mother and protector (185). In the *Collected Poems*, 'Icon' appears on the same page as 'X-Ray' (in *Gorse Fires* they were on opposite pages, mirroring each other), which underlines the continuities as regards the replacement of mother by wife, both poems troping the female body as home and haven. In the latter, the poet looks at the impossible memory, the prenatal self in the site of its gen-eration – 'I gaze at myself before I was born' – in fact an X-ray plate of himself and his twin in their mother's pregnant body. Both poems come in the wake of her death, and their adjacency highlights the iterated image of the breasts as synecdoche for the maternal and conjugal:

> I should look up to the breasts that will weep for me

> ('X-Ray', 185)

> I could not believe that when you came to die
> Your breasts would die too and go underground.

('Icon', 185)

This view of the whole generational span as a transit from uterus to tomb is complemented by the insight that a more recent poem derived from the awareness 'that "come home" in Scots can mean "be born"' (248). The ensuing perspective encompasses the different types of love that home and family may harbour, and includes the anticipation of a blissful old age and serene death (239). Such a prospect is afforded by the same middle-aged, anticipatory outlook that, in 'The Scissors Ceremony', considers with fascination the scene of an old woman clipping her husband's fingernails – 'Her / White hair tickles his white hair. Her breath at his ear' – and construes the intimate ritual, observed in a sedate suburban environment, as surrogate erotic pleasures that reverse time and conquer age (217).

To the extent that it juxtaposes the garden and the bedroom – 'What they are doing makes their garden feel like a big room' – 'The Scissors Ceremony' neatly instances the metaphoric and metonymic relationship between love and the landscape (with all its creatures) in Michael Longley's poetry, a rapport that Peter McDonald has emphasised on remarking that 'Longley's "love"-poetry and his "nature"-poetry tend towards a common point of origin and destination' (McDonald 1992: 66–7). Their interconnection enjoys foundational status in his verse, since the title poem of Longley's inaugural collection, *No Continuing City*, was also a starting point for his erotic topographies, as the soon-to-be-married poet cleared his memory of the images of past girlfriends, represented as the territory and landscape of sexual hiking: 'their small geographies', 'The hillocks of their bodies' lovely shires / (Whose all weathers I have walked through)' (16). The continuity of this representational strand, with an autobiographical content, makes such erotic correlations of humans and the natural space appear as an extension, in poems relating to later experience, of pieces on the logistics and emotions of married life. It has contributed to a pastoral element in Longley's poetry, and it has allowed tropes from agriculture and cooking to be combined with an interest in one's 'neighbour' that pertains to private feeling and social mores (besides echoing the best-known Christian injunction), as in several of the six-line poems in the short sequence 'Lares' (a sestina with no envoi). In these pieces from Longley's second collection (*An Exploded View*), 'Beds' puns on 'lazy-beds' and (implicitly) flowerbeds, 'Furrows' equates ploughing with the mechanics of a couple's bodily encounter, and 'Neighbours' represents their shared space and sleep in bed as benign trespasses in a pastoral environment (42).

The mutual erotic troping of body and space in Longley's poetry favours natural landscapes, but this referential preference is not exclusive, as indeed signalled by the title 'No Continuing City', which combines pastoral images with an urban and suburban imagining of 'Familiar avenues of love', 'my one-way streets', 'suburbs / Of experience' (17). This imagery is made necessary by the ultimate metaphor of body as house, a metaphor also of the total gift of self that precedes marriage and finds the husband-to-be, at the close of this unsolemn epithalamium, telling the bride 'To be sure of finding room in me / (I embody bed and breakfast) – / To eat and drink me out of house and home' (17). This humourous envisaging of marriage as willing expropriation of the exclusive space of selfhood is also an enabling counterpoint or foil to Longley's recurrent tropes of domicile and cohabitation. Yearning for at-homeness sometimes requires its other, an imagined challenge, or relating the emplaced self to others that are located beyond the immediate domestic pale, querying the distinctions between indoors and outdoors, location, and mobility.[11] A memorable example of this process is the half-observed, half-imagined scene of 'Caravan', in which the sheer evidence of a *mobile* home and a nomadic way of life proves compatible with Longley's imagery of insulated domesticity and identification with these easily dislocated dwellers (44).

'Caravan' is pointedly exceptional, since its effect on Longley's readers largely depends on their recognition that the poem's socially peripheral circumstance confirms the persistence in his writing of a range of representations that derive from a more conventional family situation. The poem's imagery of a quasi-oppressive cosiness, and the inherent tension between a mobile capsule and its environment, highlight Longley's affinities with Heaney's own representations of home as shelter ('we build our houses squat'; 'Roof it again. Batten down. Dig in' – Heaney 1966: 38; 1991: 56), as also the enclosed circulation that determines spatial cognition in Heaney's driving poems. It also invites comparison with Mahon's 'Gipsies', a poem in which 'caravans' and 'crockery' do not conjure a quasi-pastoral vignette of home on a road kerb, but rather a denunciation of harassment bred by intolerance. 'I have watched the dark police / rocking your caravans', avows Mahon's bourgeois persona, who, 'fed, / clothed, housed and ashamed', nonetheless equates himself embarrassedly with the segregated tinkers in view of 'the heap / of scrap metal in [his] / garden' – both the actual junk generated by his civilisational model, and a trope for the waste land in a relationship or in the dejected self (Mahon 1999: 67).

Such comparisons highlight the greater closeness between Longley's and Heaney's poetics as regards a sense of location and the emotional life; this acknowledgement holds true for their pursuit of erotic analogies between body and landscape, and yet a distinction (with a relative, rather than absolute import) should be pointed out, bearing on their respective prevalent objects and means of representation. In Heaney, such analogies occur characteristically in poems about ground and landscape, in which the erotic emerges as a source of metaphors for the self's sensorially intense contact with animals, plants, the earth; the converse practice – poems that have the erotic for their primary and ostensible object, and draw their representational resources from the natural world – emerges later and proves less recurrent in his work. Longley's poetry, on the other hand, often celebrates married love and sex using natural, topographic, territorial imagery – a referential domain which tends, therefore, to be ancillary and functional.

The range of the relation between human erotic experience and the landscape in Longley's poetry is broad enough to obtain yet further specification. It can involve an enhancement of feeling and fruition through actual immersion in the natural environment, as in 'The Swim', a poem about irrepressible lovemaking in the open (84). It can also include an extension of desire from human lovemaking to sensuous awareness of natural elements, as in 'On Mweelrea': 'When I dipped my hand among hidden sounds / It was the water's pulse at wrist and groin' (142). The erotic imagination can equally accommodate elements of communal history, as an amorous encounter on linen sheets may prompt Longley to tease out (as noted by Heaney) 'the connections between the private flax and linen of this poem ["The Linen Industry"] and the public flax and linen which had been the basis of Belfast's industrial power' (Heaney 1985a: 175). Through his 'ecocentric sense of home and history' (Kennedy-Andrews 2008: 141), Longley thus traces the route from nature to industry to 'bleach green' and the home setting as an analogy for the stages of a love story; and he adds a reminder of the fundamental moments of existence: 'Let flax be our matchmaker, our undertaker, / The provider of sheets for whatever the bed' (143). Such lines foreground yet again the closeness of desire and death in Longley's poetry; as noted above, this *memento mori* emphasis, present from the beginning, has tended to gain intensity (but also serenity) in his work since *Gorse Fires*.

Indeed, in the more recent collections, Longley's broad perspective on existence and experience often finds the means for its enabling epiphanies in the poet's observations of nature and its creatures. In 'Between Hovers' (167), an otter's relationship to its habitat gives Longley a model for understanding the course of life, from birth to death, as a transit between temporary and definitive homes. This is one of the pieces that qualify Peter McDonald's notion that 'the difference between the human and the pastoral landscapes [in Longley] [. . .] is that one involves the recognition of mortality' (McDonald 1992: 74). Years earlier, this close involvement of love, landscape, and intimations of mortality – the cautionary effect of perceiving the skeleton that structures the supple body and will outlast it – was underlined by Heaney, who noted (again in 'Place and Displacement') that 'Longley's poems count the phenomena of the natural world with the particular deliberate pleasure of a lover's finger wandering along the bumpy path of the vertebrae' (Heaney 1985a: 173). The remark remains valid for Longley's later work, but it is also one of the many instances of self-commentary that pervade Heaney's critical writings, in this case bearing on that archaeology of the skeleton that in Heaney's own work yielded 'Bone Dreams', and in Longley's the poems 'In Mayo' and 'View': 'For her sake once again I disinter / Imagination like a brittle skull' (89), 'I have put my arms around her skeleton' (151).

This hint of necrophilia will not allow Longley's readers to miss the extent to which such representations often prove challenging, extending the range of his love poetry and of its received conventions – and this does not apply only to the more transparent intersections of Longley's themes of love and death. Indeed, the cross-representation of an unquestionably *living* female body (perceived as flesh rather than bone, and usually glimpsed in the context of married life), and the natural landscape, complete with fauna and flora, often balances idealised against blatantly surprising representations of the erotic and conjugal experience. In *An Exploded View*, two short poems share a page: the first, 'Swans Mating', addresses an emblematic example of an animal coupling that has a long history as a source of metaphors for the human amorous embrace; the second, 'Galapagos', counterpoints that emblem of elegance and fidelity with (again) erotic topographies – 'you have scattered into islands – / Breasts, belly, knees, the mount of Venus' – but its animal metaphors for the woman's body as an object of desire could not provide a starker contrast to the previous poem: 'The giant tortoise hesitating, / The shy lemur, the iguana's / Slow gaze' (47).

Desire is deflected to animal forms that afford culturally surprising analogies, but Longley's search for apt physical tropes for love emotions that aspire to totality ultimately explores the animality of the human body: no location remains untouched by his verse. One of his various pieces entitled 'Love Poem' aspires to being 'lulled' by an all-encompassing soundscape, 'the noise' of the beloved's 'Lungs, heartbeat, intestines' (87). This potentially grotesque representation is matched in 'Check-Up' by the description of a peculiar medical assessment as appropriate metaphor for the love relation that the self yearns for, while a no less peculiar communion tropes the male persona's total abandon to the needs of his offspring:

> In the palm of your hand
> My testicles, future:
> Because if they had to
> The children would eat me –
> There's no such place as home.
>
> (83)

The close connection between physiology and a sense of emplacement that Longley proposed from his early work is retained and advanced in later collections in ways that reflect his sharp awareness of the passing of time and of a fittingly altered consciousness. The condition described in 'Aschy' (in *Snow Water*) – 'We are both in our sixties now, our bodies / Growing stranger and more vulnerable' (295) – has obvious and acknowledged mental homologies. This has involved both the boldness of somatic reference and a tendency to trope the self as empowered by a combination of inner serenity and immersion in the natural landscape. With regard to the death theme, the ageing poet's potential sentimentality is precluded by blatant matter-of-factness. 'The Painters' includes a funereal memory that, as so often in Longley, connects family and war history – but does so with disarming somatic frankness:

> When I shouldered my father's coffin his body
> Shifted slyly and farted and joined up again
> With rotting corpses, old pals from the trenches
>
> (308)

The brevity and regular simplicity of such lyrics becomes a formal correlative, but also a determinant, of an effect of candour that accommodates the most daring of representations (if we accord superlative transgressive power to scatology). But form is just one of the factors of this enhanced representational freedom: others include intertextual and inter-artistic effects ('The Painters' is also a poem that honours two First World War painters, while balancing the limitations of their medium against its representational potential), and, above all, the increasing pervasiveness of the Mayo natural scene as a poetic object.

Longley's minute attention to fauna and flora, his poetic record of a cohabitation in which indoors and outdoors achieve mutual definition, and the combined ethical and aesthetic relevance that his writing accords to this rapport with reality have arguably become the mainspring of his late poetics. The title poem of *Snow Water* features the poet turning 60 and choosing, for his birthday gift, a pristine 'crock of snow water' with which to indulge his taste as 'a fastidious brewer of tea', or rather a capacity to effect a convergence of the best of nature and home that also represents his ultimate ambition as a poet (287). What some have called the 'eco-pastoral' dimension in Longley's writing (cf. Agee 2004) emerges in poems whose drift is eminently conservational: as Longley has himself remarked, 'my nature writing is my most political' (Allen-Randolph 2003: 305). Such concerns are made clear by the gestural and territorial care with which the poet represents himself outdoors, negotiating and acknowledging spaces with otters or hares. This ultimately leads to a dilution of species borders, an ethical stance that emerges with some humour in poems ostensibly about human affairs, as in 'Leaving Atlanta': 'I shall miss my students and the animals' (272).

The immersion in nature cherished by his eco-pastoralism has a sexual edge to it, manifested in particular in lines about swimming in a sensorially rich environment, as also in a poem dedicated to someone who 'honeymooned in a tent' on an island that is the closest it gets to 'heaven' (290).

This reveals the mystical streak in Longley's reverential rapport with his west of Ireland environment: a few poems are explicitly offered as 'prayers' for the preservation of places (249, 253). Ultimately, the place held by death in Longley's poetics is inflected by this representational complex, as a celebratory note (e.g., in 'Ceilidh' – 291) is substituted for the mournful tone in evocations of the dead. Characteristically, immersion in nature alternates with the excited contemplation of it from the domestic capsule, a favourite belvedere: 'And we rationed our binocular moments / Behind the curtains of the bedroom window' (296).

This contented, though exigent relation to his locales can also become the object of a metapoetic reflection on the current stage of the poet's writing: 'Is this my final phase?' (324). The question, posed by the closing poem in *Snow Water*, identifies a poetic voice that wonders about mortality and continuities, but the brief poem offers a complex, ambivalent answer:

> Is this my final phase? Some of the poems depend
> Peaceably like the brown leaves on a sheltered branch.
> Others are hanging on through the equinoctial gales
> To catch the westering sun's red declension.

> (324)

The concern with finality is echoed by lexical choices – 'depend', 'declension' – with secondary acceptations that involve languor and decline. However, the grammatically dynamic import of 'declension' allows this word, when qualified by the 'red' light of the setting sun, to endow the poet's hypothetical 'final phase' with the vitality of the passionate outburst (rather than resigned dwindling) signified in the poem's final image: 'I can imagine foliage on fire like that'. Partly a conjecture, partly a confident vow, this closing line, by combining an image of fiery passion with the rootedness of the tree, 'the huge beech tree in our garden', slyly toys with Yeatsian tropes, and hence with the notion of late-life intensities. Indeed, the sturdiness of the tree, and the dependable quality of its 'sheltered branch' also make the poem a reflective description of organic structure that relates the ageing poet's self-addressed interrogation to his unwavering sense of emplacement and the generational continuum – and further, through the poems' equivocal 'depend[ence]', also to that 'life-support system' of writers, a tradition (Crawford 1989: 23). 'Leaves' is thus an apt cue for a venture into the rich world of inter-authorial rewriting, which has steadily made its mark upon his poetry and the representation of its favourite locales.

4.2   The empathies of rewriting

The 'dependence' of texts on other texts, and a sharp awareness of literary transmission, are emphatically recurrent notions in this book, but their particular manifestations vary with each of the poets addressed. Michael Longley's difference resides, firstly, in the frankness with which he acknowledges literary relations, extending his familial pieties to the intellectual and moral structure of his writing self. His favourite tropes of love, death, generation, and an emplacement that is confirmed by acknowledgement of the locale and its defining elsewheres are often rhetorically enhanced by a textual and scriptural undercurrent of metaphors: inscription, palimpsest, the material book. Some of the early poems adopt a self-referential quality to construe writing as a way of 'reading' the past, of figuring one's forebears. 'In Memoriam', the first of many elegies for his father, opens with an apostrophe that includes the plea: 'the slow sands / Of your history delay till through your eyes / I read you like a book' (30). Also in his inaugural collection, 'The Hebrides', an early *Ars Poetica* addressed to fellow poet Eavan Boland, included the lines: 'I can, through mist that miscontrues, / Read like a palimpsest / My past' (25).

Longley's poems for fellow poets are themselves instances of a relational understanding of writing that, concomitantly, tend to take writing itself for their object and represent it as creative intersection or coalescence: thus, the self is troped as a melting pot in another poem from *No Continuing City*, 'A Personal Statement – *for Seamus Heaney*' (27). Longley is keenly aware that poems featuring discussions of poetics with a named audience of friends and writers could easily lay him open to charges of self-serving sterility (like any poet living and working in difficult contexts). This perception is the source of his ironies in the aptly titled 'Alibis' (already from his second collection), in which a persona successively committed to various disciplines and arts (later equated with 'telephone calls from the guilty suburbs') is imagined 'drafting appendices / To lost masterpieces, some of them my own', and announces that 'My one remaining ambition is to be / The last poet in Europe to find a rhyme' (76–7). Such ironical acknowledgement of a reputation for formal skills was pursued in the following poem, 'Options – *for Michael Allen*' (dedicated to a major expert in prosody), reviewing poetic alternatives for addressing 'the ideal reader' and 'that outer circle / Of critical intelligences', and for tackling 'My life of make-believe' (79).

These ironical pieces appear in the same collection, *An Exploded View*, that featured the already mentioned sequence 'Letters', which probably made Longley the most conspicuous practitioner of the epistolary address to fellow poets (whose prevalence in Irish writing of his generation was already noted at the time – cf. Dunn 1975: 81). However, 'Letters' cannot in any way be described as a poetic exercise for a self-centred intelligentsia, since it combines scriptural self-reference with a sharp attention to historical circumstances: the sequence includes one of the best-known and bitterest remarks ever on the troubled six counties of Northern Ireland, Longley's pun on 'the sick counties we call home' (60). This territorial awareness is confirmed in the spatial tropes favoured throughout the sequence, beginning with its epigraph, two lines by the war poet Keith Douglas on the notion of a return (implicitly, to a known place) over a 'nightmare ground.'[12] The first of these 'Letters', a piece collectively addressed 'To Three Irish Poets', once more assumes a private standpoint upon the civic crisis. In this case, the pivotal event is the christening of a son (a 'godchild' of the addressees, who are thus brought into the inner circle of the poet's relations). This prompts a metaphorical equation of tensions in 'our province' with the baby's 'pulsating [. . .] fontanel' and the suggestion that the christening might have the power to appease 'the / Malevolent *deus loci*' (53). The poem's main relevance to this study resides, however, in the metaphors of appropriated selves, territory, and language that Longley employs in the self-representation of a writing that grows out of inter-authorial relations:

> In order to take you all in
> I've had to get beneath your skin,
> To colonise you like a land,
> To study each distinctive hand
> And, by squatter's rights, inhabit
> The letters of its alphabet
>
> (54)

Long before Translation Studies (in particular with its 'cultural turn') came to theorise its ostensible object as fundamentally identical to any other writing, construed (from within Derridean poststructuralism) as always already appropriation and rewriting (cf. Lewis 2004; Derrida 2004); and long before the discipline's intersection with postcolonial studies made the translation-as-colonisation metaphor a familiar trope (cf. Bassnett and Trivedi 1999), Longley thus prefaces a poetic sequence that half-humorously calques the addressees' style and diction with lines that represent the ensuing verse letters as territorial occupation. The sequence's first, collective letter also signals the continuity between this relational and appropriative poetics and the overall lyrical consequence of Longley's emotional universe, since it describes the naming of the christened child as setting off a possession by spirits: 'Lost relations take their places', 'People my head like a ghost town' (54). An intra-familial metempsychosis – which Longley was to echo when he remarked, in an interview, 'Genetically each one of us is a ghost story' (Healy 1995: 561) – is thus juxtaposed with the inter-authorial design. In both cases, the poet becomes a medium or a revenant for other identities and voices.

The three verse letters that follow embody the tension between tribute to the diction and concerns of each of the addressees, an element of benign mimicry, and the temptation for the poet to read himself in(to) them (a strategy not devoid of risks, as proved by the mixed responses obtained by Longley's dedications – Brearton 2006: 55, 80–92). Thus, 'To James Simmons' hails a poetry of intimate encounters balanced by personal boisterousness, commissioning from the addressee 'some octosyllabics / [. . .] redolent of death and sex', and urging him to 'Play your guitar while Derry burns' (the 'Nero' topos mentioned above) (56–8). 'To Derek Mahon' evokes the shared condition of 'Two poetic conservatives / In the city of guns and long knives', haunted and harassed by the place's sectarian polarity, and evokes a trip to the west of Ireland that emphasises, rather than Longley's own acquired at-homeness in a natural setting, the embarrassment (marked by language and religion) of not belonging (58–9). Conversely, the letter 'To Seamus Heaney' is sent 'From Carrigskeewaun in Killadoon', but the temptation to signal the poets' fraternising in a 'cottage' of the imagination is balanced by the need not to downplay a history of 'broken bones and lost scruples' – a historical awareness that eventuates in a reverential circuiting of an ancient locale towards which their imaginations converge, 'A wind-encircled burial mound' (60–1).

Correspondence, in a variety of senses, therefore emerges as a principle of Longley's writing. His work is thus construed largely as an afterwriting, punctuated from the outset by poems that gloss, extend or otherwise rewrite pronouncements by his literary 'ghosts'. These prominently include the Classics; long before Homer and Ovid emerged as his recurrent objects of translation, Longley's first collection featured a series of pieces – 'Odyssey', 'Circe', 'Nausicaa', 'Narcissus', 'Persephone' (14–21) – that were offshoots (in the voices of the *personae* in their respective titles, and possibly with a con-comitant Joycean resonance) rather than versions of Classical sources; none-theless, they anticipated later strategies. 'An Image from Propertius', in *An Exploded* View; and two more poems, 'Peace – *after Tibullus*' and 'Sulpicia', in *The Echo Gate*, moved firmly in the direction of translation, practised either conventionally or (as explained in Longley's note on 'Sulpicia', appended to *Poems 1963–1983* but not to the *Collected Poems*) mixing 'a collage of origi-nal lines and free translations' (1985: 206).

Longley's readers will hardly have been surprised, therefore, when trans-lation emerged as a key organising process of his writing in his post-1991 collections, refracting and connecting all the thematic and metapoetic con-cerns identified above. In *Gorse Fires*, a relatively small group of translations from *The Odyssey* becomes the major device for clarifying the coherence of the volume, while in *The Ghost Orchid*, over a third of the poems are either translations, poems prompted by Longley's own translations of other texts, or rewrites of previous works in one way or another. *The Weather in Japan* and *Snow Water* have also pursued this practice (if not with the same struc-turing import) in ways that signal the coherence of this poetics of the inter-textual and inter-authorial. Longley's choices of texts, his basic options as a translator, reveal his long-standing thematic concerns, as he himself admits when he points out that *The Odyssey* has always interested him because 'what drives Odysseus is the urge to get home' (Wilmer 1994: 117).

In *Gorse Fires*, this interest organises the book around seven poems that, in Longley's own words (in a note not included in the *Collected Poems*) 'combined free translation from Homer's *Odyssey* with original lines', purporting to do so 'with varying degrees of high-handedness but always, I hope, with reverence' (Longley 1991: 52). In 'Homecoming', 'Tree-House', 'Eurycleia', 'Laertes', 'Anticleia', 'Argos', and 'The Butchers', the emphasis falls on the return of the hero and the repossession of his places and people. Longley's selective translation of relatively long passages from *The Odyssey*, which he renders into much shorter poems, produces an enhanced emotional and rhetorical intensity, be it with regard to the bloodshed that marks Odysseus's return home or the poignancy of his reunion with wife, son, and father. His synoptic versions favour the dominant themes of the translator's 'own' poetry, in particular marital and filial emotions, experienced as joy or pathos, and interacting in complex ways with the violence and mayhem that frame the arousal of those emotions. A metapoetic complexity is never far away, taking the form of a reflective consideration both of the poet's formal procedures and of his intertextual and inter-authorial dealings (which include his translation strategies). And Longley's prosodic options for rendering Homer – in particular his assumption of a rather looser verse line than previously – have also proved seminal for his poetic writing in this and ensuing collections.[13]

'Laertes', an 18-line version of *Odyssey* XXIV: 225–350, is a case in point. Anachronism is used discreetly rather than blatantly, as when old Laertes, active on his farm, is described 'in his gardening duds' (a phrase more appropriate to a retired suburban grandfather than a farmer of the Ancient world). As befits a lyrical rendering of a passage from an epic, Longley's abridgments affect the narrative content of the passage far more than the representation of Odysseus's and Laertes's highly strung emotions at the moment of recognition and reunion. Indeed, his translation strategy becomes a means of attaining 'intensity of utterance and formal compression', a fundamental aspect of his aims as a lyric poet (as he explained in an interview – Allen-Randolph 2003: 294). The source text's account of Odysseus's initial maintenance of his disguise, and the crafty dialogue that precedes the disclosure and confirmation of his identity, are mostly dropped, as Longley substitutes the two lines: 'So he waited for images from that formal garden, / Evidence of a childhood spent traipsing after his father' (182). The first of these lines is mostly self-referential, a metapoetic description not only of Odysseus's recollection of a topography and its associated experience, but also of the poet-translator's equation of that reminiscence with the moment of verbal creation, proposed as the inspirational and belated consequence of duly awaited 'images'. This sense of the derivative nature of writing is matched by the content of those 'images', which themselves refer back to a memory of following the begetter as precursor. Readers of contemporary Irish poetry are bound to recall an antecedent for this representation in an iconic piece by the best-known of Longley's contemporaries (rather than in an Ancient text) – Heaney's 'Follower', with its childhood memory of 'stumbl[ing]' in the paternal 'wake', following 'in his broad shadow round the farm' (Heaney 1966: 12). The fame that this trope enjoyed, and the fact that it was being retrieved by Heaney (in connection with the elegiac evocation of his father in *Seeing Things*) at around the same time that Longley wrote the poems and versions that were to appear in *Gorse Fires*, suggests a combination of accident and intent that itself buttresses the critical argument for the exceptionally close intertextual and intratextual knit of contemporary Northern Irish poetry.

Translation indeed seems to bring out the various forms of poetic convergence that bind Longley to his contemporaries, in particular to Heaney. *Gorse Fires* and *Seeing Things* were published almost simultaneously (in 1991), and this contemporaneity reveals the complexity of the affinities within this poetic generation, extending far beyond the notions of priority and derivation favoured by conventional understandings of 'influence'. Both collections include in their appropriative designs tales of filial and marital devotion related to the realm of the dead. Heaney translates Aeneas's address to the Sibyl, from Book VI of the *Aeneid*, begging permission to go safely down to Hades for 'one look, one face-to-face meeting with my dear father' (Heaney 1991: 1) – a text that explicitly recalls how 'Orpheus could call back the shade of a wife', anticipating his later version of Ovid's account of 'Orpheus and Eurydice' (Hofmann and Lasdun 1994: 222–5). Longley, in his 'Anticleia', translates part of Circe's instructions to Odysseus on how to go down to Hades (*Odyssey*, Book X), juxtaposed with the actual descent, in Book XI, 'to recognise among the zombies your own mother' (183).

Perhaps most significantly, both poets also coincide in a vignette of mature married life by bringing in the passage from Book XXIII of *The Odyssey* in which Odysseus reminds Penelope of how their bed and bedroom had been built around an olive tree – a secret about the centredness and rootedness of their place that, once mentioned, allows Penelope to cast aside all suspicions regarding the newcomer's identity as her husband. Heaney refers explicitly to this Homeric episode (which he does not translate) in the sestet of one of his 'Glanmore Revisited' sonnets. Openly seeking a precedent in a narrative of homecoming seems doubly appropriate to a poetic revisitation of the site where the poet once grounded his pastoral of love and secluded writing; but Heaney shores up this middle-aged retrieval with the vigour of the olive tree in Homer, 'a living trunk', and its perennial quality once imaginatively dislocated to the poet's northern latitude and reimagined as 'ivy, / Evergreen, atremble and unsaid'. Further, the potentially risible implication of literary, hence vicarious love (the sonnet's title is 'Bedside Reading') is attenuated by a rapport with the precursor that represents itself as fluidity and freedom: 'I swim in Homer' (Heaney 1991: 36). In Longley's poem, a comparable sense of freedom is achieved firstly by the latitude of his translation, but freedom is in this case equated with rigorous craftsmanship. Longley's version transparently seeks a correlative in the power associated with Odysseus's skilled carpentry, described in detail in eight of the 11 lines of 'Tree-House', taken up with the recollection of 'how he had built the ingenious bedroom' (177). Training and tradition will not have allowed Longley to miss the etymologically-ensured synonymy of 'room' and 'stanza', just as the prosodist in him could not have failed to identify with a master work described as 'tightly set', 'well-hinged', 'smoothed', 'plumb' (177). The ambition to balance the accomplishments of the poet-translator's verbal art against the epic carpenter's craft is also gauged by the delighted and erotically charged response to the detailed recollection of the hero at work on his 'tree-house' – a response that (with the final line) includes ascribing to Odysseus one of Longley's treasured self-descriptions:

> She believed at last in the master-craftsman, Odysseus,
> And tangled like a child in the imaginary branches
> Of the tree-house he had built, love poet, carpenter.

> (177)

The love poem is not, however, the only lyrical environment into which Longley brings these passages from *The Odyssey* dominated by the joys and woes of the hero's return, and thereby consolidates the cohesion of his work and the breadth of its relations – within and beyond his immediate tradition. The first of Longley's translations in *Gorse Fires* bears the title 'Homecoming' (a theme and title that also recur in Mahon and Heaney).[14] In Longley's poem, the harbour at Ithaca becomes a metonym for home, as both the place where the self is welcomed and stabilised in the surety of its bonds, and where paradoxically it enjoys the greatest freedom: 'Haven where complicated vessels float free of moorings / In their actual mooring-places' (171).[15] These versions also bring Odysseus to the translator's home, by means of refractions both at the level of representation and of particular linguistic options – such as the occasional use of Irishisms and other forms peculiar to the English spoken in Northern Ireland. As argued in earlier chapters, such strategies can hardly be described as unqualified 'domestication', in the sense that the word has gained in Translation Studies since Lawrence Venuti; for while Longley's versions indeed aim to produce a text with lexical and discursive traits peculiar to the target cultural and socio-linguistic system, they do not attempt to gratify their most immediate readers with the comfort of nearness and the confirmation of their cultural and political expectations and prejudices. His versions seem designed rather to generate a defining distance that will afford his readers a sudden realisation that their surrounding circumstances can be represented by such apparently remote texts.

This is broadly the strategy that Michael Longley adopts to refract the theme of Odysseus's return through the Northern Irish Troubles, but he also draws for this public tale on images and emotions otherwise to be found in his lyrics of private experience. The violent consequences of a homecoming, and full repossession of house and family, are thus the theme of the closing poem of *Gorse Fires*, a translation of passages from Books XXII and XXIV of *The Odyssey*, on the death of 'widow' Penelope's pretenders, and all their accomplices, at the hands of Odysseus, Telemachus, and some faithful servants. However, the refractions this Homeric episode undergoes in Longley's verse ultimately result in a reconfiguration of the passage's ethical implications. In *The Odyssey*, the hero's feats are exultingly narrated and the violence of his revenge is validated by the gods and integrated into the longer span of the epic plot; in the economy of Longley's 28-line version, the brutal details of the massacres, including the mutilation of Melanthios's 'nose and ears and cock and balls, a dog's dinner', and the atrocious hanging from a single wire of 'the disloyal housemaids' (the women who collaborated), cannot but become an object of revulsion. This is intensified by Longley's chosen title, 'The Butchers', which, besides the generically negative judgment it involves, acquires specific resonance with regard to sectarian practices in Ulster during the Troubles.[16] The last line of the poem/translation (and of the collection as a whole) describes Hades in terms often used by Longley to evoke home, with a close and equivocal relation between the living and the dead: 'Where the residents are ghosts or images of the dead' (194).

This gloomy closing note of *Gorse Fires* is only in part sustained in the translations that similarly help define the structure and dominant concerns of Longley's following collection, *The Ghost Orchid*. A disturbing conflation of home, family and brutality re-emerges in Longley's ironically synoptic rendering of Hector's farewell to his son (*The Iliad*, Book VI): 'Then kissed the babbie and dandled him in his arms and / Prayed that his son might grow up bloodier than him' ('The Helmet', 226). However, the poem that precedes it is one of several in which Longley reacts promptly to specific political developments, in this case the promise of peace that forms the backdrop against which *The Ghost Orchid* was written. Longley chose the title 'Ceasefire' for this piece, which is yet another synoptic translation – in this case, of the passage from Book XXIV of *The Iliad* in which Priam ransoms the dead body of his son Hector from Achilles. Here, it is construed as a moment of truce and reconciliation:

> Put in mind of his own father and moved to tears
> Achilles took him by the hand and pushed the old king
> Gently away, but Priam curled up at his feet and
> Wept with him until their sadness filled the building.
> [. . .]
> 'I get down on my knees and do what must be done
> And kiss Achilles' hand, the killer of my son.'
>
> (225)

At the time of its original publication in the mid-1990s (a moment of high hopes in the Northern Ireland peace process), this poem gained a remarkable prominence, as a contribution given by a poet to a civic cause by refracting a Classical text through a dire political situation.[17] The very fact that Longley uses translation (the celebration of literary memory) to construe proper remembrance as the ability to honour the dead without the hate-inducing memory of their killing, suggests that this practice is a valuable cultural and political resource against 'privacy, peculiarity, isolation', a defence against that 'resistance to the foreign' which may itself be equated with an 'incapacity to translate' (Warren 1989: 3).

Longley's continued demonstration of his *capacity* to translate, understood as a means of asserting an urge (if not a 'rage') for order, which emerges itself as an ethical imperative, has accommodated and extended the intersections of private emotion and public predicament that have consistently characterised his poetics. 'War & Peace', a version of a passage in Book XXII of *The Iliad* that Longley included in *Snow Water*, is a prime example of this practice. The Homeric passage narrates the combat between Achilles and Hector, and the latter's death, in gory detail. Longley, however, focuses instead on the moment when Achilles is chasing Hector along the walls of Troy, passing the idyllic spot where in peacetime the women would 'rinse glistening clothes' at the convergence of two fountains, one 'steaming like smoke from a bonfire, / The other running cold as hailstones, snow water' (310). Again isolating a vignette that has little significance in the narrative economy of the war epic, Longley refracts the literary resonance of *The Iliad* by balancing (hence, vindicating) the pastoral of peace against his readers' perception of (Hector's) imminent slaughter. He does this by employing images and phrases that endow the redemptive side in this equation with metapoetic significance, introduced by the water streams (which evoke the crafts of peace, but also poetic inspiration) and reinforced by his use of the collection's title, 'snow water', to describe one of the pristine fountains.

In formal and discursive terms, 'War & Peace', like a few of the other Homeric pieces in Longley's oeuvre, comes across as a fairly 'straightforward' version, without any of the radical departures that can so often be encountered in contemporary poetic rewritings of the Classics (comparison with the equivalent passages in standard versions of *The Iliad* – for example, E. V. Rieu's – easily confirms this perception). Yet one cannot infer from this that Longley's relation to his Classical sources is fundamentally reverential. On the contrary, there is often great irreverence in his selective strategies – in the way short passages are abstracted from their epic environment and made into autonomous lyrical pieces that become synecdoches of the larger textual body of their origins (a body on which Longley's readers are bound to project new meanings, derived from his translation of certain passages). Further, Longley's translations generate and coexist with other poems that relate to his confrontations with the Classics in a variety of ways. These include poems that mix lines of translation with lines of the poet's 'own' making; wholly original poems that reflect the combined effect (in the poet's consciousness) of translation and empirical circumstance; as well as parodies and pastiche – in short, various examples of what I have generically termed 'afterwritings'. Indeed, Longley's collections since *Gorse Fires* are characterised by metonymic transfers of meaning between translations and other poems that epitomise the central relational theme of this book.

The Weather in Japan includes a series of adjacent poems that illustrate these textual contiguities. 'In the Iliad' is characteristic of this dimension of Longley's appropriative poetics: the title suggests a version of a scene 'in' Homer's epic, whereas in fact the first of the poem's two quatrains evokes a remembered interaction between the poet as young father and 'our first-born', who once, 'in the small hours', tried to feed from his nipple – a private paternal memory that, in the second quatrain, refracts the literary memory of how 'In the *Iliad* spears go through' male nipples (250). An intimate memory of a child's misdirected search for its mother as source of life and food is thus disturbingly juxtaposed with an awareness of timeless tales of pierced and slain fathers. Longley has often taken an interest in the cultural construction of gender and occasionally (as in this poem) represents himself at the centre of the ensuing perplexities, teasing out the difficult borders between maternal, paternal and filial; between passive and active roles. These interrogations of gender may also be productively related to the transits between *genres* highlighted by his reworking of epic as lyric.

Occasionally this querying of gender and genre takes on a playful tone, as in two poems involving Helen, 'destroyer of cities, destroyer of men' (251), an agent of mischief among the warriors. She is herself a reminder of her clandestine, ultimately fatal transit to Troy, and in both pieces brings other dislocations to the translator's mind. In the first, 'Heartsease', Helen is breezily (anachronistically) described '[slipping] the lads a Mickey Finn of wine and heartsease', an incident that reminds the poet as naturalist of the meanings accorded to the plant in his title (otherwise known as the wild pansy) 'where I hail from – beyond / The north wind, Hyperborean, or nearly' (251). In the second, a single-sentence, six-line piece entitled 'The Parody', the title describes not a slanted textual relation, but rather Helen's mischievous behaviour when 'Imitating the voices of absent wives' of Greek warriors that she suspected might indeed be inside the (Trojan) horse.[18] 'The Parody', however, becomes another instance of the poet's self-implication, and indeed a love poem that hinges on the rhetorical question: 'If [. . .] Helen / Had impersonated you [. . .] / Would I have fallen for the parody, cried out / And turned death and destruction inside out?' (252). Other Homeric spin-offs in *The Weather in Japan* include 'A Poppy': imbricating text and human adversity, remote and contemporary history even further, the poem traces the migration of 'An image in Homer', the afterlife of a simile that 'Virgil steals' and Longley's historical and poetic consciousness redeploys, construing the flower (whose imaginative clout is enhanced by its emblematic value for mourning and remembrance after the First World War) as a metonym for each and every dead soldier (255).

Longley's alertness to the impact of war and death on the Western imagination inevitably brings him to confront the mutual challenge posed by the fluidity of the verbal (so clearly celebrated in the tropes of transit and motion which prevail in 'A Poppy') and the supposed permanence and fixity of memorials in other media, such as stone. This confrontation between the temporal flow of verbal art and the spatial stasis of visual representation (a cultural commonplace, ever since Lessing's influential and controversial argument in *Laocoon* – 2005: passim) emerges at its clearest in another Homeric piece in *The Weather in Japan* that combines translation and its reflective aftermath. 'The Horses' draws on the episode in Book XVII of *The Iliad* in which Achilles's horses, mourning the death of Patroclus, 'refuse to budge' and, weeping, remain 'Immoveable as a tombstone' – this simile in fact following Longley's opening reflection:

> For all of the horses butchered on the battlefield,
> Shell-shocked, tripping up over their own intestines,
> Drowning in the mud, the best war memorial
> Is in Homer

> (260)

Longley here extends his interest in remembrance and commemoration to another species – precisely the species that has long shared with humans the fate of brutal slaughter on the battlefield, though it usually features in memorials as an adjunct rather than an object per se. By selecting and highlighting this Homeric passage, Longley in fact endorses a contemporary cultural concern with interrogating the ethics of inter-species relations[19] – and anticipates the extensive poetic reflections on the rapport between humans and horses in war scenarios that have since emerged in collections by Ciaran Carson and Paul Muldoon (as described later in this book). As regards the means and media of his commemoration, he nevertheless exposes the pointlessness of a belief in the supposed greater solidity of the built memorial *vis-à-vis* verbal evocation: 'the best war memorial' for slaughtered horses consists in a representation of stone-like and *yet living* horses, crafted and preserved many centuries ago for our acknowledgement in a verbal work of art that is celebrated as the very starting point of Western literary traditions. But the successful struggle of the verbal for prominence as an apt medium for memorialisation is also pursued in Longley's lines by the dynamic images employed to represent the suffering of the commemorated species – a dynamics of indignity, of ordure and ordeal.

It is not mere wordplay to insist that a certain *humanity* is required in order to empathise with the fate of horses slaughtered as a result of human hatred: any artist willing to provoke sympathy (or co-suffering) for the plight of animals is arguably bound to draw on representational resources that were first developed to respond to the pathos of a predicament experienced by beings of the same species. It is conceptually alluring that such perceptions are afforded by some of Michael Longley's recent poetry in connection with another design that challengingly sets same against other – the eminently relational textuality of translation. And this is compounded when the translational venture takes for its object the most famous textual exploration in Western literary memory of imaginative homologies, hybridities and permutations between humans and animals.

Ovid's *Metamorphoses* is of course one of the most influential books in history. If Homer proved fundamental for the structuring of Longley's *Gorse Fires*, we might be tempted to suggest that Ovid occupies an equivalent position in *The Ghost Orchid* – were it not for the challenges to structural clarity that Ovid's fictions of transformation inevitably pose when appropriated into a work so closely attuned as Longley's to the imbrication of form and representation. 'Form' is, indeed, the title of the four-line opening poem in *The Ghost Orchid*; readers prompted by the title to expect self-reflective writing will be enthused by the first line, with its apparent promise of a bid for totality and achievement – 'Trying to tell it all to you and cover everything' – only to discover that this is in fact (or rather, also) an animal poem: lines two to four make clear that 'form' is in this case the name for the hollow in which a hare lives and sleeps (197). The collection finds its incipit, therefore, in a suggested equation of poetic form and animal shapes.

Longley's animal poems are the result of a combination of empirical awareness and different types of mediation. These involve other areas of personal experience; impingements from the public world; the amateur naturalist's self-education (cf. Corcoran 2000), and, of course, the poet's vast reading, from the Classics to his contemporaries. (As pointed out in earlier chapters, both Heaney and Mahon have invoked Ovid as an enlightening precedent, respectively in 'Exposure' and 'Ovid in Tomis'; although both have tried their hand at his shape-changing tales, Ovid emerges most memorably in their respective oeuvres as the musing exiled writer of *Tristia*, rather than the buoyant narrator of the *Metamorphoses*).[20] These various co-determinants of Longley's animal poetry prove relevant to the approach to Ovid featured in *The Ghost Orchid*, and, more generally, to our reading of the sizeable and peculiar menagerie that inhabits the collection. Given Longley's earlier pratice as a translator, it comes as no surprise that his Ovidian poems are markedly diverse in their proximity to Ovid's text: some are versions that will not strike readers as radical, while others are significant departures from the source text, with translated lines and Longley's 'original' writing blending into one another to varying degrees. This *metamorphic* diversity is all the more noticeable within the group of seven pieces that were commissioned for the 1994 anthology *After Ovid: New Metamorphoses*, a collection of new versions of Ovid by 42 contemporary poets (including all the Northern Irish poets studied in this book) to which Longley was the most prolific contributor.[21] Announced by its editors, Michael Hofmann and James Lasdun, as a response to a current 'boom' in Ovid as much as in 'the notion of poetic translation', the anthology, in its appearance and reception, was itself a confirmation of the chord struck by Ovid with contemporary literary audiences, his perceived capacity to echo 'contemporary values' (Hofmann and Lasdun 1994: xi).

'Baucis & Philemon', the first version Longley was asked to contribute to 'After Ovid', arguably reflects the translator's awareness of his commission,[22] combined with a sense of thematic congeniality, in that it is the least surprising (the least irreverent) of his Ovidian pieces in *The Ghost Orchid*. Longley maintains the title by which this tale is traditionally known; his poem takes on a narrative thoroughness that makes it the longest of these versions – reflecting the tale's length in the source text, but also the fact that the translator at no point seems to adopt (as he does elsewhere) a verbal economy predicated on the assumption that his readers are bound to know the story already. Its themes, however, contribute to its seamless incorporation in Longley's work: it is a tale of divinely rewarded hospitality, and of domestic pieties that are matched by lifelong conjugal love. The absence of conspicuous departures from the piece's narrative sequentiality, and its fairly uniform tone indeed suggest the translator's moved endorsement, also reflected in the poem's diction, which calls attention onto itself only with occasional 'demotic elements' (Brearton 2006: 192), and a few descriptive details suggestive of an Irish dislocation: 'Not far away lies bogland' (212). This is, significantly, the Ovidian tale that Mahon years earlier alluded to in a few lines of 'A Garage in Co. Cork' – 'A god who spent the night here once rewarded / Natural courtesy with eternal life', the 'old man and his wife' changed, in this sardonic version, 'to petrol pumps' (Mahon [1982] 1999: 131); while it would be perverse to account for Longley's options in 'Baucis & Philemon' as a reaction to Mahon's brief parody, the two poets' continued dialogue and heightened mutual awareness lend that precedent some critical relevance when we consider the relative (ir)reverence of their Ovidian appropriations.

From that perspective, it is noteworthy that the two poets overlapped in their contributions to *After Ovid* and that the tale in question was that of Pygmalion. Mahon's 'Pygmalion and Galatea' is a fluent and dutiful version of this tale of an artist's passion for his art finding its ultimate emotional and erotic reward when his creation is made human and living, hence able to be possessed for love and further *procreation* (Hofmann and Lasdun 1994: 237–9). Longley, however, provides a subversion (rather than a straightforward version) of this tale, by means of a textual conflation that shows his wariness of the artistic solipsism that may derive from infatuation with one's own craft and its products. In his 'Ivory & Water', the master-craftsman, whose artistic zest and erotic love for his statue of a girl makes it/her worthy of being translated from art into life, has his achievement balanced by the punishment of erotic frustration – since Longley brings together the tale of Pygmalion (from Book X of the *Metamorphoses*) and those of Cyane and Arethusa (from Book V). Launched by an 'If' clause that makes the poem a cautionary tale (either prospective and hypothetical, or predicated on a described, renewed plight), 'Ivory & Water' is addressed to the 'lonely bachelor' who 'fall[s] in love with [his] masterpiece and make[s] love to her'. The single sentence that makes up the poem (a technique that Longley has often employed) contains lists of gestures and objects that render the growing frenzy of Pygmalion's love for the statue that he ecstatically feels coming to life. However, that very moment coincides, in the poem's own terms, with 'the end of the dream', when the girl (Cyane- or Arethusa-like) becomes liquid and flows out of the hands of the punctilious artist-as-lover, who is left with the 'nothing' that follows a literally wet 'dream' (206).

To the extent that Pygmalion's ambition involves 'the perfect specimen', and that Longley's poetics is known for its close attention to formal values, 'Ivory & Water' may suggest the poet's ironical self-implication. This is qualified, however, by a fundamental opposition: as against the hubristic misogyny and isolation that in this version characterises Pygmalion, able only to love the outcome of his own creation and ultimately punished with denial and emptiness, Longley's aesthetics and ethics celebrate and yearn for the fruits of *relation* in life, love and art. This is, after all, borne out by the integrative, fluid view of nature and existence propounded in the Pythagorean disquisition from Book XV of the *Metamorphoses*, which, in Longley's 'According to Pythagoras', becomes an overall manifesto not only for the Ovidian strand in *The Ghost Orchid*, but indeed for the collection as a whole – arguably predicated on 'the fundamental interconnectedness of all things' (202). Longley translates Pythagoras's speech economically, and with corresponding rhetorical clout, offering a rather compressed account of the teeming life to be found in the most crystalline as in the most soiled hotbed of generation, and he closes the piece with characteristic tongue-in-cheek assurance, as regards the authority of his facts as also of his borrowed first person: 'I could go on and on with these scientific facts. / If it wasn't so late I'd tell you a whole lot more' (202).

The ironies that pervade the speaking and narrating voice(s) in these Ovidian versions often highlight a variously directed sense of artistic congeniality and emulation. Such is the case of 'Perdix', an example of a formally straightforward translation whose theme indirectly adds to the metapoetic emphasis in Longley's writing. It is the least well known of the tales involving Daedalus ('inventor, failure's father'), better remembered for the tale of Icarus. It recalls Daedalus's murderous envy of his brilliant nephew (arguably a case of 'anxiety of succession'[23]), and the young craftsman's rescue and mutation into a partridge – because Pallas Athene 'supports the ingenious' (201). Longley's carefully considered diction means that it is surely no accident that 'ingenious' occurred in an earlier translation, 'Treehouse', in connection with 'the master-craftsman, Odysseus' (177), in that capacity a transparent object of the poet's emulation.

Unsurprisingly, therefore, ironic self-implication tends to emerge in poems that also foreground the relational emphasis – be it intertextual, familial, erotic, or all of these. A case in point is provided by 'Spiderwoman', which puzzlingly opens, 'Arachne starts with Ovid and finishes with me'; this is the first of the two isolated lines that bracket the poem, otherwise made up of two five-line stanzas. The first stanza renders Ovid's description of Arachne's transformation, but the second embodies the poet's proclaimed contribution to the tale, a textual output that becomes represented as a sexual act, and indeed (in a blend of attraction and revulsion before female genitalia) as a matter of '[making] love on her lethal doily', impregnating her while '[avoiding] the spinnerets – navel, vulva, bum' (205). The trope of metamorphosis applies unequivocally to his poetic identity, since Arachne '[entices] the eight eyes of my imagination'. The ironical element in what I have been calling the poet's self-implication resides predominantly in his retrieval into some of his Ovidian versions of what in earlier poems had already emerged as the blunt lexicon of the body, presented in the fullness of its somatic and sexual forms and functions – and relating in challenging ways to Longley's considerate and tender representations of marital love. The poem's detached closing line – 'She wears our babies like brooches on her abdomen' – consummates the poet's metamorphic inclusion in Arachne's tale, which becomes a tale of relation, generation, and continuity. And yet this closing line relates equivocally to the poem's opening proposition, which seems to announce a literary transmission that 'finishes' with the present-day poet-translator. That first line, however, may both suggest an arrogation of authorial closure (what 'starts' with Ovid reaches completion with Longley) or, in hindsight, the poet's announcement of his assumption into this metamorphosis that confirms a maker of fertile webs (where one 'dangle[s] sperm / Like teardrops'), or rather textures, texts that ensure furtherance and continuity.

This authorial inclusion in the metamorphic design, supplemented with tropes of generation, is pursued in even clearer terms in 'Phoenix', which construes the fabled bird in the homely Ulster terms of 'a duck that renovates and begets itself / Inside my head as the phoenix' (220). While Hibernicising Ovid's tale by rendering it as a narrative featuring local characters, 'Phoenix' includes autobiographical references and images that are all too familiar from earlier poems: the 'double-yolk', reminiscent of the poet and his twin, the continuity of fatherhood and filiation economically represented through parataxis in 'His cradle, his father's coffin' (220). Further, the transformations brought by age to one's physical self are humorously invoked at the opening of 'A Flowering' – 'Now that my body grows woman-like [. . .] [I] hide / Among Ovid's lovely casualties' – as if writing about the death of young, beautiful Adonis and his changed continuity as an anemone required from the consciously aged poet a self-satirical twist (205).

Longley's interest in transformation and dislocation, bearing on mediated images of the self, acquires an intermedial characteristic that coexists with the Ovidian strand in *The Ghost Orchid*. Longley has regularly published poems that reveal his interest in the visual arts as a source of representations for his verbal art, and two such pieces involve portraits of the poet by painters Jeffrey Morgan and Edward McGuire, who are also the dedicatees of these ekphrastic ventures (in the latter case, as a posthumous dedication). The first, 'Watercolour', notes the 'continuation' in the portrait between its human object and surroundings that materialise the poet's interest in fauna and flora, considered in its circularity of life and death: 'a chicken's wishbone', 'a dolphin's skull', 'lazy beds', 'wintry grasses' (198). Conversely, 'Sitting for Eddie' notes the *absence* of such natural elements from the painting, all the more so since the poet, knowing Edward McGuire's penchant for including foliage and birds in the background of his portraits (cf. Fallon 1991: passim), which thus include features of the still-life genre, opens the poem by confessing: 'I had suggested a spray of beech leaves behind me / Or a frieze of birds' (198). Longley goes on to pun on 'our / Still lives, Eddie's and mine' – the ungrammatical plural form (the plural of the pictorial genre 'still life' is 'still li*fes*') emphasises the poet's interest in the permutations between subject and object, the living and the dead. Having noted the painter's 'mistake' with regard to 'the colour of my eyes', he closes the poem with the line: 'Me turning into a still life whose eyes are blue' (198). 'Sitting for Eddie' is thus about a series of changes or metamorphoses, involving the transit between the living and the dead – alert as Longley is to the philological, he cannot have missed that the equivalent phrase to 'still life' in several other European languages could be rendered as 'dead nature' (as in French 'nature morte'). But the piece also concerns a transit between forms and colours, and between the living, dynamic shape of a practitioner of a verbal art and a visual representation of that shape by a practitioner of a visual art, whose effort is then reciprocated by his fellow artist and portrayee in the form of an ekphrastic poem.

It is ironic, and hardly accidental, that these two poems on paintings (that happen to be portraits of the poet) appear in the *Collected Poems* on the opposite page to a satirical gloss on a celebrated passage of Horace's *Ars Poetica*, possibly the most often quoted Classical source of pronouncements on the rapport between literature and painting. Longley's poem bears the equivocal title 'After Horace' (a formula that usually indicates a translation, but has increasingly been employed to indicate other forms of derivation or succession). He offers a whimsical version, not of the *ut pictura poesis* (As is painting so is poetry) dictum, which for centuries was the primary reference for the notion that poetry and painting were 'sister arts' (Mitchell 1986: 43–3 and passim), but rather of equally influential opening lines of Horace's text. In the source passage, Horace tries to impress a sense of decorum on his readers by first asking them to imagine the (indecorous) composite image of a being made up of parts from different animals, and then prompting them to take such a grotesquerie as a visual analogue to an equally indecorous text where (to quote from a standard academic version of Horace's passage) 'the author's idle fancies assume such a shape that it is impossible to make head or tail of what he is driving at', since he goes 'to the point of associating what is wild with what is tame, of pairing snakes with birds or lambs with tigers' (Dorsch 1965: 79). Longley's satirical rendering of this famous opening, inserted in a collection that abounds in tales of shape-changing beings and humans sentenced to live on in animal shape, is couched as a denial of the decorum that Horace's text takes for self-evident. This denial glosses parts of Horace's text fairly closely and is offered, with gleeful assurance, in the first person plural:

> We postmodernists can live with that human head
> Stuck on a horse's neck, or the plastering of multi-
> Coloured feathers over the limbs of assorted animals

> (199)

If this opening might sound like a proud programme for formal and representational iconoclasm, the second stanza makes clear that it is ironical, since the reasons given by this collective persona for favouring hybridity and denying literal representation are respectively intellectual failure and the technical inability to do any better:

> Since our fertile imaginations cannot make head
> Or tail of anything, wild things interbreed with tame,
> Snakes with birds, lambs with tigers

– 'because we can draw that', the persona adds (199). This imputed admission of incompetence posing as playful incongruity, and as a programme for inventiveness, thus becomes the satirical exposé of a debasement, which the poem's closing lines take to its scatological nadir:

> Ultimate post-
> Modernists even in the ceramics department we
> May have a vase in mind when we start, or a wine-jug,
> But, look, as the wheel goes round, it ends up as a po.

> (199)

Readers who associate Longley with a conservative poetics based on the intellectual makeup of a Classicist, a preserver of formal values, will hardly be surprised (if confronted with such a poem in isolation) at this laughing exorcism of hybridity and representational unruliness, this satire of postmodernism taken in some of its trademark features. This sense of confirmation may even seem reinforced by Longley's fairly recent remark, when confronted once more with a question on the legacy of the well-made poem, that 'if it's not well made [. . .] then it isn't a poem' (cited in Brearton 2006: 246). As firmly pointed out above, though, the context in which 'After Horace' was first published, a context retained in the line-up of the *Collected Poems*, strongly dilutes the sharp distinction between agents and targets of laughter that constitutes a staple aspect in conventional definitions of satire as a literary mode, one supposedly grounded on a set of clear 'standards' and 'norms.'[24] The contiguities that Longley has created for 'After Horace' in the collections that include it invite readers to recognise that the poem *also* bears on the poet's own recent practice, playfully drawing on his assumption of the shape-changing theme and its formal correlative in the transits and dislocations that are proper to translation. Acknowledging that the laughter prompted by the poem is also self-directed is the same as describing it as comic rather than satiric – if one accepts that the comic stands for inclusive rather than exclusive laughter, that it is integrative and predicated on the notion that 'truth is a plurality', and that 'comic humans are incomplete'.[25] This is complemented, with regard to the (equivocal) fluidity and hybridity that are laughably re-invoked in 'After Horace', by the perception that 'the grotesque is a vivid celebration of *interconnectedness*' (Stott 2005: 89 – my emphasis). The notion that Longley explicitly invoked in his version of the Pythagorean discourse in the *Metamorphoses* ('the fundamental interconnectedness of all things') is again a key to this dimension of his late poetics: relation consistently proves central to the humanness and humaneness of his project. And this is a project that, though never despairing of the attainment of 'rational and benign order' (as argued by fellow poet Douglas Dunn – 2000: 32), construes such order as akin to that which is restored by comic rather than tragic endings (to pursue the dramatic analogy). It is a sense of order that accommodates contradiction and incompleteness as defining elements of the human.

Fran Brearton has claimed that Longley's penchant for 'experimentation' and 'risk-taking' brings him perhaps closer to 'that postmodern generation [of Muldoon and Carson]' than to the poetics of his strict contemporaries, and that indeed Longley's 'accommodation of difference' is fundamentally different from Heaney's 'reconciliation of difference' (Brearton 2006: 9, 33). The argument itself may prove too neat for the complexity it seeks to describe – and much of what I have already proposed in this book points rather in the contrary direction, emphasising the tense affinities that bind

Longley to his generation. But reading Longley as *also* a crucial link with poets who began their writing careers (sometimes in a spirit of iconoclasm) when he and his coevals had already begun to lay a strong mark on their tradition provides an apt cue for this study to move on and consider, in Chapter 5, the poet who has wilfully epitomised paradox on the complex but cohesive scene of contemporary Northern Irish poetry.

5
Words in Transit: Paul Muldoon

'I've been fascinated by the art of translation since I was a teenager in Armagh' (2008: 9). This avowal comes with the opening sentence of Paul Muldoon's preface to his pamphlet *When the Pie Was Opened*, published as part of a series whose declared ambition is 'to make available new explorations in writing, in translating, and in the areas linking these two activities'.[1] Muldoon's contribution to this venture consists of nine pieces: four original poems and five translations ranging from Old English to medieval Welsh, from Classical Latin to modern Greek. The interrelations that hold them together are deftly presented by Muldoon in his preface through the rather loose process of verbal and conceptual association that he often tantalisingly suggests is a basis for his poetics. But the notion that poetic writing rests on the random and accidental is in fact countered from the beginning of the pamphlet by the early memory that Muldoon retrieves and shares as the source of his opening remark. Recollecting how a former teacher encouraged a classroom of teenage students to translate Irish poems into English and then submit them for publication, he comments:

> The confidence he had in us, mere schoolboys, was transformative. It was as if we were ourselves somehow translated into writerdom, with a sense that writing was, among other things, a job of journeywork for which we were eligible to apply.
>
> (2008: 9)

This narrative of authorial inception may appear surprising. Many readers of contemporary poetry would not primarily think of Muldoon as a poet-translator; for despite his now global critical renown, his interlingual versions have attracted less attention (and indeed proved less numerous) than those of other Northern Irish poets. However, he reveals in this preface that he first thought of becoming a writer because of a translation chore, and elects translation as an apt metaphor for this poetic awakening. Muldoon has long been known for a playfulness that seems to reveal spontaneity – and yet he acknowledges here that his mental construction of a poetic calling, from an early stage, involved the planned and staid deliberateness of 'a job of journeywork'. His reputation has included an irreverent attitude towards some of the commonplaces of Irish poetic identity – and yet the paragraph in which Muldoon expands on the 'journeywork' analogy sees him evoke his father's experience 'as a hired labourer', 'a daysman', and refer to 'the use of the scythe as a weapon' (2008: 9). Such an account in fact recalls Heaney's own narrative of poetic awakening, and of the writer's descent from rural labourers (combined with the simile of the spade as gun) as expounded in 'Digging', as also in his later tribute to 'the journeyman tailor who was my antecedent' (Heaney 1966: 1–2; 1996: 67).

This chapter will inquire into Muldoon's writings and rewritings, as also into his relation to other poets, without losing sight of this tension between a reputation for iconoclasm and gestures that inscribe him within the tradition he often seems to be breaking with. The fact that Heaney, Mahon and Longley are contemporaries and shared important areas of their formative experience suggests that a chapter on Muldoon should mark a turning point. However, this expectation is only partly fulfilled by the reading that follows. While Muldoon can indeed be found to seek definition by swerving from the poetic modes represented by his immediate Northern Irish predecessors, a careful reading of his output also yields arguments for continuity (albeit pursued by distinct conceptual and formal means). Undoubtedly, it is the elements of distinctiveness, if not contrariness, in this set of ambivalent relations that are most immediately apparent. They prominently include Muldoon's ostensible, almost flaunted avoidance of the civic-political concern (whether in the form of the sombre musings on poetic responsibility that informed Heaney's protracted dilemmatic reflections, Mahon's often tortured sense of artistic isolation, or Longley's emotive bonds to a poignant reality, his assumption of a duty to record and memorialise). If such concerns can be glimpsed behind the whimsical façades of Muldoon's writing (and this chapter will suggest that they indeed can), they have to be read against the grain of his ludic evasion of political and poetic allegiances. The conditions that have made Muldoon the (paradoxically canonical) *enfant terrible* not only of Irish poetry but of global contemporary verse are largely the same that have earned him the reputation of being a defining exponent of postmodernist verse. They include his transgressive appropriation of conventional forms, the equivocal referentiality of his writing, his interest in crossing the boundaries of genres and media, and his overall ambivalence vis-à-vis the precedents and models afforded by tradition.[2]

Muldoon's relation to Heaney has been pivotal in the definition of his own singularity, and has proved one of the most intriguing inter-authorial designs in contemporary poetry.[3] While this certainly reflects the qualities that have allowed the work of these poets to appeal to a vast readership, it is also, collaterally, a measure of the global interest that (albeit to different extents) has focused on their public personae. Muldoon's own fame has to some extent integrated the tension between proximity and rivalry vis-à-vis the older poet, as publicly perceived. The well-known account of the young Muldoon having been briefly taught at Queen's by Heaney; of his publication of a first collection at the age of 21, by Faber, with Heaney's support and encouragement; some parallel developments in their global and institutional acclaim (academic positions held in America, and Muldoon becoming Oxford Professor of Poetry in 1999, a decade after Heaney was elected for the same Chair); the witty mutual allusions that both have embedded in their poetry and criticism – these features of their relational narrative have undoubtedly contributed to expectations of *emulation* that (with the full ambivalence suggested by the term) neither poet has failed to gratify.

Although the rich implications of this rapport have contributed to perceptions of Muldoon's distinctiveness, the case for his exceptionality is duly buttressed by an enviable publication record. In 2006 he published his tenth collection (*Horse Latitudes*), not counting 'a number of small, interim publications', as he referred to such other short volumes in the 'Author's Note' to his *Poems 1968–1998*. For this 500-page compilation, he shunned the title 'Collected Poems', possibly because he was no older than 50 at the time of its publication (in 2001). In view of his reiterated interest in acts and utterances that defy all boundaries, the omission of 'opera libretti written in verse, verse drama, poems for children' and other generically discrete verse writings from this anthology was one of the book's surprises. Other remarks that arguably confirm his penchant for contradiction include his avowal:

> I have made scarcely any changes in the texts of the poems, since I'm fairly certain that, after a shortish time, the person through whom a poem was written is no more entitled to make revisions than any other reader.
>
> (Muldoon 2001: xv)

This passage from the 'Author's Note' (which taps into a recurrent concern, as seen above in connection with Mahon's and Longley's diverse attitudes towards revision) reflects a tension between authorial control and the denial of agency, a tension that has tended to re-emerge in Muldoon's critical prose and arguably informs his poetic writing. Both the notion that poets can be 'entitled' to rewrite their verse *and* the implicit denial (by whom?) of that right rest on normative assumptions; they involve an attention to ownership, as much as a concern over the extent to which (any)one can tamper with a poem, a concern that requires a heightened sense of the text's integrity and stability. Needless to say, such assumptions are at odds with Muldoon's reputation for a postmodern poetics predicated on an erasure of authorship and a palimpsestic, unstable textuality.[4] The suggestion of authorial effacement in his definition (in the same passage) of a poet as 'the person through whom a poem was written' is couched, moreover, in terms that evoke an inspirational poetics – rather than the notion that 'writing is the destruction of every voice, of every point of origin' (Barthes 1977: 142). And, if Muldoon's definition seems to have little to do with poststructuralist scepticism regarding source and presence, it hardly proves compatible either with his own more recently declared attraction, in *When the Pie Was Opened*, to an understanding of poetry as 'a job of journeywork' (2008: 9). (This view of his craft was, in fact, pointedly materialised in one of Muldoon's 'small, interim publications', *The Prince of the Quotidian* – a provocative title that balances singularity against the ordinary; written in January 1992, it honoured the resolve 'to write a poem each day' – Muldoon 1994).

The picture that emerges from an overview of a few critical remarks by Muldoon is anything but coherent, and yet the emphasis on craftsmanship that stamps his declared congeniality to the figure of the journeyman, and his plea for the poem's imperviousness to authorial intervention once it is written and published, are consistent with the theoretical cast he explicitly invoked in a 1998 essay that remains possibly his most sustained critical self-description. The model he then cited was avowedly New Critical (involving, therefore, sympathy for the self-contained, self-validated 'verbal icon', '[which] is detached from the author at birth and goes about the world beyond his power to intend about it or control it' – Wimsatt and Beardsley 1967: 5). However, this was balanced in a complex way against an argument for the prerogative of the author as 'first reader' that also assisted Muldoon's vocal dismissal of poststructuralism:

> it's the poet's job to take into account, as best he or she is able, all possible readings of the poem. I know this seems to be a mere rehash, perhaps a mere hash, of New Criticism, with its insistence on the autonomy of the text, that it flies in the face of much contemporary criticism. Let it. Let the theorists get over themselves. Let Barthes claim that there is no 'father-author'. Let Derrida proclaim against 'phallologocentrism'. Let them try to get round the ungetroundable fact that the poet is the first person to read or, more importantly, to be read by, the poem.
>
> (1998: 120)

This comes, coherently, from the writer who a few years later (in a piece of occasional poetry) was to refer satirically to 'theorists' in academia as 'so many dwarfs working in the tenure mines near Saussure'[5]. However, he has also been hailed as the poetic correlative of the theories he here denounces, in view precisely of his usurpations of authorship and his parodies of famous contributions to literary and intellectual history.

Indeed, and with unparalleled persistence, textual appropriation emerges in Muldoon as a precondition for writing, yielding a range of forms of rewriting that resist classification and include (mis)quotation, burlesque and ironical plagiarism. Such procedures have earned him many admirers, but have also attracted criticism – remarks that can sometimes be turned on their heads (e.g., John Carey's damning quip, 'If all previous literature vanished, Muldoon's poetry would instantly suffocate' [Carey 1987: 56], can also be cited as proof that Muldoon epitomises the ineluctably intertextual condition of all writing). His equivocal textuality is bound up with the challenges posed by his poetry with regard to representation. On the one hand, it seems to destabilise all reference by often conflating the textual and the extra-textual, as authors and their writings coexist in his poetic fictions with circumstances, persons and objects from a variety of cultural and geographic backgrounds. On the other, such referential instability seems to be offered a stay in the form of images drawn from the geographic and cultural space of the poet's Northern Irish origins – despite the fact that Muldoon, having lived in America since 1987, has pointedly distanced himself from the emotionally defined bonds to local origins carried by the traditional nationalist narrative of 'exile'.[6]

It was undoubtedly a proleptic sign of the tension between cognitive assurance and diffidence in the poet's delineation of his circumstance that Muldoon's first publication was a pamphlet entitled *Knowing my Place* (1971).[7] His poetry foregrounds the discourses and images of a global, supposedly anti-atavistic culture; but these are made to relate, in ways that often defy the supposed laws of geography and history, to a named territory, recognisable in its topography and socio-politics – all the more so when one reads Muldoon after considering other Northern Irish poets. The dislocations afforded by Muldoon's forays into translation, and his willingness to explore the relations between his writing and artefacts in other media, arguably further this tension by confirming both his singularity, and the strength of what binds him to his tradition.

5.1   Deformation, displacement, liminality

Muldoon's inaugural collection, *New Weather* (1973), drew its title and rationale from the curious knowledge of self as cognitive subject, combined with a peculiar relation to one's natural, phenomenal environment, proposed in the opening lines of its second poem, 'Wind and Tree':

> In the way that the most of the wind
> Happens where there are trees,
>
> Most of the world is centred
> About ourselves.
>
> (4)[8]

This ironical epistemology is summoned to the collection's title via the poem's closing statement: 'by my broken bones // I tell new weather' (5).

In these lines, the self-centredness announced from the outset is reinforced by the eminently lyrical, though casually made claim that the world's sensorial impact on the subject is one of fracture and pain. This subtly announced poignancy is enhanced rather than countered by the playful tones in which it is often couched throughout the collection. But 'Wind and Tree' proves an apt critical starting point because the relation to the real that it describes makes clear that Muldoon's inaugural collection is something other than the poetic record of the traditional rurality otherwise promised by several titles on its list of contents: 'Blowing Eggs', 'Hedges in Winter', 'Cuckoo Corn', 'The Cure for Warts'. Between the 'Contents' page of *New Weather* and the poem that gave the book its title readers are offered, however, 'The Electric Orchard', a piece that stamps the collection's opening with the uncanniness of an elsewhere in a no less indefinite, remote time: 'The early electric people had domesticated the wild ass' (3).

Such a pointed departure in these early poems from an empirically recognisable world will have been especially important for Muldoon's assertion of his particular poetics in view of the epigonal expectation that might otherwise have surrounded his poetic début – he had, after all, studied with Heaney and counted on his support, and was now publishing a book with a title (*New Weather*) that seemingly echoed Heaney's own *Wintering Out*, published the previous year. It is arguable, however, that the effect of 'strangeness' imposed by Muldoon on his autochthonous frame of reference can also be read as a Heaney theme, in view of the older poet's interest in the tension between the space of his personal origins and the formative consequences of academic training, literary career and cosmopolitan experience. (Through the title of his later poem 'Making Strange' Heaney was in fact to associate this tension, as actually experienced when welcoming a foreign poet as a visitor to his home ground, with the effect of 'estrangement' or defamiliarisation that the Russian formalists proposed as defining literary language[9] – Heaney 1984: 32–3).

Before focusing on the overwhelming extent to which Muldoon's writing depends on textual and authorial relations, however, this chapter will concentrate on the trans-spatial and interlocal element in his writing, its relational topography and geography. A poem also from Muldoon's first book bears an Irish place name in its title, 'Dancers at the Moy', but it opens with the discovery in a small Irish town of a spatial arrangement – 'This Italian square' (10) – that is emblematic of the Mediterranean south. The poem then evokes a dimly remote historico-political misunderstanding: the frustrated expectation, with catastrophic effects on the local economy, of a massive business deal with foreign customers rumoured to be buying horses for 'one or other Greek war' (10). When that prospect of wealth brought by a distant war failed to materialise, the animals were left to die, but their remains were to lend buoyancy to the ground, '[giving] their earthen floors / The ease of trampolines' (11). Muldoon thus retrieves the trope (employed by several Irish poets, including Heaney and John Montague) of a past predicament remaining materially and imaginatively as an energising layer of the home ground; and the poem also constitutes an example of the plight of equines treated as analogues, fellow sufferers, or foils to human beings in a situation of conflict or distress – a recurrent theme in this book, in Muldoon's case bearing especially on his collections *Mules* (1977) and *Horse Latitudes* (2006).

'Dancers at the Moy' is also a clear example of Muldoon's contrapuntal play between conflict elsewhere and frustration or decline at home. From this perspective, it can be seen to counter the long tradition of poetry about fighting on/for the Irish soil. But arguably it also evokes the Joycean trope of paralysis, as well as the representations of stagnation and ineffectuality that recur in some mid-twentieth-century Irish poetry: Austin Clarke's inert Dublin (in which spiritual and cultural decline finds a trope in human cruelty to horses), or Patrick Kavanagh's spiritually and sexually starved countryside.[10] When Muldoon, with characteristic indirection, writes about conflict in Ireland – and in particular about the sectarian socio-political landscape of the Northern Irish Troubles – the scene is hardly one of excitement or even productive energy. In *Why Brownlee Left* (1980), the five-line poem entitled 'Ireland' raises the doubt as to whether the clandestine business of a 'Volkswagen parked in the gap' concerns 'lovers' or guerillas, but the lack of distinctiveness of either venture contributes to the deflationary combination of title and vignette (82–3). On the other hand, the fact that poems whose titles point to autochthony and emplacement coexist with pieces named after remote places compounds their mutual implication. 'Cuba' (78–9) derives its title from a crucial news item in 1962, the missile crisis, invoked as a concomitant worry (nearly an aggravating circumstance) by a father who is moved by the repressive ethos of Irish Catholicism to berate his daughter across the breakfast table for arriving late from a dance. The familial, the local and the global juxtapose and refract one another, with ironical consequences for one's perception of the crises that register in distinct spaces.[11]

The spatial relations evident in Muldoon's poetry prominently include the themes of departure and travel. Episodes of actual or frustrated mobility abound, and their starting point is usually the Irish countryside – although Muldoon's iconoclasms set him apart from the conventional nationalist narrative of emigration as a tale of historical injustice and oppression, with clear causes and culprits. In the title poem of *Why Brownlee Left*, Brownlee has suddenly departed, leaving behind a scene of relative affluence (rather than poverty and dispossession). He has abandoned his team of horses halfway through his ploughing – the accuracy and completeness of which were a point of honour for the traditional Irish peasant (as we know from Heaney, and before him, Kavanagh). He thus makes his departure a provocation and an enigma: 'Why Brownlee left, and where he went, / Is a mystery even now (84).

The following poem in the collection alludes to a frustrated departure – '[my father] took passage, almost, for Argentina' (85); but this piece of (actual) family history combines with imaginary transits: 'he has gone no further than Brazil' (85). This poem, whose title, 'Immrama' (employed twice in the same collection, respectively in the singular and plural forms), designates travel narratives in the Irish tradition, indeed claims for the poetic self an experience of quest and wandering: 'I, too, have trailed my father's spirit' (85).

Muldoon's interest in travelling or errant designs converged, from the 1980s, with the 'American' drift of his poetry – and not just *North* American, since Argentina, Brazil, Chile, Bolivia or Peru now broadened his range of place names, and often signalled, provocatively, the uncertainty of fictional (dis)locations.[12] As later suggested in the poem that gave *The Annals of Chile* (1994) its title, 'if not Brazil, // then Uruguay', 'If not Uruguay, then Ecuador' (327). The New World emphasis became especially noticeable from 'Immram', the long poem that closed *Why Brownlee Left*, and was definitively confirmed with *Meeting the British* (1987). The title poem of this collection focused on the interlinked transits of colonialism, trade and disease, and also pursued the strategy of 'estrangement' mentioned above by being couched in the voice of a native American. This was one of Muldoon's many poetic ventriloquisms, but one that appropriated a topos – the point of view of a culturally alien figure on European behaviour, especially as regards the use of power – with a long tradition in fictions that resort to a defamiliarising strategy. Muldoon's explorations of the alien gaze also allow him to broaden this defamiliarisation so as to encompass the 'strangeness' that marks an Irishman's experience of global culture, as much as global perspectives on Irish atavisms. This tension is the feature selected by the editor of a recent collection of critical studies of Muldoon precisely to claim that he remains (paradoxically, as it were) 'a typical modern Irish poet' (Kennedy-Andrews 2006: 1); which also seems to confirm the persistence of the notion, jokingly expressed by another scholar, that 'Being Irish is Being Abroad' (Serpillo 1987: 27).

The broadening of Muldoon's relational range (in culture, geography and history) was accompanied by an increase in formal experimentation. 'Immram' combined the design proper to the narrative of travel or pilgrimage, evoked by its title, with discursive markers from the American detective novel, and, in closing *Why Brownlee Left*, it became the first major instance of Muldoon's penchant for the long poem, confirmed and extended over the two following decades. Muldoon's option to close his collections with an extended narrative digression, in which a whirling intertextuality combines with the free play of signifiers, found its culmination – and also its point of rupture – in *Madoc – A Mystery* (1990). The long title poem (or sequence) occupies 246 of the book's 261 pages. Its *raison d'être* is an oblique fiction on pantisocracy, the American utopia espoused by Coleridge and Southey;

and it takes the form of a long sequence of short texts placed each under the aegis of a major figure in Western intellectual history. 'Madoc', ostensibly referring to a political dream of redemptive dislocations, is also an extensive intertextual ramble, epitomising the growing indistinction between empirical and textual space in Muldoon's poetry since the late 1980s.

Some of the key notions that inform this tendency were to be explored by Muldoon in the more sustained essay writing that he undertook at the turn of the century prompted by institutional commitments – critical ventures that often involve instances of self-reading. A case in point is provided by the Clarendon Lectures that Muldoon gave at Oxford in 1998. This was the year before he was elected Oxford Professor of Poetry, although the lectures were published during his term as holder of that honorary Chair (1999– 2004). The choice of title – *To Ireland, I* – was hardly devoid of irony. The Irish poet duly borrowed from Shakespeare (*Macbeth* 2.3.135–6) for his series of pronouncements delivered from a seat of academic Englishness; but the borrowed phrase points to the *other* island, and is followed in Shakespeare's text by the reflection: 'Our separated fortune / Shall keep us both the safer'. Muldoon constructed the lectures in *To Ireland, I* around an argument for the specificity, and hence separateness, of the Irish literary tradition; but that supposed specificity in fact involves opting out of a definition based on contrariness, or in any way informed by a sense of polarities. Muldoon states his interest in 'promiscuous provenance', in an 'essential liminality', and announces that he will focus on 'a range of strategies devised by a range of Irish writers' for which he coins notions such as 'imarrhage' and 'conglomewriting' (Joyce epitomises these metamorphic and eclectic practices). He further proposes that the Irish tradition is marked by an attraction to 'a figure who is neither here nor there, at some notional interface' (Muldoon 2000: 5, 8).

In their prevailing emphasis as in their chosen phrasing, such remarks leave no doubt of their author's awareness of current critical mores, and of his willingness to make this apparent through the use of certain favourite tropes. These include hybridity ('promiscuous provenance', in Muldoon's words), a trope that since his collection *Mules* (1977) has continually marked his poetics (cf. Gregson 1996: 39–60); and 'liminality', ultimately favoured as the source of the overarching rationale of *To Ireland, I* – judging from the term's recurrence throughout the book. Both these tropes derive favour from their affinity with the enabling concerns of a variety of critical discourses,[13] but readers will not find these explicitly acknowledged in *To Ireland, I*, nor elsewhere in Muldoon's critical prose. One may wonder how deliberate the oxymoron that lurks behind his phrase 'essential liminality' may be – or indeed, in view of Muldoon's express defence of New Critical tenets in the 1998 essay quoted above, to what extent his apparent endorsement, in and through his poetry, of aspects of poststructuralist theory may serve a parodic purpose.

Readers of *To Ireland, I* will not find Muldoon extending his reading of liminality to his own poetic generation nor to his own work, despite his earlier plea for the privileged condition of the author *qua* reader. (In fact, Irish poetry since the 1960s is totally and conspicuously left out of the map of Irish literature drawn in *To Ireland, I*). The discreet knowingness regarding present critical tendencies that marks Muldoon's essays makes it reasonable to surmise that he is not unaware of the perplexities that may beset his argument for a constancy of traits in Irish writing (even if such traits are defined precisely by their lack of definition), and that the perplexities in question are not just literary, but also cultural and political. The playfulness that pervades Muldoon's claim that Irish writing is defined by a 'tendency towards the amalgam' and a 'disregard for linear narrative', that 'a central tenet of the Irish imagination [. . .] [is] that what you see is *never* what you get' (Muldoon 2000: 74, 107, 6) does not prevent it from coming bafflingly close to the old trope of the Celts' dreamy irrationality (duly offset by Saxon pragmatism).[14] Anyone who ventures an argument for the 'essential' features of his/her country's culture can expect to find him/herself under the shadow cast by resilient national stereotypes, the burden of any project for national definition.

Muldoon's *poetry*, however, is plainly at odds with such a project and its attendant burden. His scepticism with regard to poetry's ability to make anything happen and his refusal to endorse identity politics do not indicate indifference to the civic plight.[15] 'The Boundary Commission' is a slanted representation of sectarian division in all its absurdity, from the civic charade of a *'village where the border ran / Down the middle of the street, / With the butcher and baker in different states'* to its natural correlative, the uncanny rarity of 'a shower of rain // [that] Had stopped so cleanly across Golightly's lane / It might have been a wall of glass', in front of which one of Muldoon's enigmatic characters is left 'to wonder', faced with the starkness of a divide that defies belief, 'which side, if any, he should be on' (80).[16] This short poem might be said to anticipate by several years the civic allegories that were to mark Heaney's *The Haw Lantern*, and indeed Muldoon's and Heaney's thresholds and crossings often seem to relate mutually in ways that, on the part of the younger poet, come very close to parody. The liminal situation in Heaney's poems involving the angst of going through checkpoints that, once crossed, leave you 'as if you'd passed from behind a waterfall' (Heaney 1987: 6), is transparently mimicked in 'Unapproved Road', a poem in Muldoon's much more recent *Moy Sand and Gravel* (2002): 'When we came to the customs post [. . .] / I was holding my breath / as if I might yet again be about to go // underwater' (4). This is a poem, however, that sets the concern with territory, boundaries and troubled transits in Northern Irish poetry up against perceptions of mobility and barriers in the age of global alertness to migrants and refugees, fortress Europe and its elsewheres. It features an initially mysterious nomadic character, later identified as 'the

Tuareg', who describes the migration of his flock-tending forebears 'through Algeria, Mali and Libya all the way up to / Armagh, Monaghan and Louth / with [. . .] a total disregard for any frontier' (2002: 5).

In Muldoon's recent collections images of diffuse boundaries and their free traversal may also bear, more generically, on human cognition and the ensuing processes of representation. A few lines in the opening poem of *Hay* (1998) draw on Magritte's *Le Modèle Rouge*, the painting chosen for the book's original cover, ostensibly to make an epistemological point on the limits of self and world. By entering an interauthorial and intermedial relation, Muldoon emphasises the porous limits of an artistic imagination; and by implicitly endorsing Magritte's remark (made in connection with that specific painting) on our assumption of 'monstrous habit' as normal, and on how 'the scariest things can be made to look completely harmless through the power of negligence',[17] he endows the uncanny challenge posed to the boundaries between body and environment with a whole set of social, civic, and political implications:

> it was hard to judge where the boots came to an end
> and the world began, given how one would blend
> imperceptibly into the other, given that there was no fine
> blue-green line
> between them.

('The Mud Room' 396)

There may also be personal, blatantly autobiographical implications to his liminal scenarios, right from his early collections, as in his account of his parents' distinct backgrounds – 'My father was a servant-boy', 'My mother was the school-mistress'. This distinction determined the ironical title 'The Mixed Marriage' (traditionally employed to refer to cross-sectarian marriages), and the poet's bemused representation of his in-betweenness: 'I flitted between a hole in the hedge / And a room in the Latin Quarter' (60). In more recent volumes, confrontation with the great limina of birth and death can either mitigate this offhand manner in the service of a sensitivity that is nevertheless still wary of sentimentality, or add to its brutality and make it the rhetorical formula for understated pain. An example of the former comes with a poem that, while heralding the birth of a son, pretends it is centrally about the brief stopover (yet a liminal moment) of birds in the course of a migration ('Redknots', 2002: 71). The *other* practice emerges when a poignant piece on the ravages of cancer ends on the brutally offhand note: 'Yesterday she drove to Newry to buy a bit of a wig' ('The Goose', 2002: 67). The refusal of the verbal conventions for solace and comfort is radical and stark – Muldoon has in fact argued against 'the notion of poetry as a moral force, offering respite or retribution' (1998: 127) – but unsurprisingly it is to that starkness that the poem owes its peculiar emotional effectiveness.

In spite of charges of lack of feeling,[18] Paul Muldoon's work of the past two decades has often drawn (though with characteristic indirection) on private grief. His elegiac evocations of the artist Mary Farl Powers, with whom he lived, and his mother (respectively in the long poem 'Incantata' and the vast sequence 'Yarrow', both in *The Annals of Chile*) correspond to a mode of writing whose continuity reflects not only direct experience but also the development of the poet's relational poetics. Increasingly, private sorrows integrate a design that allows them to be imaginatively exchanged and overlapped with public predicaments and absurdities – Irish, as much as of the global world.

Muldoon's collection *Horse Latitudes* (2006), and its title sequence in particular, is an elaborate case in point for this poetic practice, and one that provides important links with the authorial and textual transits to be discussed in the second part of this chapter. Equine forms – and the transformations and analogies they prompt in the poet's mind – have long recurred in Muldoon's poetry; indeed they were the focal point for the fascination with hybrid identities in *Mules*, irradiating to the whole book from the rhetorical question posed by the title poem: 'Should they not have the best of both worlds?' (67). As Clair Wills remarked in 1998, 'states of suspension or indeterminacy [. . .] are the logical extension of the concerns of *Mules*' (Wills 1998: 136): *Horse Latitudes* confirms and extends this view. Before it deals with horses verbally, the book seeks a pictorial mediation by reproducing a painting of horses on its cover: *Mares and Foals without a Background* (*c.* 1762), by George Stubbs. *Horse Latitudes* thus promises from the outset the greatest *latitude* for all that the equine comes to represent – the clean slate of a vacant background that converges with the primary sense of Muldoon's title: 'an area north and south of the equator in which ships tend to be becalmed, in which stasis if not stagnation is the order of the day, and where sailors traditionally threw horses overboard to conserve food and water' (2006: blurb).

This equation of 'horse latitudes' with the doldrums, and the suggestion of free floating vessels that have their pursuit of a course suspended in a stagnant environment, are substantiated by the book's title sequence of 19 sonnets, all named after battles, all beginning with a 'B', whose texts may at first seem unconnected to their titles, since they seldom offer recognisable representations of the historical events in question. 'Baginbun' epitomises the poetics of this sequence and volume, especially as regards the collapsing of distances in space and time, and between historical and personal memory. From the reference to Nashville in its opening line, the poem equates present-day capitalism with medieval warfare: there are the 'freebooters'; the 'mire and murk' of contracts that impede rivals' moves, much as the 'cows' stampeded into one's opponents; the fortifications put up on their respective grounds – in present-day urban space, the massive concrete structures that clutter the skyline and cause it to 'hem and haw' (2006:4). This phrase gains other implications throughout the sequence, when it mutates into 'heehaw': this extension to the asinine suggests that 'horse' is here a synecdoche for the equine in general, with no rigid borders to the species; and this combines with repeated references to Muldoon's old keyword and concept of 'mules'. Several allusions to drugs remind us that 'horse' is also slang for heroin: in this sense, 'horse latitudes' is where you go when you 'go on a trip'.

Such connections, however, do not lead 'Horse Latitudes' in the direction of a tripping idyll: Muldoon's readers may recall an association between horses and hallucinogenic substances, with an allegorical drift, in 'Gathering Mushrooms' (in *Quoof*, 1983), where it involved dark allusions to the discourses and ordeals of the Troubles (105–6).[19] The lurid family fictions and complex ramblings of 'Immram' also included the admission, by the persona of that long poem: 'My father had been a mule' (101) – that is, a drug carrier. Weird transits, personal relations that resist exegesis, and above all pain, mutilation and death haunt 'Horse Latitudes'. An Italian grandfather is intriguingly associated with pack mules on a waterfront, until the closing poem explains: 'Her grandfather's job was to cut / the vocal cords of each pack mule / with a single, swift excision' (2006: 21). His granddaughter is Carlotta, the lover of the male persona; her ordeal (Carlotta has breast cancer, as readers gradually learn) is interwoven throughout the sequence with memorable aspects of the various wars, such as those temporary fortifications on battlegrounds called 'breastwork[s]' (2006: 4, 13).

The permanent overlap or adjacency of these two levels of concern is unified by a perception of the apparent continuities between memory and discourse. These continuities are twice referred to in the sequence as 'age-old traduction(s)' (2006: 4, 17) – the word carrying the meanings of betrayal, dislocation, translation, all with a bearing on the semantic shifting proper to Muldoon's poetics. And the topical impulse for such procedure bobs up regularly and unmistakably, at its most explicit in lines from 'Blackwater Fort' that combine references to Xenophon, 'the 5th Marines', 'the old Sunni Triangle', 'the price of gasoline', 'a Texaco star' and (to clinch it all) 'the gross / imports of crude oil Bush will come clean on / only when the Tigris comes clean' (2006: 19). The Iraq war becomes an integrative reference, the public crisis that prompts the retrieval from memory of ancient and modern campaigns (their names all beginning with a B, as in Baghdad, the missing twentieth sonnet). The mutually troped public and private ordeals have their sources emblematically juxtaposed when the reflection of the star, logo for an oil company, falls on the breast that houses an expanding tumour.

The overriding sense of hurt and wound, personal and political, humanises a sequence that ostensibly takes horses for its object and otherwise seems to revel in its own textuality. The reader who has been through the whole sequence and returns to the opening sonnet, 'Beijing', sees this confirmed when the male speaker, awakening at Carlotta's side, recalls the terracotta army of warriors and horses in Emperor Qin Shihuang's mausoleum, finds a homology with his lover's body, and remarks: 'Proud-fleshed Carlotta. Hypersarcoma' (2006: 3). Imminent earth and yet living flesh coalesce in her; the 'pride' of her body, suggestive of erotic opulence, itself takes on the significance of a *memento mori* – but can also be found to have an altogether humbler meaning. Indeed, 'proud flesh' is a pathological condition, a form of keloid scarring to which horses are especially prone,

> normal tissue that has become overactive. In an attempt to heal wounds rapidly, the surrounding tissue reproduces so quickly it accumulates more tissue than is needed. The process moves at such a rapid rate it has trouble stopping. The resulting mound of tissue will protrude beyond skin level[20]

'Hypersarcoma', despite its bloodcurdling ring, can be just a gloss of the phrase that precedes it – 'proud flesh' meaning 'excessive flesh'; technically, sarcoma is a malignant tumour that grows from 'connective tissue' (*Oxford English Dictionary*). This realisation lends the line a self-referential value, and also makes it an epitome of Muldoon's textuality – connecting and proliferating on itself as on other matter of textualised experience, challenging ordinary morphology. The passage, one might say, is about *hyperflesh*, and its verbal correlative and apt representation is 'proud text' or hypertext, the semantic, lexical, prosodic, and referential surfing that has become a hallmark of Muldoon's poetics (cf. Phillips 2006). In a later poem in *Horse Latitudes*, faced with another dimly hinted cancer ordeal, the poet cannot stop himself from entering a bookshop to pick up a dictionary and '[trace] the root of *metastasis*' (2006: 94) (unmentioned in the poem, the word's root meaning is – of course – 'transition').

Equating flesh with text might entail a desensitisation to suffering, when the wayward growth of diseased flesh is represented as interchangeable with a textuality that sometimes stands accused of playfulness and self-gratification. But an undercurrent of suffering, verbally served by pained reticence, underlies Muldoon's verbal practices: the biological analogy is tantamount rather to a *sensitisation* of the text, and this invests a sequence like 'Horse Latitudes' with a lyrical/elegiac core to which the political drift (the battles, the unsaid 'Baghdad') lends an epic inflection, satirically modulated.[21] The effectiveness of this poetics depends crucially on Muldoon's 'traductions', the poignancy of a connectivity in which textual and somatic processes provide apt mutual tropes, in full awareness of their 'age-old' pedigree as of their ceaseless proliferation.

5.2   Transition, transmutation, traduction

> I've sometimes run a little ahead of myself, but mostly
> I lag behind, my footfalls already pre-empted by their echoes.
>
> (198)

The passage above comes from the prose poem, revealingly entitled 'The Key', that opens Muldoon's most challenging volume to date, *Madoc*. It emphasises – from within the brief fiction that it sketches – a concern with precedence and lateness, priority and derivation. This concern has obvious relevance for Muldoon's practice as a translator – or rather, in broader terms, for the various ways in which his writing substantiates his recent claim (quoted at the beginning of this chapter) that his literary awakening happened when he became 'fascinated by the art of translation.' However, that passage from 'The Key' introduces the book whose title sequence consists of intriguing glosses on a long gallery of major intellectual figures, and this calls for some preliminary attention to Muldoon's confrontation with the shadow cast by forebears, biological or literary.

In one of his lectures as Oxford Professor of Poetry (collected as *The End of the Poem*), Muldoon has words of praise for Harold Bloom's theory of influence, hailed as 'one of the most illuminating contributions to our understanding of the working of poets and poetry' (2006a: 41). His professed admiration for a reading of literary history based on an Oedipal struggle for prominence between 'ephebes' and influential 'strong poets' is hardly surprising in a poet who has so often exhibited an ambivalent relationship with predecessors – a relationship that literally begins at home. An early poem, 'The Waking Father', opens with a pastoral vignette of father and son fishing, but promptly leads to a parricidal fantasy: 'When my father stood out in the shallows / It occurred to me that / The spricklies might have been piranhas'; the ensuing wish to 'have his grave / Secret and safe' can be both a form of tribute and emotional redress for that fantasy, or reflect the need to conceal it and ensure that the father is indeed dead and buried (9–10). The obviousness of such fictions can make readers wonder about their earnestness, and the same doubt has to occur in the face of Muldoon's later representation of his parents as involved in a struggle that extends to the grave: 'my mother's skeleton / has managed to worm / its way back on top of the old man's, / and she once again has him under her thumb' ('Oscar', 329). A familial landscape of resentment and embarrassment has also included poems about the young male's discovery of images and narratives from the youth of his forebears that thicken the Oedipal plot, reveal the skeletons in their closets, or just cast them in ridiculous or hypocritical roles ('Cheesecake', 'Ned Skinner', 'Ma' – 47–9).

The ambivalence that the poet flaunts with regard to the memory and legacy of biological forebears extends 'naturally' to literary predecessors, glossed, parodied, and rewritten. Predictably, this has often involved Seamus Heaney – who has hardly been passive himself in this authorial relationship: 'Widgeon', a poem on the experience of finding a dead bird, blowing into its voicebox and thus resurrecting its voice, was dedicated to Paul Muldoon, arguably mixing poetic tribute with a sly allusion to the dedicatee's multiple echoes of other poets (Heaney 1984: 48). Muldoon was to reciprocate with 'The Briefcase' (in Part I of *Madoc*), dedicated to Heaney and in fact an echo of his 'The Schoolbag', which was a reminiscence of setting off for school that became implicitly a narrative of poetic birth (202). 'Something Else' (in *Meeting the British*) was more openly satirical, bearing on Heaney's 'Away from It All': Heaney, curiously prompted by the pre-meal view of a lobster, reflected in that poem on the traps of political commitment by citing (once 'quotations start to rise / like rehearsed alibis' – Heaney 1984: 16) some admired lines by Czesław Miłosz; Muldoon is brought by a similar view to recall that the *poète maudit* 'Nerval / was given to promenade / a lobster on a gossamer thread', and ultimately committed suicide. The lines that follow this narrative of artistic ineffectuality and dubious closure could hardly be more dismissive of poetry's ability to refer – whether to texts or the world – in terms that are reminiscent of a Derridean endless deferral (yet another instance of Muldoon's ambiguity towards theory?): 'which made me think / of something else, then something else again' (173).

Muldoon's querying of the authority associated with authorship, and his willingness to do so through strategies that prove relevant to a study of his rewritings, has often been general rather than specific – bearing on intellectual and literary history, its records and its fictions. A poem in *Moy Sand and Gravel*, 'Famous First Words' (2002: 39–40), seems to take up the uncertainty mooted in 'The Key' between being 'ahead' or 'behind' by simply substituting 'first' for 'last'. The poem in fact consists of a list of *last* words, either recorded or apocryphally attributed to 26 famous individuals, from Archimedes to Zola – one of Muldoon's several alphabetical lists. The fact that the brief deathbed *dicta* are repeatedly given as 'first words' reinforces the notion that (in spite or because of the banality of many of them) they are character-revealing, an epitome of their authors' legacy. Through this design and verbal practice, this two-page poem echoes one of the principles on which the earlier, monumental title sequence of *Madoc* (subtitled 'A Mystery') seemed to be based. It is only for its attitude towards authorial inscription and rewriting that 'Madoc', a 'mad history of western philosophy' (Kendall 1996: 158), 'impossible to categorise in terms of genre' (Wills 1998: 146) or to be given its due without an extended discussion, can be mentioned in this context.

Muldoon's poetic fictional enactment of Coleridge's and Southey's unrealised pantisocratic project runs intermittently through a sequence of 233 cryptic musings prompted by the names of as many thinkers (from Pre-Socratic philosophers to the present). It is deliberately constructed to be taken at a variety of levels – including a historically informed reflection on utopia and colonialism, with a slanted relation to Northern Irish politics.[22] 'Madoc: A Mystery' is relevant for an understanding of Muldoon's translational poetics because, apart from relating obliquely to the original Madoc legend (of a twelfth-century Welsh prince's voyage to America), and to Southey's retrieval of that legend in his verse epic *Madoc* (1805), the sequence illustrates the broadest possible range of ways in which others' writings can be incorporated into one's own. All the variously sized sections bear the name of an author or philosopher as a surtitle, between square brackets – as if to signal the contingency of this nominal connection. Some read like narrative episodes of the pantisocratic fiction, but in many other cases they can be taken as glosses – or radically compressed *versions* – of emblematic works, characteristic pronouncements, or lapidary descriptions of the intellectual legacy of the named authors.[23]

'Madoc' thus promotes the insight that any writing is inevitably underlaid by others' writings, even when it seems to be self-substantiating, and, concomitantly, that writing about other authors amounts to rewriting them. However, this involves a fair measure of irony, perhaps even savage satire. A sequence that seems designed to be a playground for the poststructuralist critic includes major names of poststructuralist criticism in its often caricatural design; the section surtitled 'Kristeva' reduces the high priestess of intertextual theory to three anapaests: 'Signifump. Signifump. Signifump' (321) – a satirical representation of the rebarbative metalanguage of some post-1960s French criticism. This is as ambivalent as Muldoon's text is markedly metalinguistic and metapoetic: allusions to the invoked author's particular significance combine throughout 'Madoc' with an objectified prosodic keenness, yielding lines that only signify within the sequence's enigmatic framework: 'De dum, Te Deum, de dum, Te Deum, de dum' (224).[24]

This fascination with the possibility of endowing words with new or private meanings, and their circulation beyond the spaces where that re-signification occurred, was suggested from an early moment in Muldoon's career. The title poem of *Quoof* dealt with words in transit, and the exchangeability of words and things – 'How often have I carried our family word / for the hot water bottle / to a strange bed' (112) – and the shared night with 'a girl who spoke hardly any English' pitted the strangeness of words against the immediacy of tactile, human communication. More recently, 'Errata' (in *Hay*) played with verbal relations that ostensibly concern error and revision, though in reality they propose correspondences based on a variable logic, meanings that slide metonymically between adjacent terms with a clear inscription in Muldoon's poetic universe: 'For "Antrim" read "Armagh," / For "mother" read "other"'; 'For "ludic" read "lucid"'; 'For "religion" read "region"' (445).

However, the already quoted 'The Key' arguably contains the aptest cues for Muldoon's translational poetics. In this narrative covering little more than a page, the narrator and protagonist is in 'a dubbing suite in Los Angeles', watching utterances being juxtaposed with others, ideally in such a way that the original pronouncement is fully calqued by its version. The character operating the equipment, Foley, 'was having trouble matching sound to picture' (197), but the narrator (discursively similar to Muldoon's poetic persona elsewhere) chews over bits of dialogue, mingled with fragments of his own inner discourse, dabbles in etymologies and truncated verbal echoes: 'I found myself savouring the play between "both" and "bathy-", "quits" and "mesquite", and began to "misquote" myself' (197). Misquotation is all too familiar from Muldoon's earlier writing, often involving iconoclasm, as in two lines in 'Lull' – 'Tomorrow is another day, / As your man said on the Mount of Olives' (81) – that have Christ ventriloquise through *Gone with the Wind*'s Scarlett O'Hara. But 'The Key' represents this verbal practice in a combination with visual and auditory ('trouble matching sound to picture') that has come to play an important part in Muldoon's poetics of translation and/as misquotation.[25]

Two of Muldoon's most striking examples of intermedial translation are ekphrastic renderings.[26] Both poems are about double portraits of unconventional married couples, feeding into Muldoon's recurrent theme of mismatch, and they both appropriate the titles of the paintings in question, combined with the name of the artists, suggesting the interchangeability of source and target representations and the 'transparency' of the ekphrastic relation. This compounds the readers' surprise if they do what no reading of the poems per se requires, and decide to check the texts against their visual referents. The first, 'The Bearded Woman, by Ribera', provides *Mules*, and that collection's theme of hybridity, with its 'most powerful family image' (Kendall 1996: 57). Besides describing the peculiar seventeenth-century painting – noting the woman with a 'luxuriantly black' beard and a manly face, yet suckling a baby with a 'bared [. . .] pap', which contrasts with a 'willowy and clean-shaven' husband, 'in the shadows' – the poem also registers the poet's attraction to 'this so unlikely Madonna' and raises the question: 'Might this be the Holy Family / Gone wrong?' (57–8). This brazen rhetorical question is certainly a confrontation with the iconography of his *Bildung* that shows Muldoon contributing to the 'deconstruction' of 'Catholic Ulster' (Longley 1994: 52), but it also underlines the poet's alertness to 'wrong' renderings, the possibility of a wayward or incompetent attempt at a pictorial genre in sacred art. The sense of norm that this involves further encourages readers to look for a reproduction (or go to the Prado museum) so as to gauge the painting's deviation from conventional Holy Families, and assess the relation between José de Ribera's painting and Muldoon's rendering. Readers who do so will realise that the poem departs in fundamental ways from its proclaimed object. Muldoon reconfigures the painting, deliberately mistranslates it (misquotes it?) indeed to domesticate it, that is, to bring it home into the representational range of his writing. Further, his deviant rendering is both intersemiotic *and* interlingual, since the painting itself features a Latin inscription detailing the circumstances that in 1631 led Ribera to portray Magdalena Ventura, who years earlier had suddenly grown a beard and moustache. This verbal account was included in the visual source for the sake of verification and authenticity, so that those to come would not falsify, misrepresent – or mistranslate – a tale that was thus both verbal and visual.

The second ekphrastic poem and intermedial translation involving an unusual couple appeared in *Moy Sand and Gravel* as 'Anthony Green: *The Second Marriage*' (2002: 32). The poem was originally commissioned by the National Museums and Galleries of Northern Ireland: several poets were asked to respond to art work and the results were published in *A Conversation Piece*, a collection where each poem appeared next to a reproduction of its pictorial referent. The poems were thus written in full knowledge that readers would have simultaneous access to source and target – as is the case, in interlingual translation, with bilingual editions. It is hardly irrelevant either, as regards Muldoon's contribution, that the title (of poem and painting) promises a '*second* marriage', somehow qualifying expectations of the original, singular or virginal: this piece on (or *after*) Anthony Green's painting is indeed secondary in the sense that its theme has important precedents in Muldoon's work, including the poem on Ribera's painting. This does not cancel the most immediate sense of Green's title, apparent in the middle-aged features of his couple. And the painter seems only too conscious of other ways in which his double portrait is *secondary*: it has antecedents, the most famous of which is Van Eyck's *Portrait of Giovanni Arnolfini and his Wife*, acknowledged in the editorial notes to *A Conversation Piece*.[27] But Muldoon's poem writes a narrative of transgression and imminent sentencing into an otherwise decorous wedding scene:

> they're reminiscent less of a blushing bride and a nervous groom
> than a pair of con artists summoned before
> a magistrate inclined to throw
> the book at con artists

(2002: 32)

Muldoon's verbal rendering inscribes Green's painting with a figure of authority and definitive pronouncements – a judge, there for reasons other than a wedding. The ekphrastic gesture entails that, for the sake and within the space of his poem, the poet is indeed (to retrieve Muldoon's critical dictum in his 1998 essay) 'the first person to read' the painting and to pronounce on it – a pronouncement that is magisterially conveyed by the phrase, 'to throw / the book at' (32). Indeed, through this intermedial translation 'the book', as a metonym for texts, is *thrown* at other *artists*. Further, Muldoon's chosen phrasing for an authority that is verbally conveyed suggests that all the artists involved in the intermedial process are somehow 'con artists', placed under a suspicion of illicitly appropriating and defacing another's creation – all the more so since the court case that Muldoon risibly inscribes in Green's *The Second Marriage* becomes one of receiving stolen goods, 'that silver cigarette urn [. . .] in the center of the room' (32).

Muldoon's chosen themes for these intermedial versions of strange couplings obviously echo his representations of the family as weird and dysfunctional, which prevailed (for example) among the delirious 'American' ramblings of 'Immram', featuring a disappeared father, a force-fed mother, a 'child-bride' (96). His hallmark themes also pointedly resonate in his choices as an interlingual translator. Muldoon's interlingual versions, however, seem to allow him sometimes to change discourse and register in distinct ways: either by adopting a more conventional diction than when writing under his own name, or a directness and explicitness that he has otherwise shunned. This can be noted both with regard to formal procedures and to the poet's attitude to civic and political concerns: on the side of prosody, Muldoon's version of Paul Valéry's 'Pomegranates' (2002: 24) is a considerably more regular sonnet than one commonly finds in Muldoon's frequently transgressive variations on the sonnet form, both in average line length (with consequences for layout) and in its exact replication of Valéry's rhyme scheme;[28] on the side of politics, his version of 'The Hands', a sonnet by the German poet Erich Arendt on the mutilation and murder of a Spanish peasant by the Guardia Civil constitutes an example of a rarely committed, denunciatory tone that seems to emerge in Muldoon's work only through translation (110).

This notion that translation can release the poet from his own shape-shifting, endlessly ironical persona into a greater directness also applies to private emotions – and, again, family matters. 'The Mirror – *in memory of my father*' (108–9), a translation of a poem by a contemporary, the Irish-language poet Michael Davitt, takes the form of an elegiac celebration, climaxing in a suggested continuity of spiritual presence that allows father and son to bond, without any of the ironical twists that characteristically preclude sentiment in Muldoon's evocation of family emotions. In *The Annals of Chile* (a collection strongly centred on life and death, forebears and offspring), a version of a poem by César Vallejo – originally entitled 'Piedra Negra sobre una Piedra Blanca' [Black Stone on a White Stone], but rendered by Muldoon as 'Testimony' (343–4) – is immediately preceded by poems about pregnancy and childbirth, and constitutes a self-elegy, an anticipation of death with a candour that proves rare in this poet.

A case that deserves closer attention is Muldoon's translation of Eugenio Montale's 'The Eel' (included in *Moy Sand and Gravel*), both because it is an intriguing combination of self-effacement and assertiveness on the part of the translator, and because Montale's poem was the object of one of Muldoon's Oxford lectures (collected as *The End of the Poem*). On one hand, Muldoon calques the poem's formal mimicry of the eel's meandering course with a single 30-line sentence; indeed this feature is exacerbated in his version, as made immediately apparent by its more marked variation in line length. On the other, he clinches this translation with a rhyme – 'can't you take in / her being your next-of-kin?' (2002: 59) – for which there is no ground in the source text (whose ending rhymes with a line situated four lines above it). Muldoon's couplet lends a quasi-parodic ring to the poem's closing rhetorical question, and makes it diverge markedly from most other English versions of the poem, including the ten different ones that he cites in the text of his lecture; invariably, such other versions render *sorella* (Montale's closing word) literally as 'sister' – as in Jonathan Galassi's: 'can you fail to see her as a sister?' (cited in 2006a: 217).

The singularity of Muldoon's ending should be considered against the highly detailed – and highly intertextual – close reading pursued in his lecture '*L'Anguilla* / The Eel', whose object is indistinctly Montale's poem and the multiple versions that materialise its English 'afterlife'[29]. His reading of 'The Eel' appears framed and interspersed by broader critical remarks that include ambitious claims for translation: Muldoon argues the case for 'poetic translation' as 'itself an "original" poem'; for 'the "original" poem' as 'itself a "translation"'; and also for the understanding 'that both "original poem" and "poetic translation" are manifestations of some ur-poem' (195) – a remark that may owe something to Benjamin's concern with 'ultimate essence' and the 'nucleus of pure language' (Benjamin 1999: passim). As always, Muldoon seems undaunted by the difficult compatibility of such remarks on source and essence with his proposed dilution of distinctions between original and derivative, which would seem to require a critique of origin and presence. And he continues:

> The 'activity of translation' is a form of criticism, surely the most exiguous form of close reading we're ever likely to experience, with one exception. That exception is the form of close reading which occurs simultaneously with what might be termed 'close writing'.
>
> (2006a: 195)

These remarks are self-referential in several respects; they equate translation's defining skills with Muldoon's practice as a critic – *The End of the Poem* offers a series of minute line-by-line readings of poems in which, however, any notion of self-containment is cancelled by the many insights that Muldoon derives from consideration of a broad range of other poems and authors. But the passage above also suggests the fundamental affinity between this critical exercise and Muldoon's poetry, whose rampant intertextuality poses as nonchalance, but is rather the lightly worn craft of one who nonetheless ensures 'every rift's loaded with ore' (to cite Muldoon's sardonic rephrasing of Keats's famous injunction – 2002: 32). Later in the lecture Muldoon quotes Octavio Paz approvingly on the notion that poems are 'translations of translations of translations', but the relinquishing of authorship that this might suggest is duly balanced by another quote from Paz, pointing out that poet-translators 'almost invariably use the foreign poem as a point of departure toward their own' (2006a: 201, 204). This tension allows Muldoon to theorise the position of the reader as 'stunt-writer', and of the original writer as 'a "stunt-reader", standing in for subsequent readers, foreshadowing them, determining the impact of those words and those lines' – again echoing his 1998 apology for the author as 'first reader' (1998: 120). It is also from this tension that issues a reading of Montale's 'The Eel' which is not only intertextual, but eminently inter-authorial, involving Lowell's version of Montale, but also, explicitly, Lowell as appropriated by Heaney – a two-tier example of the self-supportive manoeuvring that Muldoon imputes to consciously canonical figures (2006a: 197–200).

Such relational play empowers Muldoon's own bid for authority as reader and rewriter of the poem that he translates as a part of *Moy Sand and Gravel* and discusses in *The End of the Poem*. In the Oxford lecture, his diagnosis (in no uncertain terms) of 'the failure of Lowell as translator' (220) concerns the 'crucial moment' of Montale's ending – precisely the moment in Muldoon's own version of 'The Eel' where he conspicuously diverges not only from Lowell's, but in fact from all the ten versions that he cites; the overall theme of 'the end of the poem', whose various meanings Muldoon debates in the course of the lectures, finds here a particularly literal focus. It is no less significant that, discussing in great detail Montale's poem and its various translations, at no point does Muldoon as much as allude to his own. His perception (mooted in one of the lectures – 323) of the tasks of poet and professor of poetry as mutually exclusive does not seem to be mitigated enough by the all-inclusive 'task of the translator' for Muldoon to change his practice of self-exclusion from critical or editorial work – as he controversially did when he left himself out of his *Faber Book of Contemporary Irish Poetry* (1986), as also indeed of *The Faber Book of Beasts* (1997).

An editor's prerogatives, however, may afford Muldoon a scope for indirect self-commentary similar to that we have found in his published criticism. Introducing *The Faber Book of Beasts*, Muldoon begins by remarking that 'in poetry, as in life, animals bring out the best in us' (Muldoon 1997: xv). He furthers this by arguing that *anagnorisis* comes through comparison and contrast with other species, which helps secure the place of animal poetry in the lyric (under its conventional understanding as defined by a focus on the self): '[the] ongoing question of "What am I?" is [. . .] central not only to animal poetry but to all forms of poetry' – xvii). Such keen attention to the interface between man and beast, combined with his emphases on blurred boundaries, hybridity, and shape-shifting, make it predictable that Ovid's *Metamorphoses* should also interest Muldoon as a translator – although he has to date rendered only one episode, his contribution to the 1994 anthology *After Ovid*. This translation of Ovid's account of Leto's encounter with the churlish Lycian peasants, and of how she takes revenge by turning them into frogs (Book VI, ll.313–81), obtains from Muldoon a translation that is not characterised by radical departures, in prosody or diction, from the expectations defined by contemporary (academic) versions of Classical texts – and, indeed, the same can be said of Muldoon's other translations of Latin verse, in particular of two odes by Horace included in *Moy Sand and Gravel* (2002: 55–7).

Prosodically, these versions show a compromise between freedom and regularity that Muldoon has used on occasion: regular rhyme – couplets in the versions of Ovid, interpolated rhyme for Horace – is balanced against the discursive flow of lines of varying length. In the episode of the *Metamorphoses*, occasional demotic lexical choices become rhetorically relevant precisely by being isolated occurrences (rather than systematic anachronisms): Leto arrives in Lycia 'completely whacked / from her long travail', she is treated with no generosity by 'local yokels' (326). But the relevance of this Ovidian version in Muldoon's oeuvre is defined, above all, by positional and thematic factors that confirm how integral such translations can be to the design of the books in which they appear. It features as the opening piece of *The Annals of Chile*, almost like an extended epigraph; this prefatory position in a collection that mourns women in the poet's life (including his mother) is thus given to a tale of a goddess who was the mother of Apollo (god of poetry) and was forced by Hera's jealous persecution to roam the Ancient world with her children. Further, this translation appears in the volume immediately before one of Muldoon's familial fictions involving New World dislocations: 'When my mother snapped open her flimsy parasol / it was Brazil: if not Brazil, // then Uruguay' (327).

The main emphasis in and around this Ovidian piece is therefore human, rather than animal. However, Muldoon's vast bestiary includes a few more translations, such as the two Rilke poems on animals that he included in *Hay*, 'Black Cat' and 'The Unicorn', and they often take on a metapoetic significance – as if fulfilling the revelatory function that Muldoon attributed to animals in his *Faber Book of Beasts*. 'The Unicorn' is a considerably free version, as if the unlikely beast and its fiction were coterminous: 'the beast that has never actually been' is said to have been 'allowed such latitude' (a phrase that could here refer to the translation itself) that 'its essence shrugged off mere existence' (403). As for 'Black Cat', it reflects the interest in cat lore that recurs through *Hay* and, more specifically, appears as a companion piece and a dark, more enigmatic counterpart to the confidence and high spirits of a poem about a *white* cat, Muldoon's translation of the medieval Irish poem in which an anonymous monk celebrates his mouse-hunting companion, 'Pangur Bán.' The piece is one of the most widely translated of its kind, both for its general appeal and for its reputation as an item of marginalia inscribed in the vernacular by a monk taking a break from his scribal Latin duties. Several contemporary Irish poets have offered versions – including Thomas Kinsella, Ciaran Carson and, most recently, Seamus

Heaney; as Heaney acknowledges, this is 'a poem that Irish writers like to try their hand at, not in order to outdo the previous versions, but simply to get a more exact and intimate grip on the canonical goods.'[30] Such appropriations inevitably focus on the monk's witty characterisation of his own craft as analogous to the cat's predatory ventures for food, and Muldoon's version acknowledges features of the translator's writerly persona in lines such as, 'I muse / on something naggingly abstruse', as also in the inclusion of the odd present-day colloquialism to represent the rapport between scholar and cat: 'And so we while away our whiles, / never cramping each other's styles' (436–7). Yet the passage in this version that proves most relevant as an indirect acknowledgement of Muldoon's poetics comes with the lines, 'much as Pangur goes after mice / I go hunting for the precise // word' (436).[31] This formula for authorial control, via the *mot juste*, converges with Muldoon's interest in 'close reading' and 'close writing' (as manifested in *The End of the Poem*), and works *against* the assumption that his postmodernity would rather be tantamount to a celebration of the random, arbitrary and imprecise.[32]

Much of the above has focused on the productive tension, in Muldoon's translations, between a measure of deference towards the source and elements of iconoclasm. These characteristics may coexist in a variable balance, or one of them prevail. The latter possibility arguably characterises the two only ('interim') volumes of poetry translations that Muldoon has published: *The Astrakhan Cloak* (1992), a bilingual volume of poems by Nuala Ní Dhomhnaill, and the already mentioned short motley collection *When the Pie Was Opened* (where the few 'original' poems are presented as offshoots of the translations). The reasons for their marked difference in tone are all too apparent: idiosyncratic or radically refractive versions usually occur with regard to canonical texts, and (as previously argued in this book) often depend on readers' knowledge of other, more conventional versions with which to gauge the refraction in any one target text. Muldoon's translations of the work of a contemporary – Ní Dhomhnaill – themselves a contribution both to making her work available to a much wider readership, and, more generically, to making work originally written in the Irish language obtain a broader recognition, cannot be expected to register the irreverence and appropriative transgressiveness that so often characterise contemporary versions of canonical authors. This does not mean that Muldoon's versions in *The Astrakhan Cloak* do not include verbal markers of his recognisable style, even of his referential range: slang peculiar to the target language emerges occasionally – 'the life of Reilly', 'all's hunky-dory' (1992: 31, 43); ludic onomatopoeia – 'so full of vrouw-vroom' (35) – reminds the reader here and there of the translator's distinctive verbal inventiveness; in one or two cases the translator opts for aspects of layout and lineation that deviate from his calquing of Ní Dhomhnaill's stanzaic arrangement (33, 75); and Muldoon cannot resist the inclusion of a few discreet allusions to his 'own' work, most

prominently through the phrase 'the acrostical capercaillie', which unequivocally refers to his acrostic poem 'Capercaillies', in Part I of *Madoc* (198–9).[33]
These aspects are, however, the exceptions that prove the rule: Muldoon's
versions of Ní Dhomhnaill's poems broadly abide by the discretion proper
to the ancillary role, literary as much as cultural, that the imbalance in
global circulation between poetry written in Irish and in English inevitably
prescribes for an ethically and politically aware translation into the global
idiom, by a male poet, of the work of a woman poet writing in the minority language of their common culture – which was in fact the language in
which the young Muldoon wrote his first poems.[34]

When the Pie Was Opened, however, presents a quite different case.
Although some of the poems that Muldoon opts to translate can hardly be
said to be well-known, they are canonical (some of the more arcane pieces
are credited with a foundational or iconic value within their respective
literary traditions) and historically or culturally remote. This helps justify
the dislocation that coincides with the transit of the gaze from left to right
of the facing pages (besides *The Astrakhan Cloak*, this is the only other case
in which Muldoon publishes translations in a bilingual format). One of
Muldoon's thematic emphases in the pamphlet is (in the terms of his preface) 'the sexual life of a male' (2008: 10), glimpsed from the perspectives
afforded by poems originally in Latin, Old English and medieval Welsh, and
in different registers – among which humour arguably prevails.[35] Muldoon
revisits Ovid, although this time to render one of the best-known episodes
of the *Amores* (1.5) (also translated by Derek Mahon as section I of his 'Ovid
in Love' – Mahon 1999: 79). Muldoon's version has similar features to his
other translations from Latin sources: the regularity of interpolated rhyme
is balanced against flowing narrative lines, with the occasional present-
day colloquialism ('We'd soon be dog-tired' – 2008: 25). The poem's very
content, and the humorous cynicism of Ovid's account of an afternoon
sexual tryst, entail, however, that this appealing but otherwise unobtrusive
version easily acquires a broader resonance in the semantic economy of a
brazenly androcentric pamphlet. Indeed, the overarching tone of *When the
Pie Was Opened* queries rather than stands qualified by the female speaker
of the enigmatic 'Wulf and Eadwacer', an Anglo-Saxon verse complaint
that Muldoon reads as concerning 'a woman caught between two very hard
men indeed' (10); but its most resonant expression is to be found in 'The
Cock', the fourteenth-century Welsh poet Dafydd ap Gwilym's address to
his penis. In Muldoon's version, the poem opens with an exasperated *interrogatio* – 'For crissakes, cock, must you be kept under lock / and key round
the clock [. . .]?'– followed by the rhetorical tour-de-force required by the
attempt to match and convey the source text's characteristic procedures.
These include a heavy dependence on alliteration, assonance, internal
and end rhyme, which, once replicated in English, leave the poem poised
between outrageous celebration and outraged invective: 'bud-tip, jerking

fore and aft, / bandy and blunt, godawful post / central pillar for which no girl is hindmost' (2008: 15).

The subject matter of 'The Cock', together with its rhetorical ambivalence – self-address, or expostulation with an external entity? – is pursued but fundamentally inflected in Muldoon's 'own' poem 'The Balls', which combines rumination on the modern male's sexual and social identity with a confessional feature: the scary prospect of a testicular tumour. However, the poem also includes a transition from private (parts) to public, as information on the average position of left and right (testicles) combines with the etymological insight that *testis* can mean 'witness' – which places the poem also in the domain of political awareness and civic concerns. This is the other main dimension of *When the Pie Was Opened*, materialised in two more translations and one related poem. In 'Gypsies', from Canto VII of a sequence by the twentieth-century Greek poet Kostis Palamas (author of the Olympic anthem, hailed by some as the national poet), Muldoon selects a few stanzas on tinkers that allow him to bring the poem to bear on the 'travellers' of the Irish social landscape (who also emerge in the pamphlet's title poem). In fact, 'Gypsies' – a piece on nomads, peripheral presences in a variety of locations – is preceded by 'The Wandering Navvy', Muldoon's version of a traditional Gaelic song on the predicament of a figure who embodies the subaltern condition in the Irish historical imagination. These two versions (one from the Irish tradition, another from a distant, Mediterranean literature) confirm that Muldoon finds it possible in his translations to include politically informed lament or denunciation with a degree of explicitness that is pointedly absent from his poetry. He thus ventriloquises on how some were 'forced to part / With what little [they] had already' ('The Wandering Navvy', 2008: 33), and also, with an even rarer prospect of redress, hails 'Music' (an obvious metonym for poetry) for showing 'how the displaced and dispossessed may come into their own' ('Gypsies', 2008: 37).[36]

Earlier chapters have strongly suggested that the release, in and through translation, of discourses that the poets otherwise repress can be enhanced by a shift in genre – and that drama, in particular, has more easily proved an apt generic medium for the committed voice. Muldoon's ventures into dramatic forms already amount to a significant part of his oeuvre, and they will be the focus of the remainder of this chapter. They comprise his play *Six Honest Serving Men* (1995), his translation of Aristophanes's *The Birds* (1999), and three texts that, although they are not translations, are scripts of an intermedial nature whose affinities with translation I will be strongly arguing: his libretti *Shining Brow* (1993), *Bandanna* (1999) and *Vera of Las Vegas* (2001). *The Birds*, the only interlingual translation among these, is also Muldoon's only version of Classical drama, and it is hardly irrelevant that (unlike other Northern Irish poet-translators in their Classical appropriations) Muldoon opts for satirical comedy, rather than tragedy.

The choice of comedy suggests a wish to steer clear of the more solemn sources of *pathos*, and it may be seen as coherent with the editorial simplicity of *The Birds*: the text is presented without any critical apparatus. This is a mute argument for self-sufficiency and an unencumbered reading, irrespective of whether one comes to Aristophanes's play for the first time and (so the translator implicitly vows) will find in the text all that one needs to understand it, or has a specialist's knowledge of it already, and will in that case be pitting Muldoon's version against other translations of this Athenian Old Comedy. As with Heaney's and Mahon's dramatic versions, the book's cover gives Muldoon the prominence usually accorded to an author, with a relevant addition: Muldoon translated Aristophanes 'with Richard Martin'. The acknowledged support of a Classicist indicates that Muldoon does not claim to have translated (alone) from the Greek, but (unlike Mahon) he has not opted either to work only intralingually from other English translations of the play.

Muldoon dedicates *The Birds* to fellow Northern Irish poet Tom Paulin, also a translator of Classical drama and an outspoken commentator on Ulster political traditions, the dedication suggesting Muldoon's willingness to confront Northern Ireland more directly in a satirical comedy than elsewhere in his work. Athenian Old Comedy was, after all, characterised by violent and nominal mockery of the ills at the heart of the *polis*, and Muldoon's Aristophanic version duly abounds in topicality, as a result of a systematic refraction that begins with names. These include puns on birdnames ('the Merganservant'), on types in contemporary youth culture ('a Birdnik'), on the forms and institutions of advanced democracy ('an Ombirdsman') and, of course, on famous characters in Irish lore, one of which has her name rewritten in a way that queries her ability to bring empowerment: 'Queen Maybe, *a birde-to-be*' (1999: 7).[37] Further, the name eventually coined for the 'new city-state' in the clouds confirms Muldoon's satirical domestication: 'Nebulbulfast' (1999: 42). The combination in these names of a strong Northern Irish reference with allusions to rather more global conditions is pursued in the verbal inventiveness of Muldoon's dialogues, which show the translator's awareness that Aristophanes writes a comedy of invective, for which Muldoon relies on a profusion of abuse that can be both locally specific in its Irishisms, or non-specific, but in every case energised by the consonantal emphasis of enumerative and alliterative insults: 'You hopeless hoor. You gomeril. You glipe'; 'Supergrouse, stoolpigeon, summons-server' (1999: 9, 66).

The play's abundant references to Belfast draw both on the city's former economic and civic traditions, and on the circumstances and discourses of the Troubles. Euelpides and Peisetairos introduce themselves as coming from 'a notable ship-building town', and the effort to build the new city in the clouds brings noises that are reminiscent of such activity ('the place sounded like a shipyard'), in which some of those who excel in their industry and commitment wear garments that allude to the masonic strand in Ulster Protestantism: 'the ducks laying bricks, wearing their mason's aprons' (1999: 14, 56). The language of the Troubles, on the other hand, emerges in its formulas of intolerance – as when a mock prayer is addressed to 'the sacred finch of Notaninch' (1999: 44), or when the 'geometer and astronomer' who proposes to carry out a land survey, asked if he thinks he is 'Gerry Mander', asks in turn whether there's still 'civil unrest' there, only to be told that they agree on one thing: 'They don't like dopes. Fuck the Dope. No Dope Here' (1999: 49–50). But the commonplaces of the peace process also emerge in Muldoon's text ('Come and gather up all this decommissioned material'; 'We won't be calling off the cease-fire' – 1999: 26–7), often intersecting with sceptically considered external mediations: the 'Ombirdsman' emerges as an opportunistic UN official, and the character that in other versions is called 'Iris, *goddess of the Rainbow, daughter of Zeus*', is here derisively hailed, and made a lewd offer: 'As for you, Miss Rainbow Warrior, [. . .] I'll ram and board you' (1999: 59).[38]

Muldoon's *The Birds* is also self-referential, carrying a host of discreetly planted literary references that foreground the play's own making, and involve allusions to variously situated texts and authors. The very project to set up a bird city in the clouds is described as 'both sweet and useful' (an echo of Horace's famous description of poetry's dual goal, *dulce et utile*), which suggests the unlikely political project in the dramatic fiction is interchangeable with its verbal account (1999: 23). And the play may retain, in a mild form, the potential for lampoon that characterised Aristophanic comedy: the emergence, at late stages in the plot, of a 'bard of high degree / and honeyed words / and strict measures', who quotes from Homer and claims to have 'been singing the praises of this city for a long time now'; and of the poet Kinesias, a self-styled 'highly renowned chorus master', who claims that 'poetry is airy, at once dark and shot through with light', and proposes to 'hurry [north] plowing the ether's furrowless furrow', provide readers with enough clues to infer that they may be satirical likenesses respectively of Longley and Heaney (1999: 45–6, 64–5) – in the latter case, reinforced by an echo of the formula 'walking on air', that Heaney and Muldoon have playfully hurled at each other.[39]

The Northern Irish Troubles, satirically evoked in passages of *The Birds*, had four years earlier been the direct subject matter of *Six Honest Serving Men*, centred on the clandestine activities of 'an Active Service Unit' of the IRA – and a completely different text from Muldoon's Aristophanic venture. It consists of a succession of 36 scenes, six times the number six mentioned in the title, which comes from an unlikely source, a poem by Rudyard Kipling in which the 'honest serving men' are the six interrogatives: 'Their names are What and Why and When / And How and Where and Who.'[40] The sequence of short scenes defines a paranoid setting, in which different groups of IRA men (and one woman, Kate) are watching one another and being watched, and speculating on the act of betrayal that led to the death of 'the Chief'

(Kate's dead husband). Their musings, mostly in rhymed verse (which relates eerily to the text's brutal or cynical tone), are dense in quotations – from Kipling, Shakespeare, Yeats, George Moore, nationalist ballads, even the American anthem. And indeed this play (as all the texts for performance that Muldoon has published, except *The Birds*), despite its liminal Irish setting, 'on the border of counties Armagh and Monaghan' (1995: 9), has an emphatic American connection. The transit, between Ireland and America, of some of the IRA volunteers seems to be somehow linked with the moment when 'The Chief was rubbed out in Omagh' (1995: 33); and those selfsame characters will reappear on the singularly American set of *Vera of Las Vegas*. *Six Honest Serving Men* 'was originally commissioned and produced by McCarter Theatre, Princeton, NJ' (1995: 8); and this setting for its première will certainly have lent a risqué but equivocal note to the moment in the play's first scene when one of the IRA men, prompted by wordplay, intones, in a stage-Irish accent (at whose expense is the joke?), the opening lines of 'Star-Spangled Banner'.

Muldoon's 'American drift' is nowhere more strikingly apparent than in his three published libretti. The operas not only result from a collaboration with American composer Aron Daric Hagen, they were also commissioned by American institutions, and their plots are constructed around American settings and (in two cases, at least) American themes. *Shining Brow*, *Bandanna* and *Vera of Las Vegas* deal with figures and circumstances proper to the American scene in all its diversity: high and popular culture, native Americans and WASPS, illegal aliens and pillars of the Establishment. But they also confirm the perception that the American scene in Muldoon's writing continues to be played out against a steady undercurrent of Irish reference. It is also tempting to argue a connection between the range of Muldoon's work and the space of his experience, as his move to the great American expanse is matched by texts whose actualisation depends on extensions from the verbal matter on the page to other spaces and other media.[41] With the exception of the intralingual rendering to be found in *Bandanna* (as described below), these libretti are not translations in any of the senses explored above; nor are they 'afterwritings' or intermedial renderings of previously existing work, but rather parallel, collaborative enterprises. And yet they are artefacts that await a full dramatic and musical staging (an activity that *has* been called 'translation' – Bassnett 1998: 94), and the intermedial relations that take place at various levels between composition and performance have strong affinities with some of the forms of intertextuality and re-signification studied in this book.

Muldoon's interest in diffuse boundaries and an equivocal arrangement of geographic and social space is common to the three libretti, in spite (or because) of their various historical and cultural settings: *Shining Brow* (1993) deals with a crucial episode in the life of a cultural icon of 'white', European-derived America – architect Frank Lloyd Wright – in a privileged social context and at a time of imminent change, the years before the First World War. *Bandanna* (1999) stages a private crisis against the backdrop of a troubled community in a 'tiny town on the border of the US and Mexico' in the internationally momentous year of 1968. And *Vera of Las Vegas* (premièred in 1996, published in 2001), set in the cultural and political present, puts on stage IRA volunteers, illegal immigrants in the US chased both by the immigration authorities and by rogue secret agents, as they spend a day in transit at the peculiar (or quintessential) American location, world capital of simulacra.

In *Shining Brow* the thematic relevance of space is inherent in Wright's professional ambition to organise space for the sake of art and human fulfilment. In the sonorous pleas for his art that Muldoon writes for the opera's protagonist this becomes tantamount to an obsession with 'integrity', with an 'organic' understanding of architecture, and with a belief in the universality of certain aesthetic and functional values. This universality can support inter-artistic and intermedial arguments, as when Wright refers to 'the poetry of architecture'; and it can also claim an intercultural, interlocal, transhistorical basis: 'the Sioux and the Shoshone / might have taught the Greeks and Romans / a lesson in harmony' (1993: 4). In the course of the opera, Wright repeatedly invokes native American tribes as models for the integration of his works in the landscape, and suggests that his art combines lessons from cultures in touch with nature with the more cerebral traditions of Western culture. Wright's claims to cultural and artistic syntheses include his invocation of a Welsh ancestry as another empowering element – hence his choice of a sixth-century bard's name, Taliesin (whose English version is 'Shining Brow'), for the house in Wisconsin where he briefly lived with Mamah Cheney, formerly the wife of a wealthy client. And the Celtic trump card, always potentially ironical with Muldoon, is also played by Wright with regard to the Irish origins of his former mentor, architect Louis Sullivan (1993: 73).

However, Muldoon's text and plot do not allow Wright to emerge as a coherent practitioner of a synthetic and eclectic art. His insistent recitation of native American names suggests that they have for him a totemic rather than substantial value. Further, the Celtic element translated to the New World proves ironically fatal: the Welsh house on a hill, Taliesin, becomes a death trap for Mamah Cheney and her children when it is set on fire by a man from Barbados with the name of a controversial Irish writer, Carleton – the cook about whom Mamah had mused: 'Can it be / that all the natives of Barbados / speak with an Irish brogue?' (1993: 62).[42] The text also suggests that the cook's disaffection and rage may have derived from Wright's and Mamah Cheney's racism (1993: 64), a serious shadow cast over Wright's claims to a culturally integrative art. Despite the inclusiveness of his discourse, Wright obtains in Muldoon's text a characterisation that suggests the creation rather than the crossing of boundaries, and is represented by the (fatal) confinement of walls.

The theme of boundaries and difficult transits is all-defining in *Bandanna* – indeed, the text arguably suffers from overuse of such phrases as 'the liminal zone', 'a liminal place', 'the thin red line', the '*zona media*'. This may reflect the currency of the concept of liminality in a variety of discourses, but conditions in the Tex-Mex borderline town make it clear that the divide is here no mere concept or verbal construct. The opera's Prologue indeed features 'the chorus of the Dispossessed and the Disappeared' and a small crowd of 'Illegal Immigrants' trying to cross by night the heavily guarded border, the time being that no-man's land of the *Dia de los Muertos*. The border's brutal actuality foregrounds also the distance between the privileged scene of *Shining Brow* and the deprived community of Latinos, 'white trash' and a few strays from other social groups that make up the social landscape of *Bandanna*. However, the two texts cannot be construed simply as seeking their enabling references respectively in high and popular culture. Indeed, the range of intertexts for *Bandanna* is broad, and it prominently includes high tragedy – Shakespeare's *Othello*, for which it provides a starkly simplified intralingual translation, discernible from the start in the opera's list of *dramatis personae*: if the name of Morales for the town's 'Latino chief of police' does not give the analogy away (at least until one realises the affinity between his name and 'Moro' or 'Moor'), 'Morales' white lieutenant' is called Jake (for Iago), 'Morales' white wife' is Mona (for Desdemona), her 'best friend' and 'Jake's Latino fiancée' is Emily (for Emilia), and 'Morales' Irish-American captain' is called Cassidy (for Cassio).

The Hiberno-Hispano-American dislocations of the English play set in Venice and Cyprus acquire clear contours from the start, and may in fact enhance some of the dimensions of conflict in Shakespeare's tragedy. Muldoon's libretto is obviously a less complex textual and dramatic artefact than Shakespeare's *Othello*; but this also means that the tragic design is all the more visible. An example can be found in an additional retributive element: Mona is strangled with the bandanna, the Tex-Mex version of Shakespeare's 'handkerchief', supposed hard evidence of Desdemona's (here plain Mona's) betrayal. Further, the inter-ethnic tension involves in *Bandanna* more than the central couple, through the derogatory remarks on Hispanics made by the Irish-American police officer who broadly corresponds to Cassio (1999: 8). This character (who thus invites an ethical indictment that hardly impends on his Shakespearean prototype) shows Muldoon alert to how complex the structures of prejudice can be: the oppressed in one part of the world can become the potential oppressors and promoters of discrimination elsewhere.

Cassidy is thus an example of how identities vary as a function of the relationships proper to the spaces within which we read them. He is not the only Irishman to prove this in Muldoon's libretti: in *Vera of Las Vegas*, two IRA terrorists who have been living illegally in the US have their bloody deeds gradually confirmed by themselves in snatches of dialogue and soliloquy (verifying the suspicion that impended on them in *Six Honest Serving Men*); nonetheless, their 'translation' to the medium and setting of *Vera of Las Vegas* reveals them as tacky, inadequate, almost endearing fools. This seems to be validated by the ultimate decision to rescue them from the hands of rogue secret service agents made by Doll, 'an undercover agent for the Immigration and Naturalization Service', and Vera, whose visiting card equivocally reads 'lapdancer' or LAPD – and whose gender proves equally elusive. But even before the two Provos benefit from such unlikely female/ maternal protection, their names construe them as (albeit dark) comedy characters. Since few readers will recognise that 'Taco' is the name for a rifle telescope, his name is bound to suggest the homonymous Mexican snack – as confirmed by his full name, Taco Bell; this formula also makes it more difficult for the lethal implications of his friend's name, Dumdum (a type of bullet), to be taken seriously (2001: passim).

The ambivalence of their names absolutely fits the uncertainty of these characters' situation in America, and even more the context in which they appear in this 'nightmare cabaret opera'[43]: New York to LA travellers in transit at Las Vegas, capital of kitsch and elusive images, where the vision of gorgeous Doll is enough to make the two Irishmen revise their assessment of the place from 'the middle of nowhere' to 'the centre-*fold*', 'the heart of America' (instances of a use of wordplay with which Muldoon disproves Auden's view that librettists had better avoid 'puns or double meanings' – Auden 1968: 92). The triumphant arrival of Afro-American Vera 'galloping out of the Celtic mist' (2001: 18) announces and anticipates a dumbfounding experience for which Dumdum can only seek an analogy in his home topography and climate: 'Mist is the word, Taco. We're in a bog. We're lost in a mist. / It makes no sense' (2001: 50). This theme of perplexity is recurrently balanced against a perception of pattern – in *Vera* as in the other libretti. If in *Bandanna* the Shakespearean source text provided a design that Muldoon retained and extended schematically in its Hispanic dislocation, *Vera of Las Vegas* has an underlying structure provided by diverse but hardly arbitrary musical, filmic and literary references. These often belong to mass culture – the music of U2, Neil Jordan's film *The Crying Game* – but Vera and Taco prove learned enough to know Shelley's 'Ozymandias' (an apt reference for a city which is itself a colossal body in the middle of a desert – 2001: 25), while Doll reveals that her mother, a down-and-out actress, named her after Dol Common, the prostitute-cum-swindler in Ben Jonson's *The Alchemist* (2001: 23). This facilitates the perception that all the characters' names are 'meaningful' – again, a major sign of a central unifying concept, at odds with the postmodern model of growth by random accretion whose inevitability the Vegas setting might suggest.

For reasons that go deeper than the tempting pun, 'design' is crucial in *Shining Brow*, and this theme is especially served by Wright's regular pronouncements on his art. They manifest his ambition for authorial original assertion, to leave a 'mark / on the clean slate of America' (1993: 14); his wish for an art of necessity, precision and balance: 'Form follows function. Form and function are one' (1993: 71); his plea for the artist's exceptionality, serving 'some new vision of order' (1993: 47). Some of these values would seem to be echoed in a text often quoted above, Muldoon's 1998 essay in which he half-apologetically subscribes to a few postulates of New Criticism and lambasts aspects of poststructuralism. But Muldoon provides a framework for Wright's verbal gestures that makes their excess and the man's self-infatuation apparent. On the scene of the Taliesin disaster, Edwin Cheney, former client and Mamah's deceived husband, opposes Wright's pretensions and forces upon him an acceptance of 'the haphazard', 'the randomness of things': Wright's weak rejoinder, 'The *seeming* randomness of things' (1993: 80), is followed by an acknowledgment of hubris, but leaves this crucial issue at an inconclusive point.

For this inconclusiveness to be itself pressed home as a compositional principle one may have to turn to Vera, embodiment of the liminal and hybrid. Discussing the deftness and ambition of gamblers, a chorus of casino girls announce Vera's power in terms that oppose her ease to the totalising designs of proponents of systems – who get 'caught up in schemes and scams and strategies and the so-called "study of form"' (2001: 29). However, the character's defining ambivalence remains to the end: her blasphemous self-description – 'I, Vera of Las Vegas, am the Way, / the Truth and the Light' – precedes an apparently essentialising plea: 'it's only through their outward forms / that things truly show themselves'; but this 'verity', predicated on the expectation that external design will reflect an inner essence, is promptly qualified by the acknowledgement that 'truth's a business that needs a little illusion, a little sleight-of-hand' (2001: 45). And this is itself a truism that most readers are bound to recognise as doing justice to the verbal and imaginative range of this poet and translator.

6

The Hand, the Voice, the Map: Ciaran Carson

The work of Ciaran Carson is an apt point of arrival for the reading proposed in this book for various reasons. The first, and simplest, is chronological. Although Carson is not the youngest (born in 1948, he is Paul Muldoon's senior by three years), he emerged as an influential voice in Northern Irish poetry at a time when the poets studied above had already become defining presences on the scene. This perception of a relatively late start is also due, rather peculiarly, to the attention obtained by his *second*, rather than his first collection. Indeed, the success enjoyed by Carson's *The Irish for No* (1987), published after a silence of 11 years, has meant that critical accounts of his work have made it a *de facto* inaugural book; and although its success prompted the relaunch (in 1988, as an expanded edition) of his 1976 collection, *The New Estate*, neither this retrieval of his first volume nor the inclusion of it at the beginning of the *Collected Poems* (2008) have revoked the perception that *The Irish for No* marked the inception, in diction as much as in themes, of a distinctive poetic writing.[1]

The critical currency of this notion of a deferred beginning, combined with Carson's own sharp attention to the dynamics of literary transmission and canonisation, has contributed to his alternating attitudes (assimilative or reactive in turn) towards a variety of literary models, Irish and otherwise. The strain of creating a distinctive voice from within a tradition so strongly marked by the previous generation was compounded by the fact that he first attracted attention with a piece of critical rather than poetic writing. With his much-quoted review of Heaney's *North*, in which he vehemently denounced the book's mythopoeic design and dubbed its author 'the laureate of violence', 'an anthropologist of ritual killing', 'a mystifier', Carson, a year before he published his first collection, began by inscribing his name on lists of *secondary* rather than primary sources for contemporary poetry (Carson 1975). The fact that his subsequent literary career earned him the position (in 2004) of first director of the Seamus Heaney Centre for Poetry at Queen's University, Belfast, with its appertaining professorship, confirms both the complexities of the Northern Irish literary scene and how central to it Carson has become over the past two decades (he is, after all, one of the two Northern Irish poets in this book who have not emigrated).

In its chosen referents, formal options and generic breadth, Carson's oeuvre helps explain its author's acquired centrality to the tradition and the critical pertinence of addressing it in the closing chapter of a book on poetry, space and translation in Northern Irish writing. Carson has consistently focused on linguistic perplexities, questioning both the internal relations within the language system and the ability of language to refer to the dire reality of a site of struggle and differing narratives of identity. The titles of his collections have pursued his interest in the politics of language, often taken from the perspective of verbal particularities, as with *The Irish for No*: the phrase refers to an interlingual discontinuity, since, as Carson himself has explained, the Irish language has no words for 'yes' or 'no', which entails that affirmation or negation have to be signified in more indirect ways (Brandes 1990: 84). Carson's alertness to the politico-historical complications of language is sharpened by the unusual relationship between Irish and English as (respectively) the first and second languages of his personal, linguistic and literary *Bildung* – a biographical particularity that has come to the fore in some of his work, notably in *First Language* (1993). This was Carson's fourth collection, and the combination of private and public implications suggested by its title is characteristic of this poet's practice: Carson's personal experience (unusually, even among nationalists) of having spoken no language but Irish in the first few years of his life converges with an allusion to facts of territory and power, since the book's title also refers to the first official language (Irish) of the Republic, prompting reactions of identification or rejection in a Northern Irish context. Carson's interest in uses of language that bear on prevalent practices in the territory of his experience and imagination was also present in the title of his third collection, *Belfast Confetti* (1989), derived from a local colloquialism for 'The subversive half-brick, conveniently hand-sized, [which] is an essential ingredient of the ammunition known as "Belfast confetti"' (179);[2] a festive designation is thus found to refer ironically to the violence of local politics. A similar coalescence of celebration and aggression occurs in *The Twelfth of Never* (1998), since the title chosen by Carson for his sixth collection of originals points jokingly to a utopian circumstance, in time and in space – which is yet firmly inscribed in the calendar, in the territorial sense and the sectarian practices of Ulster, since it evokes the date (Twelfth of July, aka 'the Twelfth') when Protestant groups march to commemorate William of Orange's 1690 victory at the Boyne.

The way in which his titles foreground the intertwinings of language, territory, history, and politics also reveals Carson's playfulness, which he combines with an obsessive interest in designs, indeed in master plans. The tense relation between these two dimensions has led critics to discuss the relevance to his writing of notions of the postmodern;[3] this, then, links his work to Muldoon's, one of several affinities between the two poets that were especially highlighted in the earlier years of Carson's career (cf. Brandes 1990: 79). In Carson's work, however, a concern with plan and pattern has proved more persistent – or at least more transparent – than in Muldoon's; prominent examples include the alphabetical sequences that frame his collection *Opera Et Cetera* (1996), 'Letters from the Alphabet' and 'Opera'; the glosses on the work of a pioneer war correspondent that structure and inform *Breaking News* (2003); and the two sequences of 35 poems, employing exactly the same titles and in the same order, that make up *For All We Know* (2008). This element of design has also characterised Carson's translations, which, in their scale, range and regularity, have become arguably an even more defining part of his output than that of his Northern Irish forebears and contemporaries. It is indeed design that stands out from *The Alexandrine Plan* (1998), a collection of translations of sonnets by Rimbaud, Baudelaire and Mallarmé arranged in two sections of 16 interpolated with two sections of 18 sonnets. But the 'plan' or 'design' in his translations concerns more than pattern and arrangement – it also involves an appropriative purpose, arguably in the service of self-canonisation. If *The Alexandrine Plan* demonstrates formal mastery in the rewriting of verse that historically laid the ground for poetic modernity, Carson's more recent major translations – of Dante's *Inferno* (2002) and of *The Táin* (2007) – show him aiming at major works respectively of Christendom and of Gaelic culture. The compounded bid for centrality that this reveals would seem to emulate Heaney's translational projects (rather than the postmodern Muldoon's), and indeed the blurb of *The Inferno of Dante Alighieri* claims that Carson's version 'deserves comparison with Heaney's *Beowulf* and Hughes's *Tales from Ovid*' (Carson 2002: n.p.). Before addressing the relational play of Carson's designs as a translator, this chapter will, once again, interrogate the relation between the work of a contemporary Northern Irish poet and the empirical and imaginative territory of his writing.

6.1   A poetics of wandering

As mentioned above, Ciaran Carson is one of the two poets studied in this book who have spent most of their lives in their native city – the other being Longley; but, whereas Longley's choice space is home, and the home from home provided by a natural landscape in the west of Ireland, Carson makes the outdoor scenarios of Belfast a dominant reference in his poetry. Although this concern was already apparent in *The New Estate*, Carson's fascination with the meanders of the city, and with mapping as the prime model for other representations of the urban layout, was just one of the strands that appear in the varied diction of his first collection. Carol Rumens's characterisation of early Carson as 'a quiet, solid worker in the groves of Heaney' (Rumens 1999: 86) may reflect such features as his attraction at that stage to the epiphanies of daily life, to metaphors of creation drawn from the skills of traditional craftsmen ('Shaping it out of the darkness' – 27), or to the mouthed harshness of a consonantal diction where 'coarse-grained syllables [. . .] squelch and rasp like shingle' (36); but one might as well find in poems from *The New Estate* a hint of Mahon (in the bleak landscape of 'a terminal moraine' or of life on 'the new industrial estate' – 34–5), or indeed of Longley (in the domestic keeping of 'things needed for a wedding or a funeral', emblems of family and memory such as 'The Patchwork Quilt' – 28, 72–3). In hindsight, though, the anxious urban settings that were to prevail in the distinct formal environment of Carson's poetic refashioning (after 1987) can already be found in an earlier poem like 'The Bomb Disposal'. The title is itself a reminder that Carson is one of the few Northern Irish poets who have regularly drawn on the concrete consequences of terrorism on daily life – the consequences that are eerily hinted at in a conflation of mechanical and somatic, as the bomb's 'body' and 'heart' are listened to (40). Confrontation with the destructive device, an all-too-physical presence that spells absence, is here troped as fraught communication, an attempt to 'read' a 'message', as the bomb's 'threaded veins' are visually considered, 'like print'; and the textual analogy, employed for the bomb's layout, is promptly followed by the cartographic, as the urban setting under threat of erasure is seen as indistinct from its representation: 'the city is a map of the city' (40).

Language and the city, in their mutually mirrored circuits, prevail in Carson's work from his second collection onwards, the very relevance acquired by *topography* highlighting its root meaning as a 'writing of place', which Carson considers at various historical stages. Data from local history regularly emerge in his poetry from the late 1980s, assisted by the narrative propensity of the unusually long line that first characterised *The Irish for No* and remained a staple of his prosody for more than a decade (apparently abandoned in *Breaking News*, only to be retrieved in *For All We Know*).[4] This narrative/historiographic drift has incorporated etymological inquiries into place names, as instances of a rapport between language and territory that is found to depend partly on chance, partly on determination: a prose piece on the river Farset – the name of which accounts for the second syllable in Bel*fast* – considers in succession (and in terms that consciously verge on the pedantic) all the possible root meanings of a watercourse that divides the sectarian territories of the two traditions. Such riven territory can also be known or reconnoitred visually, the poet offering temporally aware accounts of the distinct views presented by the city. At least two poems – 'Patchwork' and 'Ambition' (119–22, 138–42) – evoke the childhood experience of an uphill climb that allows the city to be seen from the heights, in its mixture of 'terraces and furrows' (the description owes its pastoral overtones to the supposedly retrieved gaze of the child, combined with the suggestion that elements of rurality survive in the urban plan); and this broader recognition of the urban topography (otherwise encountered piecemeal and at close range) expressly prompts the analogy with gazing at a map. However, the actuality of the city, even when visually considered as layout, becomes distinct from its cartographic representation by virtue of the dynamics of urban renovation and the obliterations brought about by terrorism: 'Today's plan is already yesterday's' (125); 'I glimpsed a map of Belfast / In the ruins' (99). Subject to 'rubble and erasure', 'Maps and street directories are suspect' (165).

Immersion in the urban space ultimately entails a knowledge that ranges from the abstract to the fully sensorial. The city wanderings of the ostensibly autobiographical subject afford both tactile immediacy and a cognitive gain that bears concomitantly on space and self. Indeed, these perambulations are presented as a formative experience that balances the ambition of totality against a perception of trauma and truncation, which accords with the scarred territory over which such acknowledgement of self unfolds: 'I know this place like the back of my hand, except / My hand is cut off at the wrist' (101). This experience involves not only a relation between self and environment, but also between self and others, with some emphasis on a particular presence/absence that conflates private and public histories: the poet's father. Carson conjures him into several poems, including one entitled 'Ambition' – 'I think I'm starting, now, / To know the street map with my feet, just like my father' (141) – and also the closing piece of the sequence 'Letters from the Alphabet': 'I am in the archaic footprints / Of my postman father' (309). Carson's descent from a man whose job involved circulating self and scripts through the urban maze is thus included in his coterminous explorations of identity, space and language; and it clinches the connections between roaming, reading and knowing – all the more so when the 'postman father' is revealed to have been a fervent supporter of Esperanto, and the person who ensured that Irish was the young Carson's 'first language'.[5]

The first stages in the poet's formative trajectory are in fact evoked in a poem entitled 'Second Language', an account of the half-remembered, half-imagined transition from 'English not being yet a language' to the empowerment brought by control of the medium that was to define his craft. It is troped in epiphanic terms: 'I woke up, verbed and tensed with speaking English; I lisped the words so knowingly'; 'The future looms into the mouth incessantly' (216–17). The dreamlike mindscape sketched in this account, in which hindsight lends some narrative coherence to inevitably dim memories, is represented with a profusion of linguistic and metapoetic images. Although the strictly monolingual stage (that of the 'unforked tongue' and 'a single star' glimpsed from the window) is imagined as preconscious, the hazy verbal and visual surroundings of the young child's earliest memories include his forebears' interest in a 'convoluted genealogy' represented as 'wordy whorls and braids and skeins and spiral helices', and this rich synaesthesia is extended to bolting 'Alexandrine tropes', the star's 'acoustic perfume' and a 'stanzaic-papered wall' (214). But the awakening brought by English and formal schooling is remembered as coinciding with an awareness of a specific and very material landscape, beyond the cocoon provided by family and nursery – the Belfast industrial landscape, its iconic shapes and mechanisms consistently assimilated to the measures and rhythms that inscribe them in verse, the phonetic and prosodic resources that provide them with verbal correlatives:

> Shipyard hymns
> Then echoed from the East: gantry-clank and rivet-ranks,
> Six-County hexametric
> Brackets, bulkheads, girders, beams, and stanchions;
> convocated and Titanic
> [. . .]
> Ratlines, S-twists, plaited halyards, Z-twists, catlines; all had
> their say.
>
> (214–15)

This compressed account of the poet's *Bildung* thus incorporates echoes of MacNeice's 'Carrickfergus' (with its grudging acknowledgment of a Belfast origin, and of a skyline of 'mountain' and 'gantries' – MacNeice 2007: 55), but also of the 'lines of script like briars coiled in ditches', and the 'pre-reflective stare' of Heaney's 'Alphabets' (Heaney 1987: 2–3); and ultimately of Joyce's *Portrait*, in particular when 'Latin conjugations' combine with the Angelus to become, in a later passage of Carson's poem, synecdoches of a Catholic education: 'I inhaled *amo, amas, amat* in quids of *pros* and *versus* and *Introibos / Ad altare Dei*' (215). The enhanced cultural and literary resonance that the poem ultimately acquires confirms the notion that the poet derives the resources that allow him to characterise his circumstance directly from the materially highlighted sounds and inscriptions of the evoked early development of a combined sense of language and self.

In an interview given in 1991, at a time when *The Irish for No* and *Belfast Confetti* had already consolidated his insistence on reading reality and the urban layout as graphic material, Carson offered a remark that fully converged with the understanding of mapping as representation that has prevailed in postmodern geography: 'For a map to work, it has to use shorthand, or symbols, or metaphors, and in this it resembles poetry' (Ormsby 1991: 5). One of the poems that had impressed this perception on Carson's readers was 'Linear B', titled after the name of an ancient system of writing, but possibly also bringing in the initial for Belfast (and jokily balancing a sinuous trajectory through the city, mimicked by cryptic inscriptions, against the implied straightness of a 'beeline'). Under this metascriptural title,

Carson's persona observes the familiar 'zig-zags circle' of another's repeated route through the city – 'Threading rapidly between crowds [. . .], reading / Simultaneously, and writing' – authoring a maze of inscriptions: 'Squiggles, dashes, question-marks, dense as the Rosetta stone' (95). The mutual mirroring of walking and writing suggested by their dual practice sets out more clearly a tension experienced in both ventures – between aimlessness and linearity, communication and encryption. Carson puzzles over the meaning that may lurk behind punctuation marks or other graphic signs that uncannily become detached from the verbal (con)texts in which they ordinarily play their ancillary role towards signification: the figure observed in 'Linear B' is said to be 'writing', and yet the inscribed page yields no text.

When the urban setting for such physical and verbal rambling is also a site of mayhem, this uncertainty over goal and meaning becomes specified as doubt over the ability to signify in a context of random obliterations, as city and text are seen concomitantly to explode into their (now discontinuous, hence no longer meaningful) constituent parts:

> Suddenly as the riot squad moved in, it was raining exclamation
> marks,
> Nuts, bolts, nails, car-keys. A fount of broken type. And the
> explosion
> Itself – an asterisk on the map. This hyphenated line, a burst
> of rapid fire
>
> (93)

The cartoon-like scene envisioned in these lines from 'Belfast Confetti' has its playfulness cancelled by the perception that graphic exuberance is here the correlative of terror and its blights on the city – as on the flesh of its denizens (a disturbing nexus between apparently ludic writing and human suffering that we have also found in Muldoon). Tropes of language and print are systematically used to represent the consequences of acts of terror (and the forms of state harassment that it spawns), as streets are 'blocked with stops and colons' and the self as citizen and writer experiences aporia, identity puzzlement, disorientation in an otherwise familiar urban setting: 'What is / My name? Where am I coming from? Where am I going? A fusillade of question-marks' (93).

This closing line is one of the various occurrences of interrogation (by police or militia) in Carson's Troubles-related writing, and such use of language in the city compounds the stark perception that the poet's wanderings are no *flânerie* – both because they are ruled by anxiety, rather than ludic unconcern, and because mobility cannot be carefree and indeterminate.[6] Carson is certainly aware of Northern Irish precedents in the poetic representation of checkpoint incidents, prominently recurrent in Heaney: as memories of intrusive police control in 'The Ministry of Fear' (1975: 64–5), as hypothesis ('a faked road block?') for the sectarian murder of a cousin in 'The Strand at Lough Beg' (1979: 17), and as civic and scriptural allegory in 'From the Frontier of Writing' (1987: 6). Carson's most extended take on this topos emerges as sectarian interrogation in 'Question Time', another apparently autobiographical piece that comes across as an instance of lyrical journalism, the use of prose compounding its sense of stark actuality; however, the element of report is mitigated and qualified by Carson's interest in exploring the metaphorical interrelations of text, self and map. Ironically titled after a parliamentary routine, 'Question Time' records the menacing informal checkpoint faced after an unthinkingly casual crossing of sectarian lines: knowing the space one moves in, and control over every move is here a matter of life and death, the perception of danger enhanced by the fact that the harassment is carried out by activists from the poet's own community. Proof that he belongs to the tribe, crucial for Carson's autobiographical persona to be released unharmed, is provided by verbal cartography, close description of a neighbourhood, street by street, house by house – a test that sees the map, elsewhere troped as exchangeable with the space it represents, enter a new metonymy and become the self under threat of erasure:

> I am this map which they examine, checking it for error, hesitation, accuracy; a map which no longer refers to the present world, but to a history, these vanished streets; a map which is this moment, this interrogation, my replies. Eventually I pass the test.
>
> (170)

A polarised territory, defined by sharp dividing lines, confronts the autobiographical subject with the risks that inhere in a detachment from the binary geography of sectarianism; revealingly, a poem in the same book includes the (literally graphic) remark: 'I am a hyphen, flitting here and there' (163).

The possibility of half-way, hybrid positions that can be acknowledged without discomfort is consigned to the realm of vision or utopia in 'The Ballad of HMS *Belfast*', where metaphors for the ship's dual engine are literary – 'each system was a back-up for the other, auxiliarizing verse with prose' – and passengers consist of 'Catestants and Protholics' that are 'bribe[d] with the Future' and hanker for 'Zanzibar and Montalban', 'Vallambroso or Gibraltar' (274–6). But the persona awakes to find himself a convict 'on board the prison ship *Belfast*' (277), and his delusion of release and world travel a refashioning of the *aisling* or 'vision' of the Gaelic poetic tradition. Offering more frequent and literal representations of his Belfast here and now than other contemporary Northern Irish poets, Carson has nonetheless regularly balanced his place against a variety of actual or imaginary elsewheres; this has happened both in his verse and prose, and such spatial play is often combined with a temporal correlative. For the title of his poetry collection *The Twelfth of Never*, Carson picked a phrase that signifies the opposite of the set meanings that a special date (a red-letter day) will usually evoke. A formula that would otherwise involve memory and commemoration is given a content that makes it prospective, evoking (rather than a fixed past, in time and meaning) an indefinite and unrealisable future, a *uchronia* – with potentially libertarian implications that also carry a spatial import: 'There is a green hill far away' (351).

These are the opening words of the collection, from a poem where Carson also declares that, in this world, 'everything is metaphor and simile'. The nexus of substitution and dislocation suggested by this rhetorical description overarches the various historical settings and scenarios represented throughout the collection, in the consistently pursued format and rhythms of the sonnet in alexandrines. It is about Ireland, certainly, with some emphasis on the 1798 rebellion, the folk song and balladry associated with it, and its revolutionary French connection. But the volume's places and times can be more remote, including imperial but also present-day Japan, the intriguing setting of the Opium Wars, and a few other allusions to British colonial history. These become related to the Northern Irish imagination and its iconography through the poppy, a powerful insignia of remembrance and mournful commemoration of war scenarios, with their multitudes of the fallen, besides being 'the emblem of Peace' (352). But it is also as the source of opium, and the delirium or hallucination that this provokes, that the poppy rather jokily accounts for the dislocations – in time and settings, texts and media – on which the collection repeatedly draws. This is a connection for which Carson also has a Northern Irish precedent in Paul Muldoon's allusions to 'magic mushrooms' and 'horse', apropos of moments in which ordinary relations of time and space are suspended.[7]

The trope of delirious transit is particularly prominent in two of Carson's prose works, *Fishing for Amber* (1999) and *Shamrock Tea* (2001), which defy classification, to varying degrees blending fictional plots with autobiography, memoirs and cultural commentary – often brought together by a mock erudite, over-informative attitude. The narrating voice slides over times, places, events, areas of knowledge, sometimes prompted by a coincidence or the loosest of associations, the source of which can be an altered perception. In *Fishing for Amber* the Dutch Golden Age, and the rise of genre painting that marks it, provide the historical and visual backdrop for such referential surfing (for reasons that also explicitly include Amsterdam's current reputation for easily available intoxications). A passage in the opening chapter recalls a childhood belief linking an envisaged abrupt dislocation with perceptions that defy 'objective' sensorial apprehension: 'So, as children, we believed the mirrored altitude of puddles [. . .] were portals to Australia, through which we could dive, had we the correct magic formula, to emerge in a water-mirage trembling in an arid desert'. The 'dream voyage to this nether world' swiftly connects with the present circumstances of the adult author-narrator, en route to the Netherlands, who acknowledges on the same page that 'I wake with a jolt as my KLM flight hits an air-pocket over Amsterdam' (1999: 6).

Carson's following prose book, the equally intriguing though (this time) unequivocally fictional *Shamrock Tea* (2001), also centres on vision in its combined physical and metaphysical senses. In *Fishing for Amber* the pictorial emphasis materialised in descriptions of a large number of seventeenth-century Dutch paintings, but in *Shamrock Tea* it takes the form of obsessive attention to a single – but probably the best-known – fifteenth-century Flemish painting, Van Eyck's *Portrait of Giovanni Arnolfini and his Wife* (which around the same time, by coincidence, became an implicit reference in Muldoon's 'Anthony Green: *The Second Marriage*'). *Shamrock Tea* does have a narrative plot, based on the fantastic adventures of youthful characters that, in mid-twentieth-century Ireland, prompted by adults with a half-esoteric, half-political agenda, take the inebriating 'shamrock tea' and (through the focal point provided by the convex mirror on the back wall of the Arnolfini portrait) get sucked into Van Eyck's scene and (literally) go on a trip, travelling in time and space to fifteenth-century Flanders.

In a self-reflective passage of *Shamrock Tea*, Carson signalled his attraction to 'serendipity' (Horace Walpole's famous coinage for 'curious or happy chains of events') since his characters, 'as they travelled, were always making discoveries, by accident or sagacity, of things they were not in quest of' (2001: 137). Carson's penchant for the unexpected, liminal and ambiguous, often conjured through language whose inventiveness mimics its object, has signal affinities with Paul Muldoon – although Carson's acknowledged closeness to the setting of the Troubles is one of the features that keep his poetics distinct from Muldoon's ostensible aloofness. Muldoon is certainly a presence behind Carson's decision, a decade after *Mules*, to centre the narrative design of 'Dresden', the opening piece of *The Irish for No*, on two twins named respectively Horse and Mule (77–81). In the same book, the notion of lineage and family becomes subject to an apparent triviality that nonetheless provides the basis for a relational construction of identity in terms that Muldoon might not repudiate: 'He had / A second cousin's hands, or a cousin's twice removed, an uncle's way of walking: / In other words, he was himself' (114). And this play of shifting identities also occurred in the sequence 'Letters from the Alphabet', in *Opera Et Cetera*, through wordplay on one of the letters – 'I call you Double You' – after which the persona declares: 'I think I know ambivalence' (306).

Carson, however, confronts division and sectarianism in more openly (and nominally) political terms than one would find in Muldoon, as made clear by his lines on a borderline situation in '*Jacta Est Alea*': 'It was one of those puzzling necks of the wood where the South was in the North'; 'my heart lay in the Republic // While my head was in the Six, or so I was inclined'; 'We end up talking about talk. We stagger on the frontier. He is pro. I am con' (316). Indeed, it is arguable that, despite Carson's apparent departure from Heaney's discourse of identity and place, Heaney may prove an enabling reference for the element of anticipated redress, even of ecumenicism in the younger poet's continued confrontation with Northern Ireland; an instance of envisioned hope can be glimpsed in the (apparently flawed) hypothesis, mooted in one of Carson's toponymic ramblings, that 'Belfast' and 'Dublin' might be etymologically related, two versions of the same place name, polarisation and distance overcome by the lore of language (155–6).

Uplift was the defining spirit of 'Envoy', in which Carson, at the close of *The Twelfth of Never*, recalled the collection's allegorical journey 'through the Land of Nod and Wink', and presented its motley gallery of 'beings from the lowest to the highest rung' as standing now 'with their long ladder propped up against the gates of Heaven', 'queued up to be rewarded for their *grand endeavour*' (427 – my emphasis). This joking assumption of the chiliastic theme, explicitly associated with the effects of '*papaver somniferum*' (the poppy), was arguably pursued in the prose of Carson's two following books, *Fishing for Amber* and *Shamrock Tea*. However, readers would be hard pressed to detect it in the stark concision and dark settings that characterised his next verse collection, *Breaking News* (2003). And yet an ethical and political aspiration, hence a concern with the future, superimposes design and a sense of 'endeavour' on what otherwise might seem the book's brooding and fragmentary review of ruined and death-stricken scenarios.

Breaking News flaunted an immediately apparent difference *vis-à-vis* Carson's earlier verse through a discursive and prosodic characteristic: instead of the long (very long) lines favoured by Carson in previous books, his gaze on experience, identity and history in this collection emerges in such short lines that a whole poem may contain a shorter utterance than any one of his earlier distichs. The ensuing sense of fragmentation is sometimes reinforced by parataxis and scarcity of punctuation – although Carson's writing retains a regular syntax. The clipped diction that results from this new prosodic and graphic option is proper to a rhetoric of understatement that is again in direct contrast to the verbal profusion of earlier Carson: where the sonnets of *The Twelfth of Never* often aimed to expose the brutality of a historical predicament beneath a playful and garrulous surface, the hyperconcise poems of *Breaking News*, arranged like vertical lines on a nearly empty page, derive their rhetorical clout from the silent suggestion that this is the only acceptable verbal response to the book's chosen subject matter.

And the subject is war, gloomily considered from the dismal standpoint of an area of Belfast where (when the book was written) urban development was about to erase streets whose names, remote but for their long-standing inscription on the city plan, were mementoes of past imperial campaigns (dear to the unionist sense of history), now uttered, on the verge of their disappearance, like a roll call of the dead: 'Sevastopol / Crimea // Inkerman /

Odessa // Balkan / Lucknow' (466). A now familiar strategy entails that a book evoking distant locations, and paying tribute to a nineteenth-century Anglo-Irish journalist who covered the Crimean war, begins with a poem entitled 'Belfast'; while, through a meaningful symmetry, its most explicit and concise phrasing for Carson's design when setting up a tension between the near and the far occurs under the title 'Exile', where the persona walks the streets, lists their names and declares:

> all lie
> in ruins
>
> and
> it is
>
> as much
> as I can do
>
> to save
> even one
>
> from oblivion
>
> (466)

These closing lines leave no doubt that they serve a purpose of memorialisation, which monumentalises the poems themselves.

Memory and a strong sense of design likewise inform Carson's collection *For All We Know* (2008), but in this case the focus is on a private story – albeit with prominent historical backgrounds. The book's underlying narrative of the meeting of a couple at a second-hand clothes shop, and their subsequent love story (until the woman's death in a car crash) has to be organised in the reader's mind from the retrospective but non-sequential account as it emerges, its episodes in an intricate order, through the two sequences of 35 poems, each sequence with the same line-up of titles. The sense of an unfolding plot (even if it has to be reconstructed from a complex master plan) is assisted by Carson's return to the sprawling, discursive line out of which he opted in *Breaking News*. In the same way that an understanding of the book's temporal design requires reordering (re-collecting), so the challenges posed to the reader's attention also derive from the various spaces against which the couple's relationship unfolds.

The book's locales include Troubles-stricken Belfast, the sound of helicopters a recurrent synecdoche of the city (here as elsewhere in Carson); Paris, captured in vignettes both of May 1968 and (long before the love story's present time) of V-E Day[8]; East Germany, from the aftermath of the Second

World War to reunification, through the Cold War; and snowy Alpine settings that concern both the woman's origins and the couple's joint experience, and suggestively relate to the Mont Blanc pens sold by the recurrent figure of a travelling salesman.[9] References to these particular artefacts contribute to the presence of scriptural tropes as a part of the overwhelming emphasis on language – the 'forest of language' (496, 516) – throughout the collection, ranging from fictional redeployment of Carson's family tale of a father and mother who speak different languages, to the uses and perceptions of foreign tongues (mostly French and German) in various contexts, wordgames, and a penchant for the rhetorical figure of diaphora (with the shifting meanings between homonyms that it affords).

> You're not from around here, I said. No, from elsewhere, you said.
> As from another language, I might have said, but did not.
>
> > (503)

These lines equating the local with the linguistic as grounds for a sense of identity, and the foreignness of places with that of languages, occur in the first of the two poems entitled 'Pas de Deux', which records the pair's first meeting – and this makes the equation they encapsulate a fundamental semantic strand in the book.

For All We Know obsessively rehearses the perplexities of language and identity as exchangeable: the puzzlement in several poems about 'double lives' (496) and the uncanny experience of confronting a *Doppelgänger* (510, 523) runs parallel to an uncertainty over communication that accommodates a pun on 'lingua franca' (498) as easily as it does the casual phrase, gauge of a strained relationship: 'Sometimes I wonder if we speak the same language' (556). The verbal is itself a site of struggle – 'Still the interminable wrestle with words and meanings', as acknowledged (first in the interrogative, then in the affirmative) in the two poems entitled 'Le Mot Juste' (506, 553). This sense of the strain involved in a meaningful use of language appears bound up with the collection's obsessive relation to secondariness: the couple meet when buying second-hand clothes, and sport a recurrent interest in heirlooms, used or repeatedly worn; some of these prompt analogies between indoor and outdoor experience, erotic and civic life, epitomised in the equation of maps with quilts (525, 573) – an interest again redolent of Longley, whose quilts epitomise the comforts of continuity and transmission.[10] As regards verbal recurrence, however, the comfort of the known is replaced with a measure of anxiety over the fact that *true* repetition can hardly occur without difference. The book's first poem (which bears the teasing title 'Second Time Round', duly repeated at the beginning of Part II) includes the remark: 'For one word never came across as just itself, but you / would put it over as insinuating something else' (493). And the no less aptly entitled 'The Shadow' (Part I) reflects on the giveaway signs of those who lie (who will always 'get their story right every time'), as against the verbal shifting that supposedly spells honesty: 'when they tell the truth it's never the same twice. They / reformulate' (508). One could hardly wish for a more appropriate – and apologetic – cue to proceed to a reading of Carson's rewritings.

6.2   Crossings and circuits: Text, space and translation

> I used to lull myself to sleep with language, [. . .] till, wavering between languages, I would allow my disembodied self to drift out the window and glide through the silent dark gas-lit streets.
>
> (Carson 1997: 234)

Carson's persistent writing about language is often suggestive of a translator's perspective when confronted with a verbal peculiarity. As already noted, even the titles of his collections tend to give the foreground to linguistic transits, the most conspicuous being *The Irish for No*, which converts a trait of the Irish language into a synecdoche for a whole cultural conformation: the impossibility of producing affirmation or negation with the unequivocal impact of monosyllables is construed by Carson as signalling the difference of Gaelic culture vis-à-vis Ulster Protestant culture, notorious for the emphatic negations of its verbal insignia, identity-endowing mottoes of the citadel under siege: 'Ulster says No!', 'No Surrender!', 'No Pope!', 'Not an Inch!'. The book's title poem explicitly addresses the translation problem apropos of a commercial inscription on the cityscape – 'We were debating / [. . .] how to render *The Ulster Bank — the Bank / That Likes to Say Yes* into Irish' – and rehearses versions that are rendered back into English for the readers' sake: '*The Bank That Answers All Your Questions*, maybe?' (110). The linguistic troping of the urban meandering pursued by Carson's persona is thus regularly invested with a translational content, largely determined by his bilingual consciousness.

In a poem included in *Belfast Confetti*, Carson recalled his young self's relation to verbal, printed matter, and represented it as a progress that was also somatic: 'I ate my way from *A* to *Z*' (127). A few years later, however, Carson's use of A to Z sequences was to suggest, rather than the scattering and obliteration of a devoured alphabet soup, a perfect verbal metabolisation, or an ordered restitution in which no single letter is left out. The sense of thoroughness is compounded by the poet's command of a variety of media, hence the sequences 'Letters from the Alphabet' and 'Opera', mentioned above (the latter based on the particular code for communication employed by radio operators). *Opera Et Cetera* (1996), in which those sequences become framing devices, may reasonably be seen as the textual epicentre of this ambition for totality, which it nonetheless does not fail to qualify: in its orotund Latin title, the canonising solemnity of *Opera* (Works) is followed by the dispersiveness of 'and other things'. Carson's alertness to the mechanisms of language, from its basic constituents to elaborate codes and formations, shows him balancing demonstrations of rigorous craft against the otherwise considerable formal freedom of his poetic practice. Carson's prosodic choices reflect, indeed, the wish to devise models that combine the boldness of iconoclasm with an acknowledgement of sound-scapes, in particular as regards rhythms, originating in different linguistic environments. *The Twelfth of Never* (1998), with its debts to a repertoire of popular verse forms in English and Irish, is a sustained manifestation of this sensibility – the relevance of which for Carson's interlingual work, and especially for his interest in calquing the prosody of the source text, has since become explicit in the Introductions to his versions of *The Midnight Court* (2005) and *The Táin* (2007).

Although it emerges rather late in Carson's oeuvre, his translation of Brian Merriman's *The Midnight Court* is a good starting point for a critical reading of his work as a translator. This is largely due to the close relation between Carson's enlightening Foreword and the actual translation strategies to be found in his version of this eighteenth-century satirical romp on the (economically determined) phenomenon of Irish celibacy, the sorry consequences of which – as sexual and emotional deprivation – are exposed by an outspoken woman before a law court presided over by the 'Queen of the Fay'. A discourse of affinities prevails in the Foreword: Carson makes much of his empathy with Merriman, based on that predecessor's reputation as a virtuoso of traditional music (Carson has long taken an informed interest in Irish music[11]); but he also describes his prosodic options for his version as a result of a perceived affinity between Merriman's verse in *Cúirt an Mheán Oíche* and Merriman's music, the rhythms of the jigs he played. Carson believes he found a correlative for those rhythms in the dactyls that he eventually opted for to render Merriman's satiric verse – his version ultimately reflecting a coalescence of 'the nursery rhyme, the jig, and my picture of Merriman the fiddler' (2005: 12). Towards the end of his Foreword, Carson offers a self-fictionalisation that is transparently calqued on Merriman's tale, recalling how, on 'the two hundredth anniversary of Merriman's death', he (Carson) 'dreamed about Merriman' – indeed a dream vision of his own that echoes the mock *aisling* experienced by Merriman's persona and becomes a sly tribute to a predecessor.

The celebration of authorial empathies, the perceptions of formal proximity and the ensuing calqued solutions described in the Foreword do not, however, generate in the translator the confidence that he has found adequate matches, satisfactory correspondences: in the same way that the closing lines of the Foreword record the poet's disappointment on awakening from his dream vision, earlier pages are self-deflationary. Carson even pronounces some of Merriman's diaphoric effects in the source text – 'of near-homophones collapsing into one another, of meanings slithering into one another' – ultimately 'untranslatable' (13), a surprising judgement from a translator whose strategies elsewhere hardly conform to the normative assumptions, such as those proper to equivalence-based understandings of translation (cf. Venuti 2004: 147–79), that usually underlie verdicts of 'untranslatability'. He also describes his Irish as not being up to the challenge, and discusses the nature of his relationship with the two languages of his literate and literary consciousness:

> I hesitate to call myself a native speaker: true, Irish is, or was, my first language, but I learned it from parents for whom it was a second language [. . .]. Compared with my English, my Irish is impoverished. Yet I can remember a time when English was foreign to me.
>
> (2005: 14)

The diffidence of these remarks is arguably belied by the rhythmic vigour and zest in diction ensured by Carson's prosodic and lexical options as they materialise in the rhymed couplets of his *Midnight Court*. Examples range from the opening lyrical celebration of a summery environment – 'The trout on the rise with its mouth to the light, / While the perch swims below like a speckledy sprite' (19) – to grotesque descriptions, such as the female bailiff's appearance, 'Broad-arsed and big-bellied, built like a tank, / And angry as thunder from shoulder to shank' (20). The deftness of Carson's use of dactyls and anapaests to set a lively pace throughout is possibly at its clearest in moments of invective, in the enumerative, consonantal ranting that seems such an important part of the verbal pleasures afforded by Merriman's text: 'A flibbertigibbet, a bird-witted geck, / A loudmouth, a mope, or a gibbering wreck' (26), 'Befuddled and boozed in a bibulous Babel' (39).

This rhetorical sharpness is well-served by Carson's use of anachronism, rather prominent in a satire of economic ills (or rather 'financial disease' – 19) that couches Merriman's lambasting of corruption in the financial jargon of advanced capitalism: 'Hush money, slush funds', 'backhanders' (21). Elsewhere in the text, a group of neighbours are said to have 'formed an ad-hoc committee' (38); and a benign acknowledgement of female vanity includes an offhand allusion to 'The essential accessories every girl loves' (26). These anachronisms in lexicon and diction combine with the occasional insertion of extraneous references, as when the old man who inveighs against the young female plaintiff includes a 'fancy kimono' among her ill-earned finery, and refers to his supposed bastard child as 'the bambino' (35, 39). Earlier chapters suggested that translators might feel freer to adopt iconoclastic practices when they do not command the source language (some of Derek Mahon's translations lent themselves to this judgement); Carson, familiar with Merriman's Irish, is avowedly intent on calquing his prosody as closely as possible, but with regard to lexical and referential range rather obviously values the preservation of the text's satirical effectiveness above a concern with temporal and cultural accuracy.

Carson's major translation of an Irish text, his version of *The Táin* (2007), shows these concerns in a rather different light, reflecting the text's distinct generic features and its historic resonance, its authority as 'Ireland's central traditional heroic narrative' (Tymoczko and Ireland 2003: 22). The more reverential approach that this suggests gains in complexity with the awareness that *The Táin* already had a well-known version, published in 1969 by a respected Irish poet, Thomas Kinsella; this was a decisive publication for consolidating Kinsella's standing as also a scholar and translator of Irish, and to confirm his known commitment to 'healing' the Irish tradition from the 'broken' condition that he saw as resulting from the loss of the ancestral language (Kinsella 1967). In his Introduction Carson pays an emphatic tribute to Kinsella, acknowledging his English version as one of his sources (parallel to editions of the Irish texts), declaring unequivocally that 'the present translation would not have been possible without Kinsella's ground-breaking text', since without it 'there would have been no public consciousness of *Táin Bó Cúailgne*', and adding his hope that his own version, self-consciously 'a commentary on Kinsella [. . .] will also be taken as a tribute' (2007: xxiv–v). Such vocal awareness of this antecedent is either compounded or mitigated by Carson's attention to the motley, uneven, heterogeneous nature of the texts of which *The Táin* consists; one of the recensions he collated is described as 'made up of several linguistic strata, and [it] includes many interpolations, re-writings, palimpsests, redundancies, repetitions, narrative contradictions and lacunae', while in general the text reveals a 'history of being rewritten and edited by various hands' (2007: xiii, xxvii).

The poet-translator's description of these challenges certainly magnifies the task in hand, but it also leads to a claim for *The Táin*'s place in literary history that sharpens one's perception of the self-canonising effect of offering a new version of this foundational text: remarking on its constant shifts in register, Carson argues that 'it has no parallel in Irish literature, with the possible exception of another multilayered, polyphonic tale, James Joyce's *Ulysses*' (2007: xx–i). Equating the Urtext of an archaic Irishness with the ultimate modern classic, the latter construed by many as the quintessential record of a perplexed identity and one of the key sites where modernity paves the way for postmodernity, helps define a sense of rightfulness and necessity for a translation by an exponent of the postmodern in Irish writing; it sounds as if *The Táin* has found its translator at the point when (in Benjamin's phrasing) it 'reached the age of its fame' (Benjamin 1999: 72). Further, this tension between the integrative design inherent in rewriting *The Táin* in the light of Joyce, and the realisation that what allows for the equation is the characteristic *un*-integrity of the texts in question, is replicated in the translator's avowed concern with preserving the source's distinctive features – including a much-emphasised variousness.[12] Carson indeed argues the difference (hence, the necessity) of his version by claiming, 'I wanted to preserve in the translation some of the formal aspects of the poems', as against Kinsella's option for 'relatively free verse';[13] but he makes clear that this concern was driven by the ambition to give 'some notion of the stylistic heterogeneity of the text' (2007: xxvi).

In order to retain the variety of prosodic arrangements in the texts' verse passages, Carson resorts to a variety of forms ranging from rhymed quatrains to rather enigmatic verse, whose intermittent nature is marked on the page by caesurae – defining patterns that generate a different reading experience from that afforded by Kinsella's version. But the particularities of his version are broader, and involve a creative lexical practice, in some cases etymologically glossed in extensive notes. A signal example is Carson's coinage for Cú Chulainn's ability to twist or contort his appearance, a transformative seizure that precedes some of the hero's more exceptional feats, translated by Kinsella throughout his version as 'the warp-spasm' and dubbed by Carson 'the Torque' (2007: 37, 213n. and passim); another example concerns the name for one of Cú Chulainn's martial tricks or 'feats', descriptively rendered by Kinsella as 'his feat of the stunning-shot' (Kinsella 1970: 91) and by Carson with the coined compound 'his "ricochet-stun-shot"' (2007: 49). This version of *The Táin* also abounds in constructions that are peculiar to Hiberno-English – 'he'd *break my head for me* with a stone', 'Cú Chulainn slung a stone at him and *opened his head for him*' (2007: 55–6; my emphasis) – but the environment into which Carson's domestication brings the Old Irish text is sometimes not so much Northern Irish culture, as, more specifically, his own poetic writing and that of his contemporaries: a phrase discussed earlier in this book, 'neither here nor there', recurs in this version, first in Medb's voice, then in Cú Chulainn's (2007: 13, 129), and this cannot but remind Carson's readers of its use both by Heaney and Muldoon.[14]

The world of the human experience and imagination to which *The Táin* belongs is so obviously archaic that readers can hardly fail to be aware at all times of its ethical, political, and representational remoteness. The terms in which that very distance can be signified are no less obviously variable. Some features of Carson's version leave no doubt of the time and circumstance for which the Old Irish text is being rewritten, a context that can in some respects be significantly different from the late 1960s of Kinsella's version. The late twentieth-century and early twenty-first century interest in representations of somatic processes, in the discourses and cultural practices that concern sexuality and scatology, is reflected in Carson's more demotic use of language. Examples include the description of how '[Cú Chulainn] squeezed him [Láríne] till the shit ran out of him' (2007: 91); recurrent mention of 'a woman's arse' (92 and passim); and the tendency for basic physiology to match the grotesquely massive slaughter recounted throughout this epic (massacres are at one point declared 'beyond computation' – 110), as in the description of Medb's no less massive emptying of her bowels at a location reportedly named 'Medb's Piss-pot' (250).[15] Another translation option that reflects current discourses on the body involves Carson's rendering of the passages describing the anal impaling and visceral destruction of Lóch and Fer Diad (from which they die, after single combat with Cú Chulainn); Carson coins the phrase 'the rear portal' (2007: 95, 151), justifying the latitude of his option with an etymological note that shows the Irish source could indistinctly mean 'anus', 'ministration', and/or 'the act of going to and fro' (221). The passage and the gloss bring critical concerns of the translator's time and culture to bear on the Old Irish text, both by mimicking the 'fanciful etymology' (2007: xxvii) that already marks the source texts in order to enhance the element of wordplay and increased ambivalence (a pervasive concern of most poststructuralist criticism), and by extending the sexual mores to be glimpsed in the archaic, heroic world of *The Táin*.

There is, however, an aspect of *The Táin* that has a much more constant presence in the text, and which prompts complex linguistic inquiries, in response to a culturally current concern in the target context. As Carson argues with undisguised fascination in his Introduction, 'The *Táin* is obsessed by topography, by place-names and their etymologies'; and it appeals to present critical mores by verbalising, textualising its referential space – 'The landscape is a source-book' – as also by spatialising its plot, which according to Carson should be considered 'not as a straightforward story-line running from A to B, but as a journey through a landscape' (2007: xv–xvii). More specifically, *The Táin* provides the spatial politics that this study has been tracing in contemporary Northern Irish verse with the validation of a remote ancestry, a cultural bedrock; by consistently offering explanations for the genesis of place names with reference to particular events, most of which concern the deaths of individuals or collectives, it binds place to memory and memorialisation, and proposes a tumular understanding of the bond between language and place.

The overview of Carson's writing offered in the first part of this chapter showed his consistent interest in topography and toponymy; his most recent major translation, *The Táin*, offers a confirmation of this interest, and the pages that follow will review the presence of Carson's spatially alert poetics in his earlier rewritings of texts from a variety of times and traditions. But they will also trace the close involvement between the unfolding of this interest and the poet's positioning on the terrain of his tradition, with regard to his forebears: Carson in fact juxtaposes space and lineage when he declares *The Táin* 'a space inhabited by many generations, each commenting on their predecessors' (2007: xiv). His major versions of Irish texts relate to forebears either by conspicuous tribute or by conspicuous silence. As regards *The Táin*, he pays homage to a senior Irish poet (Thomas Kinsella) who preceded him in translating a text that is arguably the very beginning of an Irish poetic tradition, and offers this acknowledgement in a context in which critical attention to Kinsella's work has dwindled;[16] incidentally, Kinsella was also one of the most vocal opponents of the notion that Northern Irish poetry might have an identity and a dynamics of its own.[17] As regards Carson's earlier version of an Irish text, *The Midnight Court*, more attentive readers may notice the absence from Carson's Foreword, or from the list of earlier translations cited in his Acknowledgements, of any reference to Heaney's *The Midnight Verdict* (1993, reissued in 2000), a slim volume of translations published under the same imprint, which included a substantial part of Merriman's text and hardly went unnoticed. Silence (from none other than the director of the Seamus Heaney Centre for Poetry) may in this case prove no less eloquent than encomia in the struggle for canonical prominence through high-profile translations of culturally influential texts.

Heaney's *The Midnight Verdict* alternated passages from Merriman and versions of Ovid, at a time (the early 1990s) when indeed all the poets studied in this book were contributing to Michael Hofmann and James Lasdun's *After Ovid* anthology. Carson's own response to the Ovidian challenge occurs at a time when he had notably been experimenting with poetic form. He contributed four versions to that anthology (a number surpassed only by Longley's seven and matched by Hughes's four contributions). These translations (included in *First Language*) do not acquire the structuring role in Carson's oeuvre that characterised Longley's Ovidian appropriations; and the metamorphic theme is less pervasive and defining in his writing, both as regards form and representation, than in Muldoon's. Nonetheless, Carson's rewritings of the Persephone (Proserpina), Hecuba, Aurora, and Marsyas episodes stand out for the thoroughness of their refraction through recognisably Northern Irish scenarios – as also through the (re)writer's own craft.

The topography and language of the Troubles emerge at their clearest in the analogies and marked lexical forms employed in the Proserpina episode, where the girl's enforced fast in the underworld (or rather 'Pluto's no-go zone') is evoked as 'a hunger strike', and Ascalaphus, who reports on her infringement, is dubbed a 'stoolie', his metamorphic punishment described as turning him into 'the scrake-owl, Troubles' augury for Auld Lang Syne' (225). More discreetly but no less satirically, Aurora's plea to Jove for her son Memnon, 'commemorate him in some memorable way', leads to consistent wordplay on some of the catchphrases of Ulster's memorialising culture, as the warring flocks of birds that arise from the smoke produced by 'Memnon's bonfire', dubbed 'the Remember Memnon birds', are compared to 'Prods and Taigs' that 'every year [. . .] come back to re-enact / Their civil war', 'revel[ling] in it' (262). This topicality, however, combines with broader allusions, a case in point being the phrase, in the Proserpina episode, 'strange fruit' (225): readers of Irish poetry may be reminded of Heaney's poem of that title in *North*, but Heaney was of course citing a song (made famous by Billie Holiday) that denounced lynchings in the 1930s in the American South, as a part of the temporal and spatial coalescences that defined the 'myth of North'. By adding to this already complex layering of references, Carson makes his refraction of the *Metamorphoses* politically broader and more diffuse, and it is also at this less specific referential level that his version of the Hecuba episode, with its anguished interrogations – 'New funerals? New death?' (251) – but no more explicit allusions, has to be understood.

Carson's fourth Ovidian poem, however, is of a different nature: it renders the episode of the flaying of Marsyas in the first of its seven sections, but it departs from it to offer a reflection on writing, self and world (with Australian references, obscure in origin, that account for the poem's alternative titles – 'Down Under' in *After Ovid*, 'Latitude 38° S' in *First Language*). From the tale of Marsyas's fatal rivalry with Apollo as a flute player, an insolence for which the satyr is punished by losing his skin – including that of his agile fingers (Carson's perception of the impairment is surely enhanced by his own flute-playing skills) – the poem drifts to images of cutting one's finger while writing, and the person holding the quill may be a copyist: 'he'd been trying to copy the *Inquit* page off the Book / Of Kells, as if it were a series of "unquotes"' (270). In a poem that is openly derivative with regard to the Ovidian episode from which it departs, rewritings are accorded a particular 'genuineness' by the vividness of cut skin and shed blood; but the tension between original and secondary inscription is experienced in a setting that includes 'expectant academics', research routines, 'the elaborate / Machinery of books' in a modern library, an apparatus that becomes both self-referential and a magnified reminder of predecessors and sources (270–1).

This is all the more striking for appearing before the dislocated persona so far from the Old World of Antiquity, in the newness of 'Down Under', '38° S', rather than on the shores of the Black Sea to which the Roman poet was famously banished (an exile that, as seen in earlier chapters, has also struck a chord with Heaney and Mahon): 'There's a shelf of *Metamorphoses*. Commentaries. Lives. *The Mystery of Ovid's / Exile*' (271).[18] The poignancy of human suffering and the plight of art, mutually mirrored, are confirmed in the final section's recollective reflection on stories 'of the cruelty of gods and words and music' (271). But the poem's close, with its reference to 'the fluteplayer's outstretched fingers', that flaying has rendered ineffective, gains a self-referential edge from a quotation, "clearest in that Realme", marked by inverted commas but otherwise unreferenced, that research shows to belong in Arthur Golding's 1567 description of Marsyas's brook in his translation of the *Metamorphoses* (VI: 510): by inserting a passage from the first English translation of Ovid's text in a piece that began as translation and drifted into an afterwriting, Carson includes his own dual craft in the referential scope of the poem's concluding reflections.

Carson's dominant prosodic instrument for his poetry translations of the early 1990s, including Ovid, is the extra-long line that from *The Irish for No* onwards became his formal trademark. Empowering as this resource can be for its sheer distinctiveness, its sustained practice for the translation of a variety of authors is hardly devoid of problems – since the visibility that it affords the translator is achieved at the expense of the varied dictions and forms of the appropriated source texts. *First Language*, which includes versions of Ovid, Rimbaud, Baudelaire, and Irish-language poet Seán Ó Ríordáin – all rendered into the same type of verse line – is the collection in which the strengths of a homogeneous model are most clearly offset by the arguable impoverishment of exchanging the various for the same. Eliding the formal (and visual) particularities of the source text also jeopardises part of the attractiveness of collections that intermingle translations with 'originals', an attractiveness that largely rests in the surplus of meaning brought by the coexistence of different voices, identified not just by a varied referential range but also by distinct measures and rhythms.

However, Carson's work in this period in fact shows his alertness to 'the drunkenness of things being various',[19] which arguably reflects on his concern, as regards formal achievement, with balancing experiment against tradition. His extra-long lines occasionally accommodate graphically rearranged ballad quatrains, while otherwise presenting a layout that, as recognised by Carson, suggests the space of the longest-lived of lyrical forms, the sonnet (cf. Brandes 1990: 84). Ironically the best-known of 'fixed forms', the sonnet has been the object of the loosest, most ductile experiments in Carson's work – and also a crucial element in his translational poetics. 'Sonnet' and 'Four Sonnets', in *First Language*, are poems whose entitlement to that name rests solely on their 14 (very long) lines; the same collection also includes versions of sonnets by Baudelaire that are in fact made up of four couplets – which, through their graphic overspill, approximate the form's conventional length. Five years later, though, Carson proved that the freedoms taken with the sonnet did not reflect any lack of prosodic competence: in 1998 he began by publishing, as *The Alexandrine Plan*, 34 regular versions of sonnets by Rimbaud, Baudelaire and Mallarmé; and then, as if the 'plan' included an extended inflection, he published the 77 sonnets in alexandrines that make up *The Twelfth of Never*. These two books, published in the same year, highlight in concomitant ways the tension between homo- and heterogeneity in Carson's poetic designs, and the extent to which it bears on his translational poetics.

A signal demonstration of how productive this tension can be was provided by two texts with a particular connection: they are alternative versions of the same poem, published with an interval of five years. From its title, the source text would seem designed to epitomise the translation nexus: 'Correspondances', the sonnet by Baudelaire that Carson translated for *First Language* (243) under the original title (even the French spelling is maintained, suggesting that the same should happen with pronunciation), and retranslated for *The Alexandrine Plan* as 'Coexistences' (1998: 71). These alternative versions – the first, in four rhymed couplets of lines averaging

20 syllables; the second, in alexandrines, organised (like the source) into two quatrains and two tercets – matter less for the detailed conclusions that their comparison may afford than for the way they throw into relief the contingent and pragmatic nature of translation. The distinctiveness of these two renderings by the same translator ostensibly reflects the immediate context of their publication (in this case, the programmatic traits of the collections in which they feature); and, above all, they preclude the translator's (hypothetical) claim for his craft of a creative singularity grounded on notions of the poem's unique and unrephrasable quality. The translator's sense of authorship is further reconfigured when he translates himself (or rather, his own translation), since it is inevitable that his version of a few years earlier becomes also a source text for the second translation.

In *The Alexandrine Plan* Carson acknowledges his debts with an accuracy that often cannot be found in contemporary poetic translation: a closing note to the collection references editions and other English versions that the poet used, recognising that his sources are not just in the poems' original language – although this collection is bilingual, inviting readers to compare the French sonnets and Carson's renderings. Carson observes in this case the (French) sonnets' conventional format; and yet his versions retain elements of the appropriative boldness found in earlier ventures, in particular by introducing in Baudelaire, Rimbaud and Mallarmé referents that are either Irish or characteristic of an Anglophone literary culture. Besides, the mastery of the sonnet form demonstrated throughout the collection involves an economy of verbal resources that occasionally allows Carson to 'fit more' into his alexandrines than could be read in the source lines – which leads to a rather frequent use of amplification. One need look no further than the first sonnet in the collection, Rimbaud's 'Au Cabaret Vert' / 'The Green Bar', to find Carson dislocating the scene of drink, food and flirtation from Charleroi to Kingstown, and from the source's 'Octobre [18]70' ambiance to a 'tacky '50s décor'; with the comparative verbal economy of English leaving the translator with space enough to accommodate extra descriptive and expressive elements, as the waitress is compared to 'an unexpected Lady Day', and the sonnet requires extra onomatopoeic feet to achieve regularity and completeness: '*Glug. Glug. Glug. Glug*' (1998: 13).

Carson's ability to retain his characteristic diction under the formal regime of the regular sonnet was to find a more extended demonstration when he moved from the versions in *The Alexandrine Plan* to the (in most cases, original) sonnets in *The Twelfth of Never*: the fact that the two collections were published in the same year highlights the continuities, but also the latter book's broader range of cultural and historical references, and appropriated literary models. *The Twelfth of Never* opens its hexametric sonnets up to the Irish traditional ballad but also to the *haiku*, to arcane scholarship as to old and current journalism. One of the few examples of interlingual work in this collection is Carson's version of 'Pangur Bán' (one of the most frequently translated of Gaelic poems, as seen above).[20] As in earlier collections Carson had rendered poems in a variety of forms into his sprawling lines, so his 'Catmint Tea' (the title brings this version in line with the overriding theme of intoxication) translates the source's eight quatrains into a sonnet in alexandrines, the standard form in *The Twelfth of Never*. The poet's craft, matched against the cat's, is here construed as lexical surfing, a verbal desire: 'I consult thesauruses; he forages for mice', '[I] rummage through the OED's delights'[21]; and the poem's closing lines suggest that its refraction in Carson's writing lights up the mark left by his Ovidian versions, since the piece culminates in a metamorphosis not to be found in other translations: 'We rolled in serendipity upon the mat. / [. . .] / Then he became the man, and I became the cat' (372).

Tropes of transformation converge with the book's theme of intoxication (justified by the poppy leitmotiv), and find a verbal correlative in a particular transit: intralingual renderings. Several sonnets bear titles that are recognisably those of traditional songs or ballads – 'The Rising of the Moon', 'Wrap the Green Flag Round Me', 'Let Erin Remember', 'Dark Rosaleen' – and these texts evoking mostly anonymous sources are undecidedly poised between translation and gloss, rewriting and afterwriting. But *The Twelfth of Never* includes, under the title 'Spraying the Potatoes', a striking intralingual appropriation of a twentieth-century poem, specifically of one of Patrick Kavanagh's contributions to the renewal of the pastoral in contemporary Irish poetry – in tune with his denunciation of 'an essentially sentimental Ireland' as 'a thoroughgoing English-bred lie' (Kavanagh 1967: 13), and his proneness to represent rurality in terms that veer from bitter exposure of the Irish peasant's spiritual and sexual starvation to an exalted lyricism of the ordinary. Carson's use of Kavanagh's title generates an expectation of identity between the texts, rather than mere citational proximity; but the two texts have only a partial overlap, despite the pervasiveness of Carson's unacknowledged literal citation. Whole passages are directly lifted from the earlier poem, with Carson's reliance on his readers' memory of it probably accounting for Kavanagh's absence from the book's list of Acknowledgements (which includes, however, references to specialised publications on Japanese poetry and on Napoleonic lore): a surmise of universal recognition delineates the uneasy border between plagiarism and tribute. Carson's intralingual 'version' renders Kavanagh's eight quatrains into the octave (the two first quatrains) of a sonnet; crucially, though, Carson's sestet replaces Kavanagh's sketched narrative of an old man's memories of lost love, 'Remembering his youth and some Ruth he knew', with the narrative of a hanging, the execution by English soldiers of a figure whose colouring is suggestive of Irish nationalism: 'I watched him swing in his Derry green for hours and hours' (423). Thus, the refraction carried out by this version begins with Kavanagh's 'popular' tetrameters rendered into Carson's alexandrines, and ends in Kavanagh's rural simplicity intersected, unexpectedly, by a vignette of historical adversity which might have migrated from the balladry that pervades most of the collection. But the volume's apologetic 'Envoy' places all that came before it under the influence of hallucination and torpidity – 'Now you've travelled through the Land of Nod and Wink / And sucked the pap of *papaver somniferum*' – alludes to the possible variants of any narrative, and underlines once again (even through an occasionally deviant grammar) the uncertainty of all inscriptions and imputed meanings:

> These words the ink is written in is not indelible
> And every fairy story has its variorum;
> For there are many shades of pigment in the spectrum,
> And the printed news is always unreliable.

> (427)

These lines in the closing piece of *The Twelfth of Never* echo an insight that Carson voiced in earlier writing – a prose poem in *Belfast Confetti*, suggestively entitled 'Revised Version', offered the remark that 'everything is contingent and provisional' (173); and 'Second Language' prescribed 'the *Tipp-Ex* present at the fingertips' (217). But the communicational topos in Carson's allusion to texts as 'printed news', combined with the territorial basis of his insistence on contingency (whether perceived in the grim city, or in the 'Land of Nod and Wink'), also points forward to his collection *Breaking News*, and in particular to its focal sequence, 'The War Correspondent'. As with the preceding collection, *Breaking News* has ostensibly little to do with translation – only one of its poems is proposed as an interlingual version – and yet it is pervaded again by an appropriative logic. Three ekphrastic poems (intersemiotic versions of paintings by Géricault, Goya, and Edward Hopper) are made to serve the collection's overriding concern with war scenarios. And the book also contains the most brazen, provocative example to date of an intralingual translation in Carson's oeuvre, offered with exactly the same formula that would conventionally indicate interlingual work: 'The Forgotten City – *after William Carlos Williams, "The Forgotten City"*' (461); this English version of a well-known poem of the English language (by one of its canonical poets) renders a narrative of reconnoitring the site of a natural disaster as a narrative of a socio-political disaster, on the landscape of the Troubles. Albeit less provocatively, 'The War Correspondent' has also much to do with rewriting in the same language, since, as recognised by Carson in his final note, with regard to the pioneering war journalist William Howard Russell, 'in many instances I have taken his words *verbatim*, or have changed them only slightly to accommodate rhyme and rhythm' (591); besides, of course, the sequence's contribution to that spatially defined 'translation' by which the Crimean place names (on which Russell reported) are encountered on the Belfast street plan.

The tribute to the dead in *Breaking News*, and the collection's imaginary wandering through the places that saw their demise (or commemorate it), are a vivid reminder that a year earlier (in 2002) Carson published his version of the most influential account in world literature of a circuitous visitation of the dead: Dante's *Inferno*. Carson's readers, used to his evocations of the urban maze of Troubles-stricken Belfast as a gloomy, occasionally gruesome space, could hardly be surprised by this poet's attraction to the Dantean text, and its encounters on the walks and circuits of hell with the shadows of agents of violence, treason, and all forms of human impiety. This attraction was occasionally explicit, as in the simile he used for a scene of nocturnal labour in a poem in *Belfast Confetti*: 'Walking the slippery catwalk from one bake-room to the next – like Dante's / Inferno, the midnight glare of ovens' (128). Further, his earlier representations of the urban maze were informed by a sense of precedence and repetition, that others had been on that path before: this involved autobiography ('the zig-zag precedents' of his 'postman father' – 309), but also textual and authorial relations.

The pervasiveness of Carson's interest in replication and recurrence shows it to be foundational rather than incidental, although he seems to waver between the contrary notions of singularity and derivation; his poem 'Two to Tango' included the dictum, 'not to repeat yourself is not real life', but this came from one of the voices involved in an inner dialogue that also echoed the Ancient injunction 'know yourself', a fundament for the self's discreteness and autonomy (223). This tension between the yearning for self-determination and uniqueness, and the provocative (postmodern) suggestion that, ultimately, the self's defining assertion in/as 'real life' (equated with its verbal manifestation) is always already repetition crucially defines the position of a practitioner of the lyric who is also a translator, and recognises the increasing coalescence of his two crafts. In the poetic economy of Carson's work, this tension could hardly find a more revealing focus than his *Inferno*, for Dante's canonical magnitude, certainly; but also, correspondingly, for the overall effect of a version that on many occasions might be labelled 'repetition with a critical distance' (Linda Hutcheon's formula for parody – Hutcheon 1985: 6, 37).

Carson's awareness of Dante's massive literary impact, his long shadow over all forms of writing in Western literary traditions, emerges in various ways in the text and critical apparatus of *The Inferno of Dante Alighieri*. Within this translator's immediate literary space, the manifold consequence of the 'second center of the canon' (Bloom: 1995: 76) is most obviously to be found in the work of Seamus Heaney; as seen above, Heaney's response to Dante has included versions of the 'Ugolino' episode and the first three Cantos of the *Inferno*, the *Commedia* employed as a model for 'encounters with familiar ghosts' in 'Station Island' (1984), a study of priority and descent in the essay 'Envies and Identifications: Dante and the Modern Poet' (1985), and vocal appreciation (in interviews) of the empowerment that the culturally

Catholic poet derives from Dante's work.[22] Introducing his *Inferno*, Carson recognises that he is 'almost completely unfamiliar with the Italian language' (2002: ix),[23] and had to resort substantially to several English versions. One can hardly expect Heaney's versions of three Cantos, and of sections of two others, to be acknowledged in Carson's paratexts – and yet the blurb of *The Inferno of Dante Alighieri* includes a reference to Heaney; it describes Carson's as 'the first ever version of Dante by an Irish poet', and claims that it 'deserves comparison with Heaney's *Beowulf*'. This bid for canonical equivalence, through translation, gives a particular edge to the insight that 'to trace one's poetic lineage to Dante is tantamount to claiming the poet's laurels against all other contenders' (Freccero 1986: 4). It also offsets what otherwise might remain unnoticed – that the absoluteness of the 'first ever' claim on Dante, true only if taken as referring to an *integral* English version by an Irish poet,[24] effaces the *partial* versions by the older writer, previously responsible (as poet, translator, and essayist) for making Dante a prominent presence in the space of contemporary Irish poetry and criticism.

The relevance of tracing these silences and ambivalent remarks accrues with the emergence in recent years of a 'Carson vs Heaney' critical topos, centred on the former's supposedly distinct confrontation with historico-political adversity. Alex Houen, in *Terrorism and Modern Literature*, argues that Carson (unlike Heaney) avoids producing an indistinction between 'the city's exploding cartography' and its verbal exploration (Houen 2002: 270ff.); while Michael Hinds claims that Carson's version of the *Inferno* preserves the historic and geographic specificity of Dante's text:

> Carson insists on the essentially Florentine character of the poem, on its ultimate refusal of translatability into other places. [. . .] he makes it very clear that *Inferno* is an engagement with a history that is particularly Florentine and particularly Dantean.
>
> (Hinds 2004: 71)

Hinds might have in mind Eliot's famous observation that 'No one is more local' than Dante;[25] his claim, however, proves baffling (even before one considers the translation in any detail) when matched against Carson's own Introduction, which could hardly be more explicit as to the conscious Northern Irish dislocation of his *Inferno*:

> I imagine being airborne in the [British Army] helicopter, like Dante riding in the flying monster Geryon, looking down into the darkness of that place in Hell called Malebolge. [. . .] I see a map of North Belfast.
>
> (2002: xi)

This is compounded by the translator's claim of a particular imbrication of his circumstance and Dante's text, a mutual implication of textual progress and empirical, bodily dynamics: 'The deeper I got into the *Inferno*, the more I walked [. . .] I'd leave the desk and take to the road, [. . .] I'd head for [. . .] one of Belfast's sectarian fault lines' (2002: xi).

Hinds's claim that Carson's *Inferno* retains an exclusively Italian reference is thus untenable in the face of the translator's avowed domestication, but it is also true that the degree and the forms taken by that domestication vary greatly from Canto to Canto. The Italian location is indeed often *dis*located or erased: Dante's place names are occasionally omitted (XV.113, XVIII.61), and not for the sake of concision – since they are 'replaced' with descriptions. Telluric and topographic references are also a case in point for this erosion of the source's particularities: where in the Italian text one reads 'terra', Carson persistently opts for 'bog' and 'muck.' These lexical choices, so commonly used in (Hiberno-)English to refer to the soil of Ireland, easily carry a colloquial and jocular sense that is neither supported by the Italian text nor to be found in other English translations; examples include 'the stinking bog below', 'the muck-bound prisoners' (VI.12, 15), 'the horrible bog', 'the sinners who gobbled the muck in wads' (VII.128–9). The Northern Irish domestication of the infernal territory is explicit, through amplification, in Canto XXXI, which Carson translated first (2002: ix); this is also the Canto in which the dislocation is most obvious, when the giants in their pit are described 'as in some Irish bog, / collectively immobilized by muck' (XXXI.32–3). The simile becomes even more conspicuous for being coupled with another one, present in Dante's text and retained in translation, involving both topography and architecture – in the form of 'towers' erected by powerful families in medieval Tuscany. In Carson's text, the giants are thus equated with famous landmarks on the Italian landscape, but the soil in which they are buried up to their navels is *also* compared to an Irish bog. Political allusions seal this relocation through particular lexical options: in a Northern Irish context, Carson's rendering of Dante's 'gente [. . .] sommersa' as 'muck-bound prisoners' (VI.15)[26] summons a particular penal and excremental reference, acting as a reminder of the famous 1976 'dirty protest' carried out by IRA inmates at the Maze prison.

Language can itself become a politically relevant object (and not just an instrument) in Carson's version: indeed, the translator's keen interest in unusual verbal occurrences makes it predictable that two passages of the *Inferno* may epitomise the appropriative design. The passages in question are traditionally glossed as 'unintelligible' and most usually left untouched by the translator, or otherwise rendered only to maintain the *terza rima*: Pluto's shout at the beginning of Canto VII, 'Papè Satàn, papè Satàn aleppe!' (VII.1), and Nimrod's in Canto XXXI: 'Raphèl maì amèch zabì almì' (67). In both cases Carson opts to 'translate' these nonsensical shouts in terms that ensure a (varying) degree of recognition in an Irish context, rescuing the two utterances from their supposed 'unintelligibility'. In the former instance, Carson keeps close to the morphology of the source text, rewriting it as '*Pappy* [or *Poppy*] *Satin Papish Satan Alibi!*',[27] a formula that summons characteristic elements of a Northern Irish unionist discourse and imaginary. In the latter case, Nimrod's shout is completely rephrased as '*Yin twa maghogani gazpaighp boke!*', Carson's note describing his strategy as 'further garbling Nimrod's gibberish into a mixture of Ulster Scots, pseudo-Gaelic Irish, and Ulster English' (2002: 290). The explanation is potentially contradictory, since this lexical mixture, even if resulting in an absurd utterance, may obtain from Irish readers an effect of recognition (even if vague and confused), rather than of increased incomprehension – as an instance of Irish linguistic ecumenicism, ironically voiced by the builder of Babel.

The blatant Northern Irish dislocation of Canto XXXI sets in relief the generally uncharacteristic way in which, in Cantos XXXII and XXXIII, Carson renders the Ugolino episode – famously translated by Heaney in 1979. Heaney's version was conspicuous for its political refraction of Dante's text; an exercise in comparison shows that the corresponding passages in Carson's text avoid the striking temporal and spatial incongruities that elsewhere punctuate his *Inferno* – and the absence of that strategy is all the more conspicuous in view of the politically fraught history of appropriations of the Ugolino narrative, as well as (more specifically) the resonance that the theme of starvation so obviously finds in the Irish historical consciousness. If it is true that Heaney's version belongs within the set of texts that Carson's translation elides by declaring itself 'the first ever version of Dante by an Irish poet', it is also arguable that his text comes to find a muted consequence in Carson's version of the Ugolino encounter by contributing to a relative 'neutrality' of tone, when compared to the adjacent Cantos.

Indeed, *The Inferno of Dante Alighieri*, a rewriting of a text characteristically grounded on a sense of design and order, resists the delineation of a single, organising strategy: if such a principle can be found in Carson's text, it is bound to be, paradoxically, a concern with the plurality of cultural reference and of linguistic resources. This is a dimension of Carson's writing that has occasionally been identified as Joycean (Butler 2003: passim), and the procedures that verbalise it, absent both from the Italian text and from other recent English versions, include lexical imports from French or Spanish – which counter and balance, with a predominantly ludic effect, the Hibernicising strategy noted above. Thus, the simoniacs of Canto XIX, tormented by fire on their feet (or rather, 'soles flambés' – XIX.42), are described in their frantic movement as 'quivering in [. . .] a mad fandango' (XIX.26); the devils that Dante and Virgil escape from in Canto XXII through XXIII, styled by Dante 'ministri della fossa quinta', are proposed by Carson as 'seigneurs / of the fifth arrondissement!' (XXIII.55–6); while one of the same devils attracts the comment: '[his] AKA was Señor Slick' (XXII.109). Even more curiously, Carson employs Italian words that are *not* in Dante's text, adding them either for their high-culture implications – for example, terms for musical notation, in passages such as 'accents doloroso', 'terrible crescendo' (III.25, 27), 'fortissimo' (XVII.118) – or because in today's global culture they are synecdoches of a stereotyped 'Italianness'; hence, a list of treacherous characters includes 'a mafioso' (XXVIII.81).

Elsewhere, referential anachronism and register shifts abound, with risible effects, in passages where 'cranes go honking' and 'doves [. . .] paraglide' (V.46, 82); Virgil upbraids Dante for his lack of forwardness: 'What's up with you, you timid little newt?' (II.121) – a rebuke that becomes also self-directed, through the translator's identification with an author (Dante) that, here as elsewhere, reverentially acknowledges an alternately exacting and benevolent forebear (Virgil); and an unexpected festive tone surrounds the entrance in the central pit of Malebolge, to the stentorian sound of Nimrod's horn, in lines where both the film/TV reference and the musical onomato-poeia are provocatively out of place and time:

> but as I peered into that twilight zone
> I heard the mad *ta-ra-ra-boom-di-ay*
>
> of some gargantuan bugle-megaphone
>
> (XXXI.11–13)

Such passages give us examples of a playfulness afforded by anachronism and by the insertion of the popular and colloquial into a text that many readers associate with gravity and solemnity. But laughter may also arise from the archaising ring and the 'literary' commonplaces that, with ironical knowingness, Carson allows the prosodic demands of *terza rima* to impose on the syntax of his text: 'he confined himself to attics dim' (II.105), 'awash with anguished tears aplenty' (XX.6), 'and there, I fell into depression deep' (I.15). This last example shows the tension between the mock-'literary', archaic effect of postposition and the radically modern ring of a popularised use of the clinical term 'depression' – where Dante has 'paura', and other English versions 'dread', 'fear', or 'terror'.[28] The literary self-referential marks of Carson's text also involve the use of critical terms and tropes to describe the landscape, as when a castle is said to be 'encircled by a periphrastic creek' (IV.108).[29] And the movement of both the denizens and visitors of hell derives analogies from the very dynamics of the verse that carries out their representation: the devils in Canto XXI '[march] off like syllables of verse' (XXI.137 – another of Carson's interpolations); while the arduous set-ting of Canto I, that hinders Dante's progress, sees him with 'one foot firmly set / below the other in iambic stress' (I.29–30).

These are some of the ways in which Carson's version foregrounds its own strategies – its play with time and space, its shifting registers, its lexical and prosodic particularities – never or rarely permitting that, as is so often the case with versions of canonical texts, readers experience the illusion of unmediated access to the source (cf. Bassnett and Lefevere 1998: 9). This seems to be borne out by Carson's remark, in his Introduction, that 'some of us expect translations to sound like translations, and to produce an English which is sometimes strangely interesting' (2002: xix). The remark is itself double-edged: precluding the illusion that the text was originally written in the target language spells respect for the foreignness of the source; but the 'strangeness' of the version makes it an object of autonomous attention, shifting the emphasis to the translator's new authorship, and away from a perception of the source. Carson's reminder that 'Dante wrote vernacular' (2002: xix) extends this duality: the source text's linguistic, cultural and geographic specificity is invoked to validate its dislocation towards *another* vernacular, another specificity – that of the target context; tribute to the source easily converts into an endorsement of its radical rewriting. This is done by equating the circumstances of author and translator – if 'Dante wrote vernacular', 'I spoke Irish (with its different, curious and delightful grammar) before I spoke English' (2002: xx) – and reclaiming the pattern for a dislocated vernacular from the Hiberno-English ground layer previously explored in *The Twelfth of Never*: 'So I tried to write a *terza rima* crossed with ballad' (2002: xxi). The translator's resulting *visibility* is compounded by the risible, demotic elements highlighted above, which also qualify the reading experience: some of the translator's more radical rewritings bring Carson's version close to a meta-*Inferno*, a text to be fully enjoyed by readers who have already read the *Inferno* in other, more 'conventional' versions. Further, the translation's salience or opacity (arguably a characteristic trait of postmodern parody[30]), and its frequent ludic features, may entail an attenuation of the more sombre and awesome traits of Dante's text, of the terrible import of the figures and spaces visited – at the risk of jeopardising one of the dimensions that attracted Carson to the *Inferno* and justify its Northern Irish dislocation.

This dimension of gloom, however, was arguably stressed by Carson in texts published a year after his *Inferno*, as part of *Breaking News* – which can thus be construed as a site of afterwritings, that extend the space occupied by Dante's shadows in the poet's imagination as Carson's persona walks 'night / after night' through 'the smouldering / dark streets', to note that 'all lie / in ruins' (466). This remark, combined with the intermittent, interrupted flow of discourse suggested by the very short lines Carson favours in this book, may seem directly evocative of Eliot ('These fragments I have shored against my ruins'), by implication also of his famous apology for the 'mythical method',[31] and, in general, of the Modernist perspective on culture and history. The yearning for reintegrative designs that inheres in such an echo, a yearning that may be likewise gratified by the translator's assumption of canonical voices, arguably qualifies the notion of a Carson 'as happy amids the indefinite indeterminacies of post-structuralism as a leprechaun in clover' (Smith 2005: 211), his art 'rampantly [turbinating] with the relativity and contradictions of multi-perspectivism' (Gillis 2003: 183). In Carson's appropriation of Dante as a structuring model, bearing on writing but also on history and experience, are we not faced, again, with a juxtaposition of distinct places and times, with an appertaining elision of historical specificity – and is the ensuing sense of order not magnified by the assumption of a text, Dante's, that epitomises a sense of faith and of design, and has a long history of appropriations by causes with a literary extension (cf. Havely 1998: 2–3)? Carson has in the past seemed averse to such master narratives: such aversion was the starting point for an association in the critical domain between his name and Heaney's, the unmentioned predecessor in the paratextual space of some of his translations, and the author whose invocation of Dante has been described as a late instance of the Modernist concern with instituting design and order in the face of the 'futility and anarchy' (another Eliotian phrase) of contemporary history (O'Donoghue 1998: 247). It is true, however, that Carson's *Inferno*, if taken on its own, may contain enough parodic self-subversion to balance the canonical claim that inheres in the assumption of Dante. And a fundamental doubt with regard to break or continuity has long ago been identified as 'the inaugural narrative act' of a consciousness of post-modernity (Jameson 1991: xiii).

One of the prevalent tensions in this study balances canonical desire against a textual practice that would seem to illustrate, in a quasi-programmatic way, the precariousness of references, of inscriptions, and of authorial presence. Arguably, though, it is precisely the ambivalence that persists in Carson's poetry that contributes to rescuing it from that diagnosis of 'exhaustion' and of loss of creative impetus that some have associated with postmodernist writing – in the less enthusiastic strand of its critical description (cf. Barth 1982: passim; Jameson 1991: passim). The conditions for that rescue from inconsequence cannot be dissociated from the sense of purpose that Carson derives from the insistent grounding of his writing in his circumstance; nor from the extent to which that grounding is paradoxically reinforced by a writing of dislocations. This confirms translation as an integral part of this poet's output, and an enabling factor of his ethical and political positioning with regard to his time and place.

7
Conclusions – and Some Extensions

I am
as much at home here as I will ever be.[1]

This passage from a poem by Sinéad Morrissey (1972–) epitomises a relation between self and place to which the body of poetry considered above ultimately tends. The poet is neither ecstatic nor dismissive about her home-ground, but rather placidly accepts it, an attitude that is implicitly based on knowledge of a variety of elsewheres. An experience of global realities inflects the relationship with one's origins in such a way that it arguably becomes more concessive than assertive, and is tinged with an irony that is often derived from textual mediations. To differing degrees, the poets studied in this book have arguably evolved towards this more diffuse sense of location, with notable textual correspondences. This applies even to those whose poetics were emphatically defined, at the outset, by locally specific bonds (as was prominently the case with Heaney).

The emplacements of identity found in the work of these five Northern Irish poets have varied considerably in their particular expression, but have much in common as regards their source and their proven continued appeal. Indeed, the historically grounded uncertainties of Ulster identities saw their perception and representation greatly intensified by the local and global causes of the 1960s and early 1970s – a decisive formative period for the poets in question. However, the persistence of such concerns, several decades on, has much to do with the current cultural and intellectual context, which has proved amenable to them. This contextual dimension also helps explain the continued resonance of the theme of (dis)location in the work of younger poets. Sinéad Morrissey's remark comes from a poem entitled 'In Belfast', the opening piece of her second collection, *Between Here and There*. Neither the poem's title nor the collection's are bound to appear as novel to readers of the chapters above; and yet the poetry written by Morrissey and other younger authors from present-day Northern Ireland cannot in any way be described as a mere reiteration of the models provided by the poets born in the middle decades of the twentieth century – models that are themselves still fluid and in progress. These closing pages will offer a round-up of the main emphases of the preceding chapters, and briefly suggest some of their inflected continuities in three poets born in the 1970s: Morrissey, Alan Gillis (1973–) and Leontia Flynn (1974–).

One of the reasons for this book's focus on the five poets studied above is their proven capacity to avoid the perpetuation of a trademark poetic mode, while retaining (formally and referentially) the lineaments of a distinctive diction. Their commitment to innovation obviously varies in degree, and reflects such elements as relative canonicity, the vagaries of history and experience, and sheer idiosyncrasy. In every case, a balance between innovation and continuity (an important factor in maintaining reader loyalty) has derived strength from their interest in the tension between home and elsewhere, an interest that is matched by the range of their intertextual bonds, emerging most clearly in their translations. The translational poetics of Heaney, Mahon, Longley, Muldoon and Carson all derive their raison d'être and cultural clout from a favourable critical and intellectual environment (as suggested in my Introduction and endorsed throughout the ensuing readings). The acclaim that radical appropriations by contemporary poets generally attract is of course part and parcel of a broader attitude towards textual production that has found favour in recent years; this includes challenges to notions of originality and authorship; representations based on abrupt juxtapositions of distinct times and places; programmatically uncertain extensions of the notion of 'text'; and the concomitant rise to prominence of Descriptive Translation Studies. This has emerged as an overarching discipline predicated on the indefinite contours of its object, a focus on the target system, and the contingent and non-definitive status of the translated text.

For poets from Northern Ireland who recurrently combine their 'original' output with the practice of translation, such overall features of a cultural moment are compounded by the particularities of the place that locates their origins and their dominant representations. It is not surprising that discourses of belonging or uprootedness fostered by a fraught history have contributed to a tendency for self-definition afforded by homologies with other places. But it is nonetheless paradoxical that the continued appropriation of texts that originate in (or represent) a variety of elsewheres bolsters the argument for the specificity of Northern Irish writing. Critical support for the notion of a unitary Irish tradition made that specificity unpopular in significant areas of opinion in the 1980s and early 1990s; however, the consistency and diversity of this body of writing, combined with current 'theory'-based notions of anti-essentialism, dispersal and plurality, have since contributed to a broader acceptance of its particularity. The sheer scope and breadth of the rewritings carried out by Northern Irish poets have ensured that translation has become a significant aspect of this critical vindication.

As suggested already, one of the attractions of these poet-translators is their ability to preclude perceptions of 'more of the same', evident not only in their respective oeuvres, but also in the combined effect of their work (in anthologies, for example). Balancing continuity against novelty is clearly a general concern, but it becomes particularly sensitive in the case of Seamus Heaney, reflecting his long-acquired canonical prominence. The poet's sharp awareness of this has contributed to a careful negotiation of the course of his work – a process in which the poetry itself is supplemented by his substantial critical output, and prominently by his translations. There is a cumulative canonical consequence to translating key texts from the Gaelic tradition (*Sweeney Astray* and the partial version of Merriman in *The Midnight Verdict*), Greek tragedies (*The Cure at Troy* and *The Burial at Thebes*), the foundational epic of English literature (*Beowulf*), and passages from Dante (as spiritual/literary bedrock of the Catholic consciousness). Their combined effect makes Heaney's versions an important factor in the sense of integrity and natural assuredness that have long marked the critical narrative of his authorial growth.

The range and prominence of his translations also mean that Heaney's ability to appear 'very sure of his place'[2] can extend from autochthony, a sense of territory and cultural tradition, to the terrain of literary lineage. Such an extension was not impaired by his 'swerve', in the 1990s, from the telluric emphases of his earlier work to a celebration of metaphysical and reimagined topographies. Since this 'swerve' allowed Heaney to mitigate (if not completely outgrow) the brooding mode of his earlier verse, it is hardly surprising that he has seemed more recently (both as poet and critic) to favour benign rather than agonistic models of literary transmission. The mediations afforded by his translation work appear instrumental in the authorial trajectory that has led him to this perspective. The linguistic and cultural redress sought by Heaney's *Beowulf* (as argued and envisaged in his Introduction to that acclaimed translation) claim a specifically 'Britannic' scope; but such a (re)integrative rationale is of one piece with the more universal celebration of poetic forebears and peers, which, like a secular hagiography, has tended to punctuate his poetry collections. And the poet's sense of the aptness and necessity of his officiation is suggested by the metaphor of gift and incorporation, a 'transfusion', that he applies to his quasi-intralingual translation (or rather, 'retelling') of Robert Henryson's Middle Scots *The Testament of Cresseid* (2004a: 7–8).

The 'transfusion' metaphor suggests that the inter-authorial bonds created by translation make the source author and the translator into 'blood' relations. This notion could be congenial to Michael Longley, in view of the place held in his poetry by tropes of family, generation, and the emotions associated with consanguinity. In Heaney, however, the focus is on literary lineage, with regard to which the biological metaphor is merely functional; indeed, this distinct arrangement of object and means of representation may arguably be noted whenever Heaney and Longley combine images of writing and private emotional experience. Nonetheless, this particular shared dimension marks them off from their other contemporary, Derek Mahon, whose representational universe is far removed from organic imagery and placid tropes of benign transmission. His personal background (in a community that found itself in a historical cul-de-sac during his formative years) is the ostensible source of his trademark disaffection, but his sense of uprootedness is certainly compounded by literary relations. This involves both an attraction to *poète maudit* figures from several traditions, and a stance towards his Northern Irish contemporaries that ensures definition by difference (notwithstanding elements of personal camaraderie that have always persisted).

As argued above, the emplacement and permanence that Heaney has come to epitomise (both formally and referentially) has provided a foil for a writing that flaunts its malaise and instability. This also occurs at a basic textual level: Mahon's constant rewriting of his work makes revision a matter of principle, almost a token of professional fastidiousness. The contingency of the poetic text suggested by this practice brings his versions of himself into line with his varied translational work – ranging from gravitas to riotous iconoclasm. Mahon is a case in point for this book's interest in poet-translators whose work refuses to stay put; moreover, the time and mode of his translations (lyrical and dramatic) relate recognisably to the development of his poetic career as gauged by his collections of originals. In both dimensions of his writing, Mahon takes pains not to conceal (possibly even foregrounding) elements of contradiction and inconsistency. These include the difficult management of anachronism in his two versions of Molière from the mid-1980s; but also the ethical uncertainties highlighted by his attention to the contrary impulses of the Apollonian and the Dionysian, order vs release, that find their textual focus in the tragedies he translated in the 1990s, and in the afterwritings that these versions generate in his poetry collections of the same period. In close relation to this, Mahon's exposure of the banality and hype of postmodernist culture results in an exploitation of the very devices he ostensibly satirises. This strong element of unrest and doubt remains a trait of Mahon's particularity, as proved by the surprise that readers may experience at the tone of vivacity of the ecological plea in some of the poems in *Life on Earth*. Nonetheless, this tone coexists in the collection with Mahon's more characteristic sombreness, which emerges in a variety of pieces that prominently include translations.

In general terms, the ecological concern can be said to be common to Mahon and Longley, but it is expressed in markedly distinct terms: if in Mahon it has ranged from despondency to (recently) uplift, in Longley it has accompanied the tendentially pastoral serenity of poems about his place of retreat in the west of Ireland. And Longley's is a humanised landscape; in all his lyrical output (which includes his translations), textual and human relations overlap much more markedly than in the work of any of the other poets considered here. Hence, he is also the poet that is least reticent about a narrative of shared poetic beginnings, and is particularly vocal in his acknowledgement of a personal poetic pantheon. This is matched by a textual stability that pointedly includes the refusal to revise his earlier work, an aspect he shares with Heaney and which distinguishes him from Mahon. However, while Heaney's textual stability follows a literary imperative, reflecting a canonical (self-)consciousness, Longley's is experiential and ethical (through the importance of the autobiographical element), a matter of truth to self and experience. The unusually blurred boundaries between Longley's original writing and his translations brings out even more clearly that this is a poetics of *correspondence*, in all senses. The poet who has most openly cultivated the verse letter to his peers also rehearses a complex relation to the (predominantly) Ancient authors he echoes and translates, since the possibilities covered by his versions range from literalness to iconoclastic departure. One of the most surprising aspects to have emerged from my integrated reading of Longley's poetry and translations is possibly the degree of freedom that he has allowed himself with regard to his appropriations of sources (in the light of his reputation for formalism and traditional prosody), often blending these with his own lines and domesticating them into his narratives of self and family. The potential surprise is compounded by the affinity between the place held by translation in Longley's collections since *Gorse Fires* and the poet's fascination with hybridity and metamorphosis, a theme that finds its inevitable textual focus in his Ovidian versions. Longley's confrontation with the theme prompts him, like Mahon, to satirise the metamorphic fixation of some strands of postmodernism, while making productive use himself of devices that define the object of his satire; but Longley's tone is one of bemusement and amusement, rather than the exasperation that protrudes from his contemporary's confrontation with the shallowness of some of the (fluid) forms of current culture and art.

Longley's interest in hybridity and metamorphosis certainly provides a connection with Muldoon, whose writing pursues the theme with exceptional persistence, in its dominant tropes and formal options. Muldoon might seem an unlikely inclusion in this book, in view of the comparatively small number of interlingual versions he has produced. However, the sustained presence in his work of the themes of change and (often frustrated) mobility combines with his remarks on the importance of translation for his literary awakening to make him indeed a pivotal figure – for formal, thematic and generational reasons. When considered in the light of tradition and modes of literary transmission, Muldoon may surprise readers for opposite reasons to Longley: in this case, a poet with an emphatic reputation for postmodernist iconoclasm is found to take an interest – and not necessarily a subversive one – in notions of artistic responsibility, poetic lineage, and authorial control. Such concerns have become manifest in his criticism, and emerge in his poetry in equivocal ways, in view of his many transgressive appropriations (unmarked or truncated citation, ironical plagiarism). At their broadest, the contradictions embraced concern matters of intellectual history, canon and criticism, explored with a complexity that his enigmatic sequence 'Madoc' has epitomised (and arguably satirised).

Closer to home, ambivalence marks Muldoon's relation to his Irish predecessors and contemporaries, bearing in particular on the authoritative presence of Heaney – an object of tribute and mild satire, of teasing permutations of priority. Indeed, the authorial relation between Muldoon and Heaney alerts us to how frequently in recent Northern Irish poetry older poets have assimilated the example of their younger peers. Heaney's aerial, post-*Seeing Things* mode may have accommodated aspects of Muldoon's ostensible aloofness with regard to empirical reality, and again Muldoon may be glimpsed behind some of the forms taken by Longley's attraction to images of hybridity; while some of Mahon's more recent urban scenarios (e.g., in his poem on 'Brian Moore's Belfast' – 2008: 17–18) may reflect familiarity with Carson's representations of a palimpsestic cityscape. Muldoon's translations also seem to reflect his active interest in precedence and literary fame, since their tone and overall procedures vary according to the measure of cultural influence and general recognition enjoyed by the source texts, rendered with an irreverence that tends to be proportional to their canonicity. This suggests a degree of planning that can itself be surprising: critical readings of Muldoon have sometimes highlighted (on the basis of archival material) the scrupulous craft underlying the impression of randomness that characterises his textuality. Such deliberateness gains added relevance when the poet is negotiating the ways of subsuming another voice in his; and even more so when different media are involved – as is the case with Muldoon's libretti, an intersemiotic dimension of his work that has had less than its critical due. But these aspects of fastidiousness and design are screened from the reader by a rhetoric of spontaneity, accident and inconclusiveness.

An emphatic commitment to poetic master plans has become a hallmark of Ciaran Carson's writing, only in his case the design is not kept out of sight, but rather exhibited as a transparent dimension of his poetics. The difference that this suggests between Muldoon and Carson, often critically described as major exponents of poetic postmodernism, can be extended to their referential procedures. Attracted as they both are to the liminal and ambiguous, Muldoon tends to maintain a degree of fuzziness about the events and empirical settings to which his poetry refers, whereas Carson's tropes of uncertainty are employed to address and query the recognisable and indeed nominally acknowledged territory of his native place. Carson is, after all, one of the two poets studied in this book who have stayed in Belfast, and indeed the only one that recurrently draws on the city's outdoor scenarios. Thus, he is also singled out by his more open confrontation with division and sectarianism during the Troubles, and (concomitantly) by his reiteration of the postmodernist equation of text and map. The referential outwardness suggested by Carson's specific sense of location might seem at odds with the lyric's emphasis on self; but Carson's autobiographical reminiscence of first awakening to consciousness and language is itself grounded in a detailed awareness of his material, local circumstance. Ultimately, then, in exploring the locale, the resources of language and perplexities of self become coextensive endeavours, amply represented in Carson's verse – and, vicariously as it were, in his translations. Indeed, when the inscription of such wanderings (and the epiphanies they afford) coincides with a rewriting, the poet's confrontation with self pointedly becomes a confrontation with others – both the source authors, and those who have preceded him in translating them. Carson's vivid awareness of translation traditions is certainly a defining trait; it emerges in the varied translation strategies he employs (his versatility in this regard is not surpassed by any of the other poets studied above), in the models and forebears that he acknowledges, and, no less revealingly, in those about whom he is silent. It is with regard to his two major translations, *The Táin* and *The Inferno of Dante Alighieri*, that these issues prove most cogent. As argued above, his *Inferno* in fact becomes an epitome (and thus an apt point of arrival) for the textual and authorial relations studied in this book, against the 'culture of shadows' of contemporary Northern Irish poetry.

The continued imaginative pull of the space of origin evident in the work of these five poets, combined with their mutual responsiveness – shared elements that the physical absence of a few of them has not effaced – suggest that the phenomenon of a distinctive Northern Irish poetic tradition, which was so controversial in the 1980s, is unlikely to be seriously challenged today. There have of course been institutional efforts made to boost this notion,[3] and its continuity has been seen as ensured by the work of poets who began publishing around the beginning of the new millennium. The visibility enjoyed by the poetry of Sinéad Morrissey (who published her first collection in 1996), and of Leontia Flynn and Alan Gillis (who debuted in 2004), certainly reflects individual artistic success, but it cannot be dissociated either from the expectations of cultural renewal that have surrounded Northern Ireland in the recent post-Troubles period. In this regard, the recognition they have already obtained mirrors ironically the attention paid decades earlier to the poets who began publishing shortly before (or shortly after) the onset of the Troubles.

This symmetry, however, does not entail that their poetry should be read as a reflection of the recent discourses of optimism, or that it is predominantly marked by a centripetal drive.[4] In Morrissey's *There Was Fire in Vancouver* (published halfway between the 1994 ceasefire and the 1998 Good Friday Agreement), the ravages of the Troubles are very present and raw, as in the metaphor of personal obliteration, all the more poignant for the brevity of its five lines, in 'Europa Hotel' (1996: 16). But the need for the mediation of an elsewhere in order to comprehend the local and immediate (one of the most constant of the relational designs considered above) recurs throughout the volume. Examples of this include implicit identification with a protestor from Bosnia who set himself ablaze in Westminster (1996: 23); but also (autobiographically) the interlingual experience of the language teacher who surprises herself play-acting a brutal stereotype ('a gunman / On the Falls Road') in order to teach a class of foreigners 'about Northern Ireland', in the ironically entitled 'English Lesson' (1996: 18).

Morrissey's interest in spatial relations and liminal circumstances is structural rather than incidental, as shown by the title of her second collection, *Between Here and There* (2002). The second adverb ostensibly refers to sojourns abroad, in particular to the period that the poet spent in Japan, which yielded the poems in Part II; but the book's 'Here' is pointedly identified from the opening piece, the already quoted 'In Belfast'. This title cannot but recall its use by Mahon, and also, through the remark that 'the city is making money' (13), MacNeice's denunciations of Belfast (already echoed in an epithet in Morrissey's first collection, 'City compacted in faith and damage' – 1996: 57). Morrissey, however, is not offering a rehash of previous Belfast poetry: her *here* is emphatically also the *now* of post-Troubles Belfast, as seen by visitors 'from the European superstate' (in the book's second piece, 'Tourism'). Notably, the exogenous perspective does not afford the delight of a rediscovered freshness, but reveals rather an irredeemable rot: 'the festering gap in the shipyard / the Titanic made when it sank' (2002: 14). However, this note of Mahonian disaffection at the beginning of *Between Here and There* is countered, throughout the collection, by poems of emplacement that signal Morrissey's assumption of a range of poetic models within Northern Irish poetry. They include a debt to Longley in her yearning for communal liturgies in 'In Need of a Funeral', and for proper mourning and domestic comforts in 'Stitches' (2002: 22, 28); an affinity with Medbh McGuckian's poetics of women, home and familial rites (so often pictorially mediated),[5] in 'Eileen, Her First Communion' – after a portrait by Sir John Lavery, reproduced on the book's cover (2002: 15). The yearning arguably reflects the stark perception of exclusion that had a formative impact on Morrissey, from infancy to adulthood, as a consequence of biographical aspects that she has occasionally discussed – the upbringing provided by her Communist, atheist parents (against the environment of sectarian, polarised Northern Ireland), the dissolution of the family home, the wanderings of her adult life.[6]

Morrissey's representations of 'here' and 'there' also include a linguistic awareness that becomes sharper with the stark scriptural otherness that she encountered during her Japanese sojourn: hence poems such as 'To Encourage the Study of Kanji' and 'To Imagine an Alphabet' (2002: 53–5). But this alertness to language and writing only acquires a (factually) translational dimension in her third collection, *The State of the Prisons* (2005). The title sequence, or long poem in six sections, draws substantially (as an intralingual version? as an afterwriting?) on a report by the eighteenth-century penal reformer John Howard, and on elements of his biography. Offering a poetic version of a today little-known account of social iniquities can be a counter-canonical statement, in particular when it is done in such a way as to interrogate the Enlightenment values of the reformer, and their application (cf. Parker 2007 II: 229–30). As such, Morrissey's appropriation of Howard's title and (to some extent) of his text ties in with the poet's acknowledgment of enjoying the canon for its moments of imperfection, in 'Reading the Greats' (2005: 35). This relates intriguingly to the interlingual versions included in the collection, 'Polar – *after Brecht*', and 'The Yellow Emperor's Classic – *after Gong Sun*' (2005: 32, 46–7). In either case – and irrespective of the distinct expectations generated by such culturally disparate sources – the 'after' formula signals an exceptionally diffuse relation to the claimed source, made into a pre-text that yields a verbal consequence of indeterminate freedom, which it would make no sense to place side by side with the nominal target text for a parallel reading.

The book's most significant translational statement, however, is arguably an intralingual rewriting of a well-known piece by a major canonical figure, Robert Frost's 'Stopping by Woods on a Snowy Evening', rendered by Morrissey as 'Driving Alone on a Snowy Evening' (2005: 43). Her option to maintain the prosody (even some of the rhymes) of the source poem's four quatrains might suggest that the point of this version was to update Frost's horse riding to a present-day driving scene. However, Morrissey in fact replaces Frost's vignette of wonder and delight in outdoor freedom (experienced on a singular occasion) with the record of a yearning for death in a scene of entrapment; rather than magical, her snow is a stifling shroud, the blankness of oblivion; and the car no longer means mobility, its capsule an ironic icon for the book's emphasis on confinement. The boldness of this intralingual version of a contemporary poem may owe something to Carson's precedents – for example, his version of Williams's 'The Forgotten City', which (as seen above) is also about reconnoitring familiar territory under exceptional conditions. Indeed, his example seems to be present from Morrissey's first collection, in particular in her exploration of spatial dynamics in the sequence 'Mercury', which includes an image of feet that 'knew all the town's directions', walking through the city as 'through the map' (1996: 37).

In Morrissey's poetry, these possible echoes of forebears (and their spatial relations) are more often than not left for the reader to infer. They tend, however, to be considerably more explicit – and, indeed, a structural trait – in the work of Leontia Flynn. Her second collection, *Drives* (2008), emphatically alternates names of authors and places (more than a dozen in each category) in the titling of its poems. This feature runs counter to Elmer Kennedy-Andrews's reading of Flynn's work under the thematic heading of 'The Irrelevance of Place' (2008: 280) – unless one takes 'irrelevant' as meaning 'non-specific': indeed, Flynn's toponymy is global, as is her gallery of authors, although her native city is (unsurprisingly) the only place name in *Drives* that occurs in more than one title (with 'Belfast' and 'Leaving Belfast'). Her litany of names can be seen as a logical continuation of the mixture of anxiety and ambition that her first collection acknowledged with conscious, deliberate candour. *These Days* is ostensibly about the poet's *Bildung*, foregrounding (with some humour) her status as a beginner: the book's cover relates teasingly to its title by featuring a picture of the poet as a young child. The title poem, however, which is also the collection's closing piece, reports a yearning that can only be expressed through a simile of colossal scope borrowed from the centre of the canon: 'these days, like Cleopatra's Antony, I fancy bestriding the ocean' (2004: 54).

The ambition of 'These Days' laughs itself off, satirising its spacious excess by confessing it with such openness. Throughout the collection, however, the dread of being secondary or derivative recurs and prevails. It includes the unease experienced by 'The Second Mrs De Winter' (borrowed from Daphne Du Maurier's *Rebecca*), hurting under the 'implacable' stare of 'my original' (2004: 13). But it also emerges in the self-directed remark, after being prescribed tranquillisers by a Dutch doctor who finds her condition predictable (since she comes from Belfast): 'Now even your *neuroses* are unoriginal' (2004: 39). Replication seems to haunt Flynn, as suggested by her habit of giving the same title to different poems (*These Days* includes five poems under the title 'Without Me'). But the poet's ability to mock this anxiety over singularity is proved by 'My Dream Mentor', which (with understated satire) reports the dictum: 'If you can't be a prodigy, there's no point trying' (2004: 20). Other pieces perform a more explicit exorcism; the point of the autobiographical vignette 'When I Was Sixteen I Met Seamus Heaney' seems to be the ordinariness and lack of consequence of an occasion that (judging by the title) should have been momentous: indeed, the predecessor's autograph on a bus ticket was 'later lost' (2004: 19), a clear erasure of his priority. As for the writer's block recorded in 'Nocturne', it ends in protest at an epiphanic alert to precedence: 'Whaddya mean already written? What? / Louis? Louis who?' (2004: 22). These are, however, the exceptional sardonic moments in a writing that regularly acknowledges a large gallery of authors, only occasionally taking the form of rewritings – so far, always of an intralingual nature. In *These Days*, the brevity of 'Come Live with Me' makes it a textual echo, rather than an appropriation, of Marlowe's most famous lyric (2004: 4); in *Drives*, the very title of 'Sky Boats – *after Medbh McGuckian (sort of)*' (2008: 13) jokingly signals the diffuse nature of the authorial debt (hence also of the tribute).

Flynn's reflections on writing draw mostly on traditional literary culture, but it is generationally relevant that they extend sometimes to the forms and media of cyberculture, as in 'Perl Poem': the first word in the title refers to a programming language, designed for processing text (2004: 33).

This dimension is considerably more relevant, however, in the poetry of Alan Gillis, informing the scenarios and discourses of his début collection, *Somebody, Somewhere*. The referential vagueness suggested by this title[7] is belied by the recurrent, insistent reference to the poet's native Belfast. His city in fact obtains a huge variety of representations, which include construing it as a map of digitally traced locations, accessed by mobile phoning or texting ('Traffic Jam' – 2004: 28). Belfast's pubs and other social spaces are also the settings for video games, juxtaposed with virtual reality scenarios, even if they paradoxically summon key references from recent history and communal life: a case in point is '12th October, 1994', a relevant date for the Peace Process used as the title of a poem about war games at an amusement arcade (2004: 10–12). The poet's consciousness, as a hub for data and emotions that yield representations, finds an apt analogue in recording technologies that store the past and project possible futures: 'my head becomes a DVD / replaying things that were mixed with things / that might have been' ('Street Scene in Blue' – 2004: 15). Readers in search of conventional pieties, binding identity to standard features of the Irish landscape, might expect some gratification from the title of the book's first poem, 'The Ulster Way' – but they are promptly warned: 'This is not about burns or hedges. / There will be no gorse' (2004: 9). And yet the cultural ballast of traditional culture and canonical literature is *also* there in Gillis's verse, only sometimes in unlikely combinations. In 'Casualty', the liminal moment of anaesthesia is signalled by a revealing contiguity: '*The Lake Isle of Innisfree, The Forest Moon of Endor*' – Yeats converging with *Star Wars*, a conflation which is less iconoclasm than the acknowledgement of a distinct cultural moment, with altered representational needs. And 'Niamh' (2004: 24–6) combines the names of characters from Irish mythology with allusions to Pauline revelation, via Belfast's 'Damascus Street' (an alertness to the ironies of toponymy that may absorb Carson's precedent).

Gillis's postmodernism is grounded in a consciousness of incompleteness, the unlamenting knowledge that all legacies (including verbal legacies) are truncated: 'I remember things with holes' ('Thou Hast Enlarged Me' – 2004: 56). But this does not in any way diminish his writing's underlying confidence in the potency of verbal resources to propitiate meaning – to fulfil the need for inscription that, in 'Cold Flow', is expressed by means of the long-standing literary *topos* of the blank page, applied to the urban space itself: 'Belfast, under blankets of snow, lies like a letter / not yet written' (2004: 13). That confidence in the verbal can be exuberantly demonstrated: in 'Last Friday Night', Gillis employs quasi-phonetic writing to offer a demotic account of riotous nightclub behaviour (2004: 27); in 'The Lad', a piece from his second collection, *Hawks and Doves*, he summons a prodigious array of lexical resources to provide a list of more than 120 epithets for a penis (2007: 41–3).

Finally, the range of Gillis's textuality includes translation of various types. Two interlingual ventures from his first collection concern poems on seascapes, but have only this referential aspect in common. 'Deep in the Coral Forest – *after Arno Holz*' (2004: 41–3) is a version of 'Barocke Marine', a poem of a 100 years ago that Gillis can afford to translate fairly literally (only updating some of its references) and yet make it look outrageously postmodern – in the fluidity of its lines, in its exclamatory diction, in its rampant lexical inventiveness – precisely because the source was (for its time) radical and idiosyncratic, 'an attempt to find a natural rhythm for poetry free from the restrictions of traditional metrics' (Forster 1959: xxi). By contrast, 'Waverly and the Rolling Tasman Sea' (2004: 49–50) looks conventional in diction and in the formal containment of its six sixains, but (as Gillis reveals in a note) it is 'roughly modelled on "Le Cimetière Marin" by Paul Valéry', and includes 'a more or less direct translation' only of 'its last seven lines' (2004: 62); (as seen above, Mahon has offered a more conventional and high-profile version of Valéry's poem – a version that Gillis undoubtedly knows).

In his second collection, *Hawks and Doves*, Gillis also ventures into intralingual versions. 'After Arcadia' brings the formula for textual derivation into its title, and it is indeed a tongue-in-cheek rewriting of Sir Philip Sidney's double sestina 'Ye Goatherd Gods' (cf. Kennedy-Andrews 2008: 277–8). However, the 'after' formula also signals the post-pastoral condition of a poem that replaces the source's rarefied emotions, and the pastoral's defining theme of regenerative dislocation, with the half-crazed sense of entrapment of the urban persona, maimed by personal grief and harassed by the city's auditory aggression – who yet conceives of the *locus amoenus*, even if glimpsed only through analogy and make-believe: 'It's as if one might yet hold forth with valleys, music, mountains' (2007: 58). Starkly contrasting with this rewriting of canonical verse, Gillis's 'You'll Never Walk Alone' (2007: 14–15) has little to do with the lyrics of the popular song (known to many from football terraces), which is nonetheless the referent of its title, made relevant by the minimal neighbourly solidarity extended at the end of the poem to a woman in extreme distress; arguably, this allows the piece to be read as an intralingual version of the eponymous song. Diverse as they are, such pieces contribute to the perception of sharp contrasts suggested by the phrase *Hawks and Doves*. In spite of the eminently public (politico-military) ring of this title, the collection lays an emphasis on human relations (in particular within the family), which several poems present in dysfunctional terms. And this theme is visually glossed by the painting reproduced on the book's cover – none other than *Mr and Mrs Stanley Joscelyne: The Second Marriage*, the faux-naif Anthony Green painting of which Muldoon has published an intersemiotic version.[8]

Through his poems on a socially, economically and technologically distinct Belfast, Gillis confirms that, for these poets of the post-Troubles era, the home location has been extended within its own space to include an array of coterminous other places – both through an influx of cultural alterity and the redefined perspectives of the cyber age. Through his verbal versions and his pictorial choice for the cover of *Hawks and Doves*, Gillis, who is also a scholar and critic of contemporary verse, shows his sharp awareness of a vast body of writing which is varied and multilingual – but he approaches it with a set of practices that reflects the relational examples of his Northern Irish forebears. Indeed, the work of each of the three younger poets discussed in these closing pages promises to thrive on a set of distinctive formal and imaginative resources: Morrissey's perceptual intensities, grounded in the singularity of her experience and played out against an array of spatial relations; Flynn's recurrent concern about the derivative condition, poised between candour and self-mockery; Gillis's scenarios of technological eeriness, into which presences from the past can be evoked and reconfigured – each stands out for its particularity. However, by writing out of their immediate circumstance, experiential as much as literary, they also pointedly affirm their integration into the network of textual and authorial relations that has become a defining master-trait of contemporary Northern Irish poetry.

Notes

1   Introduction: On Rewriting as Dislocation

1. Maria Tymoczko and Colin Ireland have also argued for a historically grounded, peculiarly Irish 'translational condition' (Tymoczko and Ireland 2003: 20).
2. For recent studies of this process, see Doherty (2004) and Ó Cadhla (2006).
3. Cf. Stanford (1976: passim). See also Declan Kiberd, 'Introduction', McDonald and Walton (2002: vii–viii).
4. The phrase 'spatial imagination' is employed by Gerry Smyth in his *Space and the Irish Cultural Imagination* (2001: 1). Smyth offers a comprehensive account of the intellectual background to the rise of an interest in spatial analysis, and applies the appertaining critical tools to a study of a variety of aspects of contemporary Irish culture. These matters are also considered in some detail throughout Elmer Kennedy-Andrews's *Writing Home: Poetry and Place in Northern Ireland 1968–2008* (2008: 1–2 and passim). For a reflection on the retrieval of an interest in the study of space from a 'reactionary' association with stasis, see Massey (1994: 2) and Harvey (1996: 306).
5. Soja in During (1993: 137). Edward Soja played a crucial role in the emergence of this new paradigm with his *Postmodern Geographies: The Reassertion of Space in Critical Social Theory* (1989).
6. Cf. Barnes and Duncan (1992: 2); John Pickles, 'Texts, Hermeneutics and Propaganda Maps', and J. B. Harley, 'Deconstructing the Map', both in Barnes and Duncan (1992: (193–230) 194, (231–47) 231).
7. Cf. Hill and Hughes (1995: 1); Carter et al. (1993: ix); Kearney (1997: passim); Whelan (1996).
8. The image comes from a 'traditional' source and is used in section IV, 'A Severed Head', of Montague's *The Rough Field* (Montague [1972] 1995: 30).
9. For Matthew Campbell, a key aspect in the 'change' undergone by Irish poetry 'between the late 1960s and early 1970s and' the present is 'the typical allegorical or parabolic approach to history in these poems' (2003: 15). For Patrick Crotty, the sensitivities proper to the Northern situation have entailed a more marked wariness of identity politics: 'the suspicion of inherited attitudes to cultural identity shared by poets from both sides of the sectarian divide in Northern Ireland is not so marked in the work of their southern colleagues' ('The Context of Heaney's Reception', in O'Donoghue (2009: (37–55) 43).
10. E. Longley (1994: 51); also E. Longley in Crozier (1990: 26).
11. E. Longley (1987: 152). In *The Living Stream*, she also quips that 'the great advantage of living in Northern Ireland is that you can be in three places at once' (E. Longley 1994: 195).
12. Cf. Brearton (2003); Wheatley (2003: 250, 252).
13. John Goodby argues that 'the Southern dismissal of a specific Northern poetry as "a journalistic invention"' is counterpointed by a Northern 'assertion of the validity of an English-oriented poetic which can show indifference to poetry in the Republic'; he also queries the view of 'Northern Irish poetry as a haven of true poetic values in a world of parasitic metadiscourses' (Goodby 2000: 2).

14. Octavio Paz in Schulte and Biguenet (1992: 152).
15. Held respectively in Lisbon in November 2002 and in Sheffield in February 2004.
16. See Steiner (1992: 39–41) (on sex as a 'semantic act'); Sontag (2003: 15): 'Translation is the circulatory system of the world's literatures'; and Aaltonen (2000) for the 'time-sharing' metaphor.
17. Of the many possible references in Jacques Derrida's work, I will cite just two (the first for its influence, the second for its particular relevance as regards translation): *Writing and Difference* ((1967) 1978: passim); 'Des Tours de Babel' in Schulte and Biguenet (1992: 218–27). A key reference as regards theories of intertextuality: Kristeva (1969) (1980: 36–63). A text that is less often read than alluded to (and its key concept trivialised) is Barthes's 'The Death of the Author' (Barthes [1967] 1977: 142–8).
18. Iser (1995: 31); Edwin Gentzler, 'Foreword'; Bassnett and Lefevere (1998: ix).
19. An influence that is all the more admirable in view of his early death in 1996.
20. Cf. Even-Zohar (2004); Toury (1985, 1995).
21. Cf. James Merrill, 'Introduction', Halpern (1993: ix); Cronin (1996: 184–5).
22. Cf. Schleiermacher [1813] (2004); Venuti (1995: passim).
23. The phrase *Schattenkultur* was coined by scholars of the Göttingen project to refer to the relegation of translation to obscurity all through literary history – cf. Mueller-Vollmer and Irmscher (1998: passim).
24. On the enabling potential of translation for peripheral and insecure cultures, see Bassnett (1991: xii).
25. This passage refers, of course, to Harold Bloom's theory of influence, centrally (though not exclusively) presented in his *The Anxiety of Influence: A Theory of Poetry* (1973). For possible applications of this to readings of contemporary Irish poetry, see Brown and Grene (1989: passim); E. Longley (1996).
26. Dillon Johnston's *Irish Poetry After Joyce* (1985) epitomised this postulation of an alternative line of descent also (and specifically) as regards *poetry*. This was made particularly obvious, in the mid-1980s, by its contrast with Robert Garratt's *Modern Irish Poetry: Tradition and Continuity from Yeats to Heaney* (1986). John Goodby has more recently argued that the Yeats/Joyce duality has persisted 'largely because the polarised critical debate in Irish cultural politics requires it', although the complexity of their legacies is hardly compatible with conscripting these authors to 'set positions' (Goodby 2000: 5).
27. Cf. Heaney's two essays on Kavanagh, respectively 'From Monaghan to the Grand Canal: The Poetry of Patrick Kavanagh' (Heaney 1980: 115–30), and 'The Placeless Heaven: Another Look at Kavanagh' (Heaney 1988: 3–14).
28. Cf. Mahon's essay 'MacNeice in Ireland and England' (Mahon 1996b: 21–30); originally published as part of the collection *Time Was Away: The World of Louis MacNeice* (Brown and Reid: 1974), a landmark publication in this reclamation of MacNeice, for which both Edna Longley (as a critic) and Michael Longley, in particular with his published selections of MacNeice's work, have been vocal advocates.
29. Respectively Walter Jackson Bate's *The Burden of the Past and the English Poet* (1971) and Bloom's already mentioned theory of influence.
30. On the importance of verse letters for the generation that began writing in the 1960s, and in particular in the work of Mahon and Longley, see Redmond (1994), McDonald (1997: 110), Brown (2003: 142).
31. As pointed out by Bernard O'Donoghue in the Introduction to his *Cambridge Companion to Seamus Heaney*, 'no other current poet is nearly as much written

about as Heaney has been' (2009: 2). In his contribution to the same collection, Patrick Crotty expands on Heaney's unprecedented success with a variety of audiences: 'the congruence of wide popularity and critical acclaim has perhaps a readier parallel in mass culture (the Beatles and Bob Dylan) than in literature' (2009: 37).

32. In a Christmas 1975 issue of the *Observer* – cited in Corcoran (1998: 257).
33. (2000: 281). Goodby also cites Carol Rumens in this regard: discussing some of the grounds for a Northern distinctiveness in Irish poetry, she describes the Ulster poetic community as 'a bardic clan with its own semi-secret language of reference and allusion', which 'perceives itself as such even when scattered by emigration', nourished by a 'habit of mutual close-reading and hard-criticism [which] has never disappeared' – Carol Rumens, 'Taig-Tickling and Prod-Picking: Some Northern Irish Poets and their Critics', *Thumbscrew* 7 (1997): (20–8, 28) – cited in Goodby (2000: 320).

2   Authority and Freedom: Seamus Heaney

1. Literally his reply, in the course of an interview: 'your volumes seem to be so carefully crafted in the way they relate to one another [. . .]. Is that the poet's planning or the critics' retrospection? *SH* – Well, it's been planned retrospectively, so to speak' (Homem 2001: 24).
2. Works by Seamus Heaney will be referenced henceforth, in the course of this chapter, only by publication date and page number, unless context requires a specification of authorship.
3. On the gendering of Heaney's writing, involving the actuality of experience but also his understanding of poetic creation, see Fran Brearton, 'Heaney and the Feminine' (in O'Donoghue 2009: 73–91).
4. On the spatial dynamics proper to the pastoral mode, see Alpers (1996); Gifford (1999).
5. For Helen Vendler, the whole gallery of revenants consists of 'a series of alter egos' for the poet, lives that he might have led (Vendler 1998: 93).
6. I use this word to refer to written representations of the process of writing, writing that becomes its own object, or derives from itself its prevalent imagery. This usage has affinities with Rand Brandes's notion of 'the scribal' (as deployed in one of his studies of Seamus Heaney – 1996). My preference for the form 'scriptural' involves its provocative suggestion of textual authority – a central theme in this book.
7. This arguably shows Heaney's ability to transcend the traditional ruralist mindset and respond to a perception of place that, for Elmer Kennedy-Andrews, is characteristic rather of the work of younger poets: 'Place is increasingly viewed as the product of global, interconnecting flows of peoples, cultures and meanings – of routes rather than roots' (Kennedy-Andrews 2008: 8).
8. For several early reactions to the change, in particular in reviews of *Seeing Things*, see Hofmann (1991); MacKinnon (1991); Levi (1991); Crotty (1991/1992).
9. In 1991, interviewed by Blake Morrison, Heaney declared: 'The most important thing that has happened to me in the last ten years is being at two death beds' (Morrison 1991: 26).
10. Rand Brandes has argued for the sustained critical relevance of Heaney's titles: 'Seamus Heaney's Working Titles: From "Advancements of Learning" to "Midnight Anvil"' (in O'Donoghue 2009: 19–36).

11. Several passages in this poem, and in particular the phrase 'the jumbo a school bus', refer to Heaney's regular commuting to America, because of positions held at Harvard University since 1982.
12. Ana Blandiana, 'Inhabited by a Song,' trans. Seamus Heaney, *The Southern Review* 31: 3 (Summer 1995): 468.
13. This process is enhanced by Heaney's 'absolute concentration on lyric poetry in his criticism' (O'Donoghue 1994: 144).
14. Brandes (1988: 14). The indirection of such self-assessment arguably reflects an important formative dimension, acknowledged by Heaney in the same interview with Rand Brandes when he refers to 'my New Critically trained generation' (11). Nonetheless, the mutual consequences of Heaney's life and work (as poet and critic) have obtained considerable attention, as in Michael Parker's monograph *Seamus Heaney: The Making of the Poet* (1993); more recently, Heaney has agreed to offer an extensive integrated account of his experience and writing in Dennis O'Driscoll's *Stepping Stones: Interviews with Seamus Heaney* (2008).
15. The theme has a broad resonance, as suggested by Edna Longley's observation that 'the speech or eloquent silence of the father is an important motif in Northern Irish poetry' (1994: 65). See also her essay '"When Did You Last See Your Father?": Perceptions of the Past in Northern Irish Writing 1965–1985' (1994: 150–72).
16. The brazenness of this was compounded by the fact that, as noted by Conor McCarthy, Heaney's is 'the first full-length English version since O'Keeffe's' (McCarthy 2008: 15).
17. Congeniality has remained a strong factor behind Heaney's translational endeavours. A more recent case in point, involving a rural character who suddenly departs from his territory, is provided by his description of Ozef Kalda's short lyrics for Leoš Janáček's song cycle, *Diary of One Who Vanished* (which he translated in 1999), as a tale of 'a haunted farmer's boy' who falls in love with 'a dark-eyed gypsy', 'the standard fare of folk song' (1999a: vii, ix).
18. Heaney discusses such links in one of his recent interviews with Dennis O'Driscoll (2008: 153–4).
19. For book-length studies of Heaney's work that consistently adopt a poststructuralist, mostly Derridean perspective, see O'Brien (2002 and 2003). Heaney's own attitude to such critical tools is suggested by his remarks on 'a contest going on between Derry and Derrida', his endorsement of '[his] father's silence' as a 'counterweight to all speechifying and theory-speak' (O'Driscoll 2008: 287).
20. The latter phrase was coined by Edna Longley, who applies this duality to her study of the post-Yeatsian poetic scene – E. Longley (1996).
21. This despite the fact that Heaney himself has declared that the figure in question was rather the great Polish poet Czesław Miłosz (O'Driscoll 2008: 262).
22. On Heaney's relationship to Yeats, with particular emphasis on 'authority' and formal accomplishment, see McDonald (1996a); O'Driscoll (2008: 191–5). 'Poetic authority' is also the key theme in David Wheatley's article, 'Professing Poetry: Heaney as Critic' (in O'Donoghue 2009: 122–35). Neil Corcoran has emphasised 'the strenuousness of Heaney's ongoing engagement with Yeats', drawing on his poetry, but arguing also that 'Heaney [is] at his best as a critic' when writing about this predecessor ('Heaney and Yeats' in O'Donoghue 2009: [165–77] 165–6).
23. Dorothy L. Sayers's and Robert Pinsky's versions may prove useful terms of comparison: 'And as starved men tear bread' (Sayers 1949), 'the way the starving devour their bread' (Pinsky 1994).

24. Cf. Sayers (1949); Ciardi (1954); Musa (1971); Sisson (1980); Mandelbaum (1980); Pinsky (1994); Hollander (2000); Carson (2002); O'Brien (2006).
25. Neil Corcoran and Shane Alcobia-Murphy have provided detailed and useful commentary on this passage of 'The Flight Path' (Corcoran 1998: 190; Alcobia-Murphy 2006: 149–51).
26. The version used for this epigraph was Dorothy L. Sayers's, whose translations Heaney acknowledged as fundamental for the inception of his interest in Dante (cf. De Petris 1989: 72). For Sayers's relevance, as for a detailed critical study of the relative and varying importance for Heaney of the *Inferno*, the *Purgatorio*, and the *Paradiso*, see Fumagalli (2001).
27. Levi (1991: 12). Peter Levi's admiration was to be reciprocated in a poem in *Electric Light* that hails him as '*poeta doctus*' (2001: 7). By coincidence, Levi was Heaney's successor (from 1994) as Oxford Professor of Poetry.
28. As noted by Bernard O'Donoghue, 'This Larkin is the Movement formalist co-opted for Modernism' (1998: 248).
29. The remarkably active interest that Irish writers have taken in Greek drama has attracted considerable attention. Recent studies include (in book length) Younger (2001), and McDonald and Walton (2002), besides a large number of articles, among which: McDonald (1995); Richards (1995); McDonald (1997); O'Rawe (1997); Arkins (2003); Hardwick (2006).
30. The project was founded by Brian Friel and Stephen Rea, who were joined on its board of directors by Seamus Heaney, Tom Paulin, David Hammond and Seamus Deane. Book-length studies of the Field Day project include Richtarik (1994) and Szabo (2007).
31. For a recent discussion of Heaney's attraction to their 'moral' and 'artistic author-ity', see Justin Quinn, 'Heaney and Eastern Europe' (in O'Donoghue 2009: 92–105). Quinn is critical of what he sees as the 'overstatements and enthusiasms' in Heaney's critical assessment of Russian, Polish and Czech poets, compounded by his lack of 'proficiency in any Slavic language'; this means that Heaney read these poets in translations that Quinn finds mostly assimilative and domesticat-ing. Quinn grants, though, that Heaney's engagement with these poets has grown in sophistication over the years (93, 95, 102–4).
32. Raymond Williams comes to mind, defining drama as 'one of the most social of all art forms' (Williams 1961: 271), or Martin Esslin declaring that 'The theatre is the place where a nation thinks in public in front of itself' (Esslin 1976: 121).
33. 'Swerve' was a word employed by Heaney to describe the *Seeing Things* moment in his work (cf. Homem 2001: 28); 'redress' became a keyword in his criticism in the 1990s, as in the title chosen for lectures given during his term as Oxford Professor of Poetry (1989–94), *The Redress of Poetry* (1995).
34. Paulin's poetry translations have become noted for the extent to which poets from many different periods and traditions are assimilated to his own diction; a substantial number of examples of his radical appropriations can be found in *The Road to Inver* (2004).
35. Compare Hugh Lloyd-Jones's also recent version for the Loeb Classical Library: 'Well, I will bury my brother, and yours, if you will not; I will not be caught betraying him' (Sophocles 1994: 9).
36. This characteristic of Heaney's translation may have contributed to its conver-sion into an opera libretto. The opera, with music by the Caribbean composer Dominique Le Gendre, and directed by Derek Walcott, premièred in October 2008 at Shakespeare's Globe, in London.

37. For a study of the Newgrange complex that combines elements from archaeology, anthropology, and the history of religions, see Brendan Purcell, 'In Search of Newgrange: Long Night's Journey into Day' (in Kearney 1985: 39–55).
38. The specification is rightly made by Bernard O'Donoghue, with regard to these classicising poems on rurality, in his 'Heaney's Classics and the Bucolic' (O'Donoghue 2009: 106–21).
39. For a discussion of Heaney's relationship to notions of authority, a propos of the publication of his Oxford lectures, in terms that also involve his relationship to Yeats, see McDonald (1996).
40. Heaney had previously used the formula 'I'm all through other' in one of Neoptolemus's speeches in *The Cure at Troy* (48). The later essay, however, expands on the phrase to lend it a more positive and empowering signification. Eugene O'Brien discusses the implications of the phrase in his *Seamus Heaney and the Place of Writing* (2002: 6).
41. In this regard, Heaney '[preserves] the poem's cultural alterity' (Heather O'Donoghue, 'Heaney, *Beowulf* and the Medieval Literature of the North' – in O'Donoghue 2009: [192–205] 205).
42. Susan Bassnett calls attention to this in an essay included in a volume co-authored with André Lefevere (Bassnett and Lefevere 1998: 94).
43. Justin Quinn, otherwise critical of Heaney's invocations of Eastern European poets (see note 31 above), praises these versions as 'a symbol for the reinstatement of the poetry of the East within the European poetic tradition proper' (in O'Donoghue 2009: 103).
44. The connection between this feature of the 1996 collection and its thematic emphasis on 'translation' is made by Neil Corcoran in his chapter 'Translating Freely: *The Spirit Level*' (1998: 186–208).
45. In 'Through-Other Places, Through-Other Times: The Irish Poet and Britain', Heaney advocates the use of this form, since it 'allows equal status on the island of Britain to Celt and Saxon, to Scoti and Cymri, to Maldon and Tintagel, to *Beowulf* and the *Goddodin*' (2002: 378). Justin Quinn has also recently opted to employ the phrase 'the Britannic Isles' (Quinn 2008: 130).
46. Conor McCarthy notes the 'optimism' that underlies Heaney's endeavours with *Beowulf* (2008: 126); and Eugene O'Brien argues that for Heaney, 'to translate is metonymic of the ethical imperative: it is the quintessential form of dialogue with the other' (2002: 117).

3 Of Containment and Unmeasure: Derek Mahon

1. The phrase was employed in the mid-1980s by Mark Patrick Hederman (1985: 115) in an article in the influential periodical *The Crane Bag*. It occurs during a discussion of the implications for poetry of the notion of a 'fifth province' as a mental, additional and non-sectarian space in Ireland – a notion closely associated with the project of the Field Day Theatre Company, much discussed in *The Crane Bag*.
2. Haughton proposes that Mahon's revisions are of five different 'types' – 'changes of title', 'changes of dedication', 'changes of layout', 'cuts', and 'smaller verbal changes' (2007: 126). In this regard, see also Denman (1994) and Allen (2002).
3. Pronouncements that converge towards this critical assessment include Paulin (1980: 64–9); E. Longley (1984: 17–18 and 1991: 7–9); Garratt (1989: 263).

4. Brian Burton has argued for Mahon's indebtedness to Beckett as regards his interest in 'obliterating texts, blackening margins, darkening the page, obscuring the written word *in perpetuum* just as speech obfuscates thought', and this in order 'to express the misery of being human' (Burton 2005: 55). One of Mahon's rare critical pieces that are not book reviews deals precisely with 'the "brief scattered lights" of Beckett's poems' (Mahon 2006a).

5. Tim Kendall's review of *The Hudson Letter* and Ian Sansom's of *The Yellow Book* were respectively damning and accommodating, but both subscribed to the notion that Mahon's best work was in the past (Kendall 1996; Sansom 1998); Frank Sewell's later pamphlet mounted its defence of those collections significantly on arguments for continuity, opposing the notion that they were markedly distinct from Mahon's earlier poetry (Sewell 2000). Hugh Haughton also accounts for this critical reticence by suggesting a fundamental misunderstanding of later 'Mahon's poetics of *bricolage*', whose rampant intertextuality becomes 'a forest of contradictions' (Haughton 2007: 312–13).

6. The page numbers that follow quotations of Derek Mahon's verse up to 1999 refer to his *Collected Poems* of that year. In the case of poems that have been revised, earlier references may be provided when relevant. Quotations from other books by Mahon will be referenced by publication year and page number.

7. This perception of a marked difference between 'Seamus', who 'is very sure of his place', and himself, persistently diffident with regard to a located identity, was explicitly endorsed by Mahon in an interview given in 1981 (cited in Haughton 2007: 97).

8. Michael Parker notes that Mahon's ethical and political estrangement also reflects the global changes in post-1960s politics, which led to Ulster Protestants being perceived as bigots, similar to 'the white settlers clinging on to power in Rhodesia and South Africa' (2007 – I: 167). As regards Belfast in particular, the city's reputation for commercial pragmatism has traditionally made it a difficult object for poetry (on the difficulties posed by 'Belfast in poetry', see Hughes (2003)).

9. For the complexities of his relationship to (Northern) Ireland, see the opening and closing chapters respectively of Edna Longley's and Peter McDonald's monographs on MacNeice (E. Longley 1988: 1–34; McDonald 1991: 203–29).

10. Examples include 'Didymus, III' and 'House on a Cliff' (MacNeice 2007: 335–6, 516).

11. For a recent detailed reading of the poem's historical implications, see Klein (2007: 141–5).

12. As pointed out by Elmer Kennedy-Andrews, 'America Deserta' relates intertextually to Pound's 'Provincia Deserta', also on the decline of a reconnoitered territory (2008: 164). This contributes to the tension that Mahon sets up between the modernist legacy and the motley shapes of postmodern culture.

13. The phrase is borrowed from the title of Dillon Johnston's study of *The Poetic Economies of England and Ireland, 1912–2000* (2001).

14. Hugh Haughton's comprehensive study provides a very useful chart of Mahon's publication history, including his poetry translations (Haughton 2007: 383–90). Haughton opts not to focus on the longer translations, but pays careful attention to some of the shorter lyrical versions.

15. In this regard, see Parker (2007, I: 164); Goodby (2000: 49); Tinley (1994).

16. In 1987 he also published a translation of a novel by Raphaële Billetdoux, under the title *Night Without Day* (New York: Viking). This translation of extensive narrative fiction is outside the range of the present study.

17. Medbh Ruane, 'The Summoning of Everymahon' – cited by Hugh Haughton, '"The Importance of Elsewhere": Mahon and Translation' (in Kennedy-Andrews 2002: 162). David G. Williams cites an earlier interview (1990), in which Mahon acknowledges that his dramatic versions proved 'good practice for arriving at the kind of more conversational verse I'm aiming at now' (Williams 1999: 111).
18. In her essay 'Derek Mahon: Extreme Religion of Art', Edna Longley points out how 'again and again he [Mahon] represents the artist *in extremis*' and 'resurrects the *poète maudit*' (1995: 280–1). At several points in his monograph on Mahon, and also in an earlier discussion of Mahon's work with other critics, Hugh Haughton has evoked how 'the role of *poète maudit* appealed to Mahon' in his early days, and stressed his continued interest in the figure of the writer as detached, 'outside the business,' wary of public recognition (Ní Anluain 2000: 160, 170; Haughton 2007: 30–1 and passim).
19. Shields (2000: 145). In her chapter 'Derek Mahon's Nerval', Shields offers an attentive reading of the tension between self and other in this translation. My reading of *The Chimeras*, in the context of current practices in literary translation carried out by prominent authors, does not confirm her view that Mahon's version is highly manipulative and 'experimental' (159); nor would I agree that, through Nerval, 'he is writing about Northern Ireland' (152) – other than in the indirect terms that derive from the (limited) degree to which Mahon inscribes Nerval with his own diction. As the rest of this chapter will suggest, I do not subscribe either to Shields's view that 'as experiments Mahon's drama translations are less interesting than his translations of Jaccottet and Nerval' (146). I do agree, though, that his versions of Jaccottet provide an empowerment that comes from 'temperamental affinities' rather than a defining stark contrast (148).
20. Terence Brown's essay 'A Northern Renaissance: Poets from the North of Ireland, 1965–1980' sums up the argument that the tradition of the well-made lyric survived and thrived in post-1960s Northern Irish poetry, accounting indeed for its distinctiveness (1988: 203–21). In a 1977 interview, Seamus Heaney endorsed this notion, arguing that the legacy of the well-made poem explained the 'kind of tightmouthedness' common to his poetic generation (1977: 61). See my Introduction above, pp. 9–11.
21. Nerval (1964: 9); Mahon (1982a: 11). Literally, 'wicked old man' or 'old pervert'.
22. All the citations given below are excerpted from this 1998 edition.
23. Mahon (1996: 11). The critical deftness of Mahon's reviews, as of his Jaccottet Introduction, proves that the rarity of his criticism is strictly a matter of choice. This wariness of producing more extensive critical writing suggests Mahon's continued attraction to the writer's peripheral situation with regard to institutional 'culture', and especially to the academic world (in contrast, again, to Heaney's arguable assimilation by the academic and critical Establishment, as tokened by his substantial collected criticism and the chairs held at Harvard and Oxford).
24. The term 'commission' is here employed in the sense accorded to it in Hans J. Vermeer's *Skopostheorie*, a rhetorical and intercultural theory of translation based on the sense of purpose that guides any given translation, following the 'commission' that the translator has accepted – cf. Vermeer (2004).
25. 'Et devant qu'il vous pût ôter à mon ardeur, / Mon bras de mille coups lui percerait le cœur' (Molière 1971: 460).

26. The guiding principle would in this case seem to be what Eugene Nida once called 'dynamic equivalence,' the notion that, in translation, 'the relationship between receptor and message should be substantially the same as that which existed between the original receptors and the message' (Nida [1964] 2004: 156).
27. J. Michael Walton, 'Hit or Myth: the Greeks and Irish Drama' (in McDonald and Walton 2002: 8).
28. On these basic characteristics of the comic plot, see Northrop Frye's classic study, 'The Mythos of Spring: Comedy' (Frye 1973: 163–86).
29. On Irish appropriations of Sophocles and Euripides, and their discrete implications, see Marianne McDonald, 'The Irish and Greek Tragedy' (in McDonald and Walton 2002: 41 and passim).
30. E. R. Dodds was an important intellectual influence on Louis MacNeice, and the first editor of his *Collected Poems* (1966). Invoking Dodds, via the epigraph, furthers Mahon's acknowledgement of MacNeice's legacy.
31. Philip Vellacott's (1973) and David Kovacs's (2002) translations provide, in this regard, useful terms of comparison – and will, as such, be cited in the notes that follow.
32. Mahon (1991a: 18). 'Wherever the sparkle of sweet wine adorns their feasts, / No good will follow from such Bacchic ceremonies' (1973: 200); 'Wherever women get the gleaming grape to drink in their feasts, everything about their rites is diseased' (2002: 35).
33. Mahon (1991a: 20). 'Your wits have flown to the winds, your sense is foolishness' (1973: 202); 'At the moment you are all in the air: you are clever, but your cleverness amounts to nothing' (2002: 41).
34. Mahon (1991a: 37). 'I am ready to save you by my skill' (1973: 220); 'I'm offering to rescue you by my arts' (2002: 87).
35. Mahon (1991a: 12). 'The whole female population of Thebes, / To the last woman, I have sent raving from their homes. / Now, side by side with Cadmus' daughters, one and all / Sit roofless on the rocks under the silver pines' (1973: 192); 'All the female seed of the Cadmeans, all the women there were, I have driven in madness from their houses. Mixed together with the daughters of Cadmus they sit upon the cliffs in the open air under the green fir trees' (2002: 15).
36. 'Et, dans un fol amour ma jeunesse embarquée' (Racine 1990: 44).
37. *The Yellow Book* was the title of a magazine associated with the 'decadent' literature of the 1890s. For a recent appraisal of Mahon's assumption of the title and its implications in his 1997 collection, see Haughton (2007: 265ff.).
38. As pointed out by Elmer Kennedy-Andrews, Mahon's city is 'postmodern', the site of a 'discontinuous culture', 'when it is New York [. . .], but not at all when it is Dublin' (2008: 12).
39. The source text reads: 'dans son obscure chambre' (Rostand 1939: 230).
40. Clive James's review of the National Theatre production of *Cyrano de Bergerac* for the *Times Literary Supplement* was thoroughly damning, with a particular focus on Mahon's version – *TLS* (April 30, 2004): 18–19.
41. Respectively in translations by F. Storr (1912) and Hugh Lloyd-Jones (1994); the remarks here made on Mahon's version of Sophocles are based on comparisons afforded by these two translations.
42. 'I seem to have been only like a boy playing on the sea-shore, and diverting myself in now and then finding a smoother pebble or a prettier shell than ordinary, whilst the great ocean of truth lay all undiscovered before me' – David

Brewster, *Memoirs of the Life, Writings, and Discoveries of Sir Isaac Newton* (1855), vol. II. Ch. 27. Charleston, SC: Booksurge, 2001. 410.

4   Versions of Compassion: Michael Longley

1. Unless otherwise indicated, the page numbers that follow quotations of Michael Longley's verse throughout this chapter refer to his *Collected Poems* (2006).
2. Longley (1994: 31–42). A thorough study of this period in literary history is available in Heather Clark's *The Ulster Renaissance: Poetry in Belfast 1962–1972* (2006).
3. Longley recounts this in his contribution to a discussion panel whose proceedings were published in *Cultural Traditions in Northern Ireland: Varieties of Irishness* (Crozier 1989: 33). Earlier, in a short article in *Fortnight* magazine, he recalled how his schooldays had given him evidence only of social and economic differences within the Protestant community, rather than any direct cross-sectarian contacts (Michael Longley [1984] 1991: 121–2). More recently, Heaney has also commented at greater length on this generational dimension (O'Driscoll 2008: 101 and passim). See also Parker (1993: 52).
4. Longley (1994: 33). Both Fran Brearton and Hugh Haughton, in their authoritative studies respectively of Longley and Mahon, have produced revealing evidence (on the basis mostly of correspondence between the two poets) of the persistent and exigent dialogue between the two, in particular as uncompromising critics of each other's work – Brearton (2006: 17–18 and passim); Haughton (2007: 41, 43 and passim).
5. The best-known version of this argument was put forward by Donald Davie in his *Thomas Hardy and British Poetry*, and later pursued by John Powell Ward in *The English Line: Poetry of the Unpoetic from Wordsworth to Larkin* (Davie 1973; Ward 1991). In his 1970 edition of the Penguin anthology *British Poetry since 1945* Edward Lucie-Smith described the then budding poetic talents from Belfast as 'recognizably post-Movement and neo-Georgian' (Lucie-Smith 1970: 337). Longley has acknowledged and discussed the assumption of the 'well-made poem' by himself and poets of his generation, as in his interview with Fran Brearton (1997: 37).
6. Michael Longley, *The Poetry Book Society Bulletin* (Christmas 1979): 1 (cited in Marken 1989: 85). A later useful statement of his position can also be found in his interview with Clive Wilmer (1994: 116). The 'Nero' caveat would be pursued also by Seamus Heaney in the introductory essay of *The Government of the Tongue* (1988: xi–xxiii).
7. The massacre evoked in this poem was committed on the 5 January 1976 by a Republican paramilitary organisation, SARAF (*South Armagh Republican Action Force*), and its victims were Protestant workers travelling by bus; ten were killed, several others seriously wounded (Bell 1991: 175).
8. Longley borrows the title from a famous song cycle (1902) by Gustav Mahler, after a sequence by the German poet Friedrich Rückert (1788–1866).
9. The fundamental study to date of this aspect of Longley's writing, considered in its historical and ethical implications, is Fran Brearton's article 'Cenotaphs of Snow: Memory, Remembrance, and the Poetry of Michael Longley' (2004). Brearton emphasises Longley's awareness of the perplexities of many remembrance rituals – remembering in order to forget – and hence his concern, variously manifested

in his poetry and in prose statements, with countering their anaesthetic, amnesiac effect.

10. This plea is not unlike a line in Heaney's 'Homecomings' – 'Mould my shoulders inward to you' (Heaney 1979: 49) –, highlighting the affinities between their representations of domestic and married experience.

11. My argument that this productive confrontation nevertheless allows confirmation of the sense of self and place is distinct, in perspective rather than degree, from Fran Brearton's more radical reading of Longley's relation to self and home. She argues that this relationship is fundamentally unstable (particularly in his early work), subject to paradox, 'profound uncertainty', an unceasing quest – a reading that allows her to declare that for *both* Mahon and Longley 'identity is permanently transitional' (Brearton 2006: 34, 45).

12. The source is Douglas's poem 'Vergissmeinnicht' (Graham 1987: 111).

13. Recent studies of Longley's poetry have dedicated a significant amount of attention to his evolving prosody: see Allen (2000); Dunn (2000: 27–30); Brearton (2006: 165ff.).

14. Heaney, 'Homecomings' (1979: 49); Mahon, 'Homecoming'; 'Going Home' (1999: 33, 95–6).

15. Longley's interest in this relational tension, with seductive metapoetic implications, becomes clearer when these lines are compared with E. V. Rieu's famous translation: 'and [it] allow[s] large ships to ride inside without so much as tying up, once within mooring distance of the shore' (1986: 204).

16. As Longley himself acknowledged, this referred to 'a particularly bloody case, the Shankill butchers' (Wilmer 1994:117).

17. The poem was published in the *Irish Times* two days after the IRA's declaration of a ceasefire on 31 August 1994. Longley also read it at the close of a talk given in June 1995 to a symposium on 'Reconciliation and Community: The Future of Peace in Northern Ireland' (Longley 1995a).

18. Heaney has also written about this episode (1996: 35); the source is a recollection in *The Odyssey* (IV: 242ff.).

19. The theme of 'postmodern ethics' and 'the question of the animal' has been the object of a recent spate of publications – for example, Cary Wolfe's *Animal Rites: American Culture, the Discourse of Species and Posthumanism* (2003) and *Zoontologies: The Question of the Animal* (2003).

20. The interest that Ovid has obtained from Northern Irish poets and dramatists was noted by John Kerrigan in his essay on 'Ulster Ovids' (1992), published three years before Longley's versions came out in *The Ghost Orchid*. Kerrigan notes a variety of occurrences and offers a disquisition of the broad political, cultural and literary reasons for the phenomenon.

21. Ted Hughes and Ciaran Carson, each with four contributions, came a distant second to Longley's seven poems – although Hughes contributed longer pieces.

22. See note 24 in Chapter 3 above.

23. See the Introduction, p. 20.

24. Cf. Frye (1957: 223–4); Paulson (1967: 10); Pollard (1970: 3). The 'old theoretical consensus' on satire as defined by a clear set of norms has been challenged in more recent years by (e.g.) Dustin Griffin (1994: passim), but it remains critically influential.

25. Farley-Hills (1981); Stott (2005: 61). The classic definition of comic laughter as benign and congregative is yet Frye's essay 'The Mythos of Spring: Comedy' (1957: 163–86).

5   Words in Transit: Paul Muldoon

1. From the blurb of The Cahiers Series, published jointly by Sylph Editions and the Center for Writers & Translators at the American University in Paris. Muldoon's contribution was No. 8 in this series.
2. This characterisation of Muldoon has become too widespread in critical discussions of his work to allow for brief referencing at this point (see Bibliography). The currency of his description as epitome of a postmodern poetics can also be gauged from academic events like the conference on *Paul Muldoon and Postmodern Poetry*, held in September 2005 at the University of Leeds. For a recent overview of his work and reputation, see Kennedy-Andrews (2006: 1–17).
3. Neil Corcoran's chapter on this rapport remains a fundamental example of its critical appreciation (Corcoran 1999: 121–36); other examples include Longley (1994: 51, 57 and passim); Sansom (1996); Jenkins (1996); Kennedy-Andrews (2006: 101–26); Alcobia-Murphy (2006: 22–5).
4. Jefferson Holdridge argues that Muldoon 'is eclectic and playfully baroque in style, but [. . .] when it comes to his central philosophy of the illumination of the subject, and its place in the world, he is beholden to the modernists for his poetic, [. . .] he celebrates relativism only to a point, and not to a point of no return' (2008: 121).
5. Paul Muldoon, 'To the Threshing-Floor: A celebration of the centenary of the *TLS*', *TLS* (18 January 2002): 16.
6. His rejection of the condition of 'exile' (with all its political implications) emerged at its clearest in *The Prince of the Quotidian*, apropos of a remark made by Seamus Deane (Muldoon 1994: 36). His expatriation, nonetheless, is for Justin Quinn the key to understanding 'the major achievements and major failures of Muldoon's poetry since the 1990s' (Quinn 2008: 185). See also Elmer Kennedy-Andrews's tendentially antithetical reading of Heaney's and Muldoon's constructions of place as standing respectively for 'omphalos' and 'diaspora' (2008: 83–117).
7. Paul Muldoon, *Knowing My Place* (Portrush: Honest Ulsterman, 1971).
8. Unless otherwise indicated, the page numbers that follow quotations of Paul Muldoon's poetry throughout this chapter refer to his *Poems 1968–1998* (2001). Works not included in this collection will be referenced by date and page number.
9. The original source for the notion of *ostranenie*, or 'making strange', is a famous essay by Viktor Shklovsky: 'Art as technique' (1917), Lee T. Lemon and Marion J. Reis (eds/trans.), *Russian formalist criticism: Four essays* (Lincoln, NE: University of Nebraska Press, 1965): 3–24.
10. Revealing examples include Clarke's 'Knacker Rhymes' and 'The Hippophagi', and Kavanagh's long poem 'The Great Hunger' (Clarke 1974: 229–35; Kavanagh 2005: 63–89).
11. As pointed out by Michael Parker, the father's 'table-"pounding"' in 'Cuba' 'replicates that of Nikita Kruschev at the United Nations in October 1960' (2007 – II: 89).
12. For Jefferson Holdridge, 'a sense of exaggerated geography' is a telling aspect of America's impact on Muldoon (2008: 63).
13. These range from the denunciation of binary oppositions by deconstruction to the querying of identity boundaries within gender studies, and of ethnicity and race within postcolonial studies. The latter has emphasised the creative potential of 'liminal spaces', thus establishing further links with the kind of reflections on

the construction of space and place that have characterised 'postmodern geography'. See Bhabha (1994: 38–9 and passim); Graham (1994); Cleary (2003).

14. Seamus Deane and Terence Brown are among the Irish critics who have in recent decades written about these stereotypes: Deane (1985: 17–27); Brown (1988: 3–13).

15. For a discussion of political readings of Muldoon, centred on the argument that he endorses 'the poet's ability to diagnose rather than cure', see Kendall (2006: 77 and passim).

16. Though it alludes to sectarian conditions in Northern Ireland during the Troubles, the poem derives its title from a 'commission' created after the 1921 partition (with the Anglo-Irish Treaty) to decide on any adjustments to the borders between the Irish Free State and Northern Ireland (cf. Foster 1989: 527).

17. Quoted in Marcel Paquet, *René Magritte, 1898–1967* (Cologne: Taschen, 1995) 61.

18. Helen Vendler has famously accused Muldoon's poetry of lacking an emotional core – Vendler (1997).

19. The poem refers to the 'dirty protest' and the hunger strikes at the Maze prison (in the late 1970s and early 1980s); on the relevance of such events for Northern Irish poetry, see Alcobia-Murphy (2006: 142ff.).
As regards the hallucinogenic dimension, see Holdridge (2008: 63–6).

20. http://horsedoc_org.tripod.com/id136.htm (last visited 1 October 2008).

21. For Jefferson Holdridge, the indignation that energises the satirical dimension to Muldoon's writing brings his vision close to Swift's (2008: 27–8). As with Swift, the core concern is 'human suffering', and the poet leaves no doubt that 'human suffering is messy' (141).

22. This dimension was privileged by Clair Wills in some of the pages on *Madoc* in her *Improprieties: Politics and Sexuality in Northern Irish Poetry* (1993: 215–27), and in her 1998 *Reading Paul Muldoon* (135–56). Tim Kendall's chapter on the collection remains a balanced comprehensive assessment of the variety of readings afforded by *Madoc* (Kendall 1996: 149–74). Shane Alcobia-Murphy defends the sequence from charges of randomness, hermeticism and elitism, arguing rather that it is 'chaos by design' (Alcobia-Murphy 2006: 26–38); his reading is predicated on the understanding that 'demonstrating the logic behind [Muldoon's] intertextual references renders his work more accessible' (247).

23. This practice arguably had a miniature rehearsal in '7, Middagh Street' (175–93), the sequence that closed *Meeting the British*, whose seven sections were titled after (and apparently 'spoken' by) the artistic and literary figures – including 'Wystan [Auden]', 'Salvador [Dali]', and 'Louis [MacNeice]' – who at one point shared the New York address mentioned in the title. Muldoon's attraction to the notion of dispersing one's voice through a plurality of masks comes to the fore in his remarks on the uncertainties of poetic personality, included in his lecture on the Portuguese Modernist poet Fernando Pessoa, who wrote under many different names and identities (Muldoon 2006a: 222–44).

24. On the implications of the alternating 'Te Deum' and 'de dum' iambic units throughout the sequence, see Kendall (1996: 165).

25. Claudette Sartiliot's discussion of the transgressive 'citational practices' of 'modernist and postmodernist writers' provides a useful context for Muldoon's own practice (1993: 3, 19 and passim).

26. For more detailed readings of these poems, see my articles 'Of Beards and Breasts, Baldheads and Babies: Muldoon's Mongrel Families', Neil Sammells (ed.), *Beyond Borders: IASIL Essays on Modern Irish Writing*. Bath: Sulis Press, 2004. 178–90;

and 'Couplings: Agon and Composition in Paul Muldoon's Ekphrastic Poetry', *Estudios Irlandeses*, n 0. (Barcelona: 2005): 58–66. http://www.estudiosirlandeses.org/RuiCarvalhoHomem.pdf

27. Rice and Reid (2002: 147).
28. Muldoon's innovative practice of the sonnet form has long been noted (cf. Marken 1989).
29. The notion is here borrowed from Walter Benjamin's much-quoted essay 'The Task of the Translator', which Muldoon cites admiringly on more than one occasion (2006a: 220 and passim).
30. From the translator's notes on this version in *Poetry Magazine*, 188: 1 (April 2006): 9.
31. Compare Heaney's more recent versions of the quoted passages: 'lines that held and held / Meaning back begin to yield'; 'So it goes. To each his own. / No vying. No vexation'; 'His whole instinct is to hunt, / Mine to free the meaning pent' – *Poetry Magazine*, 188: 1 (April 2006): 9.
32. Muldoon's argument, in an interview with Neil Corcoran, that, as a writer, 'one is trying to restrict the range of possible readings' concurs with the notion of authorial control suggested by this passage on 'close writing' (Corcoran 2006: 173).
33. As pointed out by Dillon Johnston, cited in Kendall (156).
34. As pointed out in Kennedy-Andrews (2006: 3). Frank Sewell also notes, with regard to the collection's title, that '"astrakhan" is a pun on the Irish "aistriúchán" which means "translation"' (in Campbell 2003: 163). On the ethics and politics of translation in the global culture, see Venuti (1998: 8–30 and *passim*).
35. Jefferson Holdridge has emphasised the recurrent 'associations between creativity and sexual potency' in Muldoon's writing (2008: 72).
36. Versions of Palamas's sequence by George Thomson (1969) and Theodore Ph. Stephanides with George C. Katsimbalis (1975) provide apt terms of comparison.
37. In David Barrett's translation, these correspond to 'The Footbird', 'A Rebellious Youth', 'An Inspector', and 'Sovereignty – *a beauteous maiden*' (Aristophanes 1978: 153–4). Muldoon's name for the fourth of these characters puns on the mythological Queen Medbh, which indeed stands for sovereignty in Irish myths; replacing her name with 'Maybe', however, puts that traditional significance in question.
38. The alternative version cited is again Barrett's. Muldoon alludes satirically to the name of a famous ship, *The Rainbow Warrior*, owned by the environmental pressure group Greenpeace.
39. Heaney launched these exchanges by suggesting, in *The Place of Writing*, that Muldoon's 'swerves away from any form of poker-faced solidarity with the political programs of the Northern Catholic minority [. . .] have [. . .] achieved the poetic equivalent of walking on air' (1989: 52). Muldoon reciprocated sardonically in *The Prince of the Quotidian*, apropos of Heaney's swerve towards transcendence: 'the great physician of the earth / is waxing metaphysical, has taken to "walking on air"' (1994: 14). Heaney graciously accepted the inversion of poetic priority that this suggested, and declared, on no less an occasion than his Nobel lecture: 'I am permitting myself the luxury of walking on air' (1995a: 11). And in *Hay* (the year before publishing *The Birds*) Muldoon combined the reiteration of this image with an allusion to Heaney's penchant for representing himself *in mezzo del cammin*: 'I could have sworn the she-goat was walking on air, / bounding, vaulting, pausing in mid-career' (2001: 395). Recently, Derek Mahon joined the game by claiming, in 'During the War': 'even at sixty I can still walk on air' (Mahon 2005: 31).

40. Rudyard Kipling, 'Six Honest Serving Men', *Gunga Din and Other Favorite Poems*. Mineola, NY: Courier Dover Publications, 1990. 60.
41. Muldoon's interest in writing words for music has also yielded the lyrics for rock songs that he has published in *General Admission* (2006b) – an area of musical taste and cultural production that the breadth and the dramatic nature of the libretti include but also outweigh. He has been a member of a rock band since 2004 – cf. http://www.rackett.org/about.html
42. The passage takes advantage of a nominal coincidence to allude to the nineteenth-century novelist William Carleton, known for having written about actual (rather than idyllic) rural experience, but also for his sinuous political and religious trajectory. It also alludes to the persistence, in parts of the Caribbean, of an Irish accent introduced in the seventeenth century by transported political prisoners (see Kennedy-Andrews 2008: 18).
43. This subtitle appears on the jacket of the CD recording of *Vera of Las Vegas* (New York: Composers Recordings, 2002).

6   The Hand, the Voice, the Map: Ciaran Carson

1. The notion, favoured by an almost complete omission of references to *The New Estate* in critical accounts of his poetry, was to some extent endorsed by Carson himself in interview with Rand Brandes, shortly after the relaunch of his career (1990: passim).
2. Unless otherwise indicated, the page numbers that follow quotations of Ciaran Carson's verse throughout this chapter refer to his *Collected Poems* (2008). Quotations from other books by Carson will be referenced by publication year and page number.
3. Albeit from such varied perspectives as those of Neil Corcoran (1992: 215); Edna Longley (1994: 52–5); Stan Smith (2005: 203–19).
4. His 'rangy "long line" [. . .] has been attributed variously to the influence of C. K. Williams, Louis MacNeice and traditional music', and helped Carson refashion himself as 'a raconteur-poet' (Rumens 1999: 86).
5. Some of this information emerges in passages of Carson's prose, especially in *The Star Factory* (1997). On Carson's ambivalent tracing of his father's steps, between continuity and 'revision', and the motif of the 'speech or eloquent silence of the father' in Northern Irish poetry, see E. Longley (1994: 64–5).
6. Elmer Kennedy-Andrews's characterisation of Carson's persona as 'a harried *flâneur*' (2008: 207) is in fact an oxymoron: such a figure has little or none of the ease, composure and leisure of the Baudelairean/Benjaminian *flâneur* (cf. Benjamin 1999: 162–70 and passim).
7. See Chapter 5, p.145.
8. Some of these vignettes evoke known precedents in Irish poetry, including Mahon's interest in Parisian settings and, before him, John Montague: Carson's two 'Rue Daguerre' poems in *For All We Know* inevitably involve an echo of Montague's 1967 piece on his Paris address, '11 rue Daguerre' (Montague 1995: 213).
9. On the recurrence of trade names in Carson's verse, see O'Brien (1998: 191–2).
10. See Chapter 4, pp.107–8.
11. As made evident in his prose volume *Last Night's Fun: In and Out of Time with Irish Music* (1996).
12. On discontinuity and contradiction in *The Táin*, see Lowe (2003).

13. In his own Introduction, Kinsella stated his aim 'to produce passages of verse which more or less match the original for length, ambiguity and obscurity', but he believed that this was best done by making 'no attempt [. . .] to follow the Irish verse forms' (Kinsella 1970: xii).
14. See Chapter 2, p. 34; Chapter 5, p.141.
15. For the same passages, Kinsella opts for 'dung', 'backside' and 'Foul Place' (Kinsella 1970: 132, 133, 250). Maria Tymoczko has argued that the omission from earlier translations of *The Taín* (e.g., Standish O'Grady's late nineteenth-century versions) of episodes of irrational violence, sex, adultery, or scatology reflected the perception of nationalists that such features of this foundational epic would favour the persistence of demeaning stereotypes of the Irish; conversely, the inclusion of such aspects in recent translations suggests a regained cultural self-confidence (Tymoczko 1999: 22–4, 66ff.).
16. As a consequence of his much debated retreat, from the early 1970s, into a poetics of spareness and 'difficulty'. He briefly discusses this himself in a 1993 interview (Badin 1996: 194 and passim).
17. See Chapter 1, pp. 9–11.
18. On Carson's 'ambilocation' and attraction to the notion of the antipodes, see Smith (2005: 208 and passim).
19. MacNeice's famous phrase in 'Snow' (MacNeice 2007: 24). For a reading of Carson's own 'Snow' (131–2) against its MacNeicean prototype, see E. Longley (1994: 262–4).
20. See Chapter 5, pp. 155–6.
21. A particularisation of Muldoon's 'hunting for the precise // word' (Muldoon 2001: 436), and of Heaney's 'instinct [. . .] to free the meaning pent' (*Poetry Magazine*, 188: 1 [April 2006]: 9).
22. See Chapter 2, pp. 49–50.
23. All citations of the text (rather than the introductory paratexts) of Carson's version of the *Inferno* will be referenced by Canto and line numbers. Citations of the source text refer to the 1980 Rizzoli edition; other translations, cited for comparison, will be referenced by the translator's name (see Bibliography).
24. The *Inferno* was translated *into Irish* by Pádraig de Brún (clergyman, mathematician and classical scholar) and posthumously published, with annotations, in 1963 (cf. the 'Dante catalogue' at http://www.mtholyoke.edu/lits/library/arch/col/rare/rarebooks/giamatti/dantegia.htm.
25. In his essay 'What Dante Means to Me' (Hawkins and Jacoff 2001: [28–39] 38).
26. In other English versions, 'impious wretches [. . .] in the filthy field' (Sayers), 'the spirits sunk in that foul paste' (Ciardi), 'the drowning sinners of this place' (Musa), 'The wretches [. . .] where they are mired' (Pinsky), 'the wretches drowning in the filth' (O'Brien).
27. The opening word is given as 'Pappy' in the text, but glossed as 'Poppy' in a note (2002: 252–3).
28. Respectively in Sayers; Ciardi and Musa; Pinsky, Heaney and O'Brien.
29. Dante's 'un bel fiumicello' is, in other versions: 'a goodly rivulet' (Sayers), 'a sweet brook' (Ciardi), 'a sweetly flowing stream' (Musa), 'a handsome stream' (Pinsky), 'a gently flowing stream' (O'Brien).
30. Especially when used 'as a means to connect the present to the past without positing the transparency of representation' – Hutcheon (1991: 227–8); see also Hutcheon (1985: 2–3).

31. Eliot, 'The Waste Land' l.430 (1963: 79); his plea for the 'mythical method' was presented in his review-essay '*Ulysses*, Order and Myth' (1923).

7   Conclusions – and Some Extensions

1. Sinéad Morrissey, 'In Belfast' (2002: 13).
2. See Chapter 3, p.70, and note 7, p.217.
3. A commitment to poetry has long been a distinctive trait of the School of English at Queen's University Belfast, further enhanced in recent years by the creation of the Seamus Heaney Centre for Poetry. Efforts to improve the image of post-Troubles Belfast have included an emphasis on its literary traditions (countering the city's earlier reputation for commercial philistinism), and in particular on its poets (cf. http://www.belfastcity.gov.uk/tourismguides/literaryguide.asp).
4. Justin Quinn has remarked on Flynn's and Gillis's indifference to traditional frameworks, in particular those provided by a nationalist agenda, for confronting 'events unfolding around them' (Quinn 2008: 197).
5. For a discussion of this aspect of Medbh McGuckian's poetry, see my 'Looking for Clues: McGuckian, poems and portraits' (in Homem and Lambert 2006: 187–98).
6. Both Michael Parker and Elmer Kennedy-Andrews, in their recent studies, provide details of this biographical dimension (cf. Parker 2007 II: 157; Kennedy-Andrews 2008: 256–7).
7. For Elmer Kennedy-Andrews, this title is also 'an impassioned cry for an audience' (2008: 271).
8. See Chapter 5, p.151.

Bibliography

Primary Sources

Seamus Heaney

Poetry

Death of a Naturalist. London: Faber, 1966.
Door into the Dark. London: Faber, 1969.
Wintering Out. London: Faber, 1972.
North. London: Faber, 1975.
Stations. Belfast: Ulsterman Publications, 1975a.
Field Work. London: Faber, 1979.
Station Island. London: Faber, 1984.
The Haw Lantern. London: Faber, 1987.
Seeing Things. London: Faber, 1991.
The Spirit Level. London: Faber, 1996.
Opened Ground: Poems 1966–1996. London: Faber, 1998.
Electric Light. London: Faber, 2001.
District and Circle. London: Faber, 2006.

Translations

Sweeney Astray. London: Faber, 1983.
The Cure at Troy: A Version of Sophocles's Philoctetes. London: Faber, 1990.
The Midnight Verdict. Loughcrew: Gallery, 1993.
Inferno Cantos I, II, III. Daniel Halpern (ed.). *Dante's Inferno: Translations by Twenty Contemporary Poets.* Hopewell, NJ: Ecco Press, 1993a. 3–15.
(with Stanislaw Baranczak). *Jan Kochanowski: Laments.* London: Faber, 1995.
Beowulf. London: Faber, 1999.
Diary of One Who Vanished: A Song Cycle by Leos Janacek of Poems by Ozef Kalda, in a New Version by Seamus Heaney. London: Faber, 1999a.
The Burial at Thebes. Sophocles's *Antigone* translated by Seamus Heaney. London: Faber, 2004.
The Testament Of Cresseid; A Retelling Of Robert Henryson's Poem. London: Enitharmon, 2004a.

Essays

Preoccupations: Selected Prose 1968–1978, London: Faber, 1980.
'Envies and Identifications: Dante and the Modern Poet'. *Irish University Review* 15: 1 (Spring 1985): 5–19.
'Place and Displacement: Reflections on some Recent Poetry from Northern Ireland'. *The Agni Review* 22 (1985a): 158–77.
The Government of the Tongue: The 1986 T. S. Eliot Memorial Lectures and Other Critical Writings. London: Faber, 1988.
The Place of Writing: The Inauguration of the Richard Ellmann Lectures in Modern Literature. Atlanta, GA: Scholars Press, 1989.

'Earning a Rhyme: Notes on Translating *Buile Suibhne'*. Rosanna Warren (ed.). *The Art of Translation: Voices from the Field*. Boston: Northeastern University Press, 1989a: 13–20.

'Learning from Eliot'. *Agenda* 27: 1 (Spring 1989b): 17–31.

The Redress of Poetry: Oxford Lectures. London: Faber, 1995.

Crediting Poetry: The Nobel Lecture. Loughcrew: Gallery, 1995a.

'The Frontier of Writing'. Jacqueline Genet and Wynne Hellegouarc'h (eds) *Irish Writers and Their Creative Process*. Gerrards Cross: Colin Smythe, 1996b: 3–16.

'The Drag of the Golden Chain: How the Translator 'gropes along', Transmitting Meaningful Signals 'from the hoard to the herd''. *TLS* (12 November 1999b): 14–16.

'Time and Again: Poetry and the Millennium'. *The European English Messenger* X: 2 (Autumn 2001a): 19–30.

Finders Keepers: Selected Prose 1971–2001. London: Faber, 2002.

'The Cure at Troy: Production Notes in No Particular Order'. Marianne McDonald and J. Michael Walton (eds). *Amid Our Troubles: Irish Versions of Greek Tragedy*. London: Methuen, 2002a. 171–80.

'"Apt Admonishment":Wordsworth as an Example'. *Hudson Review* LXI: 1 (Spring 2008): 19–33.

Derek Mahon:

Poetry

Night-Crossing. Oxford: Oxford University Press, 1968.

Lives. Oxford: Oxford University Press, 1972.

The Snow Party. Oxford: Oxford University Press, 1975.

Poems 1962–1978. Oxford: Oxford University Press, 1979.

The Hunt by Night. Oxford: Oxford University Press, 1982.

Antarctica. Dublin: Gallery, 1985.

Selected Poems. London/Oldcastle: Viking/Gallery, 1991.

The Hudson Letter. Loughcrew: Gallery, 1995.

The Yellow Book. Loughcrew: Gallery, 1997.

Collected Poems. Loughcrew: Gallery, 1999.

Harbour Lights. Loughcrew: Gallery, 2005.

Life on Earth. Loughcrew: Gallery, 2008.

Translations

The Chimeras: A Version of Les Chimères by Gérard de Nerval. Dublin: Gallery, 1982a.

High Time: A Comedy in One Act Based on Molière's The School for Husbands. Dublin: Gallery, 1985a.

The School for Wives: A Play in Two Acts after Molière. Dublin: Gallery, 1986.

The Bacchae: After Euripides. Loughcrew: Gallery, 1991a.

Racine's Phaedra. Loughcrew: Gallery, 1996a.

Words in the Air: A Selection of Poems by Philippe Jaccottet. Loughcrew: Gallery, 1998.

Saint-John Perse – Birds. Loughcrew: Gallery, 2002.

Cyrano de Bergerac: A New Version of Edmond Rostand's 'Heroic Comedy'. Loughcrew: Gallery, 2004.

Oedipus – A Version of Sophocles's King Oedipus and Oedipus at Colonus. Loughcrew: Gallery, 2005a.

Adaptations. Loughcrew: Gallery, 2006.

Essays

Journalism: Selected Prose 1970–1995. Ed. by Terence Brown. Loughcrew: Gallery, 1996.

'MacNeice in England and Ireland'. Terence Brown and Alec Reid (eds). *Time was Away: The World of Louis MacNeice*. Dublin: Dolmen Press, 1974. 113–22.

'Watt is the Word: The "brief scattered lights" of Beckett's Poems'. *Times Literary Supplement* (3 November 2006a): 12–13.

Michael Longley

Poetry (and translations)

No Continuing City. London: Macmillan, 1969.

An Exploded View. London: Gollancz, 1973.

Man Lying on a Wall. London: Gollancz, 1976.

The Echo Gate. London: Secker and Warburg, 1979.

Poems 1963: 1983 (1985). Harmondsworth: Penguin, 1986.

Gorse Fires. London: Secker and Warburg, 1991.

The Ghost Orchid. London: Cape, 1995.

Broken Dishes. Belfast: Abbey Press, 1998.

The Weather in Japan. London: Cape, 2000.

Snow Water. London: Cape, 2004.

Collected Poems. London: Cape, 2006.

Essays/memoirs

'A Boy on a Sleeping Volcano' (1984). Robert Bell, Robert Johnstone and Robin Wilson (eds). *Troubled Times: Fortnight Magazine and the Troubles in Northern Ireland 1970–91*. Belfast: Blackstaff Press, 1991. 121–2.

Tuppenny Stung: Autobiographical Chapters. Belfast: Lagan Press, 1994.

'Memory and Acknowledgment'. *The Irish Review* 17/18 (Winter 1995a): 153–9.

Paul Muldoon

Poetry

New Weather. London: Faber, 1973.

Mules. London: Faber, 1977.

Why Brownlee Left. London: Faber, 1980.

Quoof. London: Faber, 1983.

Meeting the British. London: Faber, 1987.

Madoc – A Mystery. London: Faber, 1990.

The Annals of Chile. London: Faber, 1994.

The Prince of the Quotidian. Loughcrew: Gallery, 1994.

Hay. London: Faber, 1998.

Poems 1968–1998. London: Faber, 2001.

Moy Sand and Gravel. London: Faber, 2002.

Horse Latitudes. London: Faber, 2006.

General Admission. Loughcrew: Gallery, 2006b.

Translations

The Astrakhan Cloak: Poems in Irish by Nuala Ní Dhomnaill with Translations into English by Paul Muldoon. Dublin: Gallery, 1992.

The Birds: Translated from Aristophanes by Paul Muldoon with Richard Martin. Loughcrew: Gallery, 1999.
When the Pie Was Opened. The Cahiers Series. Lewes: Sylph Editions, 2008.

Drama/Libretti

Shining Brow. London: Faber, 1993.
Six Honest Serving Men. Loughcrew: Gallery, 1995.
Bandanna: An Opera in Two Acts and a Prologue. London: Faber, 1999a.
Vera of Las Vegas. Loughcrew: Gallery, 2001.

Essays

'Getting Round: Notes Towards an *Ars Poetica*'. *Essays in Criticism* XLVIII: 2 (April 1998): 107–28.
To Ireland, I: The Clarendon Lectures in English Literature 1998. Oxford: Oxford University Press, 2000.
The End of the Poem: Oxford Lectures on Poetry. London: Faber, 2006a.

Ciaran Carson

Poetry

The New Estate. Belfast: Blackstaff, 1976.
The Irish for No. Dublin: Gallery, 1987.
Belfast Confetti. Dublin: Gallery, 1989.
First Language. Loughcrew: Gallery, 1993.
Opera Et Cetera. Loughcrew: Gallery, 1996.
The Twelfth of Never. Loughcrew: Gallery, 1998.
Breaking News. Loughcrew: Gallery, 2003.
For All we Know. Loughcrew: Gallery, 2008.
Collected Poems. Loughcrew: Gallery, 2008.

Translations

The Alexandrine Plan: Versions of Sonnets by Baudelaire, Mallarmé and Rimbaud. Loughcrew: Gallery, 1998.
The Inferno of Dante Alighieri. London:Granta, 2002.
The Midnight Court: A New Translation of 'Cúirt an Mheán Oíche' by Brian Merriman. Loughcrew: Gallery, 2005.
The Táin: A New Translation of the Táin Bó Cúailnge. London: Penguin, 2007.

Fiction/Autobiography

Last Night's Fun. London: Cape, 1996.
The Star Factory. London: Granta, 1997.
Fishing for Amber: A Long Story. London: Granta, 1999.
Shamrock Tea. London: Granta, 2001.

Other primary sources

Aristophanes. *The Knights, Peace, Wealth*. Trans. Alan H. Sommerstein. *The Birds, The Assemblywomen*. Trans. David Barrett. Harmondsworth: Penguin, 1978.
Clarke, Austin. *Collected Poems*. Dublin: Dolmen Press, 1974.

Dante Alighieri. *Hell (L'Inferno) – The Comedy of Dante Alighieri, the Florentine, Cantica I.* Trans. Dorothy L. Sayers. London: Penguin, 1949.

Dante Alighieri. *Inferno.* Milano: Rizzoli, 1980.

Dante Alighieri. *Inferno – The Divine Comedy.* Trans. C. H. Sisson. London and Sydney: Pan Books, 1980.

Dante Alighieri. *The Inferno of Dante.* A New Verse translation by Robert Pinsky. New York, NY: Farrar, Straus and Giroux, 1994.

Dante Alighieri. *Inferno – The Divine Comedy.* Trans. Allen Mandelbaum (1980). London: Everyman, 1995.

Dante Alighieri. *The Inferno.* Trans. John Hollander and Jean Hollander. New York: Anchor, 2000.

Dante Alighieri. *The Inferno.* Trans. John Ciardi (1954, 1982). New York, NY: Signet, 2001.

Dante Alighieri. *Inferno – The Divine Comedy,* vol.1. Trans. Mark Musa (1971). Harmondsworth: Penguin, 2003.

Dante Alighieri. *Inferno.* Trans. Sean O'Brien. London: Picador, 2006.

Deane, Seamus (gen ed.). *The Field Day Anthology of Irish Writing.* 3 vols. Derry: Field Day/London: Faber, 1991.

Dorsch, T. S. (trans.). *Classical Literary Criticism – Aristotle: On the Art of Poetry; Horace: On the Art of Poetry; Longinus: On the Sublime.* Harmondsworth: Penguin, 1965.

Eliot, T. S. *Collected Poems 1909–1962.* London: Faber, 1963.

Euripides. *The Bacchae and other plays.* Trans. Philip Vellacott. London: Penguin, 1973.

Euripides. *Bacchae, Iphigenia at Aulis, Rhesus.* Edited and trans. David Kovacs. Cambridge, MA: Harvard University Press, 2002.

Fallon, Peter and Derek Mahon (eds). *The Penguin Book of Contemporary Irish Poetry.* London: Penguin, 1990.

Flynn, Leontia. *These Days.* London: Cape, 2004.

Flynn, Leontia. *Drives.* London: Cape, 2008.

Forster, Leonard (ed.). *The Penguin Book of German Verse.* Harmondsworth: Penguin, 1959.

Friel, Brian. *Translations.* London: Faber, 1981.

Gillis, Alan. *Somebody, Somewhere.* Loughcrew: Gallery, 2004.

Gillis, Alan. *Hawks and Doves.* Loughcrew: Gallery, 2007.

Graham, Desmond (ed.). *Keith Douglas: The Complete Poems,* Oxford: Oxford University Press, 1987.

Griffiths, Eric and Reynolds, Matthew (eds). *Dante in English.* Harmondsworth: Penguin, 1998.

Halpern, Daniel (ed.). *Dante's Inferno: Translations by Twenty Contemporary Poets.* Introduced by James Merrill, with an afterword by Giuseppe Mazzotta. Hopewell, NJ: Ecco Press, 1993.

Heaney, Seamus and Ted Hughes (eds). *The Rattle Bag.* London: Faber, 1982.

Heaney, Seamus and Ted Hughes (eds). *The School Bag.* London: Faber, 1997.

Hofmann, Michael and James Lasdun (eds). *After Ovid: New Metamorphoses.* London: Faber, 1994.

Homer. *The Iliad.* Trans. E. V. Rieu (1950). Harmondsworth: Penguin, 1986.

Homer. *The Odyssey.* Trans. E. V. Rieu (1946). Harmondsworth: Penguin, 1986.

Homer. *The Odyssey.* Trans. Robert Fitzgerald. New York, London, Toronto: Everyman, 1992.

Joyce, James. *Finnegans Wake.* 3rd edn. London: Faber, 1975.

Kavanagh, Patrick. *Collected Poems*. Ed. byAntoinette Quinn. London: Penguin, 2005.

Kennelly, Brendan (ed.). *The Penguin Book of Irish Verse*. 2nd edn. Harmondsworth: Penguin, 1981.

Kiberd, Declan (ed.). *The Field Day Anthology of Irish Writing*. Vol. 3. Derry: Field Day/ London: Faber, 1991.

Kinsella, Thomas (ed.). *The New Oxford Book of Irish Verse*. Oxford: Oxford University Press, 1986.

Kinsella, Thomas (trans.). *The Tain: Translated from the Irish Epic Tain Bo Cuailnge*. Oxford: Oxford University Press, (1969) 1970.

Lucie-Smith, Edward (ed.). *British Poetry Since 1945*. Harmondsworth: Penguin, 1970.

MacNeice, Louis. *Collected Poems*. ed. Peter McDonald. London: Faber, 2007.

Montague, John. *Collected Poems*. Loughcrew: Gallery, 1995.

Molière. *Oeuvres Complètes*. Paris: Gallimard, 1971.

Morrissey, Sinéad. *There was Fire in Vancouver*. Manchester: Carcanet, 1996.

Morrissey, Sinéad. *Between Here and There*. Manchester: Carcanet, 2002.

Morrissey, Sinéad. *The State of the Prisons*. Manchester: Carcanet, 2005.

Muldoon, Paul (ed.). *The Faber Book of Beasts*. London: Faber, 1997.

Muldoon, Paul (ed.). *The Faber Book of Contemporary Irish Poetry*. London: Faber, 1986.

Nerval, Gérard de. *Poésies*. Paris: Gallimard/Librairie Générale Française, 1964.

O'Keeffe, J. G. (ed. and trans.). *Buile Suibhne (The Frenzy of Suibhne), being The Adventures of Suibhne Geilt: A Middle-Irish Romance*. London: Irish Texts Society, 1913.

Ormsby, Frank (ed.). *A Rage for Order: Poetry of the Northern Ireland Troubles*. Belfast: Blackstaff, 1992.

Ovid. *Metamorphoses*. Trans. Arthur Golding (1567).

Ovid. *Metamorphoses*. Trans. Mary M. Innes (1955). Harmondsworth: Penguin, 1983.

Palamas, Kostes. *The Twelve Lays of the Gipsy*. Trans. George Thomson. London: Lawrence and Wishart, 1969.

Palamas, Kostes. *The Twelve Words of the Gypsy*. Trans. Theodore Ph. Stephanides and George C. Katsimbalis. n.p.: Memphis State University Press, 1975.

Paulin, Tom. *Liberty Tree*. London: Faber, 1983.

Paulin, Tom. *The Riot Act: A Version of Sophocles' Antigone*. London: Faber, 1985.

Paulin, Tom. *The Road to Inver*. London: Faber, 2004.

Racine. *Phèdre*. np: Larousse, 1990.

Rice, Adrian and Angela Reid (eds). *A Conversation Piece: Poetry and Art*. Newry: The National Museums and Galleries of Northern Ireland/Abbey Press, 2002.

Rostand, Edmond. *Cyrano de Bergerac* (1897). Paris: Hachette, 1939.

Sophocles. *The Antigone*. Edited with introduction and notes by Sir Richard Jebb. Cambridge: Cambridge University Press, 1891.

Sophocles. *Oedipus at Colonus*. Trans. F. Storr. London: Heinemann, 1912.

Sophocles. *Antigone/The Women of Trachis/Philoctetes/Oedipus at Colonus*. Trans. Hugh Lloyd-Jones. Cambridge, MA: Harvard University Press, 1994.

Stevens, Wallace (1972). *The Palm at the End of the Mind: Selected Poems and a Play by Wallace Stevens*. Ed. by Holly Stevens. New York: Random House.

Yeats, W. B. *Collected Poems*. London: Picador, 1990.

Secondary Sources

Aaltonen, Sirkku. *Time-Sharing on Stage: Drama Translation in Theatre and Society*. Clevedon: Multilingual Matters, 2000.

Agee, Chris. 'Of Peace and Nature'. *The Irish Times* (17 April 2004): 12.

Alcobia-Murphy, Shane. *Sympathetic Ink: Intertextual Relations in Northern Irish Poetry.* Liverpool: Liverpool University Press, 2006.

Allen, Graham. *Intertextuality.* London: Routledge, 2000.

Allen, Michael. 'The Parish and the Dream: Heaney and America, 1969–1987'. *The Southern Review* 31: 3 (July 1995 – Special Irish Issue): 726–38.

Allen, Michael (ed.). *Seamus Heaney.* Houndmills and London: Palgrave Macmillan, 1997.

Allen, Michael. 'Longley's Long Line: Looking Back from *The Ghost Orchid*'. Alan J. Peacock and Kathleen Devine (eds), *The Poetry of Michael Longley.* Gerrards Cross: Colin Smythe, 2000. 121–41.

Allen, Michael. 'Rhythm and Revision in Mahon's Poetic Development'. Elmer Kennedy-Andrews (ed.), *The Poetry of Derek Mahon.* Gerrards Cross: Colin Smythe, 2002. 111–29.

Allen-Randolph, Jody. 'Interview: Michael Longley'. *Colby Quarterly* XXXIX: 3 (September 2003): 294–308.

Alpers, Paul. *What is Pastoral?.* Chicago, IL: The University of Chicago Press, 1996.

Álvarez, Román and M. Carmen-África Vidal (eds). *Translation, Power, Subversion.* Clevedon: Multilingual Matters, 1996.

Andrews, Elmer (ed.). *Contemporary Irish Poetry: A Collection of Critical Essays.* Basingstoke and London: Palgrave Macmillan, 1992.

Andrews, Elmer (ed.). *Seamus Heaney: A Collection of Critical Essays.* Basingstoke and London: Palgrave Macmillan, 1992a.

Arkins, Brian. 'Irish Appropriations of Sophocles' *Antigone* and *Philoctetes*'. Michael Cronin and Cormac Ó Cuilleanáin (eds). *The Languages of Ireland.* Dublin: Four Courts Press, 2003. 167–78.

Auden, W. H. *Secondary Worlds.* London: Faber, 1968.

Badin, Donatella Abbate. 1996. *Thomas Kinsella.* New York: Twayne Publishers/ London: Prentice Hall International.

Barnes, Trevor J. and James S. Duncan (eds). *Writing Worlds: Discourse, Text and Metaphor in the Representation of Landscape.* London: Routledge, 1992.

Barnstone, Willis. *The Poetics of Translation: History, Theory, Practice.* New Haven and London: Yale University Press, 1993.

Barth, John. *The Literature of Exhaustion and the Literature of Replenishment.* Northbridge, CA: Lord John Press, 1982.

Barthes, Roland. 'The Death of the Author' (1967). *Image, Music,Text.* Trans. Stephen Heath. London: Fontana, 1977. 142–8.

Bassnett, Susan. *Translation Studies* (1987). Revised edition. London: Routledge, 1991.

Bassnett, Susan. *Comparative Literature: A Critical Introduction.* Oxford: Blackwell, 1993.

Bassnett, Susan. 'The Meek or the Mighty: Reappraising the Role of the Translator'. Román Álvarez and Carmen-África Vidal (eds), *Translation, Power, Subversion.* Clevedon: Multilingual Matters, 1996. 10–24.

Bassnett, Susan and André Lefevere. *Translation, History and Culture.* London: Continuum, 1996.

Bassnett, Susan and André Lefevere. *Constructing Cultures. Essays on Literary Translation.* Clevedon: Multilingual Matters, 1998.

Bassnett, Susan and Harish Trivedi (eds). *Post-colonial Translation: Theory and Practice.* London: Routledge, 1999.

Bate, Walter Jackson. *The Burden of the Past and the English Poet*. London: Chatto and Windus, 1971.

Batten, Guinn. '"He Could Barely Tell One from the Other": The Borderline Disorders of Paul Muldoon's Poetry'. *The South Atlantic Quarterly* 95: 1 (Winter 1996): 171–204.

Bell, Robert, Robert Johnstone and Robin Wilson (eds). *Troubled Times: Fortnight Magazine and the Troubles in Northern Ireland 1970–91*. Belfast: Blackstaff Press, 1991.

Benjamin, Walter. *Illuminations*. Edited with an introduction by Hannah Arendt. Trans. Harry Zorn. London: Pimlico, 1999.

Bhabha, Homi K. *The Location of Culture*. London: Routledge, 1994.

Biguenet, John, and Rainer Schulte (eds). *The Craft of Translation*. Chicago: The University Of Chicago Press, 1989.

Bloom, Harold. *The Anxiety of Influence: A Theory of Poetry*. Oxford: Oxford University Press, 1973.

Bloom, Harold. *A Map of Misreading* (1975). Oxford: Oxford University Press, 1980.

Bloom, Harold. *The Western Canon: The Books and School of the Ages* (1994). London and Basingstoke: Palgrave Macmillan, 1995.

Brandes, Randy. 'Seamus Heaney: An Interview'. *Salmagundi* 80 (Fall 1988): 4–21.

Brandes, Rand. 'Ciaran Carson interviewed by Rand Brandes'. *The Irish Review* 8 (Spring 1990): 77–90.

Brandes, Rand. '"Inscribed in Sheets': Seamus Heaney's Scribal Matrix'. Catherine Malloy and Phyllis Carey (eds), *Seamus Heaney: The Shaping Spirit*. Newark, NJ: University of Delaware Press, 1996. 47–70.

Brearton, Fran. '"Walking Forwards into the Past": An Interview with Michael Longley'. *Irish Studies Review* 18 (Spring 1997): 35–9.

Brearton, Fran. 'Poetry of the 1960s: The "Northern Ireland Renaissance"'. Matthew Campbell (ed.), *The Cambridge Companion to Contemporary Irish Poetry*. Cambridge: Cambridge University Press, 2003. 94–112.

Brearton, Fran. 'Cenotaphs of Snow: Memory, Remembrance, and the Poetry of Michael Longley'. *Irish Studies Review* 12: 2 (August 2004): 175–89.

Brearton, Fran. *Reading Michael Longley*. Newcastle: Bloodaxe, 2006.

Brown, Richard. 'Bog Poems and Book Poems: Doubleness, Self-Translation and Pun in Seamus Heaney and Paul Muldoon'. Neil Corcoran (ed.), *The Chosen Ground: Essays on the Contemporary Poetry of Northern Ireland*. Bridgend: Seren Books, 1992. 153–67.

Brown, Terence. *Northern Voices: Poets from Ulster*. Dublin: Gill and Macmillan, 1975.

Brown, Terence. *Ireland's Literature: Selected Essays*. Mullingar: The Lilliput Press, 1988.

Brown, Terence. 'Derek Mahon: The Poet and Painting', *Irish University Review* 24: 1 (Spring/Summer 1994): 38–50.

Brown, Terence. 'Mahon and Longley: Place and Placelessness'. Matthew Campbell (ed) *The Cambridge Companion to Contemporary Irish Poetry*. Cambridge: Cambridge University Press, 2003. 133–48.

Brown, Terence and Nicholas Grene (eds). *Tradition and Influence in Anglo-Irish Poetry*. London and Basingstoke: Palgrave Macmillan, 1989.

Burton, Brian. 'The Art of Failure: Samuel Beckett and Derek Mahon'. *Irish Studies Review* 13: 1 (February 2005): 55–64.

Butler, David (2003). '"Slightly out of Synch": Joycean Strategies in Ciaran Carson's *The Twelfth of Never*'. *Irish University Review* 33: 2 (Autumn/Winter): 337–55.

Campbell, Matthew (ed.). *The Cambridge Companion to Contemporary Irish Poetry*. Cambridge: Cambridge University Press, 2003.

Carey, John. 'The Stain of Words', *Sunday Times* (21 June 1987): 56.

Carson, Ciaran. 'Escaped from the Massacre'. *The Honest Ulsterman* 50 (Winter 1975): 183–6.

Carter, Erica, James Donald and Judith Squires (eds). *Space and Place: Theories of Identity and Location*. London: Lawrence and Wishart, 1993.

Clark, Heather. *The Ulster Renaissance: Poetry in Belfast 1962–1972*. Oxford: Oxford University Press, 2006.

Cleary, Joe. 'Misplaced Ideas? Colonialism, Location and Dislocation in Irish Studies'. Claire Connolly (ed.), *Theorizing Ireland*. Houndmills: Palgrave Macmillan, 2003. 91–104.

Cole, Henri. 'Seamus Heaney: The Art of Poetry No. 75'. *Paris Review* 144 (Fall 1997): 88–138.

Connolly, Claire (ed.). *Theorizing Ireland*. Houndmills: Palgrave Macmillan, 2003.

Corcoran, Neil (ed.). *The Chosen Ground: Essays on the Contemporary Poetry of Northern Ireland*. Bridgend, Mid Glamorgan: Seren Books, 1992.

Corcoran, Neil. *The Poetry of Seamus Heaney: A Critical Study*. London: Faber, 1998.

Corcoran, Neil. *Poets of Modern Ireland: Text, Context, Intertext*. Cardiff: University of Wales Press, 1999.

Corcoran, Neil. 'My Botanical Studies: The Poetry of Natural History in Michael Longley'. Alan J. Peacock and Kathleen Devine (eds), *The Poetry of Michael Longley*. Gerrards Cross: Colin Smythe, 2000. 101–19.

Corcoran, Neil. 'Paul Muldoon in Conversation with Neil Corcoran'. Elmer Kennedy-Andrews (ed.), *Paul Muldoon – Poetry, Prose, Drama: A Collection of Critical Essays*. Gerrards Cross: Colin Smythe, 2006. 165–87.

Cosgrove, Denis and Stephen Daniels (eds). *The Iconography of Landscape: Essays on the Symbolic Representation, Design and Use of Past Environments*. Cambridge: Cambridge University Press, 1988.

Crawford, Robert. 'Callaloo'. *London Review of Books* (20 April 1989): 22–3.

Crawford, Robert. *Identifying Poets: Self and Territory in 20th-Century Poetry*. Edinburgh: Edinburgh University Press, 1993.

Cronin, Michael. *Translating Ireland: Translation, Languages, Cultures*. Cork: Cork University Press, 1996.

Cronin, Michael. *Across the Lines: Travel, Language, Translation*. Cork: Cork University Press, 2000.

Cronin, Michael. *Translation and Globalization*. London and New York: Routledge, 2003.

Cronin, Michael. *Translation and Identity*. London and New York: Routledge, 2006.

Cronin, Michael and Cormac Ó Cuilleanáin (eds). *The Languages of Ireland*. Dublin: Four Courts Press, 2003.

Crotty, Patrick. 'Lyric Waters'. *The Irish Review* 11 (Winter 1991–92): 114–20.

Crozier, Maurna (ed.). *Cultural Traditions in Northern Ireland: Varieties of Irishness/ Varieties of Britishness*. Belfast: Institute of Irish Studies, The Queen's University of Belfast, 1989/1990.

Davie, Donald. *Thomas Hardy and British Poetry*. London: Routledge, 1973.

Dawe, Gerald and John Wilson Foster (eds). *The Poet's Place – Ulster Literature and Society: Essays in Honour of John Hewitt, 1907–1987*. Belfast: Institute of Irish Studies, The Queen's University of Belfast, 1991.

Dawe, Gerald. *Against Piety: Essays in Irish Poetry*. Belfast: Lagan, 1995.

Dawe, Gerald. *False Faces: Poetry, Politics and Place*. Belfast: Lagan Press, 1996.

De Petris, Carla. 'La pausa per la riflessione: Incontro con Seamus Heaney'. *Linea d'Ombra* 42 (ottobre 1989): 69–73.

Deane, Seamus. 'Unhappy and at Home: Interview with Seamus Heaney'. *The Crane Bag* 1: 1 (1977): 61–7.

Deane, Seamus. *Celtic Revivals*. London: Faber, 1985.

Denman, Peter. 'Know the One? Insolent Ontology and Mahon's Revision'. *Irish Univerity Review* 24: 1 (Spring/Summer 1994): 27–37.

Derrida, Jacques. *Writing and Difference* (1967). Trans. Alan Bass. London and New York: Routledge, 1978.

Derrida, Jacques. 'What is a "Relevant" Translation?' (1999). Lawrence Venuti (ed.), *The Translation Studies Reader*. 2nd edn. London: Routledge, 2004. 423–46.

Devine, Kathleen and Alan J. Peacock (eds). *Louis MacNeice and His Influence*. Gerrards Cross: Colin Smythe, 1997.

Doherty, Gillian. *The Irish Ordnance Survey: History, Culture and Memory*. Dublin: Four Courts, 2004.

Duddy, Thomas. *A History of Irish Thought*. London: Routledge, 2002.

Dunn, Douglas. 'Mañana is Now', *Encounter* XLV: 5 (November 1975): 76–81.

Dunn, Douglas. 'Longley's Metric'. Alan J. Peacock and Kathleen Devine (eds), *The Poetry of Michael Longley*. Gerrards Cross: Colin Smythe, 2000. 13–33.

During, Simon (ed.). *The Cultural Studies Reader*. London: Routledge, 1993.

Eco, Umberto. *Mouse or Rat: Translation as Negotiation*. London: Weidenfeld and Nicolson, 2003.

Eliot, T. S. '*Ulysses*, Order and Myth' (1923). Robert H. Denning (ed.), *James Joyce: The Critical Heritage*. vol. 1. London: Routledge, 1970. 268–71.

Eliot, T. S. *Selected Essays*. 3rd edn. (1951). London: Faber, 1969.

Esslin, Martin. *The Anatomy of Drama*. London: Abacus, 1976.

Even-Zohar, Itamar. 'The Position of Translated Literature within the Literary Polysystem' (1978/1990). Lawrence Venuti (ed.), *The Translation Studies Reader*. London: Routledge, 2004. 199–204.

Fallon, Brian. *Edward McGuire, RHA*. Dublin: Irish Academic Press, 1991.

Farley-Hills, David. *The Comic in Renaissance Comedy*. London and Basingstoke: Palgrave Macmillan, 1981.

Field Day Theatre Company (ed.). *Ireland's Field Day*. London: Hutchinson, 1985.

Foster, John Wilson. *Colonial Consequences: Essays in Irish Literature and Culture*. Dublin: The Lilliput Press, 1991.

Foster, John Wilson. *The Achievement of Seamus Heaney*. Dublin: Lilliput, 1995.

Foster, R. F. *Modern Ireland, 1600–1972* [1988]. London: Penguin, 1989.

Foucault, Michel. 'Of Other Spaces'. *Diacritics* 16 (Spring 1986): 22–7.

Foucault, Michel. *Discipline and Punish: The Birth of the Prison*. Trans. Alan Sheridan (1977). New York, NY: Vintage Books, 1995.

Frazier, Adrian. 'Anger and Nostalgia: Seamus Heaney and the Ghost of the Father'. *Éire-Ireland* 36: 3/4 (Autumn/Winter 2001): 7–38.

Freccero, John. 'Virgil, Sweet Father: A Paradigm of Poetic Influence'. Stuart Y. McDougal (ed.), *Dante Among the Moderns*. Chapel Hill, NC: The University of North Carolina Press, 1986. 3–10.

Frye, Northrop. *Anatomy of Criticism* (1957). Princeton, NJ: Princeton University Press, 1973.

Fumagalli, Maria Cristina. *The Flight of the Vernacular: Seamus Heaney, Derek Walcott and the Impress of Dante*. Amsterdam: Rodopi, 2001.

Garratt, Robert F. *Modern Irish Poetry: Tradition and Continuity from Yeats to Heaney*. 2nd edn. Berkeley: University of California Press, 1989.

Garratt, Robert F. 'The Place of Writing and the Writing of Place in Twentieth-Century Irish Poetry in English'. Hans Werner Ludwig and Lothar Fietz (eds), *Poetry in the British Isles: Non-Metropolitan Perspectives*. Cardiff: University of Wales Press, 1995. 173–92.

Gifford, Terry. *Pastoral*. The Critical Idiom. London: Routledge, 1999.

Gillis, Alan. 'Ciaran Carson: beyond Belfast'. Nicholas Allen and Aaron Kelly (eds), *The Cities of Belfast*. Dublin: Four Courts Press, 2003. 183–98.

Goodby, John. *Irish Poetry since 1950: Stillness into History*. Manchester: Manchester University Press, 2000.

Graham, Brian (ed.). *In Search of Ireland: A Cultural Geography*. London: Routledge, 1997.

Graham, Colin. '"Liminal Spaces": Post-Colonial Theories and Irish Culture'. *Irish Review* 16 (Autumn/Winter 1994): 29–43.

Graham, Colin. *Deconstructing Ireland: Identity, Theory, Culture*. Edinburgh: Edinburgh University Press, 2001.

Gregson, Ian. *Contemporary Poetry and Postmodernism: Dialogue and Estrangement*. Houndmills: Palgrave Macmillan, 1996.

Griffin, Dustin. *Satire: A Critical Reintroduction*. Lexington: The University Press of Kentucky, 1994.

Guillén, Claudio. *Literature as System: Essays Toward the Theory of Literary History*. Princeton: Princeton University Press, 1971.

Hardwick, Lorna. '"Murmurs in the Cathedral": The Impact of Translations from Greek Poetry and Drama on Modern Work in English by Michael Longley and Seamus Heaney'. *The Yearbook of English Studies* 36: 1 (January 2006): 204–15.

Harvey, David. *Justice, Nature and the Geography of Difference*. Malden, MA: Blackwell, 1996.

Haughton, Hugh. '"Even now there are places where a thought might grow": Place and Displacement in the Poetry of Derek Mahon'. Neil Corcoran (ed.), *The Chosen Ground*. Bridgend, Mid Glamorgan: Seren, 1992. 85–120.

Haughton, Hugh. *The Poetry of Derek Mahon*. Oxford: Oxford University Press, 2007.

Havely, N. R. (ed.). *Dante's Modern Afterlife*. Basingstoke: Palgrave Macmillan, 1998.

Hawkins, Peter S. and Rachel Jacoff (eds). *The Poets' Dante: Twentieth-Century Responses*. New York: Farrar, Straus and Giroux, 2001.

Healy, Dermot. 'An Interview with Michael Longley'. *The Southern Review* 31: 3 (July 1995 – Special Irish Issue): 557–69.

Hederman, Mark Patrick. 'Poetry and the Fifth Province'. *The Crane Bag* 9: 1 (1985): 110–19.

Heffernan, James A. W. *Museum of Words: The Poetics of Ekphrasis from Homer to Ashbery*. Chicago, IL: University of Chicago Press, 1993.

Heidegger, Martin. *Poetry, Language, Thought*. Trans. Albert Hofstadter. New York, NY: Perennial Classics, 2001.

Hermans, Theo (ed.). *The Manipulation of Literature: Studies in Literary Translation*. London: Croom Helm, 1985.

Hill, Tracey and William Hughes (eds). *Contemporary Writing and National Identity*. Bath: Sulis Press, 1995.

Hinds, Michael. 'Nor is He out of It: Ciaran Carson in the Wars'. *Metre* 5 (Spring 2004): 67–79.

Hofmann, Michael. 'Dazzling Philosophy'. *London Review of Books* (15 August 1991): 14.

Holdridge, Jefferson. *The Poetry of Paul Muldoon*. Dublin: Liffey, 2008.

Homem, Rui Carvalho. 'On Elegies, Eclogues, Translations, Transfusions: An Interview with Seamus Heaney'. *The European English Messenger* X: 2 (Autumn 2001): 24–30.

Homem, Rui Carvalho and Maria de Fátima Lambert (eds). *Writing and Seeing: Essays on Word and Image*. Amsterdam and New York, NY: Rodopi, 2006.

Horton, Patricia. 'Degree Zero: Language, Subjectivity and Apocalypse in the Poetry of Derek Mahon'. *Irish Studies Review* 8: 3 (December 2000): 353–65.

Houen, Alex. *Terrorism and Modern Literature: From Joseph Conrad to Ciaran Carson*. Oxford: Oxford University Press, 2002.

Hughes, Eamonn. '"What Itch of Contradiction?" Belfast in Poetry'. Nicholas Allen and Aaron Kelly (eds), *The Cities of Belfast*. Dublin: Four Courts Press, 2003. 101–16.

Hutcheon, Linda. *A Theory of Parody: The Teachings of Twentieth-Century Art Forms*. New York and London: Methuen, 1985.

Hutcheon, Linda. *A Poetics of Postmodernism: History, Theory, Fiction*. London: Routledge, 1988.

Hutcheon, Linda. 'The Politics of Postmodern Parody'. Heinrich F. Plett (ed.), *Intertextuality*. Berlin: Walter de Gruyter, 1991. 225–36.

Iser, Wolfgang. 'On Translatability: Variables of Interpretation'. *The European English Messenger* IV: 1 (Spring 1995): 30–8.

Jacoff, Rachel (ed.). *The Cambridge Companion to Dante*. Cambridge: Cambridge University Press, 1993.

Jakobson, Roman. 'On Linguistic Aspects of Translation' (1959). Lawrence Venuti (ed.), *The Translation Studies Reader*. 2nd. edn. London: Routledge, 2004. 138–43.

Jameson, Fredric. *Postmodernism, or, the Cultural Logic of Late Capitalism*. London: Verso, 1991.

Jenkins, Nicholas. 'Walking on Air'. *TLS* (July 5 1996): 10–12.

Johnston, Dillon. 'The Anthology Wars'. *TLS* (13 September 1991): 26.

Johnston, Dillon. *Irish Poetry After Joyce*. 2nd edn. Syracuse, NY: Syracuse University Press, 1996.

Johnston, Dillon. *The Poetic Economies of England and Ireland, 1912–2000*. Houndmills: Palgrave Macmillan, 2001.

Kavanagh, Patrick (1967). *Collected Pruse*. London: MacGibbon and Kee.

Kearney, Richard (ed.). *The Irish Mind: Exploring Intellectual Traditions*. Dublin: Wolfhound, 1985.

Kearney, Richard. *Postnationalist Ireland: Politics, Culture, Philosophy*. London: Routlege, 1997.

Kendall, Tim. 'Beauty and the Beast'. *Poetry Review* 86: 1 (Spring 1996): 52.

Kendall, Tim. *Paul Muldoon*. Bridgend: Seren, 1996.

Kendall, Tim. 'Paul Muldoon's Twins'. Elmer Kennedy-Andrews (ed.), *Paul Muldoon – Poetry, Prose, Drama: A Collection of Critical Essays*. Gerrards Cross: Colin Smythe, 2006. 71–84.

Kendall, Tim and Peter McDonald (eds). *Paul Muldoon: Critical Essays*. Liverpool: Liverpool University Press, 2004.

Kenneally, Michael (ed.). *Poetry in Contemporary Irish Literature*. Gerrards Cross: Colin Smythe, 1995.

Kennedy-Andrews, Elmer (ed.). *The Poetry of Derek Mahon*. Gerrards Cross: Colin Smythe, 2002.

Kennedy-Andrews, Elmer (ed.). *Paul Muldoon – Poetry, Prose, Drama: A Collection of Critical Essays*. Gerrards Cross: Colin Smythe, 2006.

Kennedy-Andrews, Elmer. *Writing Home: Poetry and Place in Northern Ireland, 1968–2008*. Cambridge: D. S. Brewer, 2008.

Kerrigan, John. 'Ulster Ovids'. Neil Corcoran (ed.), *The Chosen Ground*. Bridgend: Seren Books, 1992. 237–69.

Kerrigan, John. 'Earth Writing: Seamus Heaney and Ciaran Carson'. *Essays in Criticism* XLVIII: 2 (April 1998): 144–68.

Kiberd, Declan. *Inventing Ireland: The Literature of the Modern Nation*. London: Cape, 1995.

Kinahan, Frank. 'Artists on Art: An Interview with Seamus Heaney'. *Critical Inquiry* 8 (Spring 1982): 409–10.

Kinsella, Thomas. 'The Irish Writer'. *Éire-Ireland* II: 2 (Summer 1967): 8–15.

Kittel, Harald and Armin Paul Frank (eds). *Interculturality and the Historical Study of Literary Translations*. Berlin: Erich Schmidt, 1991.

Klein, Bernhard. *On the Uses of History in Recent Irish Writing*. Manchester: Manchester University Press, 2007.

Kristeva, Julia. *Desire in Language: A Semiotic Approach to Literature and Art* (1969). Trans. Alice Jardine, Thomas Gora and Léon Roudiez. London: Blackwell, 1980.

Leerssen, Joep. 'The Rhetoric of National Character: A Programmatic Survey'. *Poetics Today* 21: 2 (Summer 2000): 267–92.

Lefevere, André. 'Why Waste Our Time on Rewrites? The Trouble with Interpretation, and the Role of Rewriting in an Alternative Paradigm'. Theo Hermans (ed.), *The Manipulation of Literature*. London: Croom Helm, 1985. 215–43.

Lefevere, André. *Translation, Rewriting and the Manipulation of Literary Fame*. London: Routledge, 1992.

Lefevere, André. 'Mother Courage's Cucumbers: Text, System and Refraction in a Theory of Literature' (1982). Lawrence Venuti (ed.), *The Translation Studies Reader*. London: Routledge, 2004. 239–55.

Lessing, Gotthold Ephraim. *Laocoon: An Essay Upon the Limits of Painting and Poetry* (1766). Trans. Ellen Frothingham. Mineola, NY: Dover Publications, 2005.

Levi, Peter. 'Scythe, Pitchfork and Biretta'. *Poetry Review* 81: 2 (Summer1991): 12–14.

Lewis, Philip E. 'The Measure of Translation Effects' (1985). Lawrence Venuti (ed.), *The Translation Studies Reader*. 2nd edn. London: Routledge, 2004. 256–75.

Longley, Edna. 'An Ironic Conscience at One Minute to Midnight'. *Fortnight* (17 December 1984): 17–18.

Longley, Edna. '*North*: "Inner Emigré" or "Artful Voyeur"?'. Tony Curtis (ed.), *The Art of Seamus Heaney*. 2nd edn., Bridgend: Poetry Wales. 1985. 63–95.

Longley, Edna. 'MacNeice and Ireland'. *London Review of Books* (4 June 1987): 4.

Longley, Edna. 'Regional Variations'. *Irish Review* 2 (1987): 149–52.

Longley, Edna. *Louis MacNeice*. London: Faber, 1988.

Longley, Edna. 'Where a Thought Might Grow'. *Poetry Review* 81: 2 (Summer 1991): 7–9.

Longley, Edna. *The Living Stream: Literature and Revisionism in Ireland*. Belfast: Bloodaxe, 1994.

Longley, Edna. 'Derek Mahon: Extreme Religion of Art'. Michael Kenneally (ed.), *Poetry in Contemporary Irish Literature*. Gerrards Cross: Colin Smythe, 1995. 280–303.

Longley, Edna. '"It is Time that I Wrote My Will": Anxieties of Influence and Succession'. Warwick Gould and Edna Longley (eds), *Yeats Annual No.12 – A Special Number – That Accusing Eye: Yeats and his Irish Readers*. Houndmills and London: Palgrave Macmillan, 1996. 117–62.

Longley, Edna. *Poetry and Posterity*. Highgreen: Bloodaxe, 2000.

Lowe, Jeremy. 'Contagious Violence and the Spectacle of Death in *Táin Bó Cúailgne*'. Maria Tymoczko and Colin Ireland (eds), *Language and Tradition in*

Ireland: Continuities and Displacements. Amherst and Boston, MA: University of Massachusetts Press, 2003. 84–100.

Ludwig, Hans Werner and Lothar Fietz (eds). *Poetry in the British Isles: Non-Metropolitan Perspectives*. Cardiff: University of Wales Press, 1995.

Mackinnon, Lachlan , 'A Responsibility to Self'. *TLS* (7 June 1991): 36.

Malloy, Catharine and Phyllis Carey (eds.). *Seamus Heaney: the Shaping Spirit*. London: Associated University Press, 1996.

Marken, Ronald. 'Paul Muldoon's "Juggling a Red-hot Half-Brick in an Old Sock": Poets in Ireland Renovate the English-Language Sonnet'. *Éire-Ireland* XXIV: 1 (Spring 1989): 79–91.

Massey, Doreen. *Space, Place and Gender*. Minneapolis, MN: University of Minnesota Press, 1994.

McCarthy, Conor. *Seamus Heaney and Medieval Poetry*. Cambridge: D. S. Brewer, 2008.

McDonald, Marianne. 'When Despair and History Rhyme: Colonialism and Greek Tragedy'. *New Hibernia Review* 1: 2 (Summer 1997): 57–69.

McDonald, Marianne and J. Michael Walton (eds). *Amid Our Troubles: Irish Versions of Greek Tragedy*. London: Methuen, 2002.

McDonald, Peter. *Louis MacNeice: The Poet in His Contexts*. Oxford: Clarendon, 1991.

McDonald, Peter. 'Michael Longley's Homes'. Neil Corcoran (ed.), *The Chosen Ground*. Bridgend, Mid Glamorgan: Seren Books, 1992. 65–83.

McDonald, Peter. 'The Greeks in Ireland: Irish Poets and Greek Tragedy'. *Translation and Literature* 4: 2 (1995): 183–203.

McDonald, Peter. 'The Poet and "The Finished Man": Heaney's Oxford Lectures'. *Irish Review* 19 (Spring/Summer 1996): 98–108.

McDonald, Peter. 'Yeats, Form and Northern Irish Poetry'. Warwick Gould and Edna Longley (eds). *That Accusing Eye: Yeats and his Irish Readers. Yeats Annual No. 12 – A Special Number*. Houndmills and London: Palgrave Macmillan, 1996a. 213–42.

McDonald, Peter. *Mistaken Identities: Poetry and Northern Ireland*. Oxford: Oxford University Press, 1997.

McDonald, Peter. 'Lapsed Classics: Homer, Ovid, and Michael Longley's Poetry'. Alan J. Peacock, and Kathleen Devine (eds), *The Poetry of Michael Longley*. Gerrards Cross: Colin Smythe, 2000. 35–50.

McDougal, Stuart Y. (ed.). *Dante Among the Moderns*. Chapel Hill, NC: The University of North Carolina Press, 1986.

McGuckian, Medbh. *Horsepower Pass By!: A Study of the Car in the Poetry of Seamus Heaney*. Coleraine: Cranagh Press, 1999.

Mitchell, W. J. T. *Iconology: Image, Text, Ideology*. Chicago and London: The University of Chicago Press, 1986.

Montague, John. 'Work Your Progress'. *Irish University Review* 12: 1 (Spring 1982): 48–52.

Morrison, Blake. 'Seamus Famous: Time to be dazzled'. *The Independent on Sunday* (19 May 1991): 26.

Mueller-Vollmer, Kurt and Michael Irmscher (eds), *Translating Literatures, Translating Cultures: New Vistas and Approaches in Literary Studies*. Stanford, CA: Stanford University Press, 1998.

Murphy, James J., Lucy McDiarmid and Michael J. Durkan, 'Q. and A. with Derek Mahon', *Irish Literary Supplement* 10: 2 (Fall 1991): 27–8.

Murphy, Rosalie (ed.), *Contemporary Poets of the English Language*. Chicago: St. James Press, 1970.

Murray, Christopher. '"For the Fun of the Thing": Derek Mahon's Dramatic Adaptations'. *Irish University Review* 24: 1 (Spring/Summer 1994): 117–30.

Ní Anluain, Clíodhna (ed.). *Reading the Future: Irish Writers in Conversation with Mike Murphy*. Dublin: Lilliput, 2000.

Nida, Eugene. 'Principles of Correspondence' (1964). Lawrence Venuti (ed.), *The Translation Studies Reader*. 2nd edn. London: Routledge, 2004. 153–67.

Ó Cadhla, Stiofán. *Civilizing Ireland: Ordnance Survey 1824–1842 – Ethnography, Cartography, Translation*. Dublin: Irish Academic Press, 2006.

O'Brien, Eugene. 'Seamus Heaney and the Ethics of Translation'. *Canadian Journal of Irish Studies* 27: 2/28: 1(Fall 2001/Spring 2002): 20–37.

O'Brien, Eugene. *Seamus Heaney and the Place of Writing*. Gainesville: The University Press of Florida, 2002.

O'Brien, Eugene. *Seamus Heaney: Creating Irelands of the Mind*. Dublin: Liffey Press, 2002a.

O'Brien, Eugene. *Seamus Heaney: Searches for Answers*. London and Sterling, VA: Pluto, 2003.

O'Brien, Sean. *The Deregulated Muse: Essays on Contemporary British and Irish Poetry*. Newcastle: Bloodaxe, 1998.

O'Donoghue, Bernard. 'Appropriate Territory'. *TLS* (27 September, 1991): 13.

O'Donoghue, Bernard. *Seamus Heaney and the Language of Poetry*. Hemel Hempstead: Harvester Wheatsheaf, 1994.

O'Donoghue, Bernard. 'Dante's Versatility and Seamus Heaney's Modernism'. Nick Havely (ed.), *Dante's Modern Afterlife*. Houndmills: Palgrave Macmillan, 1998. 242–57.

O'Donoghue, Bernard. 'Poetry in Ireland'. Joe Cleary and Claire Connolly (eds), *The Cambridge Companion to Modern Irish Culture*. Cambridge: Cambridge University Press, 2005. 173–89.

O'Donoghue, Bernard (ed.). *The Cambridge Companion to Seamus Heaney*. Cambridge: Cambridge University Press, 2009.

O'Rawe, Des. 'Plays of Difference'. *Irish Review* 20 (Spring 1997): 143–6.

O'Toole, Fintan. *Black Hole, Green Card: The Disappearance of Ireland*. Dublin: New Island Books, 1994.

O'Driscoll, Dennis. 'In the Mid-Course of his Life'. *Hibernia* 11 (October 1979): 13.

O'Driscoll, Dennis. 'An Interview with John Montague'. *Irish University Review* 19: 1 (Spring 1989): 58–72.

O'Driscoll, Dennis. *Stepping Stones: Interviews with Seamus Heaney*. London: Faber, 2008.

Ormsby, Frank. 'Ciaran Carson interviewed by Frank Ormsby'. *Linen Hall Review* 8: 1 (Spring 1991): 4–8.

Parker, Michael. *Seamus Heaney: The Making of the Poet*. Basingstoke and London: Palgrave Macmillan, 1993.

Parker, Michael. *Northern Irish Literature, 1956–1975: The Imprint of History*. vol. 1. Basingstoke: Palgrave Macmillan, 2007.

Parker, Michael. *Northern Irish Literature, 1975–2006: The Imprint of History*. vol. 2. Basingstoke: Palgrave Macmillan, 2007.

Paulin, Tom. 'A Rare and Extraordinary Imagination'. *The Honest Ulsterman* 65 (February/June 1980): 64–9.

Paulin, Tom. *Ireland and the English Crisis*. Newcastle: Bloodaxe, 1984.

Paulson, Ronald. *The Fictions of Satire*. Baltimore, MD: The Johns Hopkins Press, 1967.

Peacock, Alan. 'Mediations: Poet as Translator, Poet as Seer'. Elmer Kennedy-Andrews (ed.), *Seamus Heaney: A Collection of Critical Essays*. Basingstoke and London: Palgrave Macmillan, 1992. 233–55.

Peacock, Alan J. and Kathleen Devine (eds). *The Poetry of Michael Longley*. Gerrards Cross: Colin Smythe, 2000.

Phillips, Ivan. 'In the Electric Orchard: Technology, Literacy and the Innocence of Experience'. Elmer Kennedy-Andrews (ed.), *Paul Muldoon – Poetry, Prose, Drama: A Collection of Critical Essays*. Gerrards Cross: Colin Smythe, 2006. 145–63.

Plett, Heinrich E. (ed.). *Intertextuality*. Berlin and New York: Walter de Gruyter, 1991.

Pollard, Arthur. *Satire*. London: Methuen, 1970.

Quinn, Justin. *The Cambridge Introduction to Modern Irish Poetry, 1800–2000*. Cambridge: Cambridge University Press, 2008.

Redmond, John 'Wilful Inconsistency: Derek Mahon's Verse-Letters'. *Irish University Review* 24: 1 (Spring/Summer 1994): 96–116.

Reynolds, Barbara. 'Translating Dante in the 1990s'. *Translation and Literature* 4: 2 (1995): 221–37.

Richards, Shaun. 'In the Border Country: Greek Tragedy and Contemporary Irish Drama'. C. C. Barfoot and R. Van den Doel (eds), *Ritual Remembering: History, Myth and Politics in Anglo-Irish Drama*. Amsterdam/Atlanta, GA: Rodopi, 1995. 191–200.

Richtarik, Marilynn J. *Acting Between the Lines: The Field Day Theatre Company and Irish Cultural Politics 1980–1984*. Oxford: Clarendon Press, 1994.

Rumens, Carol. 'The Stitches Show'. *Poetry Review* 89: 3 (Autumn 1999): 86–7.

Sansom, Ian. 'A Difference of Poetry'. *The Guardian* (Friday 10 May 1996): 6.

Sansom, Ian. 'Jaundiced'. *Poetry Review* 88: 2 (Summer 1998): 83–4.

Sartiliot, Claudette. *Citation and Modernity: Derrida, Joyce, and Brecht*. Norman and London: University of Oklahoma Press, 1993.

Scammell, William. 'Derek Mahon Interviewed'. *Poetry Review* 81: 2 (Summer 1991): 4–6.

Schleiermacher, Friedrich. 'On the Different Methods of Translating' (1813). Trans. Susan Bernofsky. Lawrence Venuti (ed.), *The Translation Studies Reader*, 2nd edn. London: Routledge, 2004. 43–63.

Schulte, Rainer and John Biguenet (eds). *Theories of Translation: An Anthology of Essays from Dryden to Derrida*. Chicago and London: The University of Chicago Press, 1992.

Serpillo, Giuseppe. "Why donsh yeh tell ush shometin about Marseille?' Being Abroad and Being Irish – Being Irish is Being Abroad'. Zach and Kosok (eds), *Literary Interrelations – Ireland, England and the World*, Vol. 3. Tuebingen: Gunter Narr, 1987. 27–33.

Sewell, Frank. *'Where the Paradoxes Grow': The Poetry of Derek Mahon*. Coleraine: Cranagh, 2000.

Shields, Kathleen. *Gained in Translation: Language, Poetry and Identity in Twentieth-Century Ireland*. Bern: Peter Lang, 2000.

Smith, Stan. *Irish Poetry and the Construction of Modern Identity*. Dublin: Irish Academic Press, 2005.

Smyth, Gerry. *Space and the Irish Cultural Imagination*. Houndmills: Palgrave Macmillan, 2001.

Soja, Edward. *Postmodern Geographies: The Reassertion of Space in Critical Social Theory*. London: Verso, 1989.

Sontag, Susan. 'The World as India: Translation as a Passport within the Community of Literature'. *TLS* (13 June 2003): 13–15.

Stanford, W. B. *Ireland and the Classical Tradition*. Dublin: Allen Figgis and Co. Ltd/ Tottowa, NJ: Rowman and Littlefield, 1976.

Steiner, George. *After Babel: Aspects of Language and Translation*. 2nd edn. Oxford: Oxford University Press, 1992.

Stott, Andrew. *Comedy*. New York and London: Routledge, 2005.

Szabo, Carmen. *'Clearing the Ground': The Field Day Theatre Company and the Construction of Irish Identities*. Newcastle: Cambridge Scholars, 2007.

Tinley, Bill '"Harmonies and Disharmonies": Derek Mahon's Francophile Poetics'. *Irish University Review* 24: 1 (Spring/Summer 1994): 80–95.

Toury, Gideon. 'A Rationale for Descriptive Translation Studies'. Theo Hermans (ed.), *The Manipulation of Literature*. London: Croom Helm, 1985. 16–41.

Toury, Gideon. *Descriptive Translation Studies and Beyond*. Amsterdam: John Benjamins Publishing Company, 1995.

Tymoczko, Maria. *Translation in a Postcolonial Context: Early Irish Literature in English Translation*. Manchester: St. Jerome Pub, 1999.

Tymoczko, Maria and Colin Ireland (eds). *Language and Tradition in Ireland: Continuities and Displacements*. Amherst and Boston, MA: University of Massachusetts Press, 2003.

Vendler, Helen. 'Anglo-Celtic Attitudes'. *New York Review of Books* (6 November 1997): 57–60.

Vendler, Helen. *Seamus Heaney*. London: HarperCollins, 1998.

Vendler, Helen. 'Seamus Heaney and the *Oresteia*: "Mycenae Lookout" and the Usefulness of Tradition'. Marianne McDonald and J. Michael Walton (eds). *Amid Our Troubles: Irish Versions of Greek Tragedy*. London: Methuen, 2002. 181–97.

Venuti, Lawrence. *The Translator's Invisibility: A History of Translation*. London: Routledge, 1995.

Venuti, Lawrence. *The Scandals of Translation: Towards an Ethics of Difference*. London: Routledge, 1998.

Venuti, Lawrence (ed.). *The Translation Studies Reader*. 2nd edition. London: Routledge, 2004.

Vermeer, Hans J. 'Skopos and Commission in Translational Action' (1989). Lawrence Venuti (ed.), *The Translation Studies Reader*. 2nd edition. London: Routledge, 2004. 227–38.

Ward, John Powell. *The English Line: Poetry of the Unpoetic from Wordsworth to Larkin*. London and Basingstoke: Palgrave Macmillan, 1991.

Warren, Rosanna (ed.). *The Art of Translation: Voices from the Field*. Boston: Northeastern University Press, 1989.

Welch, Robert. *Changing States: Transformations in Modern Irish Writing*. London: Routledge, 1993.

Wheatley, David. 'Unsuspected Shapes'. *Irish Review* 19 (Spring/Summer 1996): 125–9.

Wheatley, David. 'Irish Poetry into the Twenty-First Century'. Matthew Campbell (ed.), *The Cambridge Companion to Contemporary Irish Poetry*. Cambridge: Cambridge University Press, 2003. 250–67.

Whelan, Kevin. 'The Region and the Intellectuals'. Liam O'Dowd (ed.), *On Intellectuals and Intellectual Life in Ireland*. Belfast: Institute of Irish Studies/Royal Irish Academy, 1996. 116–31.

Williams, David G. '"A decadent who lived to tell the story": Derek Mahon's The Yellow Book'. *Journal of Modern Literature* 23: 1 (1999): 111–26.

Wills, Clair. *Improprieties: Politics and Sexuality in Northern Irish Poetry*. Oxford: Oxford University Press, 1993.

Wills, Clair. *Reading Paul Muldoon*. Newcastle: Bloodaxe, 1998.

Wilmer, Clive. *Poets Talking: The 'Poet of the Month' Interviews from BBC Radio 3*. Manchester: Carcanet, 1994.

Wimsatt, W. K. (Jr) and Monroe C. Beardsley. *The Verbal Icon: Studies in the Meaning of Poetry* Lexington, KY: University of Kentucky Press, 1967.

Wolfe, Cary. *Animal Rites: American Culture, the Discourse of Species and Posthumanism*. Chicago and Longon: The University of Chicago Press, 2003.

Wolfe, Cary. *Zoontologies: The Question of the Animal*. Minneapolis, MN: University of Minnesota Press, 2003.

Worton, Michael and Judith Still (eds). *Intertextuality: Theories and Practices*. Manchester and New York: Manchester University Press, 1990.

York, Richard. 'Derek Mahon and the Visual Art'. Elmer Kennedy-Andrews (ed.). *The Poetry of Derek Mahon*. Gerrards Cross: Colin Smythe, 2002. 131–44.

Younger, Kelly. *Irish Adaptations of Greek Tragedies*. Lewiston, NY: Edwin Mellen Press, 2001.

Zach, W. and H. Kosok (eds). *Literary Interrelations: Ireland, England and the World*, 3 vols. Tuebingen: Gunter Narr, 1987.

Zuber-Skerritt, Ortrun (ed.). *Page to Stage: Theatre as Translation*. Amsterdam: Rodopi, 1984.

Index